D1036215

The Guantánamo Files

The Guantánamo Files

The Stories of the 774 Detainees
in America's Illegal Prison

ANDY WORTHINGTON

Pluto  Press

LONDON • ANN ARBOR, MI

First published 2007 by Pluto Press
345 Archway Road, London N6 5AA
and 839 Greene Street, Ann Arbor, MI 48106

www.plutobooks.com

British Library Cataloguing in Publication Data
A catalogue record for this book is available from the British Library

Hardback
ISBN-13   978 0 7453 2665 8
ISBN-10   0 7453 2665 X

Paperback
ISBN-13   978 0 7453 2664 1
ISBN-10   0 7453 2664 1

Library of Congress Cataloging in Publication Data applied for

10   9   8   7   6   5   4   3   2   1

Designed and produced for Pluto Press by
Chase Publishing Services Ltd, Fortescue, Sidmouth, EX10 9QG, England
Typeset from disk by Stanford DTP Services, Northampton
Printed and bound in the United States of America

Contents

Acknowledgments

This book would not have been possible without the support of Roger van Zwanenberg, my editor at Pluto, who saw its potential in the summer of 2006 when I approached him with a proposal. Nor would it have been possible without the efforts of those at the Associated Press, the American Civil Liberties Union and the Center for Constitutional Rights to force the US government to release the documents relating to the prisoners in Guantánamo that formed the basis of my research. It's a testament to the importance of the American legal system—and its beleaguered Constitution—that Freedom of Information legislation exists to compel an administration bent on unfettered executive power to release documents which, on close inspection, reveal the errors, ineptitude and cruelty underpinning the Guantánamo regime.

Thanks are also due to the many people who have helped with information and encouragement, including Clive Stafford Smith, Zachary Katznelson and Cori Crider at Reprieve, Maryam Hassan, Dr. Adnan Siddiqui, Moazzam Begg and Asim Qureshi at Cageprisoners, Marc Falkoff, Candace Gorman, Anant Raut, Joshua Colangelo-Bryan, Mark and Josh Denbeaux, Anna Cayton-Holland, Shawn Nolan, Louise Christian, Katharine Newall Bierman and Joanne Mariner at Human Rights Watch, Farid Khan at the Afghan embassy, Val Stevenson, Peter Bergen, Marty Fisher, Stephen Grey, Mike Otterman, David Rose, Jo Glanville, Seth Farber, Polly Nash and Farah Stockman at the *Boston Globe*.

And finally, as with everything I do, this project would not have been possible without the support of my wife Dot and our son Tyler. I dedicate it to Tyler, in the hope that he will grow up to see a more just and less brutal world, to the children of those in Guantánamo, deprived of their fathers for so many years, and, of course, to the prisoners themselves, not only in Guantánamo but also in every other illegal prison established in the wake of 9/11. It's a sign of the current

US administration's shameful dismissal of established legal principles that, after nearly six years of imprisonment, a book like this is required to tell their stories.

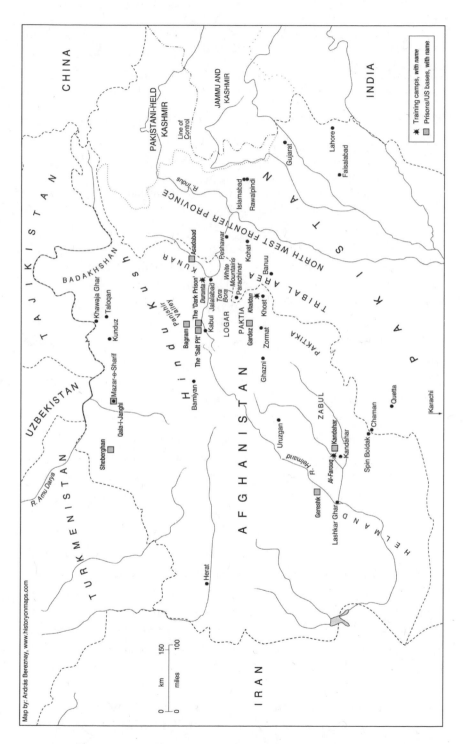

Map by: András Bereznay, www.historyonmaps.com

Legend:
- ✳ Training camps, *with name*
- ▢ Prisons/US bases, *with name*

CHINA

TAJIKISTAN

UZBEKISTAN

TURKMENISTAN

IRAN

AFGHANISTAN

PAKISTAN

INDIA

PAKISTANI-HELD KASHMIR

JAMMU AND KASHMIR

Line of Control

NORTH WEST FRONTIER PROVINCE

TRIBAL AREAS

BADAKHSHAN

H i n d u K u s h

Panjshir Valley

KUNAR

LOGAR

PAKTIA

PAKTIKA

ZABUL

HELMAND

R. Amu Darya

R. Indus

R. Helmand

White Mountains

Cities and locations:
- Khawaja Ghar
- Taloqan
- Kunduz
- Mazar-e-Sharif
- Qala-i-Janghi
- Sheberghan
- Bamiyan
- Herat
- Bagram
- The 'Salt Pit'
- The 'Dark Prison'
- Durunta
- Asadabad
- Peshawar
- Kabul
- Jalalabad
- Tora Bora
- Parachinar
- Kohat
- Banuu
- Khalian
- Khost
- Gardez
- Zormat
- Ghazni
- Uruzgan
- Al-Farouq
- Kandahar
- Spin Boldak
- Chaman
- Quetta
- Karachi
- Lashkar Ghar
- Gereshk
- Islamabad
- Rawalpindi
- Gujarat
- Lahore
- Faisalabad

km 0   150
miles 0 100

xi

Preface

> But that I am forbid
> To tell the secrets of my prison-house,
> I could a tale unfold whose lightest word
> Would harrow up thy soul, freeze thy young blood ...
> William Shakespeare, *Hamlet*, Act I, Scene 5

On January 11, 2002, exactly four months after the terrible events of 9/11, the first of 774 prisoners arrived at a hastily erected prison—Camp X-Ray—located on a US naval base in Guantánamo Bay, Cuba.[1] A territorial anomaly, leased from Cuba since 1903, Guantánamo was specifically chosen as a prison for those captured in the "War on Terror," because it was presumed to be beyond the reach of the American courts.

Until recently, it was impossible to tell the stories of these men. Held without charge, without trial, without access to their families, and, initially, without access to lawyers, they are part of a peculiarly lawless experiment conducted by the US administration, which has chosen to disregard both the Geneva Conventions and the established rules of war, holding the men not as criminals or as prisoners of war, but as "illegal enemy combatants," a category of prisoner which is recognized only by the White House and the Pentagon.

As the administration fashioned Guantánamo into what Lord Steyn, a British law lord, described as a "legal black hole,"[2] those in overall charge of the prison—President Bush, Vice President Dick Cheney and defense secretary Donald Rumsfeld—maintained such a strict veil of secrecy that for four years they refused even to reveal the names of the prisoners. Although some reporters—in particular, teams at the *Washington Post* and the British-based website Cageprisoners, run by Muslim volunteers—built up partial lists of the prisoners, and a number of shocking stories were told by some of the 260 prisoners who were released during this period, it was not possible to provide a comprehensive overview of the prisoners and their stories until spring

2006, when, in response to Freedom of Information legislation filed by the Associated Press, the Pentagon was forced to reveal the names and nationalities of all the prisoners held in Guantánamo, as well as 7,000 pages of transcripts of tribunals convened by the authorities to assess their status as "enemy combatants."

The tribunal process was, like everything else at Guantánamo, both illegal and deeply flawed. The prisoners were not allowed legal representation, and were prevented from seeing the classified evidence against them, which often consisted of allegations based on hearsay or torture, but they were at least allowed to tell their own stories, which were otherwise completely unknown. Through a careful study of these documents, as well as discussions with lawyers representing the prisoners, and an analysis of press reports, interviews with released prisoners and other reports compiled by human rights organizations, including Amnesty International and Human Rights Watch, I have been able to put together the first detailed history of Guantánamo and its prisoners.

Beginning with the US-led invasion of Afghanistan in October 2001, the chapters that follow explain, in detail, the genesis of the prison, its counterparts in Afghanistan, its development from 2002 to the present day, its role as a prison devoted to interrogation and torture, the legal challenges that have been launched against the administration, and the network of secret prisons that underpins Guantánamo's brutal illegality. More importantly, they also tell the stories of the prisoners themselves, allowing them to explain who they are and where and when they were captured. In contrast to the administration's claims that the Guantánamo prisoners are the "worst of the worst,"[3] what the stories reveal most of all—filtered through the horrendous abuse to which they have been subjected—is that very few of them had anything to do with 9/11 or al-Qaeda, and the vast majority were either Taliban foot soldiers, recruited to fight an inter-Muslim civil war in Afghanistan that began long before 9/11, or humanitarian aid workers, religious teachers and economic migrants, who were, for the most part, sold to the Americans by their allies in Afghanistan and Pakistan. These findings are similar to the results of a statistical analysis by lawyers at the Seton Hall Law School, who published a ground-breaking report on the prisoners in 2006, but I hope, in this book, to bring to life the stories behind these statistics, and to demonstrate the human cost of the administration's ill-conceived and violently executed "War on Terror."[4]

For updates on developments at Guantánamo, and additional information not included in this book, see my website <www.andyworthington.co.uk>.

Andy Worthington, London, April 2007

1
"Operation Enduring Freedom"

Osama Bin Laden: Wanted, Dead or Alive

Guantánamo was not even on the radar, when, on September 17, 2001, President Bush announced that Osama bin Laden was the "prime suspect" for the 9/11 operation. Instead, the rhetoric was pure vengeance. "I want justice," the President said. "And there's an old poster out West, I recall, that said, 'Wanted, Dead or Alive.'" On September 20, he delivered an ultimatum to the Taliban, telling them to hand over the leaders of al-Qaeda, to close all "terrorist training camps," and to "hand over every terrorist and every person in their support structure, to appropriate authorities." "The Taliban must act and act immediately," he added. "They will hand over the terrorists, or they will share in their fate." Anticipating that the Taliban would not comply with these demands, Bush was briefed on the plans for "Operation Enduring Freedom" on the following day by General Tommy Franks, the US military commander, who told him that US Central Command "would destroy the al-Qaeda network inside Afghanistan along with the illegitimate Taliban regime which was harbouring and protecting the terrorists."[1]

From the beginning, therefore, the administration equated bin Laden with the Taliban, even though this was not an entirely valid assumption. When bin Laden returned to Afghanistan in 1996 (after four years in Sudan, where he had moved after the Saudis exiled him on his return from Afghanistan in 1992), he was regarded with suspicion by the Taliban's leader, Mullah Mohammed Omar, who retained a parochial outlook and was, reportedly, furious when bin Laden announced a global jihad against the United States in 1998.

1

Ironically, when al-Qaeda bombed the US embassies in Kenya and
Tanzania later that year, Omar was finally drawn into bin Laden's
orbit: he had been in the process of betraying bin Laden to the Saudis,
but reneged on the deal after President Clinton ordered air strikes
on al-Qaeda training camps in Afghanistan. Even so, it remained
apparent to those who were studying Afghanistan closely that, at
the time of "Operation Enduring Freedom," the overlap between the
Taliban and al-Qaeda was extremely small. According to a senior US
intelligence official, "In 1996 it was non-existent, and by 2001, no
more than 50 people."[2]

As the plan for the invasion of Afghanistan developed, the
administration, anxious to avoid repeating the fate that befell the
Soviet Union—losing 25,000 lives in a ten-year war that was ultimately
unsuccessful—decided that the best way to "destroy" al-Qaeda and
the Taliban was through a proxy war, in which a few hundred Special
Forces operatives, backed up by substantial, targeted bombing raids,
would work with the leaders of the United Islamic Front for the
Salvation of Afghanistan (aka the Northern Alliance) to ensure the
victory that the loose confederation of anti-Taliban warlords in the
north of the country had been striving for over the previous seven
years. What this meant in practice was supporting Afghanistan's ethnic
minorities—the Tajiks, Uzbeks and Hazaras—against the Pashtun
majority in the south and east, crushing the Taliban while attempting
to ensure that moderate Pashtun leaders could be found to prevent
the northern victors from exacting a terrible revenge on the Pashtun
population and starting a whole new cycle of atrocious violence.[3]

In order to intervene in Afghanistan's long-standing civil war, it was
necessary for the US administration to indulge in a collective bout of
amnesia: to forget that, when the Soviet Union invaded Afghanistan
in 1979, the US had, through a strategic intermediary—Pakistan's
powerful intelligence service, the Inter Services Intelligence Directorate
(ISI)—poured billions of dollars into the creation of the mujahideen,[4]
a fighting force of tens of thousands of anti-Soviet Muslim warriors,
primarily drawn from Saudi Arabia and the Yemen. Some of these—
including Osama bin Laden—became so enamored with the notion of
a holy war that they went on to form al-Qaeda ("the base"), a warrior
corps devoted to pursuing "holy war" in other Muslim countries.[5]

It was also necessary to maintain a good relationship with America's oil-producing friends in Saudi Arabia (and to ignore its funding of the Taliban), and to embrace Uzbekistan's dictator, President Karimov, who had a reputation for boiling dissidents alive, to secure a military base that could be used until the Taliban had been driven from northern Afghanistan. Most important of all, however, was the need to form a strong alliance with Pakistan—until recently something of a pariah state, because of its nuclear program—and to overlook its role in funding and supporting the Taliban. In many ways, Pakistan was the most dubious of all America's new allies. In order to hold onto his position, President Musharraf, the military dictator who had seized power in 1999, was required to juggle a number of potentially lethal factions within Pakistani politics; in particular, the Pashtun sympathizers in the government, the ISI and the military, who, either by stealth or as a long-standing component of Pakistan's foreign policy, were pro-Taliban, and also the country's many militant Islamists, who had been providing the Taliban with a steady stream of foot soldiers through their madrassas (religious schools). Although it was easy for the US administration to threaten to bomb Musharraf "back to the Stone Age" if he did not support them, it was by no means clear that this support would be as dependable as they would have liked.[6]

Almost as alarming as these dangerous exercises in realpolitik was the amnesia that was required in order to strike up relationships with the warlords who would fight America's proxy war. The military leader of the Northern Alliance, a charismatic Tajik called Ahmed Shah Massoud, had first encountered the Americans in 1984, when he was fighting the Soviet Union, although he was deprived of American financial assistance at the time because he was implacably opposed to Gulbuddin Hekmatyar, a warlord favored by the ISI. Gary Schroen, a senior Special Forces operative who directed operations in Afghanistan during the first three months of "Operation Enduring Freedom," resumed contact with Massoud in 1996, and for the next five years he and others who were aware of the threats posed by the Taliban and bin Laden tried and failed to secure financial and military support for Massoud's struggle. During a CIA visit to his base in the Panjshir valley, north of Kabul, in October 1999, when his help was sought in tracking down bin Laden, Massoud told the delegation that the US policy was "doomed to fail," because they failed to see the bigger picture. "What about the Taliban?" he asked. "What about the Taliban's supporters in Pakistani intelligence? What about its financiers in Saudi Arabia and the United Arab Emirates?" In November 2000, after al-Qaeda's bombing of the USS *Cole*, CIA officers drew up a wish list for Massoud—including weapons, trucks, helicopters and substantial amounts of money to bribe commanders and to compete with the Taliban's Arab-funded treasury—but President Clinton refused, and President Bush only approved the plan a week before 9/11, at which point the Taliban controlled 90 percent of the country and even Massoud was feeling the pressure.[7]

Five days later—and just two days before 9/11—Massoud was assassinated by two Tunisians, working on behalf of al-Qaeda and posing as journalists, in a mission that was clearly intended to destabilize the Northern Alliance in preparation for a final push on the remaining 10 percent of the country that was under their control.[8] While his death was a significant loss to the anti-Taliban Alliance, however, his legacy was secure. Through his meetings with the CIA over the previous five years, he had essentially set the conditions for "Operation Enduring Freedom," and although the Americans were unfamiliar with his successor, General Mohammed Fahim, their relationship with Massoud provided an invaluable base on which to build a new relationship. Even more importantly, in the months before his death Massoud had strengthened the Alliance considerably, cementing relationships that would become crucial to the Americans: with General Rashid Dostum, the Uzbek warlord and former ruler of the strategically important northern city of Mazar-e-Sharif, who had been encouraged by Massoud to return from self-imposed exile in Turkey in April 2001; with the Tajik Ismael Khan, the former governor of Herat, the relatively wealthy western province which straddled important trade routes to Iran and Turkmenistan; and with Hamid Karzai, a Pashtun from the prominent Popolzai tribe, which had 500,000 clan members in Uruzgan and Kandahar provinces, who had served as deputy foreign minister in the post-Soviet government, but had been forced into exile in Pakistan by the Taliban.[9]

Where the amnesia kicked in for the Americans was in overlooking the Alliance's history over the previous nine years. When the Soviet-backed regime collapsed in 1992, three years after the Soviet withdrawal, General Dostum, who had been fighting with the Russians throughout the occupation, surrendered to Massoud's forces, allowing the Tajiks to take the capital. Although Massoud's ally Burhanuddin Rabbani subsequently became President, it was a fragile peace, and the country soon descended into civil war as Gulbuddin Hekmatyar, allied with the Hazaras, attempted to wrest power from Rabbani and Massoud. When Dostum changed sides again in 1994, allying himself with Hekmatyar, Kabul was all but destroyed as the various sides attempted to annihilate each other. Between 1992 and 1994, over 50,000 people lost their lives in the capital alone, and throughout the country human rights abuses were so widespread that in November 1994, when Kandahar was taken by a small group of Pashtun fighters—the Taliban, strict Islamists influenced by Saudi Arabia's ultra-orthodox Wahhabi doctrine—they were initially regarded as saviors. Over time, however, as they were infiltrated by the ISI and their facade of purity slipped to reveal a harrowing brutality, they became at least as reviled as their predecessors, but as they steadily took over the country in the years that followed, it was their world— a terrifying simulacrum of a medieval Islamic state, with added Kalashnikovs—that confronted the Americans as they prepared to embark on "Operation Enduring Freedom." It was perhaps too easy to forget the carnage that had come before and the part that some of their new allies had played in it.[10]

"Operation Enduring Freedom"

On the night of October 7, 2001, the American mission to "destroy" al-Qaeda and the Taliban commenced in a rain of bombs—on Taliban military facilities, and on 23 military training camps in the south and east of the country, which, in a sign of the hyperbole to come, were all alleged to belong to al-Qaeda.[11] The bombers then targeted locations frequented by bin Laden and Mullah Omar, although Omar himself had already been allowed to escape. On the first night of hostilities, he was identified, fleeing Kabul in a convoy of Taliban vehicles, by a remote-controlled Predator surveillance plane, but by the time the CIA went through the process of requesting permission to fire the Predator's Hellfire missiles—a request which had to be made through Central Command's headquarters in Florida—he had slipped away, never to be seen again.[12]

For the next month, as US Special Forces hooked up with the commanders of their proxy army, the Taliban refused to buckle, and reports of widespread civilian casualties—some that were manufactured by the Taliban for propaganda purposes, but others that were all too real—threatened to derail the war. As the US began, for the first time, to drop cluster bombs on any convenient gathering of Taliban soldiers, the UN's Human Rights Commissioner, Mary Robinson, called for a pause in the bombing to allow aid agencies access to the millions of Afghans who were threatened with starvation, and who had not managed to take advantage of the millions of dollars' worth of MREs (Meals Ready to Eat) that the Americans had also dropped on the hapless population. As the progress of the war swayed in the balance, Musharraf weighed in, insisting that the US held back from the total destruction of the Taliban front lines. "If a power vacuum was filled by the Northern Alliance," he declared, "we would be thrust back to the anarchy and atrocities we saw in the past." Overlooking the Taliban's atrocities of the previous seven years, he neglected to mention how many Pakistani officers were advising the Taliban, how many Pakistani foot soldiers were already serving alongside the Taliban, and how many others were streaming over the border to join the fight.[13]

It was not until a month into the war, when Musharraf's delaying tactics were overruled and US forces began dropping 15,000 pound "daisy-cutter" bombs on the Taliban lines, that the way was paved for what would be the war's pivotal moment, the capture of Mazar-e-Sharif on November 9. The size of a car, "daisy-cutters" incinerate everything within a radius of about 900 meters, and their effect on the Taliban was devastating, incinerating hundreds of soldiers and traumatizing the survivors. In a three-pronged attack, with Special Forces riding in with Dostum's men on horseback from the south and the Tajiks and Hazaras advancing separately from the west, Mazar fell rapidly. Although thousands of Taliban soldiers fled—mainly to the city of Kunduz, 150 km to the east—many more were massacred, and when a thousand stragglers were found in a madrassa, Special Forces called in bombers who scored four direct hits on the building, and Dostum's soldiers stormed the ruins to finish off the survivors. "When the smoke cleared," Gary Berntsen wrote in his account of the war, "Dostum's men counted 450 dead."

After the fall of Mazar, which allowed the Americans to reopen the "Friendship Bridge" to Uzbekistan and bring supplies in by road, the Taliban's collapse throughout northern Afghanistan was spectacular. Over the next few days, Ismael Khan recaptured Herat, and the Hazara recaptured Bamiyan in their central heartlands. Repeatedly hit by air strikes, the Taliban in the north-eastern city of Taloqan, which had been the Northern Alliance base until they captured it 14 months earlier, followed a long-standing Afghan tradition and changed sides, and dozens of other towns also capitulated or were captured. So swift was the fall of the Taliban that on November 13, after a number of significant defections and another will-sapping bombing campaign, in which, according to Berntsen, 2,000 soldiers were killed in 25 air strikes, the Taliban lines broke on the Shomali Plains, north of Kabul. Despite the Americans' insistence that the Alliance should hold back five miles from the capital until an anti-Taliban Pashtun leader was confirmed, to establish some kind of power balance, the Alliance commander, Bismullah Khan, was unwilling or unable to hold back his men, and they entered Kabul in triumph. Although there were a number of summary executions, there was no Mazar-style slaughter, probably because the Taliban, for the most part, had already left, after looting everything in sight, including $6 million from the national bank.[14]

The last city to fall in the north—and the first where prisoners, in large numbers, would have to be dealt with—was Kunduz, where those who had fled the fall of the other cities joined an existing army of Taliban and al-Qaeda soldiers. The exact numbers were unclear, although the Northern Alliance estimated that there were as many as 20,000 men holed up in the city, including 10,000 recent arrivals from Pakistan, and 2,000 foreign al-Qaeda fighters. Whether or not this was a reasonable estimate, the numbers were significantly reduced when, with the approval of the US administration, Musharraf was allowed to avoid political embarrassment by arranging for several planes to airlift Pakistani soldiers and intelligence operatives out of the city. According to a senior intelligence official, the operation "slipped out of control" and an unknown number of Taliban and al-Qaeda fighters also joined the exodus, which probably numbered several thousand people.[15]

Encircled by the Northern Alliance and relentlessly bombed by the Americans, three of the Taliban leaders—deputy defense minister Mullah Mohammed Fazil, his deputy Mullah Dadaullah and Mullah Noorullah Noori, the military commander in northern Afghanistan—arranged to negotiate a surrender with General Dostum in Qala-i-Janghi, a nineteenth-century fortress in Mazar-e-Sharif. In exchange for safe passage for his fighters, Fazil was prepared to surrender the city and all his heavy weapons, but left the fate of the foreign fighters for Dostum to decide. No one wanted to deal with al-Qaeda; neither the Northern Alliance, who were unwilling to face such a fanatical enemy—"They don't care about life, only death," one Alliance soldier noted, incredulously—nor, it seemed, the Taliban. Civilians who escaped the city said that, after a thousand Taliban soldiers defected, an Arab al-Qaeda commander ordered the execution of 150 others who were trying to leave.[16]

Remarkably, Mullah Fazil managed to persuade the foreign fighters to accept the terms of surrender, and on the night of Friday, November 24, a group of 450 foreign fighters set off to surrender to General Dostum in Mazar-e-Sharif. Like the many thousands of mainly Afghan and Pakistani Taliban fighters who surrendered near Kunduz over the next few days, they were to find that the terms of surrender were not as straightforward as they appeared. The first Guantánamo prisoners were drawn from these men, but, although Mullah Fazil had avoided a bloodbath in Kunduz, much more blood would be spilled before they arrived in Cuba.

2
The Qala-i-Janghi Massacre

The "Uprising"

On the morning of Saturday, November 24, in the desert near Mazar-
e-Sharif, the 450 foreign fighters who had left Kunduz to surrender
to General Dostum realized too late that they had been betrayed by
Mullah Fazil, and that they were to be imprisoned rather than being
allowed to return home. Disarmed after a tense stand-off, they were
loaded onto trucks and taken to Mazar-e-Sharif, but Said Kamel,
Dostum's security chief, neglected to search them all before they set
off, and, after arriving at the fort, one of them detonated a hidden
grenade, killing himself, Dostum's police chief Nader Ali, and a number
of his fellow prisoners. Shocked by the attack, Amir Jan Naseri, an
Alliance commander, ordered his men to tie up the prisoners' hands
and put them in the basement, but it was clear that they had not all
been disarmed. That night, fearing they were about to be murdered,
eight more prisoners killed themselves with hidden grenades.[1]

The following morning, two CIA agents—Johnny "Mike" Spann
and an Uzbek speaker called Dave—turned up to interrogate the
prisoners. Spann was filmed quizzing a truculent prisoner, dressed
in a filthy black tunic and with long unkempt hair, whose case was
to overshadow almost all other media reports about Qala-i-Janghi,
when it was revealed that he was a 20-year-old American called John
Walker Lindh. "He won't talk to me," Spann complained to Dave. "I
was explaining to the guy we just want to talk to him, find out what
his story is." "The problem is," Dave replied, "he's got to decide if he
wants to live or die and die here. We're just going to leave him, and
he's going to fucking sit in prison the rest of his fucking short life. It's

his decision, man. We can only help the guys who want to talk to us. We can only get the Red Cross to help so many guys."[2]

Soon after, while Spann was interrogating another prisoner, asking him, "Why are you here?" the man said, "To kill you," and lunged at him. Spann shot the man but was immediately set upon by numerous other prisoners, who beat him to death. As Dave escaped to the parapet, where he called in air strikes, other prisoners overpowered their guards, seizing their weapons, breaking into Dostum's armory, and freeing the rest of their companions from their overnight prison. At least half the prisoners were killed by air strikes that afternoon, but a group of 50 fighters, holed up in the basement, held out for another day. Twenty-four hours later, when Special Forces operatives estimated that only three men were still alive, oil was poured into the house in which they had taken shelter, which was then ignited. As silence descended for the first time in three days, an Alliance commander encouraged his men to descend from the ramparts. Journalist Alex Perry noted that they were "plainly spooked by the suicidal bravery of the Taliban, and had to be forced to break cover," but they soon overcame their fear and began looting the corpses, taking money, pens, cigarettes, copies of the Koran, and, in particular, the dead men's trainers. Two wounded prisoners were executed on the spot. One was "shot to pieces," and another had a rock dropped on his head.[3]

The day after, with the all-clear sounded, journalists poured into the fort, filing reports from the corpse-strewn compound and witnessing further looting, including one Alliance soldier prying gold fillings out of a dead prisoner's mouth. General Dostum also showed up, and brought Mullah Fazil and Mullah Noori with him. The Mullahs were silent, but Dostum was happy to talk. "We tried to treat the Taliban humanely," he said. "We could have tied their hands and their legs but we didn't." As he spoke, one of his soldiers kicked the body of a man to make sure that he was dead, and Justin Huggler noted, "The body rolled over to reveal that the man's arms had been tied together behind his back."[4]

The clean-up continued the following day, when it was announced that 175 corpses had been recovered. No one knew how many more were underground. After four shots rang out from the basement, and two rescue workers stumbled out, wounded, the Alliance and their

American advisors came up with a plan to finish off the survivors: a water supply was diverted, and the whole of the basement was flooded. Astonishingly, despite being bombed, burned and flooded, not every Taliban prisoner had been killed. Thirteen survivors emerged from the basement on the evening of Saturday, December 1, and were detained overnight in a container. Luke Harding reported that there were twelve Pakistanis and one Afghan, and that one of the Pakistanis asked him, in perfect English, "Could you ask them to bring us some tea? We are very hungry. We have had nothing to eat." As he peered into the container, glimpsing a man in the shadows "with no face, whose nose and mouth had been blown away," the English-speaking prisoner told him, "We wanted to surrender on Thursday. But there was a group of seven Arabs who wouldn't let us."[5]

At 10 am, another group of 73 survivors emerged. As they limped forward, one by one, to be searched beneath a ruined avenue of pine trees, a guard called out their nationalities: "Uzbekistan! Arab! Pakistan! Yemen! Chechnya!" "Where are you from?" Matthew Campbell asked a man who stopped in front of him. "I was born in America ... Baton Rouge, Louisiana—you know it, yeah?" the man replied. Later revealed as 21-year-old Yaser Hamdi, who retained his US citizenship despite moving back to Saudi Arabia with his family when he was a child, his case is discussed in Chapter 18. Luke Harding, meanwhile, spoke to Abdul Jabar, a Taliban volunteer from Uzbekistan, who explained, "It was our commander who began the fighting." He was probably referring to Tahir Uldosh, the deputy leader of the Islamic Movement of Uzbekistan (IMU), who was identified as one of the leaders of the uprising, and who presumably succeeded in his aim of choosing death over surrender. While Red Cross representatives handed out apples, bananas and pomegranates, feeding those who were too incapacitated to feed themselves, Harding spoke to another wounded survivor, a Pakistani teenager called Ijaz Latif, who told him, "There were a lot of Pakistanis with me, but most of them are now dead. I didn't see who started the fighting. We just ran away and hid in the basement."[6]

The Survivors' Stories

Of the 86 survivors, at least 50—including 21 Saudis, nine Yemenis, several prisoners from other Gulf countries and North Africa, and a dozen men from the countries bordering Afghanistan to the north—were subsequently transferred to Guantánamo, where their alleged participation in the "uprising" was used against them in their tribunals. It's far from clear, however, that the majority of them were anything more than Taliban foot soldiers, prepared to help the Taliban establish a "pure Islamic state" by fighting the Northern Alliance, but unprepared for 9/11, the US-led invasion, and a "Global War on Terror" in which they would come to be regarded as terrorists.

The Saudis and Yemenis, for example, who were mostly aged between 16 and 25 at the time of their capture, were largely recruited through a fatwa issued by the octogenarian Saudi cleric Sheikh Hamoud al-Uqla, who was condemned by the US administration for condoning 9/11, encouraging jihad against Christians and Jews, and raising money for Osama bin Laden. In the fatwa that was responsible for sending large numbers of young men to Afghanistan to fight with the Taliban, al-Uqla praised the Taliban for creating "the only country in the world in which there are no man-made laws and legislations," and explained that the jihad was "ordained by the Sharia" because it was "against the Northern Alliance which is being funded by the forces of Disbelief like America, Britain, Russia and others who are calling for a broad-based government in Afghanistan established upon a western legislative system." On the ground in Afghanistan, what this actually meant—given Dostum's history in particular— was the Russians, and it was no surprise that many of those who made their way to Afghanistan thought that they were fighting the Russians. Mesh Arsad al-Rashid, a 21-year-old Saudi, said that he went to help Muslims fight Dostum and Massoud over a year "before any problem happened in America," and pointed out that he "didn't know of any alliance between America and Massoud" and that "all that was known in the world was that Massoud and Dostum were helping the Soviet Union."[7]

With a few exceptions, the "evidence" against the Saudis and Yemenis consisted primarily of allegations that they were recruited in the Gulf, and that they trained and served with the Taliban. Very few of them, for example, were accused of training at al-Farouq, the camp established by the influential Afghan warlord and Islamic scholar Abdul Rasul Sayyaf in the early 1990s, which became closely linked to Osama bin Laden in the years before 9/11, and there were none of the exotic allegations about purported connections to al-Qaeda and bin Laden himself that were to plague many of the other Guantánamo prisoners. This is not to say that there were no "hard-core" fighters amongst the survivors, but the tribunal transcripts contain few clues to their identities. The only remotely serious allegations were leveled against four of the Saudis: 30-year-old Bijad al-Atabi was accused of being an assistant commander in al-Qaeda's Arab Brigade, 23-year-old Fahed al-Harazi was accused of traveling to Afghanistan in March 2001 and—with remarkable speed—becoming a trainer in al-Farouq, and 34-year-old Abdullah al-Yamani was accused of knowing both Abu Musab al-Zarqawi (the leader of "al-Qaeda in Iraq," killed in 2006) and Abu Zubaydah (a senior al-Qaeda operative discussed in Chapter 13). Most astonishingly of all, 17-year-old Yasser al-Zahrani (whose death in Guantánamo is discussed in Chapter 19) was accused of being "a front line fighter for the Taliban who facilitated weapons purchases for offensives against US and coalition forces." While a few of these allegations seem to be self-evidently absurd (al-Yamani, for example, was released in 2006), it's worth noting that none of them are necessarily credible, as they were obtained through a long process of dubious interrogations and hearsay "evidence" that will be looked at in more detail in later chapters.[8]

Although only a handful of the Saudi and Yemeni detainees spoke about their experiences, their recollections echoed those of Ijaz Latif. Most were wounded—either by being shot or through shrapnel wounds—and several said that they were tied up before the shooting began. Abdul Aziz al-Oshan, a 22-year-old Saudi student who went to Afghanistan to rescue his brother, told his tribunal, "You are talking about the uprising. They called it an uprising and it's not; it's some kind of massacre. I was even wounded while I was there." Ibrahim al-Sehli, a 36-year-old Saudi, who worked as a guard for the Taliban (and was later diagnosed with dementia and released in 2006), said, "They handcuffed us and put us in a court, a big open space, and there were explosions behind us. Shrapnel from that explosion hit me." Mesh Arsad al-Rashid, who was injured in his thigh and shoulder, asked, "What uprising? We didn't do any uprising. We had given up our weapons, so how could we be part of an uprising? They [Dostum's troops] were the ones that had the weapons. We tried to defend ourselves but we couldn't, because they had all the weapons."

He added that accusing men who were tied up of using weapons was a sure sign of the "betrayal" that had taken place in the fort. Yusef al-Rabiesh, a 20-year-old Saudi, who also went to Afghanistan to rescue his brother (and was also released in 2006), said, "we were taken out two by two. We were handcuffed and seated in a big field ... We sat there for about two to three hours. There was a demonstration and then the Northern Alliance started shooting at us ... We were handcuffed when the shooting started. The only people who had weapons were the Northern Alliance, and they were shooting at the detainees." He added, "I got shot and lost consciousness and my brother was killed. He was handcuffed when he was killed."[9]

The other prisoners from the Gulf and North Africa—Nasser al-Mutairi, a 24-year-old Kuwaiti (released in January 2005), Walid Ali, a 27-year-old from the Sudan, and Ali al-Tayeea, a 28-year-old Iraqi (cleared for release in 2007)—told similar stories. Al-Mutairi, who admitted fighting with the Taliban, but insisted that he went to Afghanistan for rabat (preparation) rather than jihad, said that he and other prisoners were "outside in the courtyard with our hands bound" when the shooting started, and that he was shot as he tried to make his way back to the basement. Walid Ali and Ali al-Tayeea told the most complete stories of being caught in the crossfire and suffering in the basement. Like the Saudi quoted earlier, Walid Ali, who worked as a Taliban guard for a month, stated that he went to Afghanistan to fight the Russians, and was unable to understand how Dostum had become an ally of the United States. Describing what happened in the fort, he said:

> They handcuffed us so tightly that the circulation was cut off, and I became unconscious. [Then] they were firing bullets at us while we were handcuffed and American airplanes came and started firing at us and killed a lot of us. I was handcuffed and wounded in my back with a bullet and it went to my belly where it is now. And I feel the pain of it ... While I was on the ground an American airplane fired a bomb and shrapnel hit my head and it is still there in my head. And then I went unconscious and I did not feel anything until I woke up in a room underground ... Of course, they used all [kinds of] different weapons in order to kill us. They even used water and electricity. And they threw a bomb on us. And a lot of times they opened water on us to the point [that] we had water up to our necks. Of course, the wounded ones couldn't stand up and they were killed in the water.[10]

Ali al-Tayeea explained what happened after he came out of the basement on the day that the uprising began:

> Now, all the people were outside and we hear the bomb and someone from Dostum's army had a machine gun on his shoulder. He opened fire on people. People were yelling, "please don't shoot" and he opened fire … There was nothing we could do. We were in the centre and fire came from everywhere. A lot of people died. I laid down because my hands were tied. I begged for someone to just open my hands because they had been tied for a long time with wire and they were blue and cold. They opened my hands and I went inside the shelter. There was bombing and fire for the first three days. It was dark and you couldn't see who your neighbour was. Like, 70 people had died and it smelled bad.

After explaining that some of those in the basement were still armed, he continued:

> I didn't fire because I'm not a jackass. I stayed inside. After three days, they opened the window and put fire inside the shelter and there was nothing we could do about it. Many people died in the fire and it smelled like steak. I looked and I was beside John Walker. After this they put water in through the window. John Walker was tall and he's beside my shoulder. Some of the detainees that were short were under water.[11]

In addition to the Arabs, the survivors from Afghanistan's neighbors to the north also had stories to tell, although Abdul Jabar was not among them. Like numerous Pakistanis (some of whom were probably transferred to Guantánamo but then released in 2003 or 2004 without their stories being recorded), the fate of the eleven Uzbeks who survived the Qala-i-Janghi massacre is unknown, although the most alarming possibility is that they were among the dozens of Uzbeks who were transferred to the custody of President Karimov in exchange for services rendered.[12] Instead, there were a few Tajiks, a Kazakh, four "Russian" Muslims (two Balkars from Kabardino-Balkaria, north of Georgia, and two Tatars from Bashkortostan, north of Kazakhstan), and a handful of Uyghurs who had fled from poverty and oppression in East Turkistan, a largely Muslim country bordering Pakistan, Kyrgyzstan and Kazakhstan, which was subjugated by the People's Republic of China and is now known as Xinjiang province. What's noticeable about these prisoners is that several were serving with far less enthusiasm than either Abdul Jabar or the majority of the Arabs, and others were simply in the wrong place at the wrong time.

One of the Uyghurs, 30-year-old Ahmad Tourson, who had been living in Kabul since arriving in Afghanistan with his family in 2000, was accused of traveling from Kunduz to Mazar-e-Sharif to fight the Northern Alliance. In response, he said that he was arrested for no reason, after visiting Kunduz to find out if it was easier for Uyghurs to live with Uzbeks in the north of Afghanistan than it was in Kabul: "Foreigners, bad people, good people, soldiers, fighters. Everybody walks through the street and I am passing through the road, then I am captured by General Dostum's troops. It does not explain that all these people are al-Qaeda. It is kind of funny looking. Everybody walks in the street, everybody walks." Speaking of his time in Qala-i-Janghi, he said that a Uyghur friend of his was killed in the fortress, and added, "I did not participate in the riot. They dropped bombs and I was injured. I was not a soldier. I have nothing against the Americans. Why would I participate in the riot? All Uyghurs have one enemy, the Chinese. We have no other enemies."[13]

The rest of the prisoners were scarcely more fortunate, as they were mostly coerced into service by pro-Taliban forces in Tajikistan and Uzbekistan. Although the 28-year-old Balkar Ruslan Ogidov left home partly because he had been tortured by the Russian intelligence services in 1999, and his compatriot Rasul Kudayev, a 17-year-old former wrestling champion, left home to avoid military service, the Tatars Shamil Khazhiyev, a 30-year-old police lieutenant, and Ravil Gumarov, a 39-year-old businessman, fitted the profile of religious refugees who were coerced into military activity. Gumarov's father said that his son's desire to live under Islamic law grew so strong that, in 2000, he abandoned his wife, four children and elderly parents to travel to Afghanistan. "When I asked him what he would do abroad," his father said, "Ravil said he was ready to tend sheep if he could live under the rule of Islam." Leonid Syukiainen, a Russian academic, drew parallels between the Russian prisoners and the idealistic Westerners who moved to the Soviet Union after the 1917 Revolution to help build a socialist society. "Of course, there had to be a combination of reasons for these people to flee to Afghanistan," he said, "but I believe that their strongest motive was that they sincerely sought a fair Islamic society there." Igor Tkachyov, the head of a team of Russians who visited the prisoners at Guantánamo, made even more specific comments about what happened to the men. He said that they traveled via Tajikistan, where members of the Islamic opposition to President Rahmonov helped them get to Afghanistan, and added that once they were there they "found themselves in a kind of totalitarian sect commanded by the Taliban ... They were not allowed to be alone and had to do everything together, obeying strict regulations that left no time for anything but prayers."[14]

Ilkham Batayev, a 28-year-old from Kazakhstan (released in December 2006) told a similar story. After traveling to Tajikistan to sell apples, he was kidnapped by thugs working for the IMU, and transported to Kunduz, where he was forced to work as an assistant to a Taliban cook. In the chaos surrounding the fall of Kunduz, he saw his chance to escape, and hopped in a car with some other men who were hoping to escape to Iran, but was captured by Northern Alliance soldiers and taken to Qala-i-Janghi. Sick with malaria, and in pain from a recent operation to remove his wisdom teeth, he decided to leave the basement behind everybody else on the Sunday morning, but was injured by a grenade as soon as he emerged, and then crawled back underground, where he spent the next six days hallucinating because he had lost a large amount of blood.[15]

On December 1, as a container truck arrived to take the survivors to General Dostum's prison at Sheberghan, human rights groups began calling for an investigation, suggesting that the Geneva Conventions could have been breached on two specific counts: the requirements that "prisoners of war must at all times be humanely treated," and that, if force were to be used against them, it had to be "proportionate." With hindsight, and the knowledge that the US administration was preparing to discard the Geneva Conventions altogether, it's clear that no investigation was ever likely to take place, but it also remains apparent that there was some justification for the US administration's claim that "they only bombed Qala-i-Janghi because their own personnel were under threat." Having noted this, however, "proportionate" is the last word that comes to mind to describe the colossal number of bombs that were dropped on the fort, and when it comes to other aspects of the operation the evidence of both inhumane treatment and a brutality that is far from proportionate becomes even more compelling. The summary execution of two wounded prisoners has already been mentioned above, but its callousness should not be overlooked or forgotten.

Nor, too, should the attempts by both Dostum and the Americans to suggest that few of those who were killed were tied up at the time they were shot. Although various reporters were briefed that "only" eight prisoners had been bound before being shot after the uprising started, the estimate of 250, which was proposed by Luke Harding, is more credible for three reasons: first, because a photographer "saw the bodies of up to 50 Taliban fighters whose hands had been bound by scarves, laid out in a field in the southern part of the fort," and that he "watched as Alliance fighters cut the scarves from the hands of the corpses"; secondly, because Alex Perry noted, "some of the dead had their hands bound, and Alliance soldiers used scissors to snip off the strings"; and third, and no less significantly, because so many of the survivors—whose testimony was suppressed until the Pentagon released their tribunal transcripts in 2006—also talked about being bound when the shooting started.[16]

3
The Convoy of Death

Yerghanek and Qala Zeini

On Sunday, November 25, 2001, as the uprising began in Qala-i-Janghi, a far larger group of Taliban soldiers—at least 4,500, but possibly as many as 7,000—made their way from Kunduz to Yerghanek, five miles west of the city, where they surrendered to General Dostum. What no one either knew or cared about, however, was that among the surrendering soldiers were hundreds of civilians who had been caught up in the chaos or who were fleeing the hard-core al-Qaeda and Taliban fighters making a last stand in Kunduz itself.

One of the most vivid accounts of the surrender was provided by three young Britons who fell into this latter category. Twenty-four-year-old Shafiq Rasul, 20-year-old Asif Iqbal and 20-year-old Rhuhel Ahmed—childhood friends from Tipton in the West Midlands—had traveled to Pakistan in September 2001. Iqbal was making arrangements for his forthcoming marriage to a young woman in Pakistan, Ahmed was his best man, and Rasul was planning to do a computer course once the wedding was over, but soon after their arrival, when the invasion of Afghanistan began, they made the fateful decision that an exciting adventure awaited them over the border, just a short bus-ride away. Using the money they had brought with them, they planned to provide humanitarian aid to Afghan villagers, a mission that also involved the adrenaline rush of being in a war zone, and, they hoped, the opportunity to sample the Afghans' enormous naan breads. Up close, however, the war zone was more frightening than they had anticipated. At risk from both US bombing raids and the Taliban, who were deeply suspicious of young men wandering around without beards, they tried to return to Pakistan in a taxi, but were instead taken to Kunduz. As the first groups of Taliban soldiers began to surrender, they clambered onto a truck that was leaving the city, but the vehicle was immediately shelled, and almost everyone on board was killed. With nowhere else to turn, they surrendered to Alliance soldiers who took their money, their shoes and their warm clothes, and marched them to Yerghanek.[1]

Very few of those who made their way to Yerghanek—70 at most—were eventually transferred to Guantánamo. Of these, only a handful have spoken about their experiences, and none were in the first convoys that set off for Sheberghan on the Sunday. Overwhelmed by the sheer numbers of people flooding out of the city, Dostum was obliged to keep thousands of them marooned in the desert while he arranged additional transportation over the next few days. As a result, neither the men from Tipton nor the others who ended up in Guantánamo—including Abdul Rahman, a 25-year-old shopkeeper from Kunduz, and Mohammed Saghir, a 49-year-old woodcutter from Pakistan's North West Frontier Province—had any inkling of the grisly fate that awaited them.

While the vast crowds of fighters and civilians were disarmed, Dostum's men recruited drivers to go to Qala Zeini, an old fort on the road between Mazar-e-Sharif and Sheberghan, where those transported from Yerghanek were transferred into containers for the last stage of the journey to Sheberghan. One of the drivers, who was in the fort when a convoy of prisoners arrived that evening, said that, as soon as the Northern Alliance soldiers began stripping them of their turbans and vests, tying their hands behind their backs and transferring them to the containers, some of the prisoners—those who were familiar with recent Afghan history—realized that Dostum was planning to kill them. Since 1997, when a brutal Uzbek general had first seen the viability of containers as cheap and convenient killing machines, murdering 1,250 Taliban soldiers by leaving them in containers in the summer sun, they had become a familiar weapon of Afghan warfare. When the Taliban took Mazar-e-Sharif in 1998, they disposed of their conquered enemies in the same fashion.

According to one of the drivers, a few hours after the convoy had set off from Qala Zeini, the prisoners started pounding on the sides of the containers, shouting, "We're dying. Give us water! We are human, not animals." He said that he and other drivers punctured holes in the walls and passed through bottles of water, but added that those who were caught doing this were punished. Even these gestures, however, were not enough to prevent large numbers of the prisoners from suffocating as the convoy crawled towards Sheberghan. When the first trucks pulled up at the prison and the doors of the containers were opened, most were disturbingly silent. One of the drivers recalled, "They opened the doors and the dead bodies spilled out like fish."[2]

Back at Yerghanek, other prisoners had worries of their own. Abdul Rahman's life had been unsettled for some time. Originally from Zabul province, east of Kandahar, he moved to Kunduz, where he established a small general store, after rival tribesmen seized his family's land. When the US bombing campaign began, he was reassured that "they were also dropping leaflets and telling on the radio they were coming, saying their fight was not with the public; it was only against the Taliban and al-Qaeda"; but as he set off for home on the day of the Taliban surrender he found that Tajik soldiers of the Northern Alliance had blocked the roads, and were "pinpointing Pashtuns and taking them out of cars, taking their money and beating them up." When some locals said that he and other merchants should seek US and Red Cross assistance at Yerghanek, they started making their way there, but were stopped by Dostum's men. "They told us when we see you Pashtun people, we will tie you up and beat you up," he said. "They did as promised, and a lot of Pashtun people in Afghanistan got beaten up."

Abducted and taken to Yerghanek, Abdul Rahman watched in shock as several Taliban members bribed their captors to set them free, while he and the other captured shopkeepers were tied up for the night. He became even more fearful when he heard screams during the night. "I think they buried about 50 people alive in the ground," he said. "They kept on shouting and screaming, and they kept putting dirt on them." The following day, his nightmare began in earnest. He and his companions were taken to Qala Zeini, where container trucks were waiting to take them to Sheberghan. "About 200–300 people were thrown in these trucks, and they closed the doors," he said. "We did not see any light, and there was no air in it. Due to lack of air, a lot of people died there; I fainted somehow." When they finally arrived at Sheberghan, "We were in bad shape, and they left the dead behind." Three years later, having been transported from Sheberghan to Kandahar and then to Guantánamo, Abdul Rahman's nightmare had still not come to an end. In his tribunal, repeating his story as he had so many times before, he was obliged to refute allegations that he had bought a car for the Taliban while wearing a Taliban-style turban, accompanied by his personal security force of four Taliban soldiers, explaining that this was a story that had been conjured up by the men who falsely imprisoned him in the first place. Finally, someone believed his story, and, after 40 months in detention, he was released in April 2005.[3]

Mohammed Saghir faced a similar ordeal. The woodcutter was also a missionary with Jamaat-al-Tablighi, a vast worldwide proselytizing organization whose annual gatherings in Pakistan and Bangladesh attract millions of followers. Over the years he had been involved in numerous preaching missions to Afghanistan, but on this occasion he and nine other missionaries were seized by Northern Alliance troops. Saghir was also held for a night at Yerghanek, where he "witnessed wounded and injured men buried alive with the dead," and was then taken to Qala Zeini and herded into a container. "The journey took five hours," he said. "It was dark, hot and suffocating as there was not enough air in the container. Fifty out of the 250 prisoners died on [the] way." Unlike Abdul Rahman, however, it took Saghir less than a year to convince the Americans of his innocence. He was one of the first three prisoners to be freed, in November 2002, and was the first ex-Guantánamo prisoner to speak in detail not only about the horrors of detention in Afghanistan and Cuba, but also about the death convoys.[4]

The three men from Tipton waited for another day until their transportation was arranged, and in their case the container lorries came at night, and the whole sordid spectacle was illuminated by spotlights operated by US Special Forces soldiers. Once the doors were shut, their ordeal followed a now familiar pattern. "They'd herded maybe 300 of us into each container ... packed in so tightly our knees were against our chests," Asif Iqbal said, "and almost immediately we started to suffocate." As with some of the previous journeys, ventilation was provided by Northern Alliance soldiers, who made sure that their humanitarian gesture was accompanied by more killing. "We lived because someone made holes with a machine gun," Iqbal said, "though they were shooting low and still more died from the bullets. The last thing I remember is that it got really hot, and everyone started screaming and banging. It was like someone had lit a fire beneath the containers. You could feel the moisture running off your body, and people were ripping off their clothes." When he finally awoke, he realized that he had not drunk anything for more than two days, and was seriously dehydrated. Using a cloth, he wiped the moisture off the wall and began sucking on it, until he realized he was drinking the blood of those who had died. "We were like zombies," he said. "We stank; we were covered in blood and the smell of death."[5]

Sheberghan

As the survivors spilled out of the container trucks at Sheberghan, they discovered that, although the mass executions were over, the conditions at Dostum's prison were almost unspeakably grim. Thirty-five hundred prisoners were crammed into a space that could only reasonably hold five hundred, and in order to sleep they took turns on the floor, squeezed together in four-hour shifts. Food was also a problem. Shafiq Rasul recalled that each prisoner received a quarter of a naan every day, and a small cup of water, and that sometimes prisoners fought over the food. Twenty-four-year-old Sulaiman Shah, an Afghan used car dealer, was another of the many innocents swept up by the Northern Alliance. On his release in March 2003, he mentioned his time at Sheberghan, where, he said, "life was inhuman, all the prisoners had diarrhea, some had tuberculosis, there was no food for days at a time and we were subjected to beatings and torture."[6] Despite Shah's appraisal of the ill-health of the prisoners, medical attention was non-existent. Rasul recalled, "There were people with horrific injuries—limbs that had been shot off and nothing was done. I'll never forget one Arab who was missing half his jaw. For ten days until his death he was screaming and crying continuously, begging to be killed."

To make matters worse, reporters were swarming around Sheberghan, but for the most part they were blind to the suffering of the prisoners. "All they seemed to be interested in," Rasul said, "was if any of us knew the American Taliban John Walker Lindh." No one realized that Lindh was not even in Sheberghan. Instead, he and the other Qala-i-Janghi survivors were taken to a hospital in Mazar-e-Sharif, where they were discovered by Robert Young Pelton, an American writer who was staying with General Dostum. "They were the most pathetic looking humans I had ever seen," he said, "they were all freezing, hypothermic because they were wet and it was very cold that night." Pelton talked to Lindh as he was being treated, and noted that he was "a very gentle, thoughtful, intellectual person," adding, "If you've been around fighters and soldiers a lot, that's just the wrong kind of guy you put on the front lines." When Lindh recovered, Pelton arranged to take him back to Dostum's house, and, after cleaning him up, feeding him and giving him a chance to sleep, "the next day he was blindfolded and taken to the Turkish schoolhouse where the Americans had a base." Ironically, while the Qala-i-Janghi survivors received medical treatment, the prisoners in Sheberghan continued to be deprived of even the most basic comforts. After ten days, Red Cross representatives were finally allowed to visit, but although they brought food supplies and water, several prisoners complained that it was confiscated by the guards. "The Red Cross people asked Dostum's people to feed us," Abdul Rahman said, "but they wouldn't. Those were dark nights for us."[7]

Several weeks passed before the first of the prisoners in Sheberghan were transferred to US custody, but in the meantime, as news of the massacre began to seep out, human rights organizations again called for an investigation, focusing not only on the convoys, but also on claims that the dead and wounded had been buried in mass graves at Dasht-i-Leili, an expanse of wasteland on the outskirts of Sheberghan. The graves were subjected to intense scrutiny over the next few months, as representatives of Physicians for Human Rights, and Bill Hegland, a pioneer in the field of "human rights archaeology," investigated them. Both confirmed that a massacre had taken place, but, as with Qala-i-Janghi, no official inquiry took place. *Newsweek* reported that the UN confirmed that the findings were "sufficient to justify a fully-fledged criminal investigation," but also noted that advisors warned against proceeding with the case, citing its "political sensitivity."[8]

It was left to film-maker Jamie Doran, in his documentary *Afghan Massacre: The Convoy of Death*, to present a series of explosive claims, which remain unanswered. Doran, who concluded that up to three thousand men were killed in the convoys, sought out eyewitnesses to explain what had happened. While no one claimed that the Americans had any prior knowledge of the massacre, an Afghan soldier said that, when confronted with the corpses of several hundred men, "The Americans told the Sheberghan people to get them outside the city before they were filmed by satellite." He also visited Dasht-i-Leili with a driver who said that he was accompanied by thirty to forty American soldiers when he brought wounded men to the site, who were then shot and buried, and spoke to other witnesses who said that the Americans were responsible for murders and disappearances at the prison. An Alliance soldier told him that a US soldier murdered a Taliban prisoner in order to frighten the others into talking, and explained, "The Americans did whatever they wanted; we had no power to stop them. Everything was under the control of the American commander," and an Alliance general said he saw US soldiers stabbing prisoners in the leg and cutting their tongues. "Sometimes, it looked as if they were doing it for pleasure. They would take a prisoner outside, beat him up and return him to the jail," he said. "But sometimes, they were never returned and they disappeared."[9] While these were grave allegations, the Americans' conduct over the months and years to come would do nothing to dispel fears that torture, murder and disappearances had become acceptable tools in the "War on Terror."

4
Tora Bora

Tora Bora

On Saturday, November 10, 2001, Osama bin Laden addressed a meeting of a thousand tribal leaders and their followers at the Islamic Studies Centre in Jalalabad, telling them, "The Americans had a plan to invade, but if we are united and believe in Allah, we'll teach them a lesson, the same one we taught the Russians," and that evening, at a lavish banquet, envelopes were handed out to the tribal leaders containing between $300 and $10,000, depending on the size and influence of the various clans. Three days later, bin Laden's convoy, consisting of several hundred vehicles loaded up with men, women and children, set off for the caves of Tora Bora, south-east of the city. First fortified during the war against the Soviet Union, using funds from the Saudis and the expertise of the ISI, the caves had been converted by Engineer Mahmoud, a commander serving under Maulvi Younis Khalis, an alim (Islamic scholar) and prominent Islamic leader, and the whole area was one that bin Laden knew well. He had fought nearby in his mujahideen days, when he had established his reputation as a warrior, and, while his speech in Jalalabad had focused on the forthcoming showdown with the Americans, he had specifically couched it in the context of the resistance to the Russians, promising a reprise of the guerrilla warfare that had been so successful in the 1980s. Tora Bora had also figured prominently in bin Laden's more recent history. In 1996, when he returned to Afghanistan from Sudan, it was Khalis in particular who welcomed him in Jalalabad, and later allowed him to further adapt the caves, and a compound in the nearby Milawa valley, for use as a family home and as "a command centre and logistics hub."[1]

As the Americans prepared to take on bin Laden in Tora Bora, they followed the pattern established in northern Afghanistan and recruited a proxy army, instead of risking the lives of their own men. Astonishingly, they first tried to recruit Khalis, seemingly oblivious to the fact that he was a friend of bin Laden, and had issued a call for jihad against US forces at the start of the invasion. When Khalis told them he was retired, they recruited two of his former commanders, who had both fought the Russians in Tora Bora and Jalalabad: Hazrat Ali, a semi-literate bruiser, who had flirted briefly with the Taliban before allying himself with Ahmed Shah Massoud, and Haji Zaman Ghamsharik, a wealthy, sophisticated drug smuggler, who had been living in France during the Taliban years, until he was lured back by American money.[2]

While these alliances did not augur well for the success of the Tora Bora mission, the most grievous failure on the part of the Americans concerned their unwillingness to put troops on the ground to block the exit routes leading to Pakistan. Seduced by their own hyped-up fantasies about the scale and intensity of al-Qaeda's fanatical hordes, they failed to realize that, far from being "Al-Qaeda's Last Stand," Tora Bora was actually hemorrhaging jihadi refugees at an alarming rate. The Afghans were astonished at this oversight, but the most vociferous complaints came from other Americans. Gary Berntsen, who directed the Tora Bora operation on the ground, attempted to persuade the military high command to use a battalion of 800 Rangers—the army's most highly-trained paratroops—to seal the border. Turned down by the Rangers' commander, for fear of "alienating our Afghan allies," Berntsen shouted, "I don't give a damn about offending our allies! All I care about is eliminating al-Qaeda and delivering bin Laden's head in a box!"[3]

Compounding these failures, the situation was no better on the Pakistani side of the border, where the crossings were also unguarded. The only time the Pakistani government had sent troops into the remote and effectively autonomous Pashtun tribal areas bordering Afghanistan was to put down a revolt in 1973, and it was followed by a hideously violent 18-month struggle that no one in the government wanted to repeat. As a result, it took President Musharraf several weeks to negotiate a troop deployment with the tribal leaders, and by the time two brigades arrived at the border—around December 10—it was too late for all but the last-minute mopping-up operations that are discussed in the next three chapters.

According to *Newsweek*, the Tora Bora fighters had actually been in full-scale retreat from November 16. That evening, 600 armed men, who had been led by a local guide on a seven-hour trek from Tora Bora, passed through a village near the Pakistani border. While some of the men rested, the villagers recognized several senior Taliban figures in a group that pressed on without pausing for food, including Maulvi Abdul Qabir, Mullah Omar's deputy. One local was so impressed that he decided to investigate how they had managed to escape without encountering any American bombing. He discovered that, although there were two routes out of Tora Bora—one leading down to Khost, and the other, which the fighters had taken, across the White Mountains—the Americans were only bombing the route to Khost. Working as a guide over the next month, he made five trips across the White Mountains, escorting around twenty men at a time and traveling at night along old smuggling paths. He added that one of the men told him that bin Laden and his son Abdullah had left Tora Bora on December 1 "for an unknown place," and this was confirmed by Abu Jaffar, a Saudi al-Qaeda financier, who told the *Christian Science Monitor* that he had left in early December and had sent his son Salah Uddin to take his place.[4]

By the time the ground offensive began, on December 3, the Americans' allies had managed to assemble an army of 2,500 men, vastly outnumbering their now-depleted enemy, but lacking the al-Qaeda fighters' command of the terrain, and the avowed fanaticism of those who had chosen not to flee. With the help of three dozen US Special Forces operatives, who called in targeted air strikes, they slowly gained the upper hand, but the US forces were unprepared when, realizing that the remaining fighters were still well-armed and committed to martyrs' deaths, Ghamsharik established radio contact with one of the Tora Bora commanders on December 12 and attempted to negotiate a ceasefire. Responding that they would only surrender to the UN, the commander requested extra time to discuss the matter, and said that he would get back in contact the following morning. Unsurprisingly, the return call never materialized. The Americans were outraged, arguing that the negotiations were just a ploy to allow time for the rest of the fighters to escape. They were almost certainly right, but their claim that 800 fighters escaped that night was wildly exaggerated, considering quite how many people (1,500 at least) had slipped away over the previous month through American squeamishness and inertia.[5]

The Survivors

When the Afghans took the last of the Tora Bora caves on December 16, 200 corpses, scattered around the mountains, testified to some kind of a victory, but there were few survivors. News reports at the time gave the impression that the prisoners captured at Tora Bora were the last men standing in some kind of final bloody siege, but the majority of them were in a group of recent recruits and religious students who were passing through a valley on their way to Pakistan when they were targeted in a US bombing raid. Another dozen or so were captured in the days before and after the end of hostilities was declared on December 16, and of these around 15 were Afghans, while the foreigners—ten men who were paraded in front of the world's media on December 17, six who were taken to a hospital in Jalalabad, and around 14 others—were handed over to US forces after four to six weeks in Afghan custody.[6]

Some of the prisoners were questioned by US Special Forces while in Afghan custody—specifically for information on bin Laden's whereabouts. A cameraman who was present while they spent four hours interrogating prisoners in a compound near Tora Bora reported, "From what I could see through the crack in the door, the Special Forces were asking hard questions in Arabic, but not mistreating the prisoners in any way." On the same day, the six severely wounded prisoners were transported to the hospital in Jalalabad, where they too were questioned. One of them, described as "Fehmi, a 20-something Yemeni fighter," said, "Osama was with us in Tora Bora, but he stayed high in the mountains and rarely made contact. I think he is still up there somewhere or maybe he has escaped," an insight that was about as useful as Donald Rumsfeld's comment, on December 13, "I have seen reports that people believe are from reasonably reliable sources that, in one case, suggest he's still in Afghanistan, in another case suggest he's out of Afghanistan."[7]

In truth, it was unlikely that any of those captured would have been able to provide more detailed information on bin Laden's whereabouts. Like the majority of those captured in Tora Bora, 24-year-old Fehmi al-Assani was a recent recruit to the Taliban cause, a foot soldier in an inter-Muslim civil war that had suddenly gone global. He traveled to Afghanistan in the summer of 2001, trained briefly at al-Farouq and ended up in Tora Bora, but only, he said, because "I was fleeing for my life with many other people to avoid the bombing that was imminent," and not, as was alleged, because he "was assigned to augment Taliban and al-Qaeda forces already in defensive positions in Tora Bora." He added that he was with a group of Pakistanis, trying to get to Pakistan, when they were bombed by US forces and he was "the sole survivor."[8]

The rest of the prisoners in the hospital in Jalalabad appear to have been wounded in the other bombing raid mentioned above. With a few exceptions—in particular, Ayman Batarfi, a charismatic, 31-year-old Egyptian-born Yemeni doctor, who was to assume increasing importance for the Americans over the coming months (as described in Chapter 14)—they too were recent arrivals in Afghanistan, and their role in the "War on Terror" seems to have been as minimal as that of al-Assani. Abdullah al-Anazi, a 21-year-old Saudi, who lost a leg in the bombing raid (and had his other leg amputated at Guantánamo), said that he went to Afghanistan to provide spiritual assistance to the Afghans, and Walid Zaid, a 23-year-old Yemeni who was wounded in the left foot in the raid, denied that he went to Afghanistan for "jihad readiness military training," as alleged, and said that he had just finished his final year studying Arabic literature at college, and went to Afghanistan a fortnight before 9/11 because he hoped to teach Arabic in an Afghan school. He admitted attending al-Farouq, but said that he had only done so because some Afghan acquaintances said that Afghanistan "was a country with a great deal of fighting," and suggested that he should get some training in self-defense.[9]

A rather more expansive story was told by Ghanim al-Harbi, a 27-year-old Saudi, who said that he went to Afghanistan in summer 2001 because he "felt the need to defend myself and my family." He explained that some of his family members had been imprisoned during the invasion of Kuwait by Saddam Hussein, and had subsequently moved to Saudi Arabia, and that, in 2000, when it was felt that the Iraqi leader was causing problems again, he decided that he should learn to defend himself. When his attempts to join the Saudi Navy came to nothing, his quest led him to Afghanistan. He admitted training at al-Farouq, but added, "I never completed my training because I became ill. Every week I had to travel to Kandahar to receive medical treatment or I was at the camp hospital." He also said that Osama bin Laden had spoken at the camp, but that he had not attended because "it was voluntary, I was sick and it gave me a chance to sleep," and explained that bin Laden "is a radical with radical thoughts and I didn't want to be influenced by him." While this infuriated the Presiding Officer of his tribunal, who insisted, "Al-Farouq trained al-Qaeda to kill," al-Harbi replied, "That wasn't written about it. All I know [is that] there were a lot of people in al-Farouq training. To my knowledge, Osama bin Laden was just a guest and he would give a speech and just leave." This conflicts with the received intelligence about al-Farouq as "bin Laden's camp," but it perhaps explains what the situation was actually like in summer 2001, as unprecedented numbers of volunteers arrived in Afghanistan for training.

After leaving al-Farouq, al-Harbi said that he went to Kabul and hired a guide to help him leave the country, but when the guide realized he was unable to help him cross the border, he took him to the Tora Bora mountains and turned him over to a group of 65 Arabs who were also trying to escape. He explained that he stayed with them for the month of Ramadan, and described them as civilians rather than fighters: "Some of them were teachers, some of them were running away from the war and were just regular civilians who were trying to get back to the Pakistan embassy so they could get back to their homes." Around December 13, he said that the group finally managed to recruit two guides to take them to the Pakistani border, but, as they passed through a village, the whole area was targeted in a huge US bombing raid, in which 60 to 70 of the villagers died, and "40 of the Arabs with me were killed and 20 were injured"; al-Harbi suffered serious injuries to his stomach and one of his legs.[10]

Also captured after the raid were a handful of mostly older prisoners from countries other than Saudi Arabia or the Yemen, including Ahcene Zemiri, a 34-year-old Algerian, Faiz al-Kandari, a 26-year-old Kuwaiti, Abdul Latif Nassir, a 36-year-old Moroccan,

Tariq al-Sawah, a 26-year-old Egyptian, who had been living in Bosnia, and two Tunisians, 35-year-old Riyad Nasseri and 36-year-old Abdul Ourgy. Zemiri, who had been living in Canada, said that he moved to Afghanistan in June 2001 with his Canadian wife—who was pregnant at the time—"to immigrate, live and retire peacefully," primarily because he and other North Africans were kept under non-stop scrutiny by the Canadian intelligence services. After the US-led invasion began, his wife managed to return safely to Canada, but he was trapped in the mountains, where he sustained a broken arm and shrapnel wounds in the bombing raid.[11]

Al-Kandari and Nassir were interviewed by the journalist Jon Lee Anderson in jail in Jalalabad, shortly after their capture. Al-Kandari explained, "The international community is mistaken about Arabs in Afghanistan. Not all are here for Osama bin Laden." He said that he was a businessman, adding, "I have a lot of money, and I came here to Afghanistan to help Muslims. I came to dig wells." When Jalalabad fell, he explained that he met some Arabs, who "said I should go into the mountains with them, and so I did and that's when I was caught." This is the story he has maintained throughout his imprisonment by the Americans, but it was regarded as unbelievable from the beginning. Anderson told him, "This is hardly credible," and noted that the interpreter laughed while translating his story, "and put his hand on the Kuwaiti's shoulder in a matey kind of way." Nassir told a rather different story, explaining, "I came to Afghanistan because of Afghanistan's strict Islamic rule, and because it was full of Islamic scholars." He said that he was in Kabul when it fell to the Northern Alliance, and then escaped to Jalalabad and fled to the mountains.[12]

The Tunisians—who had both been living in Italy in the 1990s—were subjected to more serious allegations. Nasseri was accused of training at the Durunta camp near Jalalabad, which was established by the warlord Gulbuddin Hekmatyar in the early 1990s,[13] and of fleeing Jalalabad for a cave in Tora Bora, where he was injured during the US bombing, and where he "and others arranged their surrender." Ourgy, who was injured in the bombing raid, said that he had been a drug dealer until he met a man in Milan who revived his faith and encouraged him to attend a training camp in Afghanistan. He admitted training at Durunta in 1997, but said that he had since settled down, and had married in 2000. He added that, after the fall of Jalalabad, when Arabs were being killed, his brother-in-law took his wife to safety in Pakistan, but he stayed behind to pack up the household goods and then volunteered to go through the mountains to Pakistan: "I couldn't go through the main road because I am an Arab. That way, when he [the brother-in-law] entered Pakistan with all these household goods there would be no problem."[14]

In the months that followed, as the Americans began mining the prisoners for intelligence, seeking out connections, drawing on developments elsewhere in the "War on Terror," and eliciting confessions that were often obtained through coercion or bribery, all the men described above came under increasing scrutiny. Zemiri was erroneously linked to Ahmed Ressam, who had planned to blow up Los Angeles airport in a "Millennium Plot" at the end of 1999 (Ressam only recanted his "confession" in January 2007), al-Kandari was mysteriously transformed into a spiritual leader of al-Qaeda, and the North Africans were linked to an alleged web of militants, scattered throughout Europe, that first began to be pieced together by interrogators working in the US prison at Kandahar airbase. While these will be discussed in the chapters that follow, it's worth noting that the only ones who admitted to any kind of sustained military involvement were Abdul Latif Nassir and Tariq al-Sawah.

In his interview with Jon Lee Anderson, Nassir explained more about his presence in Afghanistan. He said that, although he had been a businessman, he decided to become a fighter in Afghanistan, and attended a Libyan training camp in Kabul. While Faiz al-Kandari was vague about al-Qaeda's presence in Tora Bora, telling Anderson, "The al-Qaeda didn't keep their people with us. Al-Qaeda takes its people to a big secret place in the mountains. There are a lot of secret things in al-Qaeda," Nassir admitted that he had seen Osama bin Laden in the mountains. "He was in Tora Bora for a long time and he was receiving a lot of visitors," he said, adding that bin Laden told them, "Believe in us, believe in Allah, believe in me, in this jihad. We will win in the end."[15]

In contrast to Nassir, al-Sawah's military commitment was specifically directed at the Northern Alliance. A former aid worker, he was married to a Bosnian woman and went to Afghanistan to see if it was a suitable place to take his family. Once there, he succumbed to the most virulent anti-Massoud propaganda, declaring, "One time in a jihad, Massoud killed about 10,000 Muslims in an hour," and decided that it was his mission to support those who were being oppressed by the Northern Alliance. He insisted, "There are no rules in the United States to prevent it if you want to fight for religion. There are no rules to direct me not to defend people," and also pointed out that he went to Afghanistan to fight the Northern Alliance before 9/11, when it was no business of the Americans: "If Massoud and Dostum are American allies, they were not an alliance before September 11th, were they?" Charged up with his new-found fervor, he became a trainer at a military camp, but denied engaging in hostilities against the US, saying, in a comment that cut to the heart of the proxy war, "There was no fighting against Americans. If there were any American soldiers saying they were fighting in Afghanistan, bring them here to me and show the evidence." Mentioning a well-founded belief that numerous prisoners were sold for money (which is discussed in more detail in the next chapter), he explained that "because the Americans offered $5,000 to anyone who captured us, they [the Northern Alliance] were fighting us and they kept us alive to get the $5,000." Injured in the bombing raid, after spending a month in the mountains, he gave a poignant description of his departure from Jalalabad, in which he emphasized that the war in Afghanistan and the fall of the Taliban had triggered an exodus of all kinds of people, not just al-Qaeda and Taliban fighters: "We left everything. We were moving through mountains and caves; there were hundreds of families, children, women and people were climbing through the mountains. What were we to do? Some people were escaping from other fronts, near Jalalabad and Kabul. There were too many people there."[16]

The rest of those captured after the raid appear to be as inconsequential to the "War on Terror" as those detained in the hospital. Several claimed that they were in Afghanistan on a religious mission. The 27-year-old Saudi Sultan al-Anazi (released in 2006) traveled to Pakistan before 9/11 to study with Jamaat-al-Tablighi, and then went to Jalalabad on a specific mission. After the collapse of the Taliban, he said that "Afghanis would look for Arabs to hold as hostages or kill so they could take our money and possessions," and described how he fled with the other Tablighi members to a village near Tora Bora, where they waited for an opportunity to escape that never came: "When I was in the village ... it was bombed by the

United States and I decided to give up because I didn't want to die. Many people were killed as a result of the bombing of the village and I didn't want to be next. The people from Jamaat-al-Tablighi that I fled with were killed by the air raids and I was injured." Mohammed Khusruf, a Yemeni who was caught after the bombing raid, said that he went to Afghanistan to teach the Koran, and asked, "Is it really reasonable that al-Qaeda or the Taliban, in bad need of men to fight, have to go to Yemen to find men at 60 years old to fight? Is this logical?" He admitted training at al-Farouq, but said that he only did so because the man who arranged his travel told him he needed to be able to defend himself. Saleh al-Zuba, a 46-year-old Yemeni (released in December 2006), also had a non-military explanation for being in Afghanistan. Accused of fighting in Tora Bora, he said that he had coronary artery disease and went to Pakistan for medical treatment, and was only in Afghanistan because he did not have enough money for an operation, and was told that a charitable organization in Afghanistan might provide extra funding.[17]

Only one of these prisoners—Sulaiman al-Nahdi, a 27-year-old Yemeni—admitted to any kind of presence in Tora Bora that could be construed as military, but his experience hardly marks him out as a member of al-Qaeda. Inspired by Sheikh al-Uqla's fatwa, he spent a month at al-Farouq, saw Osama bin Laden in Tora Bora, when he "talked about the jihad for approximately one hour and then a senior al-Qaeda operative [identified as Ayman al-Zawahiri] made a few comments," and then went into the mountains, where he took turns guarding a foxhole with 15 other people. Responding to an allegation that he "may have fought in Tora Bora," he said, "I never fired a weapon. I was only sitting," and, when asked if he would have shot at Americans, he echoed Tariq al-Sawah's comments: "I did not see any Americans. If I had seen any Americans, I would not have shot at them. I would have only shot at them if they had shot at me first, to defend myself."[18]

The stories of the remaining prisoners—with the exception of two men whose experiences are so emblematic of the catch-all definitions of "enemy combatants" that I'm using them to close this chapter— are riddled with the kind of anomalies that arise when prisoners are captured by proxy armies and the rule of law is brushed aside, to be replaced by a shadowy series of allegations and counter-allegations.

Abdul Rahman Khowlan, a 29-year-old Saudi, denied allegations that he trained at al-Farouq and was captured in Tora Bora. He said that he was captured in Jalalabad, and explained that he went to Afghanistan to "retrieve the clothing of the Prophet Mohammed from a shrine in Kandahar with financial backing from a prominent Saudi businessman," a mission which, if successful, would have made him "more popular than Michael Jackson." (He was released in December 2006, which perhaps indicates that there was some truth in his fantastical story.) Yasin Ismail, a 19-year-old Yemeni, denied an allegation that he fought in Tora Bora. Although he admitted training at al-Farouq, he said that he was only in Tora Bora because he was forcibly taken to a house there after being kidnapped in a market place in Kabul while attempting to leave the country after 9/11. Tarek Dergoul, a 24-year-old Briton (released in March 2004), also insisted that he had not been in Tora Bora. A non-practicing Muslim, born to Moroccan parents in London's Mile End, he had been a mini-cab driver and a carer in an old people's home, and went to Pakistan for a holiday in July 2001, intrigued by descriptions of the country provided by British friends whose parents were from Pakistan. Speaking after his release, he said that, having decided, with two Pakistani friends, to invest in property in Afghanistan in the hope that they could sell it for a profit after the war, the three men were close to securing a deal, and were spending the night in an empty villa in Jalalabad, when it was hit by an American bomb. His friends were killed, and he was wounded and unable to walk, and only survived for a week—until he was discovered by Alliance soldiers—because a water tap was still working, and he had a few biscuits and raisins in his pockets. Although the soldiers treated him well, taking him to a hospital, where he had three operations on his left arm, which had been badly injured by shrapnel, they subsequently sold him to the Americans, who insisted that he had fought in Tora Bora and eventually forced a false confession out of him.[19]

The last two prisoners to be discussed in connection with Tora Bora are Fouad al-Rabia, a 42-year-old Kuwaiti, and Mahrar al-Quwari, a 36-year-old Palestinian (who was cleared for release in 2007). Married with four children, al-Rabia, who had been working for Kuwait Airways as an engineer since he was 21, explained that he regularly did relief work in his spare time, and was approached one day, at a health club that he part-owned, by a member who told him about Afghanistan's problems and asked him to visit to see for himself. Unaware that the young man, Sulaiman Abu Ghaith, was a spokesman for al-Qaeda in Afghanistan, al-Rabia took a ten-day vacation from work in June 2001 and traveled to Afghanistan "to see the refugees and to assist with their situation." He was accompanied by a religious student called Abu Muldah, who took him to meet Osama bin Laden in Kandahar, thinking that he might be an important symbolic figure in Islam, a shepherd-like leader who would guide the people to a higher calling, but explained that he was disappointed when he met him. "Abu Muldah asked bin Laden his opinion about killing innocent people," al-Rabia said. "I think Abu Muldah was referring to the [embassy] bombing[s] in Africa. Bin Laden replied, he did not order the bombing but was not shocked by it. Bin Laden cited words [in] Arabic stating, 'I do not order massacres, but I do not object if I see them.'"

After this unpromising start, al-Rabia arranged meetings with the governor of Kandahar, where he also met representatives of the UN Commission for Refugees and the World Food Program, and with officials from the Ministries of Health and Public Works, and when he returned to Kuwait, he compiled a report and approached the head of the government-backed Kuwaiti Joint Relief Council, who "was convinced from my research that Afghanistan was a genuine disaster area." He said that the charity decided that, although they would not work directly with the Taliban, they would reopen their office in Peshawar, and would appoint him as the head of the office. Having arranged for a year's leave, he set off on a further fact-finding mission to Afghanistan on October 3, 2001, arriving, with unfortunate timing, as "Operation Enduring Freedom" commenced in a blizzard of bombs. After spending a month traveling between Herat, Kandahar and Kabul, and finding that the situation for Arabs was becoming inhospitable in each of these cities, he ended up in Jalalabad, where hundreds of Arabs were escaping in mini-buses to a house on the edge of Jalalabad that belonged to a man called Abdul Qadus, who "turned out to be a very big man in al-Qaeda" (a Yemeni, Qadus was the military commander of the Tora Bora base). From there, the refugees made their way on foot into the mountains. Overweight and unable to manage the climb, al-Rabia was provided with a mule, and explained that when he reached the top of the mountain, he "could see the chaos that was going on. They did not respect people. It was way above their heads. Everything there had collapsed. They were arguing over food and things like that." Qadus told him to look after the "issue counter," where supplies were being handed out: "He told me because of my age, no one would scream, shout or argue with me. So I would sit there and say, give this person a blanket, give this person rice, and so forth ... This lasted for a week." After another two weeks, in which he oversaw six or seven mules, which were used to collect water, he was allowed to leave, and Qadus arranged for him to travel down from the mountains. After staying in a village for a week, Alliance soldiers arrived in the village, "took several people as hostages, and stated if they were not given the injured people from the village, the hostages would be killed. So, the remaining injured people were the prize—myself and the other injured gentleman that was walking with me."[20]

The "injured gentleman" was Mahrar al-Quwari, who, like al-Rabia, became involved with Abdul Qadus by accident. After traveling to Pakistan on a fruitless visit to get "official identification" for his family from the UN, he went to Afghanistan, found a job in Jalalabad, but fled the city "when the coalition forces accused the Arabs of killing Massoud." He explained that he met Qadus while fleeing through the mountains, and helped him organize food for the other refugees, and Qadus then arranged for him to be taken to a village, where he was looked after by a family who were supposed to help him to get to Pakistan. Taking up the story after the hostage-taking scenario described by al-Rabia, he said that he was driven to Jalalabad, where he was sold at a checkpoint and taken to a prison. "The next day," he said, "the commander of the checkpoint told me they would get paid $5,000 for me. He said if I could pay him more than that he would release me. I didn't have any money. The next day vehicles came and they took me from Jalalabad to a Kabul prison," where the prison commander "told me they got paid $10,000 for me," and where "they tortured us for the month we were there." When asked if anyone was with him when he was captured, he replied, "Fouad al-Rabia, he came down from the mountain with me. It was him, some Afghans and I. The same amount of money that was offered for me was also offered for him. We were given to the Americans in Bagram and I haven't seen him since."[21]

At the end of the Tora Bora campaign, when the Americans had paid millions of dollars to their Afghan allies, and had spent untold amounts on the horrific bombs—including several "daisy-cutters"—that had laid waste to the mountains, the capture of the men described in this chapter was supposed to make up for the fact that the entire leadership of al-Qaeda escaped from under their noses. While Abdul Qadus was conducting military operations against the US in eastern Afghanistan in January 2002, al-Rabia and al-Quwari were just starting their nightmare in US custody, in which al-Rabia, despite his frank admissions of how he came to meet bin Laden, was regarded as an al-Qaeda fund-raiser, and both men were partly judged as "enemy combatants" because—as al-Rabia's tribunal clumsily described it—"while fleeing to Pakistan via the Tora Bora mountains with a group the detainee admitted contained, in part, al-Qaeda fighters, the detainee did, in fact, help coordinate logistics efforts for Abdul Qadus, someone the detainee admits was, in his estimation, al-Qaeda."[22]

5
Escape to Pakistan: "Osama's Bodyguards"

The First Group of Prisoners

Despite the abject failure of the Americans to capture Osama bin Laden, Ayman al-Zawahiri or any other senior members of al-Qaeda and the Taliban during the Tora Bora campaign, the announcement that Pakistani forces had made it to the border, arresting 39 "suspected al-Qaeda" members—mostly Yemenis—on December 15 and 16 prompted celebration in the Pentagon. Donald Rumsfeld declared that "US and Pakistani officials would interrogate the prisoners for vitally needed information," and that they "should be a treasure trove" of intelligence leads.[1]

Unfortunately, it was by no means clear that the majority of these prisoners were capable of fulfilling Rumsfeld's expectations. Four of them—Ali Hamza al-Bahlul, Ibrahim al-Qosi, Abdallah Tabarak and Mohammed al-Qahtani—were regarded as major prizes, although it was apparent that none of them held leadership positions in al-Qaeda. Al-Bahlul, a 32-year-old Yemeni, was accused of being a media officer, producing videos "glorifying, among other things, the attack on the USS *Cole*," and of being a bodyguard for bin Laden, a role which apparently required him to wear "an explosives-laden suit." Al-Qosi, a 41-year-old from the Sudan, was accused of working as the deputy to Sheikh Sayyid al-Masri, al-Qaeda's financial chief, fighting in Chechnya in 1995 (after bin Laden financed his trip), and serving as bin Laden's bodyguard, driver, supplies manager and cook for his retinue from 1996 until his capture. Both were put forward for trial by Military Commission, as discussed in Chapter 18. Tabarak, a 46-year-old Moroccan, worked on bin Laden's farm in Sudan, and traveled with him to Afghanistan, where he served as a bodyguard and was apparently involved in a gem-smuggling operation that raised funds for al-Qaeda. In Tora Bora, he was allegedly involved in a ruse that enabled bin Laden to escape, making calls from his boss's satellite phone to confuse the Americans, while bin Laden slipped away. For reasons that have never been explained (but which indicate that he was a far more peripheral character than the story above suggests), he was transferred to Moroccan custody in August 2004, and released on bail three months later. Al-Qahtani, a 22-year-old Saudi, would gain a special notoriety, once it was discovered that he had recently returned from the US, where he had been deported as he tried to enter the country to meet Mohammed Atta and fulfill his alleged role as the twentieth hijacker on 9/11. Tortured in Guantánamo, he alleged that thirty of the men who were captured at around the same time as him were bin Laden's bodyguards.[2]

The full story of al-Qahtani's torture—and its ramifications for the prisoners accused by him—will be discussed in detail in Chapter 15. For now, it's sufficient to note that, long before these allegations came to light, there was little, if any evidence connecting the other prisoners to al-Qaeda. A handful admitted to attending training camps and fighting with the Taliban, but they do not seem to have been anything more than simple foot soldiers. Fahed Ghazi, for example, a 19-year-old Yemeni, left his wife and baby daughter to embark on what he thought would be a one-month trip to Afghanistan. Recruited by a cleric who stated that "Muslims had a right to train themselves for self-defence against enemies," he admitted attending al-Farouq, but said that he left Yemen on August 19, 2001, and was only at the camp for nine days before 9/11. When the camp closed, he left for Kabul with five other people—his trainer, and four other recruits, who, like him, "came from overseas to train" and "did not belong to the Taliban"—and was then taken to Tora Bora. Fleeing after a bombing raid, he joined up with a group of people heading for Pakistan, where he turned himself in.[3]

Mohammed al-Zayla, a 24-year-old Saudi (released in 2006), also admitted training at al-Farouq, but said that he didn't fight the Northern Alliance because he wouldn't fight other Muslims. He said that he went to Afghanistan because he wanted to fight in Chechnya, and an ex-Chechen fighter told him he should first receive some training in Afghanistan. Al-Zayla was not even questioned about Tora Bora. He explained that he was in Kabul, on the back lines, when the US-led invasion started, and that everyone in the house that he was staying in decided to leave for Pakistan via Khost. Another Saudi, Abdulrazzaq al-Sharekh, who was only 16 years old when he arrived in Afghanistan in late 2000, told a similar story. He also wanted to fight in Chechnya, where his brother had been killed, but explained that, although he wanted to "go over there so I can die and meet up with him," a friend advised him that he "wouldn't last one day" in Chechnya, and suggested that he went to Afghanistan instead. Al-Sharekh also admitted training at al-Farouq, and serving on the Taliban front lines with Pakistani members of the militant group Jaish-e-Mohammed, but insisted that he never fired a weapon at anyone, and that there was little activity until after 9/11, when the Northern Alliance attacked them so fiercely that they retreated. Like al-Zayla, he was not questioned about Tora Bora. He said that he went to Khost via Kandahar, and then crossed into Pakistan, where he was arrested with two Pakistani guides.[4]

There was slightly more substance to the allegations against four prisoners who refused to take part in their tribunals, but without their responses it's impossible to know how much of this supposed intelligence was also gathered under dubious circumstances. Mohammed Ghanim, a 26-year-old Yemeni, was accused of having "participated in jihad activities" in Bosnia and Yemen, before traveling to Afghanistan to fight with the Taliban, and Ibrahim Idris, a 40-year-old from the Sudan, was accused of training at al-Farouq—where he was suspected of serving as an instructor, and where he apparently "met, spoke with and shook hands with Osama bin Laden on multiple occasions"—and fighting with the Taliban for two years. Sultan al-Uwaydha, a 26-year-old Saudi, was the only one of the four accused of having been in Tora Bora. It was also alleged that he visited one of bin Laden's houses, and that he had experience of assembling and sighting anti-aircraft weapons. The most sweeping allegations were leveled against Ridah al-Yazidi, a 36-year-old Tunisian. It was alleged that he decided to join the jihad in Afghanistan in 1996 while he was living in Milan, that he trained at Durunta and at Khaldan, a training camp near Khost (established in the 1980s by Abdul Rasul Sayyaf), that he stayed at a guest house in Jalalabad that was run by a Tunisian terrorist cell, and that he fought on the front lines in 2001.[5]

Religious Teachers and Humanitarian Aid Workers

The rest of the prisoners maintained that they were not involved in any kind of conflict in Afghanistan: nine said that they went to teach the Koran, three traveled to provide humanitarian aid, and one, Samir Moqbel, a 24-year-old Yemeni, was tricked by a friend, who told him he would find a job in Afghanistan: "He told me I would like it in Afghanistan and I could live a better life than in Yemen. I thought Afghanistan was a rich country but when I got there I found out different ... it was all destroyed with poverty and destruction. I found there was no basis for getting a job there. I was lied to but couldn't return to my country because I had no money or passport."[6]

From the onset of detentions in Afghanistan, the Americans have been remorselessly suspicious of prisoners claiming they were in Afghanistan for religious or charitable reasons, and the tribunals produced numerous examples of cultural ignorance, with tribunal members often unable to understand how it was possible for Arabic speakers to teach the Koran to non-Arabic speakers, thereby missing the essential point that the Koran is considered to be the direct speech of God in Arabic, as spoken to the Prophet Mohammed by the angel Gabriel, and that to be a devout Muslim means being able to read and understand classical Arabic, regardless of one's native language. When it came to understanding that charity is one of the five pillars of Islam, comprising zakat (the requirement to give 2½ percent of one's annual income) and sadaqa (an additional, voluntary donation), the Americans again showed their ignorance, failing to understand that in the event of a humanitarian catastrophe—for example, the plight of millions of refugees following the US-led invasion of Afghanistan—a devout Muslim might collect a significant amount of money, through donations from himself, his family and others in his local mosque, and travel to the area to hand out the money to those in need.

The Americans were clearly not impressed by the claims of those captured at this time that they were in Afghanistan to teach the Koran, as none of them had been released at the time of writing.

This was clearly due to al-Qahtani's allegations, because, according to their own accounts, their only transgressions were that, in order to teach, they had to deal with the Taliban. Othman Mohammed, a 22-year-old Yemeni, who said that he traveled between Kabul and Khost teaching the Koran from March to December 2001, admitted staying at a Taliban house in Quetta, Pakistan, which was the normal entry point for volunteers who came to fight, but only because he was told that it was the only way for him to enter Afghanistan. Abdul Malik al-Rahabi, another 22-year-old Yemeni, said that he went to Pakistan with his wife and his young daughter to teach Islamic studies in 2000, and spent a year traveling around Pakistan and Afghanistan, teaching. He said that he was in Kandahar when the US-led invasion began, but that, although his wife and daughter managed to return safely to the Yemen, he was arrested and sold to the Americans after he hired a taxi to travel to the Pakistan border, where he presented himself to the authorities in an attempt to contact the Yemeni embassy. Responding to an allegation that he "admitted receiving help from the Taliban," he said that they approved of his teaching mission, and provided his family with a house, but explained the relationship as follows: "When you go into a house you have to get permission from the owner of the house." Farouq Saif, an 18-year-old Yemeni, also admitted visiting the Taliban office in Quetta, but only to gain permission to teach the Koran. Escorted to Kabul, he said that he was introduced to a man named Abdul Rahman at the Wazir Akbar Khan mosque, and that he spent the next four months teaching the Koran, before moving on to Khost, where he taught another group of children. Although he admitted handing over his passport to Abdul Rahman for safekeeping, he denied knowing that he was a member of the Taliban, as the US authorities alleged.[7]

Farouq Saif was not the only prisoner to face additional problems because he did not have his passport when he was arrested. The Americans realized that those who attended training camps did not have passports because they were required to hand them in at guest houses before training, but this inevitably meant that those who did not have passports for other reasons—either because they were lost, stolen, or abandoned in the rush to leave a hostile environment, or because they were entrusted to others in an attempt to find a legitimate way to leave Afghanistan—were automatically regarded as liars, whether or not this was the case. Yahya al-Sulami, a 22-year-old Saudi, said that he was given a contact in a village near Khost by a friend in Mecca, where he taught the Koran for four months, but was clearly regarded as lying when he said that he lost his passport in a river while following a group of Afghan refugees to the Pakistani border. Mahmoud al-Mujahid, a 24-year-old Yemeni, was inspired by a sheikh at whose institute he was studying, and traveled to Kandahar to teach the Koran. After the war began, he said that he gave his passport to an Afghan friend who took it to Kabul to try and arrange his safe return to the Yemen, but fled the country in the meantime, when he heard that US bombers were targeting Arabs: "I became afraid they would bomb a whole village because of one Arab."[8]

Khalid al-Bawardi, a 24-year-old Saudi, told the most complete tale of being a missionary, which he related with a superior moral tone that was both pompous and convincing. He explained that he took a vacation from his job with the Chamber of Commerce, and went to Pakistan to find people who were receptive to the idea of dawa, which he described as correcting the mistakes of Muslims who have "strayed from the path of righteousness." He then gave his tribunal a lecture on Jamaat-al-Tablighi, saying that, although he met Tablighi representatives in Pakistan, "They have certain procedures that they are tied down by and the procedures they follow are wrong in our religion. Their work is good and it's correct but they make some mistakes," adding, "You are not able to understand this or get a whole clear picture because you don't have a complete picture of Jamaat-al-Tablighi. Besides that, you have to know Islam to know what is right and what is wrong." Having decided to work on his own, he traveled around Pakistani villages with a guide, correcting people's mistakes (particularly to do with raised graves and good luck charms), and then went to Kabul, where the people were more in need of his help. When the war started, he was advised to leave the country, and, after explaining that he suspected that his landlord stole his bag, which contained his passport, he described a difficult journey to the border, in which a man who gave him a lift in a car "forcefully told me to get out" in the desert, and a young Afghan who took him into his house also asked him to leave: "I told him I wanted this and that and he said he was poor and that he couldn't help me." After finding a guide, he was arrested crossing the border.[9]

Those who went to Afghanistan to provide humanitarian aid were more fortunate than the teachers, as they were eventually released. Abdel Hadi al-Sebaii, a 31-year-old Saudi police officer (released in 2006), went to Pakistan "for charity purposes to build houses," but decided he would be able to do more in Afghanistan. He explained that he "didn't only go to build houses but anything that would help the poor and needy," and added that it would cost him up to $300,000 to build a mosque in Saudi Arabia, whereas in Afghanistan it would only cost about $2,000. Speaking of the circumstances of his arrest, he raised the issue of prisoners (himself included) being sold to the Americans. He said that when he entered Pakistan and asked to go to his embassy, having shown the border guards his passport and travel tickets, he was told he would first be required to fill out some forms:

> We were getting along famously. They didn't put me in prison or place any restrictions on me ... Suddenly, I was turned over to the United States. I don't know why I was turned over to the US ... My only problem was with the Pakistani government. Why did they do that? Pakistan is the reason I am here. Pakistan was greedy and wanted money, so they sold me. This might have put the US in a very precarious position.[10]

While numerous other prisoners made similar allegations, compelling evidence that this was a widespread practice both in Afghanistan and Pakistan comes from detailed analyses of US Psychological Operations and from a statement made by President Musharraf. A series of PsyOps leaflets were analyzed in depth by retired US Sergeant Major Herbert Friedman, who noted that 84 million leaflets, containing over a hundred different messages, were dropped during the first year of the war in Afghanistan. While most of these vilified the leaders of al-Qaeda and the Taliban and fruitlessly offered rewards of $25 million for the capture of bin Laden and al-Zawahiri, one particular leaflet, which, for some reason, featured a Hergé-like cartoon of an Afghan elder next to a photo of the Alhambra palace in Grenada, Spain, encouraged its readers to "Get wealth and power beyond your dreams—help the anti-Taliban force to rid Afghanistan of murderers and terrorists." On the back of the leaflet, the key to this wealth was spelled out explicitly: "You can receive millions of dollars for helping the anti-Taliban force catch al-Qaeda and Taliban murderers. This is enough money to take care of your family, your village, your tribe for the rest of your life—pay for livestock and doctors and school books and housing for all your people." For his part, President Musharraf announced in his autobiography that, in return for handing over 369 terror suspects (including those described in this chapter), "We have earned bounties totalling millions of dollars."[11]

The two other humanitarian aid workers captured at this time also complained that they were sold to the Americans. Adel Kamel Haji, a 37-year-old Bahraini (released in November 2005), took a break from his job as a clerk for the ministry of defense "to help the refugees and the poor who suffered from the war" in Afghanistan. Taking 2,500 Bahraini dinars (around $6,700) of his own money, he entered Afghanistan in a taxi from Iran in late October, passing through Herat, where he expected to see refugees but found none, and taking a bus to Kabul via Kandahar, where he discovered that the office of the International Red Cross was boarded up. In Kabul, he told the owner of his hotel that he had come to help refugees and the poor, and he "offered to show me people in areas outside the city where people were in need of help," so "I went and gave money to families living in poor small houses and things like that." A few days after his arrival, however, Kabul fell to the Northern Alliance, and the owner advised him to flee, finding a driver who took him towards the Pakistani border, dropped him off and said that if he carried on walking he would reach Pakistan. He was then picked up by an Arab called Omar, in a car with an Afghan driver, who "saw my clothes and my features, which looked familiar to him, so he stopped." On arrival in Pakistan, he handed himself in to the authorities, anticipating that he might receive "a verbal admonishment" for not arriving through the proper channels, but never considering that he would be arrested. When this was pursued by a Board Member, who asked, "Why do you think you ended up here after showing up with the proper papers?" he replied:

> I don't know what happened exactly. But it became clear to us later that ... the Pakistani police force was selling people for money [and] that the price for Arabs was a large sum of dollars. I think you have documentation to show that many of the people here had nothing to do with fighting or killing ... I think you have become certain that these people did not have anything to do with this affair. One of the interrogators told me that a lot of the Pakistanis were selling people for money ... They said these people are all from al-Qaeda and they turned them in.[12]

The man who picked up Haji on the last stage of his journey was Omar Rajab Amin, a 34-year-old Kuwaiti (released in September 2006), who studied at the University of Nebraska and then spent seven years heading a Kuwaiti charity in Croatia and Bosnia, which supported orphans from the war zone. Like Haji, Amin was inspired by the plight of the Afghan people. In October 2001, with 3,000 Kuwaiti dinars (about $10,000) donated by himself and his brothers and sisters, he traveled to the Iranian border, but didn't find any refugees. He then decided to enter Afghanistan, traveling to Kabul to find people who might need his help, secure in the knowledge that the Americans had stated that the war would be "a political war, an economical war, an information war and an intelligence war." "The Americans were not stupid," he added. "They were not going to commit all their troops to go into Afghanistan to die, like the Russians and the British." In Kabul, he found an interpreter, and said that they were "working every day from the morning until the sunset ... meeting the poor people and the orphans," until one day his interpreter advised him not to return to the city because it was about to fall to the Northern Alliance. He then began trying to escape from Afghanistan, eventually meeting up with a group of Afghans and other Arabs, who were heading to the border, where they turned themselves in and were sold to the Americans. He added that he would never have entered Afghanistan in the first place if he had known that the Americans "were not going to apply the Geneva Convention, especially to people who worked in charity organizations."[13]

6
Escape to Pakistan: Saudis and Yemenis

The Second Group of Prisoners

In the days that followed, refugees continued to pour over the border into Pakistan, and over 150 men were captured at this time and eventually transferred to Guantánamo. On the surface, they appeared to represent a microcosm of the global jihad, hailing from Algeria, Bahrain, Belgium, China, Denmark, Egypt, France, Jordan, Kuwait, Libya, Morocco, Saudi Arabia, Spain, Sweden, Syria, Tunisia, Turkey and the Yemen. On close inspection, however, they displayed many of the characteristics outlined in the previous chapters, comprising large numbers of Taliban foot soldiers recruited in Saudi Arabia and the Yemen, several dozen humanitarian aid workers from Saudi Arabia and other Gulf countries, a handful of religious students, a complex mix of jihadists, naïve idealists and economic refugees from Europe and North Africa, and, in the case of the Chinese prisoners, a group of desperately poor men caught up in the wrong war.

While a few of these men were seized by enterprising villagers or units of the Pakistani Army, the majority were captured either in one particular village, where dozens were welcomed and then betrayed by the locals, who took them to a mosque and handed them over to the army, or by Pakistani soldiers at the border checkpoints, where they handed themselves in, believing they would be questioned briefly and then escorted to their embassies. The first the media knew of these arrests was on December 18, when 156 prisoners were transported to a jail in Peshawar in three buses and two trucks. According to an eyewitness, none were handcuffed, and only a hundred soldiers were assigned to guard them. En route, a cleaner who was on the second bus recalled that some of the men "said something in Arabic among themselves, raised 'Allah-u-Akbar' … and pounced on us." After the men snatched five rifles from their guards, a firefight broke out, in which six guards and nine prisoners were killed, before the survivors fled in different directions. Twenty-one were subsequently recaptured—ten in a school—while 18 were still at large the day after.[1]

The Saudi Foot Soldiers

The stories of the 27 Saudis captured at this time largely echo those of the foot soldiers described in previous chapters. Typically, they were in their late teens or early twenties, had been recruited through fatwas, and had no experience of anything other than helping the Taliban in their long-standing civil war with the Northern Alliance. One of the most straightforward stories was that of 22-year-old Ibrahim al-Rubeish (released in 2006), who was only in Afghanistan for three months. He admitted training at al-Farouq and passing through Tora Bora on his way to Pakistan, but said that he went to Afghanistan primarily to "train for the jihad for God." When asked who he was training to fight, he replied, "Whoever fights Muslims," and when asked if he thought that this included the US, he said, "the United States is a partner with Saudi Arabia, so how could I consider it an enemy of Islam if it's a friend of Saudi Arabia?" Twenty-six-year-old Jabir al-Fayfi (also released in 2006) told a similarly simple story. Having responded to a fatwa, he said that he received two weeks' training and was then moved to the front lines, but added that "there was no fighting during my time there," and that he was soon forced to retreat, crossing to Pakistan with a group of other people. Denying an allegation that he met al-Qaeda members in Tora Bora, he said that he only passed through the area on his way to Pakistan, and pointed out that, although he met some other Arabs, he did not know whether they were al-Qaeda, because "al-Qaeda do not have a special uniform for me to recognize and avoid them." Others did not even progress beyond the training camps. Twenty-two-year-old Bandar al-Jabri, who hoped to fight in Chechnya, explained that he "had to stop training because he was experiencing asthma attacks."[2]

Twenty-two-year-old Ziad al-Jahdali, who worked as a guard after one day's training on the Kalashnikov, said that he was "provided misinformation" in his local mosque, where he was "told the aggressors in Afghanistan were not Muslims." As already noted, this was a view shared by several other prisoners, and the differences between the recruits' expectations and experiences were analyzed in a perceptive article by Sharon Curcio, a military intelligence analyst who read over six hundred transcripts of interrogations conducted at Guantánamo in 2003 and 2004. Noting that many prisoners related "vivid 'they-never-told-me-about-this' narratives" describing what happened to them in Afghanistan, Curcio explained how the imams and sheikhs in their home countries were "quick to position jihad as the panacea for lost, disenfranchised youth"—those who were unemployed, had failed in education or in business, or had family problems—and also noted that, for the educated, the call to jihad was used to play on their "desire for self-discovery and a challenge," and, for the unskilled, it was presented as "alternative employment." She explained that charitable organizations "frequently hired young men for warehouse and distribution work to provide relief materials such as foodstuffs or blankets to a local population, so the call to jihad appeared to be more of the same." She also pointed out that jihad was presented in many different guises: as an opportunity to fulfill charitable obligations, to teach the Koran, to visit a country that was a model of Sharia law, or to learn to use weapons to defend one's family, as well as the more familiar encouragement to help other Muslims fight their oppressors. Completing this thorough picture of the recruitment process, Curcio also commented on the important role played by the facilitators, who provided funding and sorted out travel arrangements, and explained the unexpected problems faced by the recruits during training: the punishing physical regime, the unfamiliarity of their companions, and, in particular, the lack of medical provision. Confused that no vaccinations were provided, even though the drinking water was unsafe, and as many as one in four of the recruits fell ill, she concluded that the leaders of the camps were so obsessed with the importance of martyrdom that they even extended it to the life and death of their recruits.[3]

Curcio's observations were reflected in some of the other prisoners' stories. Eighteen-year-old Tariq al-Harbi (released in 2006) said that the sheikhs "told him that he had to go to Afghanistan to help the poor and needy or God would punish him"; 18-year-old Fahd al-Jutayli (also released in 2006) was recruited by Sheikh al-Uqla "to fight in Kashmir and Chechnya," and 29-year-old Majid al-Qurayshi (released in February 2007) "wanted forgiveness from Allah" and was told that "the shortest way to get forgiveness from Allah is to go out on jihad." In other cases, the prisoners were confused about the nature of the jihad. Twenty-two-year-old Mazin al-Awfi, who was a traffic policeman before traveling to Afghanistan, said that his interpretation of jihad was "to support the Taliban, not to fight with them," and added, "I went with good intentions and then realized bad things were happening and I wanted to get out." Twenty-six-year-old Ohmed al-Shurfa (cleared for release in 2007) was particularly confused. In many ways a typical recruit—drawn in by a fatwa and provided with money and a contact in Karachi, he attended al-Farouq, left with 15 others after 9/11, and was arrested after turning himself in at the Pakistani border—he told his tribunal that he believed that the fatwa involved preparing for jihad rather than jihad itself, although he spelled out his doubts in the following exchange:

> *Detainee*: Preparing is different than jihad ... They [the sheikhs] said preparing but they didn't say jihad. Jihad means fighting. Isn't that correct?
> *Presiding Officer*: I think jihad means fighting but is also an internal struggle.

He also revealed the extraordinary influence wielded by the religious leaders delivering the fatwas, and the potential dangers of a system in which their pronouncements were obeyed unquestioningly:

> *Board Member*: I understand that you consider jihad an obligation?
> *Detainee*: I really do not know. I have to ask the higher religious leaders, the sheikhs. They tell us about our religion and what we are obligated to do.[4]

The most complete explanation of the sheikhs' role was put forward by 23-year-old Sa'ad al-Bidna, who was released in 2006. In an interview, he stated that he "followed certain fatwas that were posted on the internet," and became "motivated by youthful enthusiasm to wage jihad for the sake of Allah in Afghanistan." He explained that the militant fatwas tempted young people "by describing the great reward they will receive, the status of the martyrs in Paradise and the virgins that await them there," adding, "These fatwas have great influence on young people who have no awareness or knowledge that enables them to examine them and verify their validity." He said that he now knew that what he did was wrong—although he also pointed out that, when he was in Afghanistan, "what concerned me the most was that Muslims were fighting each other, and that is why I left and went to Pakistan, for in jihad a Muslim must never fight his Muslim brother"—and added that, when he returned home, he and other released prisoners "met with sheikhs and religious scholars who taught us a great deal, and who enlightened us on the tolerant directives of Islam."[5]

In contrast, others were unapologetic about their involvement in jihad. Twenty-eight-year-old Abdul Rahman al-Amri, who served in the Saudi Army for nine years, declared that it was his duty to fight jihad and that he "continues to admit to that today. He says it is all Muslims' responsibility to fight for jihad when called upon by a Muslim government (in this case, and at that time, it was the Taliban)." He also pointed out, however, that "had his desire been to fight and kill Americans, he could have done that while he was side by side with them in Saudi Arabia." Twenty-five-year-old Fahd al-Sharif, who had been a policeman in Mecca, went to Afghanistan in 2000 "for the purpose of jihad with the Taliban government," adding that he was "fighting with the Taliban to help ... millions of Afghan Muslims to return their hopes, their countries and their lives," and that he hoped to become a martyr. Twenty-three-year-old Said al-Qahtani made the most passionate case for supporting the Taliban. He attended a training camp in Pakistan in 2000, and also spent a week with the senior al-Qaeda operative Abu Zubaydah (see Chapter 13), although he added that he didn't know that he was with al-Qaeda, and asked, "just because somebody stays at someone's house, who may not be the best person in the world, does that make the people who stayed at that house bad people?" After returning home, he spoke to an imam who explained that he should help the Taliban because, after the Soviet occupation and the civil war, "they brought peace to 95 percent of the country, except the places where the Northern Alliance were at the time. I don't think there was anything wrong with helping to make peace after 30 years of fighting." Returning to Afghanistan in April 2001, he served as a guard on the front lines near Kabul before fleeing to Pakistan with around 15 other people, but pointed out that he was in Afghanistan before 9/11, and insisted, "Even if you say I am right or wrong, I don't think I did anything wrong. At the time I didn't think I did anything wrong, and I still don't. I didn't do anything illegal or bad to anyone."[6]

The Saudi Humanitarian Aid Workers and Religious Teachers

As well as the Saudi foot soldiers, around twenty other Saudis were captured at this time. All said that they had been involved in either humanitarian aid or religious teaching, and, at the time of writing, all but five had been released. Their stories demonstrate the array of influences that were responsible for encouraging young men to travel to Afghanistan in 2000 and 2001. Said al-Malki, a 32-year-old security officer with the Saudi police (released in 2006), went to Afghanistan in January 2001 after a sheikh suggested that distributing food and clothing to the poor was a worthwhile pursuit for a devout Muslim. He and a companion spent ten months traveling around Afghanistan, distributing food, clothing and "books and tapes regarding Islam," and he said of his arrest in Pakistan that the police "said I was Arabic and I was good value." Also released in 2006, 31-year-old Khalid al-Morghi, married with five children, was a clerk for the Saudi Air Force and the son of a Saudi general who fought with US forces during the first Gulf War. After taking a month's leave to help refugees and the poor, in response to TV reports and a fatwa urging support for the people of Afghanistan in peaceful ways, which he read on the internet, he traveled to Herat, but after the first week, in which he "went to see how to help the people there," he didn't dare leave the house, because of the violence between the Taliban and the Northern Alliance. He then paid a smuggler $1,000 to help him escape to Pakistan, and, after staying with families in Khost and Spin Boldak, crossed the border and was arrested by Pakistani soldiers, who sold him to the Americans.[7]

Several of the prisoners were associated with al-Wafa, a Saudi charity, based in Kabul, which was to come under intense scrutiny because its founder, Abdul Aziz al-Matrafi, was accused of being close to both the Taliban leadership and Osama bin Laden. These allegations are discussed in Chapter 16; here it's sufficient to note that the organization devoted most of its resources to humanitarian aid, and it was in this context that those captured at this time were involved. Nineteen-year-old Abdul Aziz al-Baddah, married with a two-year-old daughter, traveled to Afghanistan in October 2001, with his cousins Ibrahim al-Nasir and Abdul Aziz al-Nasir, to help Afghan refugees with donations of their own money. He admitted staying at al-Wafa's office in Kabul, but insisted that he was not an employee, and knew nothing about its supposed connections to al-Qaeda. When the bombing of Kabul began, he and his cousins went to Logar, where they stayed in an al-Wafa house for a week, but when they attempted to return to Kabul to retrieve their passports the city had fallen to the Northern Alliance, and they decided to return home via Pakistan, where they turned themselves over to the police. They were accompanied by Abdullah al-Ghanimi, a 27-year-old, who had been working for al-Wafa in Kabul, and all four were captured together, and released in 2006.[8]

Al-Wafa was not the only charity proscribed by the US because a handful of its members were allegedly diverting funds to terrorist organizations. Said al-Malki ran into problems because he sought advice from the al-Birr Foundation, a Saudi charity, founded in 1987, which was put on a US terror watchlist in November 2002, and 34-year-old Abdullah al-Rushaydan, who took a vacation from his job as a cleaner for the International Islamic Relief Organization to visit Damascus, Tehran and an Afghan refugee camp in Pakistan, was regarded as a threat because the IIRO—a global charity, backed by the Saudi government and established in 1978 to help refugees and victims of famine and other disasters—was regarded as an organization that channeled funds to Osama bin Laden. Arrested in Pakistan without having set foot in Afghanistan, he was released in 2006.[9] In addition to his alleged connection with al-Wafa, Abdul Aziz al-Baddah was also accused of being associated with the al-Haramain Islamic Foundation. Formerly one of the largest Islamic NGOs in the world, devoted to charitable deeds and education and with a turnover of $50 million, several of its offices worldwide were accused of being fronts for terrorist funding and were condemned by the US. Although US officials "privately conceded that only a small percentage of the total was diverted" and that few of those who worked for the organization knew that money was being funneled to al-Qaeda, the Saudi government was put under enormous pressure to shut down the entire organization, which it did in February 2004.[10] While this kind of overreaction seems akin to closing down the Catholic Church because some of its members provided funds to the IRA, the extent of US paranoia about terror funding through charitable organizations has had a profound effect on the ability of Islamic charities to raise vital funds for humanitarian funds and has made potential donors, looking for ways to fulfill their charitable obligations, wary of becoming associated with such a wide and undiscriminating terrorist dragnet. In Guantánamo, al-Baddah responded to the suggestion that he was connected with al-Haramain by asking why it was that none of the hundred or so employees of the charity were detained in Cuba, adding, "I don't want an answer, but these are questions you need to think about."

Like Abdullah al-Rushaydan, three other humanitarian aid workers (released in 2006) were arrested in Pakistan without setting foot in Afghanistan. After watching TV footage of refugees fleeing to the Iranian border after the US-led invasion began, Rashid al-Qa'id, a 42-year-old school principal, and two teachers, 38-year-old Wasim al-Omar and 24-year-old Anwar al-Nurr, decided to travel to the border to provide humanitarian aid. After spending a few days in Afghanistan, when they distributed money in refugee camps, they were not allowed back into Iran "due to prejudice; we were Sunni and they were Shiite." They then stayed for a month in a hotel on the border, "trying and failing multiple times" to re-enter Iran, before deciding that their only hope was to cross into Pakistan. Al-Omar explained that when they reached the border, the police told them to "go in an unofficial way, by bribing them," but they refused because they wanted their actions to be legal. As a result, when they passed through a checkpoint, "They took my passport and that's when [we were] put in prison for no reason." Describing his feelings about being sold, he said that he heard that the going rate was between $5,000 and $8,000 a head, and explained, "It's a hard truth when human beings are sold and bought. That makes us go all the way back, when humans had no value. It's a shame for all human beings in general, and all the people who believe in human rights."[11]

At the time of writing, only two of those who said that they went to Afghanistan to provide humanitarian aid remained in Guantánamo.

Abdul Rahman al-Juaid, a 21-year-old student, who was accused of being a fund-raiser for al-Haramain, said that he collected 10,000 riyals (around $2,700) and distributed it to the poor in Afghanistan, and Ziyad al-Bahuth, a 19-year-old, said that he raised 90,000 riyals (about $24,000), which he gave to the Taliban to distribute to the poor, staying for a year to monitor the project. His tribunal was noteworthy for the following exchange, which, while possibly demonstrating a healthy skepticism on the part of the US authorities, could also demonstrate how little they understood about the charitable obligations of Islam:

> *Presiding Officer*: When you were around 18 years old, you raised 90,000 riyals ... to take to a country you had never been to before to give the money to the needy and the poor people. Is that right?
> *Detainee*: Yes.
> *Presiding Officer*: That is remarkable.[12]

Those who went to provide religious teaching were generally less fortunate than the humanitarian aid workers. Twenty-year-old Saleh al-Khathami, who arrived in Afghanistan in August 2001 and traveled "from village to village staying with Afghan families and teaching the Koran," was released in 2006, but two others had, at the time of writing, failed to convince the US administration of their innocence. Twenty-three-year-old Musa al-Amri, who was accused of answering a fatwa and loading trucks for the Taliban, said that he only told the Pakistani authorities that he served with the Taliban because he was told that "if he told the truth about performing missionary work with Jamaat-al-Tablighi, the Saudi delegation would not help him," and 21-year-old Rami al-Taibi, who was arrested at the house of a Pakistani who traveled with him from Afghanistan, denied an allegation that he trained at a "terrorist camp," and said that he traveled in August 2001 to undertake religious training at a mosque in Kandahar.[13]

The Yemenis

With the exception of 31-year-old Salim Hamdan, a driver for Osama bin Laden who was put forward for trial by Military Commission (see Chapter 18), the stories of the 25 other Yemenis captured at this time were as varied—and as generally lacking in terrorist potential—as those of the Saudis. Several were recruited for jihad by Ibrahim Baalawi (also known as Abu Khulud), who escaped from Tora Bora and would clearly have been a much bigger catch than any of the foot soldiers rounded up instead. A facilitator for bin Laden, Baalawi recruited 20-year-old Mohsin Moqbill (released in December 2006) by teaching him about fatwa and jihad, which he described as the obligation "to help others, to give what you can," but Moqbill said that when he arrived at al-Farouq he regretted his decision, and pointed out that many of the militant sheikhs in the Gulf had now "recalled all their fatwas." Captured after staying in a village in the Tora Bora mountains for 26 days and then crossing into Pakistan with a dozen other people, he and his group surrendered their weapons in a border village and were then taken to the Pakistani police. Baalawi also recruited 23-year-old Abdul Rahman Sulayman with tales of the good life in Afghanistan that chime with Sharon Curcio's analysis of the facilitators' devious methods. Sulayman said that Baalawi "promised me that I'd be able to get married in Afghanistan. He may have had different intentions for me other than the marriage, but I didn't know," adding that he was told, "you can go to certain countries and they'll give you a house, even if it's an old house, and some financial assistance to get married. That's without having to contribute anything at all. It's a charity type of thing from these people. If you put yourself in my shoes, what would you do?"[14]

Others recruited by fatwas had more of a sense of what they were doing, although none graduated above the level of foot soldier. Twenty-eight-year-old Said al-Busayss (cleared for release in 2007) traveled to Afghanistan in late 2000, attended a Taliban training camp and fought on the front lines until his unit withdrew, when he was given the option of staying or escaping. Choosing the latter, he fled to Pakistan, where he "surrendered his weapon and was arrested by Pakistani police." Others traveled on their own initiative. Twenty-four-year-old Ali al-Tays (released in December 2006) admitted attending al-Farouq, but said that he only wanted to receive training to protect himself, because there were "tribal problems" in Yemen, and it was easier to receive training in Afghanistan than at home, and Yasim Basardah, a 25-year-old Shia, admitted attending al-Farouq, fighting with the Taliban at Taloqan, and staying at the al-Nabras guest house in Kandahar (one of the transit houses for Arabs training in Afghanistan), where he met Osama bin Laden and "listened to him speak words of encouragement and enthusiasm to the fighters" who were staying there. Denying an allegation that he was recruited by Jamaat-al-Tablighi, he said that he was recruited by a "jihad group," and highlighted the profound differences between the groups: "The Tablighi group say that their job is for God only, to notify people about God, not to fight. The jihad groups say it is about fighting the infidels who enter the Muslim countries." He also said, "I came in just for the money," explaining that the jihad group paid money to the families of fighters and "I was a very poor person at the time," and added that they also recruited people like him who had a history of drug use.[15]

The other Yemenis captured at this time told a variety of non-military stories. Twenty-two-year-old Issam al-Jayfi (released in December 2006) described himself as a government clerk and a wayward youth, who smoked, drank alcohol and loved the company of women, and was persuaded to go to Afghanistan by a religious friend called Sami. Never having been outside Yemen, he thought it would be like Europe, a place where he could live freely, but he explained that when they arrived Sami told him they had come to fight. He then fled to Pakistan, where some villagers turned him over to the police. Faris al-Ansari, who was only 17 when he was captured, was actually living in Afghanistan when the war began, because his father, who had fought against the Russians in the 1980s, had settled there. Although he denied having any involvement with the Taliban, he said, "The Taliban were nice to people like my father, because it is a good, humane thing to do." When Jalalabad fell, his family decided to leave for Pakistan, and he explained that his father, who could pass for an Afghan, traveled with the women and children in a car, whereas he and some other family friends set off on foot, guided by locals to villages where they were put up for the night. After crossing into Pakistan, they were welcomed in a small village, where they stayed for five days, but were then betrayed: "They bound our hands, covered our eyes and searched us. We weren't allowed to talk. If we moved they would hit us. I was ... taken to Peshawar. I got in the vehicle and I haven't seen my friends since."[16]

The only religious teacher amongst the Yemenis was 33-year-old Asim al-Khalaqi, who went to Pakistan with a friend to preach with

Jamaat-al-Tablighi, but decided to go to Afghanistan after discovering
that there were too many Tablighi representatives in Pakistan. He
explained that he and his friend were successful in their mission, but
everything changed after 9/11, when his friend "went one day to go
eat lunch and didn't return home." He then met an Afghan, who
advised him to leave because Arabs were being killed, and explained
that this man took him in his car to the foothills where he joined
a group of Arabs crossing the mountains to Pakistan and handed
himself in to the army on arrival. He was one of many dozens of
prisoners at Guantánamo whose association with Jamaat-al-Tablighi
was used as part of the "evidence" against them, as the US authorities
alleged that the missionary organization, like the charities referred to
above, was "used as a cover to mask travel and activities of terrorists
including members of al-Qaeda." If this was the case, al-Khalaqi
said, he wondered why no one from the organization's leadership
was held in Guantánamo.[17]

7
Escape to Pakistan: The Diaspora

The Jalalabad Connection: Europeans and North Africans

The Jalalabad connection centered on "the House of the Algerians," which was run by Omar Chaabani, an Algerian who was also known as Abu Jafar al-Jaziri. Killed in January 2002 in a US bombing raid on an al-Qaeda compound, Chaabani was allegedly close to Osama bin Laden, and the Americans came to believe that his house was used to funnel North African recruits into a training camp that was connected to al-Qaeda. According to a senior US Army interrogator who, from January to August 2002, was part of the team responsible for interrogating prisoners in Afghanistan, the discovery of the Jalalabad connection was one of their few significant success stories. The interrogator, who wrote a book about his experiences (with the journalist Greg Miller) under the pseudonym Chris Mackey, described how one North African prisoner, fooled into revealing Chaabani's name, proceeded to "betray many other enemy fighters," to "expose a never before understood connection between al-Qaeda and Islamic groups across North Africa," and to explain that the North Africans were training "so they could go back to their home countries and overthrow the government there." Inspired by this breakthrough, two interrogators explored the links between other North Africans in their custody, learning that, in an attempt to placate their critics, the Taliban had tried to expel all foreign militants from Afghanistan in spring 2001, but had been outmaneuvered by bin Laden, who offered them protection if they allied themselves with al-Qaeda. According to Mackey, several prisoners said that, as a result of this deal, a Tunisian group had been "tasked with killing" Ahmed Shah Massoud.[1]

Although this appeared to be a triumph for the intelligence operations in Afghanistan, it also highlighted the weaknesses in the unprecedented policy of detention without trial that the US administration was pioneering, as it was by no means certain that everyone who passed through the house was involved in the alleged terror web that had been unearthed. These doubts were laid bare in the stories of five French prisoners, who were released from Guantánamo in 2004 and 2005.

Nineteen-year-old Mourad Benchellali and 22-year-old Nizar Sassi traveled to Afghanistan in summer 2001 from Venissieux, a poor suburb of Lyons. After attending a training camp, they spent some time in Jalalabad, where they met up with Hervé Djamel Loiseau, a convert to Islam from Paris. Loiseau was a close friend of another French prisoner, Brahim Yadel, a 30-year-old Parisian, who arrived in Afghanistan in July 2001, accompanied by 34-year-old Redouane Khalid, who was also from Paris. Completing the connections between the men, Khalid, who admitted that he spent time at "the house of the Algerians," traveled in Afghanistan with Khaled bin Mustafa, a 29-year-old from Lyons, who had met him at his wedding in Paris.

From Jalalabad, the men traveled to Pakistan in two groups. Benchellali explained that he had seen Osama bin Laden in Jalalabad, when the remaining Arabs in Afghanistan were asked to choose whether "to leave Afghanistan, or to take up arms," and said that, having chosen to leave, "More than a thousand of us left by way of the mountains to get to Pakistan." He and Sassi traveled with Loiseau, but their companion died on the way. When they arrived in Pakistan, they were captured by locals and handed over to the Pakistani Army, who sold them for $5,000 each to the Americans. The other three were among the many dozens of prisoners who were welcomed in one particular village by the locals, who then betrayed them by sending them to a mosque where they were arrested by the army. Bin Mustafa explained, "I was with some other French nationals. I produced my French passport and my driving licence to the Pakistani police officers but it wasn't enough."[2]

While these are the facts of the case, the men's motivations—and the extent of their involvement with militancy—varied wildly. Benchallali, for example, came from a family with aspirations to militant Islam. His father was a radical imam who had tried (and failed) to fight in

Bosnia, his brother Menad had tried (and failed) to fight in Chechnya, and his brother, his father and even his mother had all spent time in French prisons, but he insisted that he went to Afghanistan for "an adventure" and as a way of enhancing his status, hoping that he would be "viewed differently" in his neighborhood, and that his reputation might "match" that of his brother. He admitted that his sense of adventure was "misguided and mistimed," and blamed his brother for encouraging him to go, and for arranging for him to attend a training camp. "For two months, I was there," he wrote after his release, "trapped in the middle of the desert by fear and my own stupidity." Sassi, described in the French press as Benchellali's "double," tagged along with his friend. A night watchman for the council, he was described by his brother as "a normal guy who liked to go nightclubbing," who had "no fundamental terrorist leanings."[3]

In his tribunal, Redouane Khalid was accused of training at a safe house in Kabul and a Taliban camp in Kandahar, but he said that he went to Afghanistan "to find the correct Muslim lifestyle for himself and his family," and hoped to buy a house there. He added that he "initially looked at Pakistan, but ended up choosing Afghanistan because it was a cheaper place to live and he could get a house for under $3,000." Although he stayed at "the House of the Algerians" while he was working out how to leave Afghanistan, he said that he moved to another house in Jalalabad after the owner told him that the border was closed and he would have to be patient. Whilst it was understandable that the Americans had their doubts about some of these stories, it's noticeable that, on their release from Guantánamo, all were freed on bail, except for Yadel, the only one with a track record of militancy, who was "sentenced in his absence to seven years in prison for his alleged participation in waves of attacks in France in 1995."[4]

Without the protection of a European government, the rest of the Jalalabad prisoners were left in a legal limbo in which it was almost impossible to discern the differences between hardened militants, naïve recruits and economic migrants. The Algerians were no exception. Twenty-five-year-old Mohammed al-Qadir had lived in Germany for seven years, but had spent three of those in prison. Released on bail in 2000, he feared being sent back to Algeria, and made his way to London, where he spent ten months before traveling to Afghanistan "to immigrate, make money, and find a wife." He denied an allegation that he trained at Khaldan, and said that, when the Northern Alliance were advancing on Jalalabad, the owner of the house that he was staying in asked him to leave, and he then made his way to Pakistan with other refugees, even though he was ill with malaria. Forty-one-year-old Abdulli Feghoul (cleared for release in 2007) had also lived in Germany, and traveled to Afghanistan in 2001. It was alleged that he trained at Durunta, but he denied the allegation, and attempted to call a witness, Mesut Sen, a 21-year-old Belgian of Turkish origin, to confirm that he stayed at an Algerian guest house and did not attend a training camp. Sen, however, refused to testify on Feghoul's behalf, and was released from Guantánamo in April 2005, leaving a trail of unanswered questions behind him. Presumably released through an arrangement between the Belgian and US governments, he made no statement on his release, although it was alleged that he and his father were connected with Milli Görüş, a Turkish organization regarded as an extremist group by the Belgian government, and that, in September 2000, he traveled from Germany to Jalalabad, where he lived for nearly a year at a "Taliban transit house."[5]

Twenty-five-year-old Motai Saib, 34-year-old Djamel Ameziane and 40-year-old Farhi Said bin Mohammed added other dimensions to the Algerian diaspora. Saib, who had been living in France, traveled to Afghanistan on a forged Belgian passport, and admitted staying at Chaabani's house, although he denied receiving any military training while he was there. Ameziane, who was apparently captured at a mosque after escaping from the bus that was taken over by prisoners on the road to Peshawar, was accused of the most globe-trotting exploits of all the disenfranchised Algerians: traveling from Austria to Canada on a forged Dutch passport in 1995, and from Canada to Pakistan on a forged French passport in 2000. Like Saib, he denied receiving military training, and said that he fled Afghanistan "because the non-Taliban and the opposition were killing Arabs." Bin Mohammed traveled from Rome to London on a stolen French passport in June 2001, and went to Afghanistan to marry a Swedish woman, as recommended by a Moroccan friend in London. He also denied receiving military training, saying that he did not need it because he had served in the Algerian Army as a young man, and added that he did not stay at the Algerian house, but in an Afghan house with another Algerian.[6]

While these accounts are rather inconclusive, another Algerian, 28-year-old Abdulnour Sameur, provided a more detailed account in which the differences between militants and migrants were more clearly delineated. A deserter from the Algerian Army—because, he said, he was "made to go in the streets and shoot innocent people"—he traveled via Italy to Britain, where he sought asylum in 1999. Granted leave to remain in 2000, he was living in the London suburb of South Harrow, but apparently "found it hard to live as a good Muslim in Britain." In his tribunal, he told a recruitment story that echoed those told by the Saudis and Yemenis in the previous chapter. He said that he met a man called Noor El-Din at London's Finsbury Park mosque, who advised him to move to Afghanistan because "living in England among the infidels might lead to greater things like neglecting my prayers, sinning, drinking," and added that El-Din told him that, if he liked it in Afghanistan, "he would help me figure out how to build a house there." After traveling to Pakistan in summer 2001, he was taken to the Algerian house, where he stayed for three months, but he denied receiving military training, and said that his time in Jalalabad consisted of prayer, playing football, looking after the house and doing some decorating for his elder brother, who also had a house in Jalalabad. Arrested after crossing into Pakistan with three other people, he, like Djamel Ameziane, escaped from the bus that was taken over by some of the prisoners on board, but was recaptured after being shot in the leg. After this, he said, "The United States bought me. They bought me with money from the Pakistani dogs."[7]

In the case of the final Algerian allegedly connected to the Jalalabad house, the truth is that he was never there at all. Ahmed Belbacha, a 32-year-old former professional footballer, moved to the UK as an economic migrant in 1999. He settled in Bournemouth, made a number of friends and took up work, first at a laundry and then as a waiter at the Highcliff Hotel, where, after being vetted by MI5, he served ministers and party members during the 1999 Labour Party conference. According to the *Guardian*, his friends "recall[ed] his pride at receiving a £30 tip and a personal letter of thanks from [Deputy Prime Minister] John Prescott." Accused of staying at the Jalalabad house, undertaking military training and meeting Osama bin Laden on two separate occasions, Belbacha actually took a month's holiday to visit Damascus, Tehran and an Afghan refugee camp, and by 2007 the Pentagon realized that this was the case. Despite being cleared for release, however, the Foreign Office refused to accept his return to the UK. "We're not making any moves with [the] British residents at Guantánamo," a spokesman said, and when asked how he imagined that Belbacha might ever be able to leave Guantánamo, he replied, "It has got nothing to do with us."[8]

Bearing in mind the allegation that several prisoners spoke of their knowledge of Ahmed Shah Massoud's assassination by two Belgian-based Tunisians, it was unsurprising that the four Tunisians captured at this time were regarded with particular suspicion. Two of the men—31-year-old Adil bin Hamida Mabrouk, and 33-year-old Lufti bin Swei Lagha—had, however, traveled to Afghanistan from Italy, and said that they were in search of a better life. Mabrouk, who had been working in sales and marketing, admitted staying at "the House of Algerians," where he learned to use a Kalashnikov, but insisted that he went to Afghanistan "as an immigrant," because "I became a Muslim when I was in Europe. My country was very tough on the Muslims. Afghanistan was a country where they were willing to take anybody, you don't need any money to live there, and they welcome all the Muslims." Lagha was accused of traveling to Afghanistan after being recruited for military training at a mosque in Italy, where the recruiter also gave him a Tunisian contact in Jalalabad. Adopting a more laid-back description of his activities in Jalalabad, he denied training in Afghanistan, and said that he spent his time fishing and "recreating."[9]

Whether these were realistic claims or not, Mabrouk and Lagha had more latitude for explanation than the other two Tunisians, 36-year-old Adel Hakimi and 35-year-old Hisham Sliti, who were remorselessly drawn into the plot to assassinate Massoud, which centered on Sliti's uncle Amor Sliti, who relocated to Afghanistan with his Belgian wife and daughter, and was followed by Hakimi and Hisham Sliti at a later date. The problem for the two men is that Amor Sliti was accused of providing shelter to Massoud's assassins in Jalalabad, and was sentenced to five years' imprisonment in Belgium in September 2003 for "recruiting militants and trafficking in false passports" linked to the assassination. Whether they have also been accused of being involved in Massoud's assassination is unknown. The allegations against Hakimi have not been made public, and Hisham

Sliti, who spent years in prison in Europe on drug-related offenses, has been accused of training at Khaldan and Durunta, and of being a member of a Tunisian terrorist group. It's clear, however, that they did not evade suspicion: in Hakimi's case, because he married Amor Sliti's daughter (who was pregnant at the time of his capture), and in Hisham Sliti's case, because of his blood relationship.[10]

When two of the Tunisians left Afghanistan for Pakistan, they were accompanied by Khalid al-Hubayshi, a 26-year-old Saudi, who traveled to Afghanistan in June 2001, but had previously visited in 1997, when he trained at Khaldan, and got to know its facilitator, Abu Zubaydah, whose capture is discussed in Chapter 13. The details of his relationship with Zubaydah are discussed in Chapter 20, as they shed some light on the relationship between Zubaydah and Osama bin Laden. For now, it's sufficient to note that al-Hubayshi was extremely suspicious of both bin Laden and the Taliban, and presented himself, instead, as a freedom fighter who focused on particular struggles that various Muslims around the world had with non-Muslim oppressors (the model that was largely superseded by bin Laden's declaration of global jihad in 1998). It was for this reason, he said, that he trained at Khaldan, which was not associated with either the Taliban or al-Qaeda at the time, and it was also for this reason that he returned to Afghanistan in 2001, joining "a private small camp" outside Jalalabad, which was subsequently closed down by the Taliban. He insisted, "I wasn't a member of al-Qaeda or on the front lines with the Taliban because I don't believe in what they are doing. I believe what the Taliban did in Afghanistan was ethnic war [and] al-Qaeda is a terrorist organization." He also explained:

> I think Osama bin Laden is wrong. He just wants to be famous. He doesn't care how he does it, killing people, killing Muslims, or destroying countries. I think he got what he wanted—to be famous. I don't need to meet him. I don't understand the politics. People look at the vision of Osama bin Laden and believe America is their enemy. They don't understand what is going on or what happened in Afghanistan in 1980.[11]

Other Europeans and North Africans

Not every European or North African captured at this time had stayed in Jalalabad. Around twenty others—including a handful of naïve adventurers from Europe, and several migrants from Syria and Morocco—were also seized. Only one of the Europeans, Slimane Hadj Abderrahmane, a 28-year-old Dane (released in February 2004), went to Afghanistan to receive military training, but he insisted that his intention was to fight in Chechnya, where, he said, "The Muslims are oppressed ... and the Russians are carrying out terror against them." After fleeing from the war and crossing the border, he was captured by locals who held him in a village prison before handing him over to the Pakistani authorities.[12]

The others maintained that they went to Afghanistan for religious reasons. Twenty-four-year-old Imad Kanouni (released in July 2004) was the only French prisoner with no obvious connection to Jalalabad. He said that he traveled to Afghanistan "to pursue religious education," and although he admitted that he was "ready to die for a good cause, [to] defend people who were attacked in their countries," he insisted that he did not agree with the ideas of Osama bin Laden and had never visited a training camp. Mehdi Ghezali, a 22-year-old Swede (released in July 2004), traveled to Pakistan to study Islam in August 2001, and was visiting a friend in Jalalabad when the US-led invasion began. He decided to return to Pakistan when he heard that Afghan villagers were selling foreigners to the US forces, but was captured in a village near Peshawar by locals who sold him to the Pakistani police, who in turn sold him to the Americans.[13]

Hamed Abderrahman Ahmed, a 27-year-old Spaniard from the North African enclave of Ceuta (transferred to Spanish custody in February 2004), was accused of fighting with the Taliban, but said that he went to Afghanistan in July 2001 to study his religion and to escape the drugs, violence and corruption in his neighborhood. "I've always dreamt about studying at a madrassa," he said, "where [the] Islam is the most authentic." After flying to Tehran, he made his way to an Islamic school in Kandahar, where, for two months, his dreams came true. The school was "a very pleasant place ... with luscious gardens and open space," and the owners "gave me a room and they let me attend the classes. In exchange for their hospitality, I only had to help a little in the garden, to take care of the flowers and to help in the kitchen. There were many foreigners, mainly Asians, and life was very peaceful." He explained that everything changed after 9/11, when there was talk about "possible and immediate retaliation," and everyone was told to leave. He and some of his fellow students took a car to Jalalabad, where they found that "bombs were falling everywhere," and people were desperately trying to escape. Some locals advised them to go to Pakistan on foot, as a car would be an easy target for missiles, but when they arrived in Pakistan they were "intercepted by a patrol of Pakistani soldiers," who put them in "some kind of an improvised jail" for a few days, before handing them over to the army.[14]

Also captured at this time were four Syrians—24-year-old Ahmed Ahjam, 19-year-old Ali Shaaban, 20-year-old Abu Omar al-Hamawe and 29-year-old Maasoum Mouhammed—who had been living together in a house in the Wazir Akbar Khan area of Kabul. This was one of the wealthier areas of the capital, where most of the embassies and other grand houses had been taken over by senior figures in the Taliban and al-Qaeda, but although the Americans described their house as "a safe house where five to 20 personnel armed with AK-47 rifles could be found at any time," which was used for "money and document forging operations" for al-Qaeda, Mouhammed described it as "a normal house, a place to eat, drink and sleep." Al-Hamawe added that it was close to the Pakistani embassy and that their neighbors, who worked for the Red Cross, "knew that all of us were not fighters or Taliban, just refugees." The four men certainly matched the profiles of economic migrants, drifting from country to country in search of employment, and drawn to Afghanistan by its Arab-influenced reputation for welcoming Muslims from all around the world. They said that only seven people lived at the house (themselves, the owner, and two other Syrians), and that they all put money in to keep the place running. Al-Hamawe worked at a store in Kabul, but planned to move to Pakistan when a friend sent him money from Syria, Mouhammed, who had been a policeman and a grocer in Syria, had saved some money while working, and planned to move on to Jordan, Shaaban had been an ironsmith in his father's store and went to Afghanistan because he wanted to move there, and, according to US intelligence, Ahjam worked for al-Wafa. When Kabul fell to the Northern Alliance, they fled to Jalalabad, and then made their way across the mountains to Pakistan, where they were arrested.[15]

Another two Syrians—41-year-old Abdul Nasir al-Tumani and his 19-year-old son Mohammed—were also captured after crossing the border. The father had traveled to Afghanistan in 1999 in search of work, finding a job in a restaurant in Kabul and bringing ten members of his family over in June 2001, including Mohammed, his grandmother and an eight-month-old baby. Another six family members—his uncle's family—arrived a week before 9/11, but after hearing about the attack on America the family fled to Jalalabad, where they stayed for a month, and then made their way on foot to Pakistan. On the way, their guide advised al-Tumani to let the women and children travel by car, to make them less of a target for highway robbers, but when he and his son arrived in Pakistan the local villagers handed them over to the Pakistani Army.[16]

Of the three Moroccans captured crossing into Pakistan, two—33-year-old Said Boujaadia and 20-year-old Mohammed Ben Moujan—were brothers-in-law. Ben Moujan (transferred to Moroccan custody in February 2006) went to Afghanistan to visit his sister, who was married to Boujaadia, and stayed at their house in Kandahar. He denied an allegation that he undertook weapons training in the mountains north of Kandahar, and explained that, after "fleeing from death and riots in Kandahar," he crossed into Pakistan with numerous Afghans and Arabs, and was arrested by Pakistani soldiers on arrival. Boujaadia (cleared for release in 2007) faced several dubious, and presumably groundless allegations: that he traveled to Afghanistan in July 2001 with the wife of the security chief of the Libyan Islamic Fighting Group (his own wife was not mentioned), that he attended a training camp, and that he was captured with Salim Hamdan, the Yemeni who was one of Osama bin Laden's drivers. It was also alleged that he and Ben Moujan "engaged in jihad in the Tora Bora mountains," although Ben Moujan insisted that this was invented by Moroccan interrogators who questioned him in Guantánamo.[17]

The third Moroccan, 33-year-old Younes Chekhouri, had a far more interesting story to tell. The elder brother of Redouane Chekhouri (released in 2004), he said that he spent ten years in Pakistan, Yemen and Syria, studying and undertaking humanitarian work, and arrived in Afghanistan in June 2001 with his Algerian wife. He explained that he then established a guest house in Kabul, which was specifically for young Moroccans, because they were not treated well in Afghanistan, and another house outside the city, which was "especially for people

who want to look at the sky and the stars and pray and meditate."
While this explanation was unacceptable to his tribunal, who insisted
that both houses were connected with military training, he denied
the allegations and made the following statement: "In our religion
of Islam, it teaches us to forgive other Muslims ... And the fighting
between Muslims is forbidden. The fighting between Afghans,
between themselves lasted for about 20 years. There was no value and
no good came out of that fighting." Reinforcing this viewpoint, he
said that he was not involved with al-Qaeda, and explained that from
1990 onwards, when he first visited Afghanistan, people told him to
stay away from Osama bin Laden. He suggested that bin Laden was a
double agent working for the Saudi government, and that when he was
"stripped out of his Saudi citizenship and exiled from the kingdom" in
1992, he was "shocked that this would be a new game that the Saudi
government would be playing with us." He then expressed surprise
that bin Laden became such an important figure in Sudan, wondering
how Sudan could "sacrifice a relationship with the world" for him,
and condemned his actions after his return to Afghanistan in 1996, in
particular the African embassy bombings—in which "a lot of Muslims
were victims"—and the attack on the USS *Cole*:

> In every meeting that happened, people would say that Osama bin Laden
> is dangerous ... I was one of the people that was telling others that Osama
> bin Laden is a crazy person and that what he does is bad for Islam. How can
> he be the only person in the world to say that jihad is fighting Americans?
> How could he just make that up? We were very honest in what we said
> against bin Laden. For that reason, we received a lot of threats. But that
> was not important to us.

Explaining the circumstances of his capture, he said that, after
9/11, a decision was made to close both the houses, and he then went
to Jalalabad. Having sent his wife to Pakistan, he planned to follow,
but when Jalalabad fell he went into the mountains with some other
people, stayed in an Afghan village during Ramadan, and was arrested
in a market after crossing the Pakistani border, when "somebody saw
me and noticed that I was Arabic. He started talking to me and the
police interfered and said you shall come with us, so I went with them
to the police station."[18]

Other Humanitarian Aid Workers and Religious Teachers

In addition to the Saudis mentioned in the previous chapter, another nine humanitarian aid workers and religious teachers—four Bahrainis and five Kuwaitis—were also arrested at this time. Several Kuwaitis crossed the border together on December 16, 2001, and their arrival is well-documented. *Newsweek* investigated their case and reported that the local villagers remembered them well. Although they were not the first Arabs to arrive via the precipitous snow-bound paths across the White Mountains, the villagers declared them "the softest." An eyewitness said that "the Afghan guide who brought them was furious, swearing he'd never take Kuwaitis on that trail again." Unlike other Arabs he'd guided before—fighters with experience of difficult terrain—he described the Kuwaitis as "weak, nervous, ill-clothed and inexperienced climbers," and "grumbled that he and his friend practically had to carry them."[19]

Whilst it's unclear exactly which of the Kuwaitis were referred to above, the description would fit all but one of the five men captured at this time. None had military experience, and all had jobs that did not prepare them for high-altitude trekking in civilian clothes. Only 28-year-old Abdullah al-Kandari, an engineer for the ministry of water and electricity and a father of four (released in September 2006), had a history of physical exertion: a well-known figure in Kuwait, he played volleyball for the national team. Thirty-six-year-old Mohammed al-Daihani (released in November 2005) was an auditor for the Kuwaiti government and a father of six, 28-year-old Abdul Aziz al-Shammeri (also released in November 2005) was a teacher and a father of two, and the two men who were still in Guantánamo at the time of writing—26-year-old Khalid al-Hameydani and 24-year-old Fawzi al-Odah—were largely indistinguishable from their freed compatriots. Al-Hameydani worked as a messenger at a primary school, and al-Odah was a religious teacher, whose father was a retired air force pilot and officer who had fought with the Americans during the first Gulf War.

Two of the men went to Afghanistan to teach the Koran, while the other three traveled to provide humanitarian aid. The teachers were Abdul Aziz al-Shammeri and Fawzi al-Odah. Al-Shammeri took a short vacation in October 2001 and traveled around Afghan villages teaching the Koran. He explained that he felt he would be safe in the villages, because life would be going on as normal and "would not be interrupted except on the battleground," and added that he had no idea that the Taliban government "would fall in the blink of an eye." As the situation deteriorated, he left everything behind and fled. "You know they killed some of the women as well," he explained. "And you know that women in Islam are not killed; they don't fight or participate in the fighting. So, when I hear something like that, I don't think of going back and getting my passport, I just think of my life." After escaping across the mountains, he turned himself in to the Pakistani Army, thinking they would question him and arrange for him to return home: "I didn't think they would tell me, 'Since you don't have identification or a passport, that means you're a follower of Osama bin Laden.' I have never heard of this before."[20]

Fawzi al-Odah, regarded by the Americans as particularly suspicious for some reason, also took a short vacation and traveled to Afghanistan in August 2001 "to teach and to help other people." After finding a liaison in the Taliban, which "was necessary because that was the government in Afghanistan at that time," he was "touring the schools and visiting families," teaching the Koran and handing out money, until his activities were curtailed after 9/11. He explained that in Kandahar, the Taliban representative "told me that was a dangerous place because it was the capital for the Taliban," and advised him to go to Logar, where he stayed with a family for a month, and left his passport and belongings for safekeeping, fearing that, "If the Afghans saw I had a passport indicating I was an Arab, and they saw the money and the camera I had, I would have been killed." After this, he moved to Jalalabad, where he stayed with another family, who gave him an AK-47 to protect himself, and then joined up with other people crossing the mountains to Pakistan, where he handed himself in.[21]

The first of the humanitarian aid workers, Abdullah al-Kandari, was moved by the plight of refugees fleeing to Iran after the US-led invasion began. He took a ten-day vacation and traveled to the Afghan border, where he gave $15,000 to a humanitarian aid worker who bought food and blankets for the refugees, but when he tried to return to Iran he was told that the borders were closed to Arabs. His Afghan guide then took him to Jalalabad, to look for a way into Pakistan: "He put me in a home and he went back to the border.

They told him, no, I couldn't leave the country because I am Arabic. I was then moved from home to home. The problems got worse. The people there wanted to kill Arabs. I was told to be careful and don't go anywhere. I was always stuck in a small room and never went out." When his guide gave up on the legal approach, he found two men to take him to the border, who seem to have betrayed him for money. After keeping him in a house for a few days, they took him to the mosque where dozens of others were taken by local villagers, where he was handed over to the Pakistani Army.[22]

Mohammed al-Daihani's family had a history of funding aid projects, and al-Daihani himself funded the construction of a mosque in Benin, and, in 2001, the digging of wells in Afghanistan. With unfortunate timing, he took a week's vacation to check on the progress of his project, arriving the day before 9/11. As the country slowly descended into chaos and the borders were closed, he was trapped, moved from house to house in Kabul, Kandahar, Herat and Jalalabad by his contact in the charity to which he had made his donation (the London-based Sanabal Charitable Committee, which, the Americans alleged, was "a fund-raising front for the Libyan Islamic Fighting Group"). Finally, he hired a guide to smuggle him into Pakistan with eight or nine other people, where he was handed over to the army by local villagers. Khalid al-Hameydani, who was accused of training at a Lashkar-e-Tayyiba camp, fighting with the Taliban at Taloqan, and finding time to work for al-Wafa, also came from a family with a history of funding aid projects. His parents said that he traveled to Pakistan to help repair a mosque they had funded, and added that, on the last occasion that he spoke to them, he said that he "wanted to assist the Afghani refugees" and would be home by December.[23]

The Bahrainis, for the most part, told similar stories. Twenty-year-old Salah al-Balushi (released in October 2006) and 22-year-old Sheikh Salman al-Khalifa, a member of the Bahraini royal family (released in November 2005), went to Afghanistan on humanitarian missions. Al-Balushi, who was obliged to fend off all manner of allegations about his purported associations with al-Qaeda, has not spoken since his release, and al-Khalifa, who gave $5,000 to the Taliban to distribute to the poor and needy, after hearing about their plight on the news, explained that he also went to Afghanistan to study his religion. Nineteen-year-old Abdullah al-Noaimi (also released in November 2005), the cousin of a lawyer who represents over a hundred Guantánamo prisoners, went to Afghanistan to find another of his cousins, and was captured by Pakistani guards after crossing the border with four Arabs and two Afghans.[24]

The other Bahraini, 28-year-old Juma al-Dossari, features prominently throughout the rest of this book, as he has been subjected to particularly brutal treatment throughout his imprisonment. The reasons for this remain unclear, but are probably connected with the fact that he spent time in the United States in 2001, and that every Arab who visited the US was regarded with particular suspicion. What's apparent, however, is that the US authorities do not believe his explanation of how he came to be in Afghanistan. According to al-Dossari, his local imam in Bahrain paid him to travel to Afghanistan in October 2001 to inspect seven mosques with another man named Mohammed Gul. He said that, after meeting Gul in Iran, the two of them crossed into Afghanistan by taxi, stayed for three weeks in a house owned by Gul in Kabul, and then moved on to another house that he owned in Jalalabad, before fleeing to Pakistan, where he was captured.[25]

Also captured at this time was a particularly unfortunate Egyptian, Sami El-Leithi (released in October 2005), whose suffering in Guantánamo is discussed in Chapter 15. The 45-year-old left Egypt in 1986, disgusted that democracy was not practiced in his homeland, and traveled to Pakistan, where he took a master's degree in economics and taught at various schools and universities for ten years, and then moved to Afghanistan, where he taught at Kabul University, and, despite various run-ins with the Taliban, managed to avoid serious problems until the US-led invasion in October 2001. When the bombing raids began, he suffered a head injury and was transferred to a hospital in Kabul with several other injured Afghans. After hearing that the US was also targeting hospitals, he and the others decided to seek refuge in Khost, but when they were told that members of the Taliban had also fled to Khost and that US forces would soon be targeting the area, they decided to flee to Pakistan. Although he was still severely injured, El-Leithi made it to the border via car, but was then arrested with his Afghan driver.[26]

The Uyghurs

Of all the wrongfully detained men captured at this time, the most woeful group were the Uyghurs, 18 young Muslims, mostly in their twenties, who had fled from Chinese oppression in their homeland. All made their way, between May and October 2001, to a small, isolated, rundown camp in the Tora Bora mountains, where they spent their days reading the Koran and repairing the camp's broken-down buildings (five simple houses and a mosque), and dreamed of hitting back at their oppressors. Occasionally, they fired one or two bullets from the camp's only gun, an ageing AK-47.

The men arrived at the camp in varied ways. Some went there deliberately, like 27-year-old Dawut Abdurehim, who had a business selling animal skins and who traveled to Afghanistan to combine business with training, 28-year-old Akhdar Basit, who traveled through Kyrgyzstan and Pakistan to reach the camp, and 28-year-old Abdul Ghappar, who went to "get some training to fight back against the Chinese government." Others ended up there while seeking a new start in life. Yusef Abbas, a 21-year-old farmer, learned about the oppression of his people as he was growing up, and was determined to leave to find a better life, but could find little information about other countries, except through broadcasts that were made by a covert US radio station. Having finally obtained a passport, he decided to try to get to the US. Taking $600 with him, he went first to Kyrgyzstan, where he was warned that the police planted false evidence on Uyghurs and handed them over to the Chinese authorities, but where they took $300 from him instead, and laughed at him when he told them that he wanted to go to America. He then went to Pakistan, where a Uyghur businessman, who befriended him at the airport, encouraged him to go to an Uzbek house in Jalalabad, where another Uyghur took him to the camp in the Tora Bora mountains. Twenty-two-year-old Abdullah Abdulquadirakhun wanted to go to Turkey, where he believed that the government would give him citizenship, but got no further than Kyrgyzstan, where he found a job in a bazaar. Some locals then gave him an address in Pakistan, where a Uyghur businessman told him about the camp. As he was having difficulties getting a visa for Iran, he decided to go to the camp instead. Thirty-two-year-old Abu Bakker Qassim and 27-year-old Abdul Abdulhehim told similar stories. Both leather workers, they met in a bazaar in Kyrgyzstan and hoped to go to Turkey on business, but when they could not get Iranian visas in Pakistan they took the advice of their host and made their way to Tora Bora.[27]

The men's isolated, subsistence-level existence came to an end in October 2001, when the camp was hit in a US bombing raid. Yusef Abbas, who was injured in the raid, said that one man died and "we were covered in half a bucket of his body meat." After the bombing, he was taken to a hospital in Jalalabad, where Abdul Razak, a Uyghur who worked at the hospital and occasionally brought food to the camp, took care of him, until "there was a riot in the city" and he returned to the other Uyghurs in the mountains, taking Razak with him. The men then spent a month dodging bombing raids, staying, on one occasion, in a place that "even had monkeys that were also screaming at us," according to Dawut Abdurehim. Finally, they saw a large group of Arabs making their way to the Pakistani border, and decided to follow them at a distance. On arrival, they were among the many dozens of men who were welcomed and then betrayed by villagers. Yusef Abbas explained, "It was the third day of a Muslim holiday ... the local people there welcomed us since it was a holiday. They gave us meat and good food." Abu Bakker Qassim took up the story: "In the middle of the night, the villagers told us they would take us to another place. We walked two to three hours away to a mosque. The tribe people tricked us and turned us over to the Pakistani authorities." Twenty-eight-year-old Ahmed Adil concluded the story: "At the mosque there were a lot of people, Uyghurs, Arabs and others as well. There weren't any Pakistani soldiers or anyone with rifles or weapons to capture us. When we were in the mosque, they told us to get out. We went out in groups of ten and we were taken to a car. They drove us for a couple [of] hours and we ended up in the Pakistani prison."[28]

Questioned in Guantánamo, the Uyghurs made it clear that their struggle had nothing whatsoever to do with the Americans. When asked, "Was it your intention when you were training to fight against the US or its allies?" the response of Abdul Ghappar was typical, and was echoed by many of his companions: "I have one point: a billion Chinese enemies, that is enough for me. Why would I get more enemies?" Others expressed contempt for al-Qaeda. Ahmed Adil said,

"I heard from you guys that most of the al-Qaeda people are Arabs. Those Arabs have their own country and they can live wherever they want in their own country. They are free to do whatever they want. I do not understand why they are causing trouble and making a mess for the world. I hear that those people have a little problem in their brain; it doesn't work properly." Yusef Abbas was particularly disappointed by his treatment at the hands of the Americans. Remembering the radio broadcasts he had listened to at home, he thought the Americans would help him rather than imprisoning him. In fact, the US authorities soon realized that the Uyghurs were telling the truth, but at the time of writing only five had been released: Ahmed Adil, Akhdar Basit, Abu Bakker Qasim, Abdul Abdulhehim and Haji Mohammed Ayub, who arrived at the camp after it had been bombed, and who was only 17 years old at the time of his capture.[29]

Detention in Pakistan

Once the prisoners were rounded up, they were transferred to various prisons—mainly Peshawar and Kohat—before being handed over to the Americans. The Bahraini Adel Kamel Haji explained that, having been detained for the night at the border with other foreigners, he expected to be taken to a police station for routine questioning when a military helicopter arrived instead, with about 15 officers from the Pakistani Special Forces on board. At this point, he said, "we realized that we had been betrayed by the officers at the border post." Blindfolded and bound, the men were thrown onto the helicopter and flown to Peshawar. On the way, each prisoner was assigned four soldiers, who "sat on our backs throughout the flight," and at Peshawar airport they were dragged from the plane and thrown on the ground, where "we remained in the open for about two hours without anyone uttering a word with us." They were then taken in trucks to a police station and held in cells, which were "located somewhere underground with doors made of steel." Haji explained that the cells were "very dirty," "the treatment in [the] prison was awful," and "the food was very bad," and Hamed Ahmed described it as "an awful jail," adding, "We were crowded together and they only gave us water with lentils to eat. I had diarrhoea 24 hours a day. I think I lost 20 kilos."

During their detention in Peshawar, Haji said that the Pakistanis took him and some other prisoners for what they claimed was routine questioning, but explained that they were taken to a villa where they were confronted by American interrogators, who "asked us about our names, nationalities, age, qualifications, the reason of going to Afghanistan, how we entered and when," and then returned them to the prison. Khalid bin Mustafa was also questioned by Americans. "They wore civilian clothes," he said. "FBI or CIA, I've no idea." Mehdi Ghezali, who was also taken for questioning, was told that he would be allowed to meet with representatives of the UN. "A woman was presented as a UN official," he said, but added, "When I saw her again at the airport, I understood that she was not from the UN but [was] an American soldier."

Slimane Hadj Abderrahmane described the conditions at Kohat jail, where he was taken after the villagers who captured him handed him over to the Pakistani authorities. He and dozens of other prisoners were blindfolded and bound and herded onto trucks, and after several hours' drive he "could hardly move as his legs and hands were badly swollen." On arrival at Kohat, they were made to stand for several hours in the prison yard, "still tied with ropes," and "were not given anything to eat or allowed to relieve themselves." After a brief interrogation by army personnel, he was taken to a cell, where iron rings were fastened around his ankles to which iron poles were attached which had to be lifted when walking. Ten days later, he was brought before two US interrogators, who did nothing to end his ill-treatment, and was then transferred to US custody. According to a report by Human Rights First, Kohat—and another Pakistani jail, Alizai—were actually run by Americans, as part of the "secret prison" system discussed in Chapter 16. The report stated that all the "civilian" prisoners were moved out of Kohat after the US-led invasion, and that, although "the Pakistani army maintained the external security of the prison ... US officials were responsible for the internal security."[30]

Two prisoners who suffered particularly harsh treatment in Pakistan were Abdul Nasir and Mohammed al-Tumani. Mohammed said that, while in Pakistani custody, in three separate prisons, they were "subjected to beatings and harsh torture," and his nose was broken. He added that throughout this ordeal "there were Americans present," and his story was echoed by his father, who said that the Pakistanis "were torturing us really hard," and the Americans "were looking and standing right there. The Americans were present. I am sure about that because they were the ones who interrogated us." Abdul Nasir also said that they were tortured to admit that they were on the bus to Peshawar that was overtaken by prisoners: "They said to be careful. If we changed just one word in what [we said] to the Americans, they were going to bring us back and kill us."[31]

From early January onwards, the prisoners were taken out in batches, bound and blindfolded and bundled onto planes that took them to the prison at Kandahar airport. Juma al-Dossari described the abuse to which they were subjected during the flight:

> After they closed the door, the soldiers started shouting, screaming and insulting us with the most vulgar insults and nasty curses. They started beating us and took pictures of us on a camera; I could see the flash. I had a violent pain in my stomach—I had had an operation on my stomach and there was a piece of metal in it. When I complained about the severity of the pain, a soldier came and started kicking me in my stomach with his military boot until I vomited blood.[32]

8
Kandahar

The Fall of Kandahar and the Escape of Mullah Omar

On December 19, 2001, the next phase of the "War on Terror" began in earnest, when 15 prisoners were transferred from Sheberghan to a hastily erected prison and interrogation center that was part of a newly established US military base at Kandahar airport. Here the administration's brand-new policy—centered on brutal captivity, relentless interrogation, and indefinite detention without trial and without access to lawyers or family—first came to life. By the end of February, around 450 prisoners had been processed, including those described in the previous chapters, as well as another 90 from Sheberghan and 65 from other Afghan-run prisons, whose stories are related in the next two chapters; there was also the first trickle of what would soon become a flood of prisoners captured in Pakistan, whose stories are related in Chapters 12 and 13.

The construction of the base, ten miles east of Kandahar, was the culmination of a campaign to conquer the Taliban's last stronghold, which began with six weeks of remorseless bombing raids, and was followed up, on the day that Kunduz fell, with the establishment of Camp Rhino, a US military base on a remote desert airstrip at Dolangi, 55 miles south-west of Kandahar. Originally built for the falconry expeditions of a wealthy Saudi, the airstrip was later renovated by Osama bin Laden, but it was now commandeered by a force of 1,200 Marines—the first significant commitment of ground troops in the Afghan campaign—who were flown in by helicopter from the USS *Peleliu* in the Arabian Sea. Their commander, General James Mattis, declared, "The Marines have landed and we now own a piece of Afghanistan."[1]

These were fine words, but Camp Rhino's most noteworthy contribution to the "War on Terror" was when it played host to John Walker Lindh, who was moved from Mazar-e-Sharif on December 7, after a group of soldiers blindfolded him, scrawled "shithead" across his blindfold and posed for photos with him; another soldier told Lindh he was "going to hang" for his actions and they would sell the photographs of his corpse and give the money to a Christian organization. In Camp Rhino, he was stripped naked, blindfolded, bound to a stretcher with duct tape, held in a shipping container ringed with barbed wire and interrogated by the US military and the CIA, who reported regularly to Donald Rumsfeld. Still suffering from his wounds, with a bullet lodged in his left leg that the medics at Sheberghan decided to leave in place "for later removal as evidence," he did not receive medical treatment until he was moved to the USS *Peleliu* a week later.[2]

As far as the military campaign was concerned, the Marines played their part in advancing on Kandahar from the south, but the battle to remove Mullah Omar and capture the nerve center of his failed Utopian experiment was mainly won through the muscle provided by the Pashtun warlord Gul Agha Sherzai (backed up by US firepower), and the impenetrable channels of Afghan diplomacy, in which Hamid Karzai—now being groomed by the US for future leadership—played a major part. In public, Karzai denied negotiating with the Taliban leader, but behind the scenes it was a different story. His solution was to allow Mullah Omar to slip away, having negotiated an amnesty for his troops. According to the agreement, the Taliban soldiers were to hand in their weapons and remain in Kandahar, but, although many weapons were surrendered, they too slipped away in their thousands. As Karzai's influence grew—he was nominated as the chairman of the Afghan Interim Authority (the precursor to the first post-Taliban government) at a UN conference in Bonn on December 5—the Americans were forced to rein him in when he announced, "I have declared general amnesty for all. Let there be no revenge and no vendetta," and offered to extend his amnesty to Mullah Omar, so long as he was prepared to "completely distance himself from foreign terrorists." He withdrew his offer after Donald Rumsfeld insisted,

"I have not seen or heard anything that would suggest anyone is negotiating anything that would be contrary to what our interests are," but he remained buoyant. "The Taliban rule is finished," Karzai declared. "As of today they are no longer part of Afghanistan."[3]

One man who was not pleased was Gul Agha Sherzai. The governor of Kandahar province during the carnage of the early 1990s, he was described by the journalist Peter Maass as "a large man of large appetites, not just for food, but for battle and laughter and power." After seven years of exile in Pakistan, he was eager for revenge on the Taliban who had deposed him, and when the Americans approached him in November he assembled a group of 1,500 Afghan fighters on the border, and joined up with a unit of US Special Forces who presented him with a formidable armory of Kalashnikovs and RPGs. Telling his men not to take revenge on the Taliban, but to "show no mercy" to the Arabs and Pakistanis of al-Qaeda, he then led them towards Kandahar. Like all the warlords supported by the Americans, he was supplied with large amounts of cash to pay his soldiers and to pay off or recruit the opposition, and one of his commanders explained, "We brought a car of cash with us. It was a Land Cruiser, full of money. I think it was resupplied too." Sherzai also knew when to be magnanimous. While the Americans were rounding up all manner of stragglers that they suspected of being associated with the Taliban, he refused to imprison those who surrendered. As Maass described it, "he gave them pocket money and told them to go home."

The combination of cash, Kalashnikovs, air support and Sherzai's enthusiastic military leadership was spectacularly successful. By the end of November, they had reached Kandahar airport, and a week later, after the Taliban streamed out of Kandahar, he entered the city unopposed and resumed his position as governor. Although he took Kandahar without firing a single shot, however, the airport was bought with blood. Peter Maass reported that, when journalists asked his commanders about their strategy, they said that Sherzai had ordered them "to execute al-Qaeda fighters who surrendered," but changed their story when they realized it was "not acceptable for soldiers who are fighting alongside the Special Forces to engage in such behaviour or, at least, to tell journalists about it." A week after the battle, Justin Huggler reported that the Americans and their allies "appear[ed] to be trying to cover up the slaughter of around 280 foreign Taliban fighters" at the airport, most of whom had been killed by American bombs. While Afghan spokesmen claimed that only 20 fighters had been killed, Huggler spoke to a soldier who had helped bury the 280 dead, and two other witnesses told him they "saw two bulldozers dumping earth into what they believed was a mass grave at the airport."[4]

The Prison Opens

From the beginning, the prison at Kandahar was a brutal place. According to one authoritative report, the prisoners, who arrived by plane, usually at night, were "bound together in long chains" as they disembarked. If one of them stumbled as he made his way down the ramp, the others would be pulled down with him. They were, invariably, in a parlous state. Many were wounded, and others, fearing death or punishment, had lost control of their bladders or their bowels. Once they were on the airstrip, military police (MPs) gathered around them, shining flashlights in their faces and "screaming a stream of commands and obscenities audible even over the roar of the plane as it pulled away." Watched over by armed military police in gun towers, the prisoners were led to a barbed-wire enclosure, and were "hurled, one by one, into a three-sided sandbag 'pin-down.'" MPs with rubber gloves then made them lie on their stomachs while they cut off their clothes. According to the report, they "howled and wailed and struggled to roll over, fearing there could only be one purpose for being held face-down and stripped," and their screams caused "supreme agitation" to those waiting in line. Naked, but hooded and still in chains, they were then sent through an "abattoir-like tunnel" to the next stage of processing, where they received "a quick intelligence screening," and were examined by a doctor. An MP then shouted, in Arabic, "And now for the ass inspection!" This process, which involved two MPs pinning the prisoners down with a knee in the back and a firm hand on the neck, while the doctor went about his business, "always prompted new shrieks from prisoners convinced they were about to be raped."[5]

The quotes above are not the words of a prisoner. They come from the prologue—subtitled "The Abattoir"—of *The Interrogator's War*, the book by Chris Mackey, the senior interrogator who worked at

Kandahar and Bagram from January to August 2002. Mackey was no apologist for the army's behavior. Elsewhere in his book (as will be discussed below, and in later chapters), he was critical of various aspects of the US operations in Afghanistan, and he was particularly appalled by the revelations of torture and abuse at Abu Ghraib in Iraq, which surfaced in 2004. Clearly, however, he had no complaints about the treatment of prisoners as they arrived at Kandahar, but while some of these processes—the removal of clothes and the anal probe—could, in theory, be defended as necessary for hygiene and security, it must also have been apparent that they were supremely humiliating to devout Muslims, many of whom had never been seen naked before, not even in front of their wives. It must also have been apparent that, for many of those being processed, their fear was not only that they were about to be raped, but also that they were about to be killed.

Former prisoners at Kandahar have corroborated Mackey's description of the treatment they received on arrival and during processing, although many said that the process was actually far more brutal. The first to speak out publicly was Mohammed Saghir, who "had not even had a cursory interview at Sheberghan before he was bound hand and foot, blindfolded and helicoptered to Kandahar," where, he said, "They would just pick us up and throw us out [of the plane]. Some people were hurt, some quite badly." A fellow Pakistani, Abdul Razaq, a 31-year-old English teacher, confirmed Saghir's complaints. Swept up during the fall of Kunduz, where he was on a preaching mission, he was singled out in Sheberghan because he spoke English. "One thing I've learned about the Americans," he said, "is they are very harsh when they transport people around. They had tied up my hands so tight that for two months I couldn't use my right hand ... For a long time we didn't know it was Kandahar. We thought they were going to kill us there." Released from Guantánamo in July 2003, he added, "I don't know what made them suspect me, but there were rumors that they arrested me because they thought I was a very senior Taliban official."[6]

The Bahrainis Adel Kamel Haji, Abdullah al-Noaimi and Juma al-Dossari also described what happened to them on arrival at Kandahar. Haji said that US soldiers beat him in the face and stomach as he was led from the plane, and al-Dossari said that he and the others who arrived with him were made to lie down on the runway, and were then beaten and kicked severely. He added that the hood came off one of his fellow prisoners, who "saw the soldiers pointing their weapons at us, so he shouted, 'they're going to kill us, brothers.' One of the soldiers hit him on the head with the butt of his weapon and he lost consciousness." He also said that, as they approached the processing center, the MPs "started to insult us savagely," and many of the younger prisoners were "shouting and crying because of their severe pain," but the soldiers only "increased their insults and beatings." Al-Noaimi told a similar story. He said that, while being moved to the processing center, "the soldiers kicked his legs out from under him, causing him to fall to the ground," and he "heard other detainees screaming in pain." He also explained that he and other prisoners "were ordered to stand with their backs to the soldiers, who then knocked them to the ground and held guns to their heads," and added that, during his anal probe, a female MP grabbed and held his penis.[7]

Abusive Treatment During Detention

After processing, the prisoners were moved to their "cells"—open-sided tents, ringed with barbed wire and watched over by armed soldiers, which provided little or no protection from the heat of the day and the freezing conditions at night. Each tent held 20 to 25 prisoners, and the facilities provided were minimal. Each prisoner was given two blankets and a copy of the Koran, but they had to share a toilet bucket, an experience that many found humiliating. The authorities also insisted that they were not allowed to talk to each other. "Talking to God in the cages was permitted," Chris Mackey wrote. "Talking to one another wasn't." Although Mackey justified this policy by claiming that it was necessary for the intelligence-gathering process, preventing prisoners from "passing information or coaching one another on how to handle interrogations," it was also manifestly cruel, enforcing a sense of isolation which could, over time, cause profound psychological damage. The no-talking rule also involved punishment, as described by a Pakistani ex-prisoner, interviewed by Human Rights Watch, who said, "we were not allowed to talk with each other and if we did, we were beaten and we were not allowed to sleep. For instance, if we were sleeping we were woken up or if we were covering our head with our bed cover we were beaten strongly. They would kick and punch us."[8]

Juma al-Dossari explained more about the everyday abuse that took place:

> Beatings were not the only form of torture; sleep deprivation was also used. The soldiers would wake us up at night for inspections; sometimes they would make us stand in a line, after pointing their weapons at us, [and] they would tell us that they were under orders to fire if any one of us moved. We would stand there for many hours like that in the freezing cold ... When the soldiers woke us up for inspections, if anyone did not hear their call, either because they were asleep, ill or completely exhausted, they would punish everyone in the tent. This was always their style of punishment: collective punishment.[9]

In keeping with the violent treatment to which the prisoners were subjected on arrival and during processing, their detention was also punctuated by acts of random brutality. This was unsurprising, given that the prison was referred to by the soldiers as "Camp Slappy," and that they dehumanized the prisoners by referring to them all as "Bob," so that, for example, a grievously wounded prisoner was referred to as "Half-Dead Bob," and Abdul Razeq—a schizophrenic, who was held in a cage on his own, where he ranted and raved and ate his own excrement—became "Crazy Bob." Mourad Benchellali, who spent three weeks at Kandahar before being transferred to Guantánamo, said that "conditions were terrible" at the camp. He explained that he and other prisoners were regularly beaten, that "Americans peed on detainees," that sometimes the soldiers "took photos of us completely naked," and that they "handcuffed us to hurt us. I was tied to a bar placed above my head or then they tied me up very low on my back ... I saw the Red Cross, but its representatives told me that there was nothing they could do." He also said that the soldiers "piled us one on top of the other," a precursor to a tactic that was later applied in Bagram and Abu Ghraib, when naked prisoners were piled up in grotesque human pyramids. Slimane Hadj Abderrahmane, who was also photographed naked, said that soldiers "made fun of his genitals while he was chained, hooded and naked," adding, "The Americans did it all to humiliate us. Why else should we be naked in the middle of a tent? Why should they hit me and shave me against my religion? Because it was a psychological fight."[10]

Juma al-Dossari also provided examples of more specialized brutality. He said that he was made to walk on barbed wire and had his head pushed into broken glass, and added that several other prisoners received injuries to their eyes in this manner, that "three brothers were blinded," and that many of the prisoners—himself included—had their noses broken by the soldiers. He was also one of the first prisoners to describe how the prisoners' copies of the Koran were regularly abused. He explained that some of the soldiers "treated the Koran terribly," dropping copies in the toilet bucket, scrawling obscenities on its pages, and tearing out pages which they used to shine their shoes or to wipe out the toilet bucket, and added that they also cursed Allah and the Prophet Mohammed on a regular basis. The abuse of the Koran was also noted by the Britons Tarek Dergoul, Shafiq Rasul, Asif Iqbal and Rhuhel Ahmed, and by Ehsanullah, a 28-year-old Afghan (released in March 2003), who said that soldiers in Kandahar hit him and taunted him by throwing the Koran in a toilet.[11]

Some of the other Bahrainis also had vivid tales to tell of their treatment at Kandahar. Isa al-Murbati (whose capture is related in Chapter 12) said that he was "shackled to a pole outside in very cold weather," and that, "every hour, US military personnel threw cold water on [him] while he was shackled to the pole." He explained that this took place every night for a week, and added that on one occasion he was taken to an area away from the other prisoners, because Red Cross representatives were visiting the camp, and the authorities did not want them to see him. It was also clear that al-Murbati was not the only prisoner to be exposed to the extreme cold. The Pakistani interviewed by Human Rights Watch said that "he and other prisoners were occasionally taken outside and forced to lie on the frozen ground until they were numb with cold."[12]

Abdullah al-Noaimi "witnessed other detainees being bitten by military dogs," and said that "a female soldier, upon learning that [his] brother lived in the USA, threatened to kill him." He also developed a urinary tract infection and came down with a fever, which made him vomit and left him unable to eat, but explained that, when he was taken to the clinic, "a military doctor allowed a military policeman to inject him with an unknown substance. When he began to bleed as a result, the doctor and the policeman laughed." He was then placed in isolation for seven weeks, and was ignored by the medical staff, even though his eyes were yellow and there was blood in his urine, and added that a doctor told him, "you're about to die and there's nothing we can do for you."[13]

In addition to these reports, the Syrian Mohammed al-Tumani said that his father's forehead was fractured "and the Red Cross saw this and wrote a report," and added that he received a fracture to his left hand, as well as suffering "many diseases" and "other methods of psychological torture," including sleep deprivation. Several Kuwaiti prisoners also spoke about brutal treatment. Fawzi al-Odah specifically said that he was "tortured badly" in Kandahar, and others made allegations to their lawyer, whose notes of their meetings were subsequently declassified:

> All indicated that they had been horribly treated, particularly in Afghanistan and Pakistan ... Although the words they used were different, the stories they told were remarkably similar—terrible beatings, hung from wrists and beaten, removal of clothes, hooding, exposure naked to extreme cold, naked in front of female guards, sexual taunting by both male and female guards/interrogators ... terrible uncomfortable positions for hours. All confirmed that all this treatment was by Americans ... Several said that they just could not believe Americans could act this way.[14]

Confirmation of some of the violence mentioned above was revealed in February 2006, when the American Civil Liberties Union released a series of documents, requested under Freedom of Information legislation and declassified by the military, in which the abuse of prisoners at Kandahar in February 2002 had been reported by interrogators. In one report, an interrogator "noticed several cuts and bruises" on a prisoner's face and wrote that he "also complained of pain and soreness to [his] ribs":

> [He] stated that approximately four days ago he was beaten by three to four guards. [He] said everyone in the pen was instructed to get up but he was unable due to numbness in his leg. That is when the guards approached him and began to beat him. The following two nights [he] stated that three to four guards entered the pen and kicked him repeatedly and left. I had spoken to [him] about a week prior to 1 Feb 02 meet, at which time I do not recall any visible marks on his face. It is quite apparent that between my initial meet and 1 Feb 02 meet that something had happened to [his] face.[15]

Abandoning the Geneva Conventions

Although Chris Mackey comes across as a principled man, the assumption that underpinned his perception of the prisoners' reception

at Kandahar—and, by inference, their treatment during detention—
nevertheless reflected the opinions of the US administration as a whole:
that the majority of those who arrived in US detention in Afghanistan
were Taliban or al-Qaeda fighters and a threat to US security; that they
were, in short, guilty until proven innocent, or, even more worryingly,
that they were guilty until confirmed guilty. Given that so many of
them were sold to the Americans by their Afghan or Pakistani allies,
this was a dangerous assumption, and a severely flawed start to the
whole process of interrogation and indefinite detention that was soon
to be enshrined in Guantánamo. It was also illegal under international
humanitarian law.[16]

What triggered the acceptance of the abusive treatment of prisoners
as normal behavior was the US administration's fateful decision, in
January 2002, that the Geneva Conventions—and specifically the
Third Geneva Convention Relative to the Treatment of Prisoners
of War (GPW)—did not apply to prisoners captured in the "War
on Terror," whether in Afghanistan, Pakistan, or anywhere else in
the world. While the GPW explicitly states that military prisoners
in wartime—enemy prisoners of war (EPW)—must, among other
requirements, be "humanely treated" and protected "against acts of
violence or intimidation," the administration seized on a particular
clause in Article 4, which states that the only prisoners who can be
excluded from EPW status are those who do not fulfill four particular
criteria: that they are "commanded by a person responsible for his
subordinates," that they have "a fixed distinctive sign recognizable at
a distance" (generally interpreted as wearing uniforms with distinct
insignia), that they carry arms openly, and that they conduct their
operations "in accordance with the laws and customs of war."

Arguing that these criteria were not fulfilled by either al-Qaeda
or the Taliban (which was largely accurate in the case of al-Qaeda,
but not in the case of the Taliban), the administration then ignored
Article 5 of the GPW, which states unequivocally that "Should any
doubt arise as to whether persons, having committed a belligerent
act and having fallen into the hands of the enemy, belong to any of
the categories enumerated in Article 4, such persons shall enjoy the
protection of the present Convention until such time as their status
has been determined by a competent tribunal." Until 9/11, the US
had always obeyed Article 5. During the 1991 Gulf War, for example,

the military held 1,196 "competent tribunals," and in nearly three-quarters of them the prisoners were found to be innocent and were subsequently released. The rules governing the tribunals were also spelled out explicitly in an update to the regulations governing the US military's treatment of enemy prisoners of war, which was issued in October 1997, in which it was stated that the tribunals should be composed of three commissioned officers, and that those brought before them "have a right to testify" and are "allowed to call witnesses if reasonably available."[17]

It was to be another two-and-a-half years before "competent tribunals" were introduced—as a toothless parody—in the Combatant Status Review Tribunals at Guantánamo. In the meantime, the administration's decision to deprive the prisoners in Kandahar of their rights as EPWs impacted on them in three particularly odious ways. Two of these—the acceptance of the abusive treatment of prisoners as normal behavior, and an almost universal presumption of guilt—have been outlined above. The third concerned the interrogation of prisoners, which is permitted by the Geneva Conventions, so long as it does not involve coercion, and so long as those who refuse to divulge anything more than their name, rank, serial number and date of birth are not "threatened, insulted, or exposed to any unpleasant or disadvantageous treatment of any kind." At Kandahar, however, interrogation not only became coercive; it also became an end in itself.

Interrogations

Chris Mackey was aware that removing EPW rights from the prisoners at Kandahar meant that the interrogators could demand more of them than the basic information they were "legally obligated" to provide, but he insisted that the Task Force leaders "declared from the very beginning that the camp would be operated under the rules of the Geneva Convention." What this meant in practice was that interrogators would only be allowed to employ the 16 authorized techniques in the Army Field Manual, which they had been taught in the army's intelligence course at Fort Huachuca. Based on psychological maneuvering, and designed to "break" prisoners by preying on their weaknesses to build up trust or to undermine their self-belief, the techniques allowed for a good deal of shouting and verbal abuse, but absolutely no physical contact whatsoever.[18]

It seems incredible, given the physical abuse to which the prisoners were subjected in detention, that Mackey could even claim that the interrogation rooms were violence-free zones, but there is evidence that the techniques were largely adhered to in the interrogations that he conducted or oversaw. Mourad Benchellali, for example, who reeled off a catalog of abuses in detention, did not allege that he was abused during his interrogations, which took place "several times a day." Instead, he said, the interrogators "were waiting for me to 'confess.' I repeated my story. No one believed me. I did not find out about the World Trade Center until several days before the Americans bombed Afghanistan." Even Juma al-Dossari, who was repeatedly abused during his time in Kandahar, did not claim that he was subjected to violence during his first interrogation (although he did say that the guards made him walk over barbed wire on the way there, and that the incident with the broken glass took place afterwards). "When I entered the investigation tent," he said, "I found that there were two Americans among the investigators ... I said to them, 'why are you torturing me and you haven't even started questioning me? What do you want from me? Give me a piece of paper and I will sign anything you want.'" He was, however, disappointed at the lack of concern that the interrogators showed, and said that one of them told him, "there is no torture here and there are no beatings," even though he "could clearly see the state I was in."[19]

Mackey's role as an interrogator is revealed in two set of accounts— one by Mackey himself, and the other by his prisoners—which provide a unique opportunity to compare and contrast the versions of the truth presented by both parties. The prisoners were Shafiq Rasul, Asif Iqbal and Rhuhel Ahmed, and their interrogation gave Mackey a chance to demonstrate a number of interrogation skills: playing prisoners off against each other, and indulging in a little role-play to deceive them. Wearing a maroon beret, and affecting an English accent, he fooled them into thinking he was an SAS officer, although he failed in his attempt to undermine Rasul—with a fake letter from Scotland Yard claiming that his house had been raided 16 hours after he left for Pakistan—as Rasul had rung his family from Pakistan and no such raid had been mentioned, and he succeeded only in confusing and terrifying the men with an allegation that they were members of the radical British organization al-Mahajiroun (which they were not), and with threats to send them to Belmarsh prison. He was also wide of the mark in his assessment of the men, saying that Iqbal's explanation that he went to Pakistan to get married "was so outrageous, it was almost comical," and attributing calculated guile to one of the other men, when he said that they made "a big mistake," and that they only went to Afghanistan in search of "adventure." Frustrated that they insisted on telling remarkably similar stories, he eventually conceded that they had perhaps been telling the truth.[20]

The crucial difference between the two sets of accounts, however, was in additional details provided by Rasul and Ahmed. Rasul said that, in the interrogation when the fake letter was produced, "One of the US soldiers had his arm round his neck and was saying, 'wait until you get back to the tent; you will see what we are going to do to you,'" and Ahmed said that, in his interrogation, "one of the US soldiers had a gun to his head and he was told that if he moved they would shoot him." These statements do little to confirm Mackey's moral authority (which is further undermined by Asif's assertion that he told him he was not going to be beaten "because you are with me"), although it's clear from their accounts of other interrogations at Kandahar that he was the only interrogator who did not subject them to physical abuse. Recalling the interrogation that preceded the SAS subterfuge, Iqbal recalled:

> An American came into the tent and shouted at me telling me I was al-Qaeda. I said I was not involved in al-Qaeda and did not support them. At this, he started to punch me violently and then, when he knocked me to the floor, started to kick me around my back and in my stomach. My face was swollen and cut as a result of this attack … Whilst he was attacking me, the interrogator didn't ask me any other questions but just kept swearing at me and hitting me.[21]

One major problem for the interrogators at Kandahar was that a large proportion of the prisoners refused to "break." Mackey reported that most of them said that they went to Afghanistan to seek a pure Islamic state, to find a wife, or to teach or study the Koran. Although they also admitted receiving weapons training, they largely insisted that it was mandatory and had only taken a few days. He was aware that not everyone who passed through interrogation was a "high value" suspect: within a few days of arriving at the base, he ascertained that the prisoners generally fell into one of two categories—"a small group of ideologically committed al-Qaeda types," and a "second, far larger group" of Taliban foot soldiers and others who claimed that they were not fighters at all—but conceded that "it was sometimes very difficult to tell the difference between the two." This was refreshingly honest, but it was not the kind of information required by those higher up the chain of command; in this case, the review board at Camp Doha, in Kuwait, comprising high-ranking officials from army intelligence, the military police, the CIA and the FBI, which was scrutinizing the intelligence from Kandahar for "tactical" intelligence that was useful to the war effort. It also conflicted with information contained in a document that the US administration has persistently used to justify its harsh treatment of prisoners: the so-called "Manchester Manual." This 180-page training manual, so named because it was seized by British police during a raid on the house of an al-Qaeda suspect in Manchester in 2000, provided details of all aspects of terrorist training and operations, and included key passages dealing with conduct after arrest. If captured, prisoners were urged to remain silent or to tell false or confusing stories, and, if given the opportunity, they were also encouraged to "complain of mistreatment while in prison" and to "insist on proving that torture was inflicted on them." In the "War on Terror," the manual's use has been two-fold: first, it has convinced the administration to behave like the witch hunters of the seventeenth century, treating every single claim of innocence as a lesson learned from the manual, and second, it has been used to refute all claims of torture. Lieutenant Colonel Flex Plexico, a Pentagon spokesman, has repeatedly denied allegations of abuse by released prisoners, repeating, by rote, that the allegations "fit the standard operating procedure in al-Qaeda training manuals."[22]

Given the pressure on the interrogators at Kandahar—and the prevalent atmosphere of self-righteous vengeance throughout the base—it was easy to see how, despite Mackey's principles, some of them began to embrace the kinds of prohibited activities that seemed to be commonplace in the prison as a whole: the use of physical violence, death threats, stress positions and sleep deprivation. From the reports of those detained at Kandahar, these transgressions ranged widely in their severity. Khaled bin Mustafa, for example, described how his interrogators began, slowly, to inflict physical pain. "The aim," he said, "was to make us confess that we were members or associates of al-Qaeda. It wasn't true in my case and I refused to falsely confess. I got many beatings as a result of that. I was hit with wet towels, double-folded like a bag and containing small contusive objects such as toilet-soaps. As a result of that I suffered dizziness and aches behind the ear." Other ex-prisoners—in addition to the three men from Tipton—described more blatant violence in which there was little difference between the well-chronicled behavior of the guards and that of the interrogators. They include the Pakistani interviewed by Human Rights Watch, and a released Afghan, who described how "they took me for an interrogation and before asking any questions they started beating me. One person picked me up high over his head and threw me onto a desk and made me lie there. And then two or three other persons hit me with their knees on my back and shoulders." Interviewed separately, the Pakistani described a similar scenario. "They made me lie down on a table with my face down," he said, "while two persons held me, one at my neck and the second at my feet. Both pressed me down hard on the table, and two others beat me on my back, my thighs and my arms with punches and their elbows. The beating lasted five or six minutes."[23]

Few of the Saudi and Yemeni prisoners have spoken about their experiences at Kandahar, either because they are unwilling to talk about treatment that they regard as shameful and humiliating, or, as is the case with many of those still held at Guantánamo, because the opportunity to talk about their detention in Afghanistan did not arise in their tribunals, or because they did not want to raise the issue of abuse by US forces for fear of prejudicing their possible release.[24] Those who have spoken out, however, have corroborated the statements made by other prisoners. Abdul Malik al-Rahabi, one of the Yemenis captured crossing the Pakistani border, told his lawyer that he was "tortured by beatings" in Kandahar, that his thumb was broken by US interrogators, and that he was "threatened with being held underground and deprived of sunlight until he confessed." Two Saudis, Abdul Aziz al-Oshan and Yusef al-Rabiesh, who were caught up in the Qala-i-Janghi massacre, spoke in their tribunals about their experiences. Al-Oshan said that he feared being tortured in Guantánamo because he was tortured in Afghanistan, first in Sheberghan and then in Kandahar, and al-Rabiesh, who went to Afghanistan to rescue his brother, also said that he was tortured in Sheberghan, where he was made to adopt his brother's story:

> I had to use the fake story to stop the torture and the pain they were forcing on me. My health was getting worse and worse. I was later given to the American forces and was transferred, in a very bad way, to the prison in Kandahar. The treatment was the same as before. The torture remained the same. I am ready to tell you, but I feel bad telling you, the treatment by the Americans was not as good as it was with the Northern Alliance.

Mohammed Haidel, a Yemeni captured in the Tora Bora region, also described being abused during an interrogation, which was sufficient to force a false confession out of him:

> I never received any mortar training. I was in the Kandahar prison, the interrogator hit my arm and told me I received training in mortars. As he was hitting me, I kept telling him, no I didn't receive any training. I was crying and finally I told him I did receive the training. My hands were tied behind my back and my knees were on the ground and my head was bleeding. I was in a lot of pain, so I said I had the training. At that point, with all my suffering, if he had asked me if I was Osama bin Laden, I would have said yes.[25]

Abuse During Interrogations by the CIA and Special Forces

On the other end of the scale from the mild injuries suffered by Khaled bin Mustafa—and even the beatings described above, which, although clearly illegal, would probably be regarded as "cruel and degrading treatment" if they ever came before a court of law—are allegations of treatment that is so abusive that it crosses an even darker threshold and can only be regarded as torture. While some of this treatment seems to have originated with the military interrogators, other cases were clearly taken out of their hands.

One disturbing scenario, which involved military interrogators, was described by the Algerian Aldulnour Sameur, who denied an allegation that he had prior knowledge of 9/11, and explained that he made this up when the interrogators threatened to withhold medical treatment. He also made it clear that this was not an isolated incident:

> I told them this in Kandahar during the interrogations because the interrogators were dogs ... I had an injury in my leg. I had metal sticking

out of my leg and they would not clean the wound; they would not give me treatment ... I just told them anything, whatever they wanted to hear because I wanted them to treat my leg. I saw other people whose legs had to be cut off. I did not want my leg to be cut off ... If you were in my place, if you were in Kandahar you would have done the same thing. Just like a small child.[26]

Juma al-Dossari described a number of particular brutal interrogations. On one occasion, "they poured boiling hot liquid on my head and the investigator stubbed his cigarette out on my foot. I said to him, 'why are you treating me like this?' He then took a cigarette and stubbed it out on my right wrist and said, 'in the name of Christ and the Cross I am doing this.'" His lawyers noted that he "has scars which are consistent with those that would be caused by cigarette burns," and also mentioned that he told them that Red Cross representatives, who visited him in Afghanistan, "were able to observe clear signs of physical abuse" on his body. On another occasion, "They stripped me of my clothes and lay me flat on the ground. One of the soldiers urinated on my head and my face after one of the other soldiers had raised my head by the hair. After that, a soldier brought petrol and injected it into my anus. I screamed because it was extremely painful." During another interrogation, he said that "the investigator brought a small device like a mobile phone but it was an electric shock device. He started shocking my face, my back, my limbs and my genitals." He also mentioned another brutal episode that he witnessed while he was being taken to one of the tents, when he saw an Afghan in his fifties, who was naked and lying on his stomach. "One of the soldiers was sexually assaulting him," he said. "One of the soldiers had a video camera with him and was taping this distressing scene. The investigator said to me, 'He was with the Taliban and he doesn't want to confess.' They made me really scared."[27]

Several of the Kuwaiti prisoners also mentioned "the use of electric shocks," which were "like ping pong paddles put under [the] arms," and they also said that various abusive acts were photographed or filmed. They added that some of the photos "still exist and are still used by the interrogators," an assertion that chimes with al-Dossari's statement that some of his abuse "was captured on video and I have pictures of myself in this state; an investigator showed me some of these pictures during a subsequent investigation session in Cuba." The use of electric shocks was also mentioned in one of the documents released by the ACLU, in which the military translator who made the complaint pointed out that those involved were Special Forces operatives:

> [We] took a break to regroup ... While we were out of the booth, several Special Forces members entered the booth ... [We] finished the break and went back to continue the interrogation. When we entered the booth, we found the Special Forces members all crouched around the prisoner. They were blowing cigarette smoke in his face. The prisoner was extremely upset. It took a long time to calm him down and find out what had happened ... He said that they had hit him [and] told him that he was going to die, blew smoke in his face and had shocked him with some kind of device. He used the term "electricity."[28]

Although this account confirms that Special Forces operatives muscled in on the interrogation process, it's also apparent that they were not the only "Other Government Agencies" to take an interest in the prisoners. Aryat Vakhitov (one of the Russians released in March 2004, whose story is told in Chapter 10) mentioned a specific interrogation session with CIA and FBI agents who were demanding to know the whereabouts of Osama bin Laden. According to a Jamestown Foundation report, "he promised to tell his captors where he had seen bin Laden in exchange for much-needed blankets and warm food. After receiving coffee, pizza, and two blankets, [he] told his inquisitors that he had seen bin Laden on the cover of *Time* magazine." In return, he was "punched in the face" and held for another six months before being transferred to Guantánamo.[29]

Vakhitov was not the only person to talk about the activities of the CIA and the FBI at Kandahar. Chris Mackey was complimentary about the FBI agents he met, but openly critical of those who worked for the CIA, complaining that they were "takers, not givers," always demanding intelligence but never sharing it in return. He acknowledged that they sometimes interrogated prisoners in the base, but claimed that they were always accompanied by an army interrogator, to prevent possible violations of the Geneva Conventions, and because it was the only way that they could find out what they were learning from the prisoners. Again, it's difficult to accept that there were no exceptions to this rule. Mackey's other reports of the CIA's behavior reveal the extent to which they acted with complete autonomy and impunity, taking prisoners to their own interrogation facilities in Kabul (discussed in Chapter 16) if the military interrogators "started to get some interesting information," and dumping others in Kandahar, without any supporting documentation whatsoever, leaving the interrogators to conclude that "they were turning over prisoners that they themselves couldn't 'break' or had concluded to be of low intelligence value."[30] With hindsight, and the knowledge that the CIA was to become central to the darkest elements of the "War on Terror"—the "ghost" detainees and "extraordinary renditions" discussed in Chapter 16—the only logical conclusion is that the CIA also did what it wanted in Kandahar, leading to some of the brutal interrogations outlined above.

9

From Sheberghan to Kandahar

Screening

As Chris Mackey and his team struggled to cope with the influx of prisoners at Kandahar and the demands from Camp Doha for "tactical" intelligence, they were also required to sort out who was to be sent to Cuba. In contrast to the ambiguously open-ended nature of the intelligence mission, this was an area over which they had little control. Mackey noted that the criteria were decided "at the highest levels of the Pentagon," and that all al-Qaeda personnel, all Taliban leaders, and all "non-Afghan Taliban/foreign fighters" were to be sent to Guantánamo, adding, in a single line that explains why so many innocent Arabs wound up in Guantánamo, "Strictly speaking, that meant every Arab we encountered was in for a long-term stay and an eventual trip to Cuba." He also noted that when certain groups of prisoners arrived—the Uyghurs and the Russians—their presence triggered a barrage of questions from the Pentagon, whose senior personnel were obsessed with securing prisoners who might make up for the woeful inadequacy of the intelligence agencies over the previous decade. He explained that, with the Uyghurs, the agencies were "starting from practically zero," and that the arrival of Russians, with their comments that the Chechens were not particularly aligned with al-Qaeda, and that the Russian Army was in disarray, "occasioned follow-up calls from Washington like you wouldn't believe." He also observed that only Afghans "with considerable intelligence value" were supposed to be sent to Guantánamo, but that once the decision-makers in Kuwait committed a name to the list of prisoners to be sent to Guantánamo, "it was next to impossible to get the name off."[1] In the early days, this meant that, in addition to all the Arab foot soldiers, humanitarian aid workers and religious teachers whose stories were told in the previous chapters, almost everyone else who passed through Kandahar was sent to Guantánamo as well; specifically, the majority of the largely Pashtun Afghans who were caught in the wrong place at the wrong time, including, as a clear example of how the filtering process was almost non-existent, Abdul Razeq, the schizophrenic who ate his own excrement. As other prisoners poured in, from Sheberghan and other Afghan-run jails, the same problems previously described—of accurately screening the prisoners and gathering useful intelligence—continued to plague the interrogators, and the stories related below largely confirm that they were essentially rubber-stamping a deeply flawed process.

In addition to the three men from Tipton and others mentioned in previous chapters, approximately ninety other prisoners—mostly Pakistanis and Afghans—were also transferred from Sheberghan to Kandahar, and then on to Guantánamo. They included five Saudis captured by Northern Alliance troops in the aftermath of the Kunduz surrender, whose commitment to jihad, like so many of those described in the previous chapters, focused on the long-standing inter-Muslim war between the Taliban and the Northern Alliance,[2] and Mohammed Bawazir, a 19-year-old Yemeni, who said that he was paid by a charity organization to distribute food and clothing to the poor in Afghanistan, and also spent time in Taloqan, where he traveled to the front lines with a sheikh to talk to the soldiers about their motivations. He explained that they "used to tell the Taliban fighters, before you start fighting do you know what Allah is all about? Do you know what Allah wants you to do before you even carry a weapon and go fight?" and added, "Religion is not all about fighting." Captured at a house in Taloqan, after the city fell to the Northern Alliance, he was transferred to Sheberghan, where, he said, all the allegations against him—which included a claim that he attended Osama bin Laden's daughter's wedding in Kandahar—came about because he was tortured:

> I don't know what to tell you, Sir, I really don't. I don't know if I attended his daughter's wedding or if I married his daughter. When I came to Mazar-e-Sharif they questioned me [and asked] me if I was from al-Qaeda … They used to hit me physically until they broke my skull … Then I had to

say yes I had met Osama bin Laden, that I talked with the Taliban, that I knew about nuclear rockets, and that I know everything about what al-Qaeda is up to. I really put my signature there that I said this.[3]

Afghans Transferred From Sheberghan

The screening of the 30 Afghans transferred from Sheberghan to Kandahar at this time—and then sent on to Guantánamo—was so inept that, with one exception, they were all subsequently released (mostly in 2003 and 2004). The case of Jan Mohammed, a 34-year-old baker from Helmand province (who was one of the first to be released, in October 2002) exemplified all that was wrong with the process. Mohammed explained that he was forced to serve with the Taliban, and was captured by the Northern Alliance after the fall of Kunduz. After languishing in Sheberghan for several weeks, he said that the decision to transfer him to Kandahar came about because some of Dostum's men "told US soldiers that he and nine others were senior Taliban officials." "They came and took ten strong-looking people," he told the journalist David Rohde. "Only one of those ten was a Talib."[4]

The innocent men and Taliban conscripts who were transferred to US custody with Jan Mohammed included the used-car dealer Sulaiman Shah, and two reluctant Taliban conscripts, 46-year-old Rabel Khan (released in July 2005), and 32-year-old Abdul Rahman Khan (released in December 2006). Rabel Khan, who was born in Afghanistan but had Pakistani ID, explained that he had been living in Pakistan, where he was working in the logging industry, but was forcibly conscripted by the Taliban when he returned to Afghanistan to work on his house in October 2001, and was taken to a compound in Kunduz, where he was kept under guard for 20 days. "There were armed guards outside the compound and we could not leave the compound on our own," he said. "They were sending people by numbers to fight. In those 20 days they did not get to my number and I did not fight." He also explained that he gave a false name—Habib Rasool—to the Uzbeks who captured him, "because I know that the Uzbek military are not our allies, they do not like Pakistanis. If they understand that I am a Pakistani, they would kill me because they did it before. They killed a lot of Pakistanis there." Abdul Rahman Khan told a similar story:

"I joined the Taliban by force not by choice. Everyone in Afghanistan knows if the Taliban asks you to go with them you cannot say no ... Our area was under Taliban control, so we could not fight them. We were so poor I could not move my family, that's why I stayed in the area." Held, like Rabel Khan, in a compound in Kunduz, he said that he was not obliged to fight either, but added that he expected he would have been shot if he had tried to escape.[5]

The solitary Taliban member transferred to Kandahar with Jan Mohammed was Abdul Rauf Aliza, who was identified by the US as Mullah Abdul Rauf, a Taliban troop commander. Although he claimed that he was conscripted by the Taliban, who said they would take his land if he refused, and insisted that he only worked for them as a cook, several released Afghans confirmed that Mullah Abdul Rauf was one of three Taliban commanders in northern Afghanistan held in Guantánamo. They told the journalist Ashwin Raman that he had not been so cautious with his identity while detained in Camp X-Ray, when he "repeatedly pleaded with the Americans to let many of the detainees free," saying, "These are no Talibs, I am the real Talib."[6]

While this suggests that Abdul Rauf Aliza and Mullah Abdul Rauf are one and the same, it's possible that the Taliban commander was hiding his true identity behind a false name, as was the case with one of the other 20 Afghan prisoners transferred to Kandahar at this time. Taliban commander Mullah Shahzada gave the Americans a false name and claimed that he was an innocent rug merchant who was captured by mistake. Released in May 2003, he seized control of Taliban operations in southern Afghanistan, recruiting fighters by "telling harrowing tales of his supposed ill-treatment in the cages of Guantánamo," and masterminded a jailbreak in Kandahar in October 2003, in which he bribed the guards to allow 41 Taliban fighters to escape through a tunnel. His post-Guantánamo notoriety came to an end in May 2004, when he was killed in an ambush by US Special Forces, but while right-wing commentators seized on the release of Shahzada—and five other Taliban fighters who subsequently returned to the battlefield—as evidence that no one should ever be released from Guantánamo, a rather different interpretation was offered by Gul Agha Sherzai, who pointed out that Shahzada would never have been freed if Afghan officials had been allowed to vet the Afghans in Guantánamo. "We know all these Taliban faces," he said, adding that repeated requests for access to the Afghan prisoners had been turned down. Sherzai's opinion was reinforced by security officials in Karzai's government, who blamed the US for the return of Taliban commanders to the battlefield, explaining that "neither the American military officials, nor the Kabul police, who briefly process the detainees when they are sent home, consult them about the detainees they free."[7]

If the release of Shahzada demonstrated that the US authorities were ill-equipped to decide who was responsible for military action against them, the stories of the rest of the Afghans transferred from Sheberghan reinforced another, more prevalent complaint: that they were also ill-equipped to decide who was innocent. Those transferred with Shahzada (and subsequently released) included the schizophrenic Abdul Razeq, and several more Taliban conscripts captured after the fall of Kunduz, including 24-year-old Mohammed Sarjudim, who said after his release, "America wanted to capture terrorists and Dostum just wanted the money, so he sold me"; Ehsanullah, who was mentioned in the previous chapter, and Abdul Rahman, the shopkeeper whose story was related in Chapter 3, were also sold.[8]

Pakistanis Transferred From Sheberghan

Up to fifty Pakistanis were also transferred from Sheberghan to Guantánamo via Kandahar. Like the Afghans, they were mostly Taliban foot soldiers or innocents swept up by the Northern Alliance during the fall of the Taliban in northern Afghanistan, and all but three were subsequently released from Guantánamo, mostly in 2003 and 2004. As with the Afghans, the stories of many of these men are unknown, because they did not speak to the press on their release, and the Pentagon has provided no information about the prisoners released from Guantánamo before the tribunal process began in July 2004, but it's clear from the available accounts that some were among the many thousands of volunteers—mostly from two particular militant groups—who poured over the border to assist the Taliban after the US-led invasion began in October 2001.

The first of these, Harkat-ul-Mujahideen (HUM), was founded in the mid-1980s. Focused primarily on Kashmir (and supported, as with most of the radical groups, by the ISI, who used them as a proxy army), HUM funneled thousands of trainee fighters from its madrassas into training camps in Afghanistan and Pakistan in the early 1990s, and by the summer of 1999, when the supply of young men from madrassas in the border provinces—who had been supplying the Taliban with thousands of fighters since 1994—began to dry up, the volunteers from HUM and other radical groups assumed increasing importance.[9] Hundreds of HUM soldiers traveled to Afghanistan to assist the Taliban after the US-led invasion, including the organization's leader, Fazlur Rehman Khalil, who crossed the border in early November, accompanied by a number of guards and colleagues. While Khalil subsequently escaped, many, if not most of the HUM volunteers were killed in Afghanistan. One survivor, at least, made it to Guantánamo, although he had little to tell. In his tribunal, 20-year-old Abdul Sattar (who was transferred to Pakistani custody in September 2004 and released in June 2005), spoke only to deny that he knew of any connection between HUM and al-Qaeda.[10] As he was only a foot soldier, this may well have been ignorance on Sattar's part, because connections between HUM and al-Qaeda were well established. In February 1998, Khalil signed Osama bin Laden's fatwa declaring war on the United States, and in August that year, after the African embassy bombings, HUM members were among those killed by US cruise missiles in retaliatory strikes on camps associated with bin Laden, prompting Khalil to warn that HUM would take revenge on the United States.

The second militant organization that provided warriors for the Taliban in its dying days in power was Tehrik Nifaz Shariat-e-Muhammadi (TNSM), which first came to prominence in 1994, when it led an armed uprising in support of Sharia law in the North West Frontier Province. TNSM's support for the Taliban in the last few months of 2001 was unparalleled among the Pakistani militants. Syed Farooq Hasnat, a professor of political science at the University of the Punjab in Lahore, delivered a damning verdict on the leaders of religious groups who provided support for the Taliban, explaining that they were "responsible for the slaughter of thousands of youths, who went to Afghanistan at their behest" (often without their parents being "aware of the real intentions of those who taught them at the madrassas"), and singling out TNSM as the "principal violator in this tragedy." Hasnat wrote that its leader, Maulana Sufi Mohammed, "was instrumental in leaving behind (all in the name of fighting a jihad against the United States) more than 8,000 young people in Afghanistan, while he returned to Pakistan, gasping for his life." Although he was subsequently arrested and imprisoned for three years, the fate of his volunteers was less certain. Hundreds were reportedly killed in Mazar-e-Sharif, and hundreds more were either killed or captured during the fall of Kunduz. Hasnat reported that the organization admitted that more than 3,000 of their "young boys" were missing, and subsequently sent a delegation to Afghanistan, asking the Northern Alliance to consider that Pakistan had been a "place of refuge for over two decades," and requesting that they "show the same magnanimity and large-heartedness."[11] It was unclear whether their entreaties impressed the Alliance leaders, although it's probable that a large number of TNSM volunteers were sent home to Pakistan from Sheberghan between December 2001, when the prison's population stood at 3,500, and September 2002, when only 800 prisoners remained.[12] A handful were probably handed over to the Americans, but only one, 21-year-old Mohammed Rafiq, spoke about his experiences.

Rafiq had attended one of the huge TNSM meetings at which thousands of impressionable men were recruited to fight with the Taliban, and said that he surrendered to the Northern Alliance with 500 other people, and was only taken from Sheberghan to Kandahar because he could speak English. What counted against him in Guantánamo, however, were the inconsistencies in his statements. Having first claimed that his desire to fight in Afghanistan was not motivated by anti-American sentiment—explaining that the oppression of the Pashtuns had been ongoing for twenty years, and that "the roots of this conflict have nothing to do with America and there was no mention of America"—he then contradicted himself, as the following exchange demonstrates (although what it reveals most of all is how ignorant and pliable foot soldiers like Rafiq actually were):

Q: Did you realize that when you were going to fight against the Northern Alliance that the United States was fighting on the same side as the Northern Alliance?
A: Yes, I knew that they were assisting the United States.
Q: Do you understand why that was?
A: No I don't.

Q: You were not told anything by your leadership?
A: I never saw the leaders afterwards. We just had that meeting and we just left. That was it.[13]

Other Pakistanis transferred at this time were also recruited to aid the Taliban. Their allegiances to particular organizations were not mentioned, but some maintained their militancy on their release. Hafiz Ehsan Saeed, a 23-year-old tailor from Lahore (and one of 17 men transferred to Pakistani custody in September 2004 and released in June 2005), said that, although his father died while he was in Guantánamo, he would "go for jihad again if given the chance." "I was quite upset when I heard the news of my father's death," he explained, "but I will sacrifice anything for Islam." It was also reported that "most of the other freed men reiterated Saeed's resolve to 'go for jihad again.'"[14]

These men were rumored to have been released on the orders of President Musharraf (perhaps as an attempt to prevent some of the beleaguered militant groups from directing their wrath at him), but others were as ignorant of the situation in Afghanistan as Mohammed Rafiq. Twenty-five-year-old Mohammed Ijaz Khan, who was captured leaving Kunduz, admitted that he traveled to Afghanistan "to fight the jihad," but said that he didn't know that the Northern Alliance were Muslims, and three recruits from villages in Sindh province— 20-year-old Abid Raza, 21-year-old Mohammed Anwar, and 59-year-old Mohammed Ilyas—revealed another aspect of the distorted propaganda used to recruit support for the Taliban. Raza told his tribunal that he was recruited "to join a jihad against Hindus," and added that he only found out that there were no Hindus to fight when, after 15 days in Afghanistan, he fled his position near Kunduz, and was captured in a village with other Pakistanis by an Uzbek, who kept them for two months before handing them over to US forces.[15]

The most unfortunate of all the Pakistanis associated with the Taliban was Zia Ul Shah, a 25-year-old from Karachi (released in October 2006), who went to Afghanistan to look for work, and was employed by the Taliban as a driver. Able to stipulate his own conditions, because the Taliban was in desperate need of drivers and he had his own truck, he refused to transport fighters to the war zone and mostly delivered food to a school in Kunduz that was used as a Taliban base. Denying an allegation that he surrendered to the

Northern Alliance in Kunduz, he explained, "I did not go to surrender. They asked me to take these [other] people to surrender and then they said I could go home. I took them to surrender and dropped them off, and then I left. There were a lot of other drivers that they let go, but they arrested me because I was the only Pakistani." He said that this was only the beginning of his problems, and that his truck was then fought over by different factions of the Northern Alliance. Abandoned during the wrangling over the truck, he was taken in by an Afghan who offered him food, asked him where he was from, and kept him captive for five days before selling him to another Afghan, who promptly sold him to another Afghan who "was beating me up everyday." This man then sold him to the Americans who "beat me up a little bit also [and] broke my nose. You can see that the bone is fractured. Then they took me to Kandahar."[16]

The final group of Pakistanis—those who had nothing whatsoever to do with the Taliban or al-Qaeda—were captured in Mazar-e-Sharif or Kunduz, and everything about their imprisonment, from their initial capture to the decision to send them to Guantánamo, demonstrates quite how arbitrary the whole process was. They included the preachers Abdul Razaq and Mohammed Saghir, Isa Khan (released in March 2005), and Shah Mohammed (released in May 2003). Khan, a 26-year-old doctor, was seized by the Northern Alliance after the fall of Mazar-e-Sharif. Originally from Banuu in the North West Frontier Province, he had moved to Mazar with his wife and his six-year-old son, and was running a clinic at the time of his capture. Mohammed, a 20-year-old baker from the Swat valley in the North West Frontier Province, was also captured in Mazar-e-Sharif. He said that he was "kidnapped by an Uzbek commander and sold to the Americans for a bounty," and explained that he only went to Afghanistan in search of a better job: "I was employed by the Taliban to bake bread for them, and they paid me a monthly stipend for these services. I had nothing to do with the military side of things in Afghanistan."[17]

An Australian Exception

Shah Mohammed also said that he met an Australian prisoner in Sheberghan called David Hicks. "I spoke to the Australian, he knew a bit of Urdu," he explained. "He said he had come for jihad." A

26-year-old former horse trainer from Adelaide, Hicks converted to Islam after traveling to Europe and training with the Kosovo Liberation Army in 1999. He then traveled to Pakistan to study in a madrassa, subsequently crossing into Afghanistan to continue his studies—at what he described as a "centre for Islamic revolution"—and to fight with the Taliban. On November 10, 2001, he rang his father on a satellite phone from a ditch outside Kandahar, telling him he was going to help the Taliban defend Kabul from the Northern Alliance. He then made his way to Kunduz, and on November 24, as the last bastion of Taliban power in northern Afghanistan fell to the Northern Alliance, he decided to make his escape. Climbing on board a taxi-van with dozens of Afghans, he tried to hide his blonde hair and blue eyes, but was unsuccessful. As the van made its way through the streets of Pul-i-Khumri, south of Kunduz, the driver noticed his pale skin and called the local Northern Alliance commanders. Heavily armed soldiers stopped the van at a checkpoint, seized Hicks and took him to a cell in the local garrison, where, he said, he was sold for $15,000 to the Americans, who took him to Sheberghan.

Because of his color and his nationality, Hicks, like John Walker Lindh, was singled out for particular attention by the US military, and was one of only ten Guantánamo prisoners to face a Military Commission (see Chapter 20). According to Shah Mohammed, he was treated differently from the majority of the prisoners from the moment he arrived in Sheberghan: "He was asked a lot of questions [by the Americans], more than us." Hicks himself said that US soldiers "tied his hands and feet and beat him with bare fists during two-hour sessions," and forced him to sit on a window ledge, while six soldiers pointed their weapons at him. He also explained that one interrogator, "obviously agitated, took out his pistol and aimed it at me, with his hand shaking violently with rage," adding, "I realized that if I did not cooperate with US interrogators, I might be shot." His treatment at Sheberghan was, however, just the start of his misery. While the majority of those around him were transferred to Kandahar or released through deals made by General Dostum, Hicks was one of a handful of prisoners (including Lindh) who were flown to the USS *Peleliu* for interrogation, where his American interrogators were joined by unsympathetic representatives of his home country, and where he heard other prisoners "screaming in pain" while being interrogated. He was then moved to the USS *Bataan*, where conditions became "drastically" worse, and it was while he was on this second ship that he and other prisoners were taken by helicopter to some vast, barn-like buildings in an undisclosed location, where they were forced to kneel for ten hours, and where, Hicks said, "I was hit in the back of the head with the butt of a rifle several times (hard enough to knock me over), slapped in the back of the head, kicked, stepped on, and spat on." It was only after these avenues of abuse had been exhausted that he was finally transferred to Kandahar.[18]

10
Others Captured in Afghanistan

Other Foreigners Transferred to Kandahar

The other 65 prisoners captured in Afghanistan and transferred to Kandahar at this time—40 Afghans and 25 foreigners—were, like David Hicks, mostly captured by Afghans, who imprisoned them before handing them over or selling them to the US military.

Shakrukh Hamiduva, an 18-year-old Uzbek, left Uzbekistan because of religious persecution, and traveled to Tajikistan, where he lived in a refugee camp, and then took a job with the Tajik government, working with other refugees in Kabul. At the time of his arrest, he was working as a taxi driver, and he explained that he was stopped by armed Afghans, who took his car and handed him over to "the American general" at Mazar-e-Sharif. Imprisoned for a month "in some kind of house" with 15 Pakistanis, he was then transferred to Kandahar. Abu Bakir Jamaludinovich, a 27-year-old Uzbek, was captured at Bagram air base. Married with two children, he was accused of being a member of the Islamic Movement of Uzbekistan, but said that he was actually a soldier in the Uzbek Army, who had been "fighting against this IMU and these Islamic terrorist organizations." His troubles began when he went to buy apples in Tajikistan, but lost his passport and was unable to return home. When he heard that his government was offering amnesty to refugees in Tajikistan, he took up the offer, only to discover that it was a trick, and that he and others who handed themselves in were dumped in Afghanistan instead. He explained that he made a living "buying and selling sheep, chicken and goats," and was told in December 2001 that the government was giving out ID cards to immigrants at Bagram. "There, I saw American soldiers," he said. "They just took me inside, they questioned me, and they kept me for a few days. I've been detained ever since."[1]

Two other prisoners were captured in western Afghanistan. Mahmud Nuri Mert, a 30-year-old Turk (released in March 2004), was married with four children and had been working as a lottery agent in Turkey. When the job came to an end he left the country in search of work, traveling first to Iran and then Afghanistan, where he was captured by the Taliban and imprisoned in Herat for three months before being handed over to US forces. Twenty-two-year-old Abdul Majid Mohammed, a poor Iranian well-digger (released in October 2006), occasionally dealt in opium and hashish, and explained that he went to Afghanistan in December 2001 to make money out of drugs and to bribe the military so that he would not be punished for desertion. He denied an allegation that he served as a watchman for the Taliban, explaining that the Taliban had been known to kill Iranians, and that he was particularly at risk because he was a Catholic, and said that he was captured by Northern Alliance soldiers, who thought he was an Arab and handed him over to the Americans.[2]

Three Kazakhs from the same village were captured in Kabul in December 2001. Eighteen-year-old Abdulrahim Kerimbakiev traveled to Afghanistan in 2000 with ten family members, including his grandmother, his mother and his sisters and brothers, but denied allegations that he worked as a cook for the Taliban, saying that he lived a simple life in a house in Kabul, where he spent most of his time growing vegetables. This was difficult for his tribunal to accept, and prompted one of its members to say, "We're trying to understand why you're here. The United States wouldn't detain someone for more than two years for simply growing vegetables. Can you help us understand?" Although it was quite possible to be imprisoned for growing vegetables, Kerimbakiev explained that one of the other people who came with him to Afghanistan, Yakub Abahanov, "was a cook for the [Taliban] back-up forces." The third Kazakh, 18-year-old Abdullah Magrupov, had only been at the house for five days, after studying at a madrassa in Karachi, when he and the others were captured by a Northern Alliance commander, who held them in "some kind of huge container" and "a place like a barn," before transferring them to US custody. At the time of writing, Kerimbakiev was still in Guantánamo, while Abahanov and Magrupov were released in December 2006.[3]

Feroz Abbasi, a 21-year-old Briton (released in January 2005), was captured in Kandahar. A student from Croydon, he traveled to Afghanistan in December 2000 with James Ujamaa, a black American civil rights activist who converted to Islam in the early 1990s and traveled to the UK, where he became close to the radical cleric Abu Hamza al-Masri at London's Finsbury Park mosque. Abbasi also became close to al-Masri. Inspired by his speeches, he became a volunteer for jihad, eventually living at the mosque, and "relying solely on Abu Hamza and his followers for his education in Islam." Having pressured al-Masri to allow him to fight in Kashmir, he was eventually sent to Afghanistan, where he trained at al-Farouq, and was then introduced to Abu Hafs, al-Qaeda's military commander (killed in an air strike in November 2001), who asked him, "Would you like to take any actions against the Americans and the Jews?" When he answered yes, he was sent to receive specialized training in a camp at Kandahar airport, where, he said, he was the only one of the recruits to argue that martyrdom operations should only be directed at military targets and not at civilians, a moral stance which was also at odds with the views of his mentors, but which resurfaced in his opinions about 9/11. "I've had enough of innocent people losing their lives," he wrote in a 156-page autobiography that he produced in Guantánamo. "I did not leave my home except to defend innocent people." Although he agreed to undertake a suicide mission after the assassination of Ahmed Shah Massoud, he was unable to find the office to which he had been sent to receive further instructions, and, as the aftermath of 9/11 brought a temporary halt to al-Qaeda's suicide missions, he was dispatched instead to another location in Kandahar, and ordered to await instructions to fight with other "English-speaking brothers." He was eventually called upon to defend the caves near Kandahar airport against Gul Agha Sherzai's men, a terrifying experience in which he spent his time "running around like a madman in the middle of nowhere trying to dodge missiles," and then found himself alone, as the Yemeni fighters with whom he had spent the night ran away. A few days later, having decided to undertake a freelance suicide mission, his jihadi adventure came to an ignominious end when he was caught with a grenade stuffed down his trousers by two Northern Alliance soldiers in Kandahar. "This guy's a nutter," one of them said, before handing him over to the Americans, who had, by now, established their prison at Kandahar airport.[4]

The "Spies"

The most unfortunate group of prisoners captured at this time were five men who were held by the Taliban as spies in a prison for political crimes in Kandahar: Jamal al-Harith, a 35-year-old Briton (released in March 2004), Abdul Rahim al-Ginco, a 23-year-old Syrian Kurd, Aryat Vakhitov, a 24-year-old Tatar (released in March 2004), and two Saudis, Saddiq Ahmed Turkistani, a Uyghur who was born and raised in Saudi Arabia (released in June 2006), and 46-year-old Abdul Hakim Bukhari. When the Taliban vacated Kandahar, 2,500 prisoners—including 1,800 in the political prison—were released, but the five foreigners were made to stay behind. "We want to release these men," the prison's new warden said, "but for their security we are requiring them to stay here as guests. If they walk into the bazaar, the people will think they are from al-Qaeda and will kill them."[5]

The five men had found themselves on the wrong side of the Taliban in different ways. Jamal al-Harith first revealed his story to the journalist Tim Reid, who met him at the prison and gained his trust by bringing him some antiseptic cream and a shortwave radio, which he had requested. Born Ronald Fiddler to parents of Jamaican heritage, he had converted to Islam and had changed his name in 1992, after reading Malcolm X's autobiography. A website designer, he went to Iran to learn more about his religion in 1993, and traveled to Pakistan in September 2001 for a three-week holiday to continue his studies. His problems arose when the US-led invasion began, and he decided to return home. Having paid a lorry driver to let him travel with him to Turkey via Iran, he had no idea that they were going to travel through Afghanistan, and after a few days they were stopped by three Taliban soldiers. According to al-Harith, "It all turned to hell" when they saw his British passport. Stripped of his belongings, he was accused of being a spy, beaten for three days and sent to the prison in Kandahar, where an American prisoner died after a particular brutal beating. "I am sure I would have got the same treatment," he said, "but I made sure that every time my guards saw me I was praying. The

Taliban liked me because I always had the Koran in my hands. I was beaten very badly, but not as badly as most of the other inmates."[6]

Abdul Rahim al-Ginco, who moved to the UAE when he was 13, left home after a dispute with his father. Recruited by an imam to devote himself to jihad in a religious sense rather than a military one, he ended up on the al-Qaeda trail in Afghanistan in early 2000, staying at a guest house in Kabul and attending al-Farouq. He explained that he was suspected of being a spy when he asked to leave al-Farouq after 18 days, telling the leaders of the camp that he would not fight against Ahmed Shah Massoud, and adding, "I told them the jihad does not say anything about killing innocent civilians in Afghanistan." Imprisoned in Kandahar for two years, he was tortured by the Taliban "to the extent that he had little use of his right arm," and he also said that al-Qaeda representatives tortured him for three months until he admitted that he was a spy, and sentenced him to "spend 25 years in prison because I was spying for the United States."[7]

Abdul Hakim Bukhari's story was similar to al-Ginco's. A former mujahideen fighter, who had met Osama bin Laden while fighting the Russians, he admitted traveling to Afghanistan to fight the US after 9/11, because "President Bush declared war on the Taliban" and "the Taliban called a jihad," but said that he too was suspected of being a spy after declaring that he admired Massoud, who, by this time, had been assassinated. "They got mad when I said I liked Massoud," he said. "They are crazy. They don't like him. If I had known they didn't like him, I wouldn't have spoken. For saying that, they punished me … they beat me, they hit me very badly. They accused me of being a spy. They are stupid."[8]

The fourth of the Taliban prisoners, Aryat Vakhitov, a Tatar from the town of Naberezhniye Chelny, was sent to a newly-opened Wahhabi madrassa at the age of 14 by his mother, who hoped to keep him away from the town's notorious street gangs. Within five years he became an imam, but his opportunities to spread the Wahhabi doctrine were limited in Tatarstan, which was still ruled by a heavyweight Communist, so he made his way to Chechnya, visiting several times in the years up to 1999. On the last occasion, however, a former colleague accused him of being a spy, and he was held in a pit for two months and beaten severely, until another Tatar arranged to take him home. Soured by his experience, he apparently became far more militant as a preacher, and was watched by the secret police. Soon after, the Grand Mufti in Tatarstan asked him to stand down, and the following day he was arrested for "participating in illegal armed formations in Chechnya," but was released due to a lack of evidence. Before the secret police came calling again, he fled to Afghanistan, where he and a companion were immediately arrested by Taliban soldiers, who accused them of being Russian spies and imprisoned them in Kabul. When the US-led invasion began, he was transferred to the jail in Kandahar, and when a French reporter spoke to him in December he had some particularly grim tales to tell. "I spent seven months in Afghanistan, locked in a total darkness," he said. "Two nights a week we were beaten until dawn and they screamed, 'Confess, you brute, that you are a KGB agent.' They slit my friend Yakub's throat in front of me, then hung me up by my hands and whipped me with electrical wire."[9]

Saddiq Ahmed Turkistani, whose family fled to Saudi Arabia to escape the repression of the Uyghurs by the Chinese authorities, had another, very different story of how he came to be in a Taliban jail. Stripped of his Saudi citizenship in 1997 after being arrested for possession of marijuana, he was given fake Afghan ID and deported to Afghanistan by the Saudi authorities, who flew him from Jeddah to Kabul, where Afghan officials detained him for six days before releasing him. He then made his way to Khost, where he made friends with an Iraqi, but they were soon arrested by four Arabs affiliated with al-Qaeda, who accused him of being a Saudi spy and tortured him. After 20 days of severe beatings and sleep deprivation, he made up a story about how the Saudis had sent him to kill Osama bin Laden, and was then handed over to the Taliban, who kept him in prison in Kandahar for four years.[10]

Despite these men's extremely negative experiences of al-Qaeda and the Taliban, the Americans decided to send them all to Guantánamo. Ironically, despite the Northern Alliance's decision to keep them in prison for their own safety, several of them had been presented with opportunities to escape before the Americans got hold of them. Saddiq Turkistani met with UN officials and took part in a press conference at which he expressed his hatred for al-Qaeda and the Taliban and offered to help the US in any way that he could, and Jamil al-Harith said that Red Cross representatives, who were present when some

Pakistanis were released from the jail, "asked me if I wanted to go with them, but I had no money and no way of getting back to Britain, so I asked them to put me in contact with the British embassy in Kabul." He added, "That is incredible to me now. I could have gone home on my own." In fact, he stayed with the Red Cross for a week, calling the embassy, whose staff assured him that he would soon be put on a flight to Kabul and brought back to Britain. Two days later, however, he was taken away by American operatives, who transported him to Kandahar and then Guantánamo.[11]

Other Afghan Prisoners

Of the Afghans captured at this time, at least thirty were subsequently released. Most slipped away quietly in 2003 and 2004, without their stories being told, although there were a few notable exceptions. Mohammed Sadiq, from Paktia province, was 88 years old when he was captured, apparently because his nephew had worked for the Taliban. One night in January 2002, US forces bombarded his house, blasted his door with rockets, confiscated his belongings and took him to Kandahar. Although he was one of the first prisoners to be released, in October 2002, it took the Americans eight months to decide that he did not pose a threat to them. After his release, with his house in ruins and his belongings gone, he moved in with his relatives and was "unable to come to terms with what happened to him." Forty-five-year-old Aziz Khan Zumarikourt, the father of ten children (released in March 2004), was arrested at his home in Paktia province for having four Kalashnikovs. Speaking after his release, he said of his captors, "They had very bad treatment towards us. Americans are very cruel. They want to govern the world." Twenty-one-year-old Rostum Shah and 26-year-old Mohammed Tahir (released in May 2003) were Taliban conscripts from Helmand who had been sent to fight in Bamiyan province, where they were captured by Hazara soldiers of Hezb-e-Wahdat, one of Afghanistan's two main Shia Muslim factions, who were implacably opposed to the Taliban. Imprisoned for four months, they were then handed over to the Americans. On his release, Tahir said that he suffered mentally and had "difficulty remembering things," and underlined the failures of the screening process: "I'm just angry that the Americans waited until we were in Guantánamo to interrogate us. Had they questioned us here in Afghanistan it would have saved us a lot of trouble. They could have realized a lot sooner that I was innocent."[12]

Others who spoke out told stories of betrayal. These were to become more prevalent throughout 2002 and into 2003, and they reflected badly on the ability of the US authorities to understand the complexities of the political situation in which they found themselves, and which they had largely engineered. Nineteen-year-old Moheb Ullah Barekzai (released in July 2005) was a Taliban conscript. Taken prisoner by a local post-Taliban commander, he was handed over to Ismael Khan, the governor of Herat, who, he believed, sold him to the Americans. Somewhere in this story of local corruption and American gullibility, he was accused of being the acting governor of Sheberghan for the Taliban. Twenty-three-year-old Fizaulla Rahman said he was betrayed because of a disagreement about money. Accused of working for Taliban intelligence in Mazar-e-Sharif, he said that he was taken in as a house servant by a senior member of the intelligence services, and his job was essentially a front. Although he did not want to spell out why he was taken in, it was implicit in his description of his brother and nephew as "young and pretty boys," who had also caught the eye of the Taliban officer. Twenty-four-year-old Ehsanullah Peerzai, who had been imprisoned in Iran for smuggling hashish, was accused of carrying lists of Taliban members and radio codes, when he was captured by US forces in Helmand province in February 2002. A clerk for the new government, he said that he was betrayed by two members of the Taliban in his home district, and his continued imprisonment seems to be based on the US authorities' claim that he is "extremely evasive and uses multiple resistance techniques," and their suspicion that he was recruited by Iranian intelligence to work in Afghanistan as a spy.[13]

Four other prisoners were caught up in the corruption surrounding another warlord, Pacha Khan Zadran, who had fought both the Soviet Union and the Taliban, and had been living in exile as a refugee in Pakistan until he was recruited by the Americans, who were desperate to find proxy armies to fight the Taliban in the south. Suddenly rich, he built up a personal militia of 3,000 men and impressed the Americans by pursuing remnants of the Taliban and al-Qaeda. By early 2002, he and his clan were effectively running three provinces,

Khost, Paktia and Paktika, but the honeymoon was soon over. When he tried to take over as the governor of Paktia, his appointment was fiercely resisted by the tribal council in Gardez, whose leader, Haji Saifullah Khan, insisted that he was "unacceptable." The council's dissatisfaction with Zadran stemmed from his responsibility for the slaughter of 60 people, including the inhabitants of two villages and a number of local tribal leaders, who were traveling in a convoy to Hamid Karzai's inauguration in Kabul in December 2001. According to Saifullah Khan and others in Gardez, Zadran ordered his fighters to stop the convoy and tell the elders to put pressure on Karzai to appoint him as the governor of the three provinces. When they refused, he called the Americans, told them the convoy was made up of elements of the Taliban and al-Qaeda, and waited for the air strikes that followed, a seven-hour onslaught that not only struck the convoy repeatedly, but flattened the two villages when the survivors tried to escape. Forced out of Gardez in February, and disowned by Hamid Karzai, who appointed a new governor, Zadran responded by attacking Gardez with rockets, precipitating a violent local conflict over which the Americans had no control. Although his glory days were over, *Time* reported that the US military were still sourcing his "intelligence" to track down remnants of al-Qaeda in August 2002, but few people noticed that four innocent men were being held in Guantánamo because of their alleged connections with the renegade warlord.[14]

Three members of a family of farmers—59-year-old Abib Sarajuddin, his 30-year-old son Gul Zaman and his 39-year-old brother Khan Zaman—were captured by US soldiers in a village near Khost in January 2002, allegedly because someone had fired on them, although the men, who were released in 2005 and 2006, said that the soldiers, who arrived at night by helicopter, broke into their houses and arrested them for no reason. It was not the first time they had heard from the Americans. Two months previously, twelve of Sarajuddin's family members—and 16 other villagers—died when US forces bombed his family compound, believing, incorrectly, that he was harboring the pro-Taliban warlord Jalaluddin Haqqani.[15] In his tribunal, he insisted that he had never met Haqqani, and his son and his brother suggested that a rival provided false information to the Americans. On the night of their arrest, it seems they were betrayed again. Sarajuddin was accused of working as a recruiter for Pacha Khan Zadran, but his son and his brother explained what had actually happened: when Zadran was working for the Americans, he approached the local commanders for support, and they in turn asked Sarajuddin to recruit other villagers to fight against the Taliban. Another villager, 39-year-old Mohammed Gul, a farmer and petrol station owner, who had been working in Saudi Arabia as a driver, but had returned home to care for his sick wife, was also captured as randomly as the other three men, and although none of them knew who had betrayed them, it's noticeable that the arrests took place after Zadran had provided money to the local commanders to help Sarajuddin rebuild his home after the US bombing. "Was your house eventually rebuilt?" a Board Member asked. "No," he replied. "I became a prisoner." Summing up their predicament, Khan Zaman said, "I am very surprised at the United States. They are very smart and I am disappointed that they do not know who their enemies and friends are. They look to their enemies and friends with the same eyes. Why is it like that?"[16]

The Taliban Prisoners

The Americans' pursuit of significant Afghan prisoners was not entirely fruitless, however, and they managed to round up a few genuine Taliban leaders. The first two, presumably to their own surprise, were deputy defense minister Mullah Mohammed Fazil, and Mullah Noorullah Noori, the military commander in northern Afghanistan. As two of the architects of the Kunduz surrender, they had been held by General Dostum as house guests, and Dostum had even taken them to Qala-i-Janghi to see the aftermath of the uprising (see Chapter 2). As a result, they probably expected to be freed rather than handed over to the Americans, especially as Dostum had facilitated the escape of other Taliban leaders, according to Mullah Almaj Khaksar, a former deputy interior minister. After the US-led invasion began, Khaksar revealed that he had become disillusioned with the Taliban in 1997 and had been spying for the Northern Alliance ever since, and he claimed that those released by Dostum included deputy defense minister Mullah Berader, and Fazil's deputy Mullah Dadaullah, who had returned to his home in Helmand province.[17] Dadaullah, who was another of the brokers of the Kunduz surrender, was responsible for the massacre of up to 6,000 Hazara civilians following the Taliban's conquest of Mazar-e-Sharif in 1998, and his murderous tendencies had been on show again in June 2001, when he advanced on the Hazara heartlands in Bamiyan province, burning down thousands of homes and shops. As Human Rights Watch described it, most of the civilian population "fled the Taliban advance, but those who remained behind, as well as some who had encamped in the hills, were summarily executed."

The crimes committed by Fazil and Noori were also well-documented. Fazil was implicated in the massacre of Hazara civilians in Mazar-e-Sharif in 1998, and was also present, as commander-in-chief, during a massacre of 170 civilians in Bamiyan province in January 2001, and Human Rights Watch reported that Noori was implicated in a massacre of civilian prisoners in a mountain pass in May 2000, and the execution of Uzbek civilians in Balkh in May 2001.[18] Both men claimed, however, that they were not who the Americans thought they were. Fazil protested that he was a minor Taliban military leader of 50–100 fighters, saying, "If you think this is a crime, then every single person in Afghanistan should be in prison," and Noori said that he was a tailor and "a very poor man," who, in order to fulfill his obligations to the Taliban, worked for the governors of Jalalabad and Mazar-e-Sharif, as part of a team of twelve people working "in a civilian environment."[19]

Another senior Taliban figure—Abdul-Haq Wasiq, the deputy minister of intelligence—was captured in December 2001 by five US Special Forces operatives in a potentially perilous operation in Ghazni, south-west of Kabul. At the time, Ghazni was a Taliban stronghold where the US had no support, but when Team Delta received a tip-off that a local warlord had arranged a meeting with Qari Amadullah, the Taliban's minister of intelligence, in which, it was suggested, Amadullah might provide information that would lead to the capture of bin Laden, Gary Berntsen approved the mission, although he told his men to take no chances with Amadullah, pointing out that he and other senior Taliban figures "will most likely lead the insurgency against the new government when this war is over," and advising them to call in an air strike if he refused to cooperate. In the end, Amadullah did not turn up, and clearly had no intention of doing so. Safely ensconced in Pakistan, after escaping via Tora Bora, he spoke to a journalist in late December, interrupting the interview to take a phone call, and then declaring, "I am personally requested by Mullah Omar and Sheikh Osama to go to Uruzgan and take the command of new guerrilla war preparations, which will start as soon as possible, and you will hear the news in papers and on BBC." Unsurprisingly, having given the US his itinerary as a result of this loose talk, he was killed in a US air strike a few days later. In the same interview, however, he also spoke about Abdul-Haq Wasiq. He said that Mullah Omar, who, he claimed, was living in a safe place in the mountains north of Kandahar, had asked him to visit, but he had been unable to do so, "because a lot of people know me, and I am frightened they will capture me somewhere on the road. So I sent my assistant Mullah Abdul-Haq Wasiq to Kandahar. Unfortunately he was captured by American agents in Ghazni." This suggests that Wasiq either made his own negotiations with the Americans in Ghazni, or was invited and then betrayed by the local warlord, because after the meeting he was duly arrested by the Team Delta operatives, along with his assistant Gholam Ruhani. Berntsen reported that Central Command in Florida were angry that they were not informed about the mission in advance, but noted that his CIA liaison told him that they would soon get over it, adding, "Congratulate Team Delta for me. Capturing the number two and three in Taliban intel was a good day's work."[20]

In Guantánamo, Wasiq was coy about his role, claiming that he was forced to join the Taliban, and that he sometimes acted as the deputy minister of intelligence, but only to combat "thieves and bribes." This did not convince his tribunal, who greeted him with the words, "Good afternoon, Mr. Minister. Seldom before have we had someone of such prestige and responsibility." Ruhani, however, was adamant that he was not the "number three in Taliban intel." He said that he was a Taliban conscript, who fulfilled his duties in a clerical capacity to avoid being sent to the front lines, and explained that he was asked to attend the meeting between the Taliban and the Americans because he had learned a little English while studying electronics manuals in a store run by his elderly father. "I turned over my pistol and ammunition to the American, as an act of faith, because it was a friendly meeting," he said. "I expected to leave the meeting and return to my life, my shop and my family. Instead, I was arrested."[21]

The capture of the Taliban leaders fulfilled one of the Americans' stated aims, although the decision to deprive them of their rights as prisoners of war and send them to Guantánamo was as counter-productive in its own way as the removal of PoW rights for the many hundreds of foot soldiers and innocent men who were also sent to Cuba. In the cases of Fazil and Noori in particular, the Americans could have followed the existing laws to prosecute them for war crimes, which would have given the Americans a degree of moral superiority and would also have sent out a positive message to the warlords in the new government that it was not "business as usual" in post-Taliban Afghanistan. Clearly, however, the subject of war crimes was taboo, when the Americans were choosing as allies other men who had also been condemned for war crimes. The failure to pursue these cases in the courts not only revealed, explicitly, how the new, democratic Afghanistan was little more than the old, pre-Taliban Afghanistan of unaccountable warlords (nominally presided over by an American-backed regime in Kabul), but also the extent to which the Americans' own agenda was increasingly geared not towards justice, but towards indefinite detention in the pursuit of "intelligence."

Noticeably, the Americans' decision to hold the Taliban leaders who came into their custody was often at odds with the Afghans' own approach. The clearest example of this was Hamid Karzai's pragmatic decision to avoid a bloodbath in Kandahar by offering amnesty to the Taliban, but it was replicated in other places for similar reasons. In January 2002, 1,500 Taliban soldiers and their leaders were captured and promptly released after a six-day operation in Baghlan province, run by Afghan forces with support from the US, during which Mullah Omar was alleged to have escaped on a motorbike,[22] and a particularly revealing example of the practice occurred in Kandahar, when three senior Taliban leaders—defense minister Mullah Obaidullah Akhund, justice minister Mullah Nooruddin Turabi, and Mullah Saaduddin, the minister for mines and industry—were released by Gul Agha Sherzai, a day after they had surrendered, and "hours after an American official said he expected them to be handed over to the US." Khalid Pashtoon, a spokesman for Sherzai, said, "We promised them that if they came by themselves and surrendered we would not arrest them," although he added that they would not be able to move freely "for their own security." While a US spokesman in Kandahar claimed that he was not concerned about the release of the three ex-ministers, saying, "We're not in the business of determining who should and should not be in custody," it's unlikely that this was true, given the jubilation that followed the capture of Abdul-Haq Wasiq, and the fact that Turabi, as the man responsible for the strict, Saudi-influenced Ministry of Enforcement of Virtue and Suppression of Vice, was regarded as a close associate of Mullah Omar.

11
Guantánamo Opens

"Enemy Combatants"

The first 20 prisoners arrived at Guantánamo on January 11, 2002, after a 27-hour flight from Afghanistan. Three days later, a second flight, containing 30 prisoners, touched down, and by early February, 220 prisoners had arrived in Cuba, and another 237 were awaiting transportation from Kandahar. "I call the journey to Guantánamo 'the journey of death'" the Kuwaiti Adel al-Zamel explained in December 2006. "I discreetly wished that the plane would fall to end the pain I felt." Many other released prisoners also described the misery that they experienced on the flight. Shafiq Rasul, who explained that the prisoners were transported in what he and his friends from Tipton described as the "three-piece suit," consisting of handcuffs attached to a metal belt and leg irons, said that he spent the whole journey in extreme pain because the belt was digging into his side. "When I finally got to Cuba," he said, "I lost feeling in my hands for the next six months."[1]

It's still not certain when the administration's Wild West bravado gave way to a realization that, not only would there be prisoners in the "War on Terror," but that, in order to exploit them as they saw fit, they would need to be detained outside the jurisdiction of the US courts. On November 28, 2001, the Pentagon was reportedly looking at plans to imprison captured terrorist suspects at Guantánamo or on the Pacific island of Guam,[2] but the catalyst was an extraordinary piece of legislation that was announced on November 13. Acting in his capacity as Commander-in-Chief of the Armed Services, and without consulting Congress, President Bush issued a Military Order declaring that he could designate any non-US citizen as an international terrorist, detain them at will and subject them to Military Commissions, beyond the jurisdiction of the US courts, which could sentence them to life imprisonment or even death.[3] As Michael Ratner of the Center for Constitutional Rights observed:

> The president decided that he was no longer running the country as a civilian president. He issued a military order giving himself the power to run the country as a general. Under the order he claimed the absolute power to arrest non-citizens anywhere in the world, even in the United States, and hold them indefinitely and without charges or a lawyer until the so-called war on terror was over, which could be fifty years or forever.[4]

Initially, it seemed that those designated as "enemy combatants" would only be major players—perhaps Osama bin Laden and Ayman al-Zawahiri, if they were ever caught—and on November 14, Dick Cheney suggested that the designation might only apply to prisoners captured on US soil. "The basic proposition," he said, "is that somebody who comes into the United States of America illegally, who conducts a terrorist operation killing thousands of innocent Americans ... is not a lawful combatant. They don't deserve to be treated as a prisoner of war. They don't deserve the same guarantees and safeguards that would be used for an American citizen going through the normal judicial process."[5] By the time Guantánamo was set up two months later, however, the definition of an "enemy combatant" had mutated beyond recognition, as the administration, pursuing the skewed logic that had prevailed from the start of "Operation Enduring Freedom," decided to ignore any distinctions between Taliban and al-Qaeda prisoners, and to regard everyone who came into their custody as an "enemy combatant."

By late December, when Donald Rumsfeld confirmed that Guantánamo was the location chosen for the imprisonment of those detained in the "War on Terror," the Marines began building the prison that would be known as Camp X-Ray: a dozen rows of steel-mesh cages, each measuring just two meters by two meters, which were open to the elements and encircled by a razor-wire fence. In a press conference, responding to a journalist who was aware that the base had, contentiously, been used to imprison Haitian refugees in the mid-1990s, and who pointed out that the US government had "gotten into trouble every time you've tried to use Guantánamo Bay in the past to hold people for other reasons," Rumsfeld evaded the subtext—that the administration's intention was to keep the prisoners away from the jurisdiction of the US courts—and responded, "I would characterize Guantánamo Bay, Cuba, as the least worse place we could have selected. It has disadvantages, as you suggest. Its disadvantages, however, seem to be modest relative to the alternatives."[6] Despite the administration's enthusiasm, however, when the first arrivals were forced to their knees in front of the world's media in orange jumpsuits, wearing blacked-out goggles, surgical masks and headphones, the reaction of all but the US news outlets was one of revulsion. The administration was shocked. Rumsfeld, typically, understated the issue by declaring that it was "probably unfortunate" that he had allowed the photos to be released, but it demonstrated a growing gulf between public opinion in the US—for whom the President's spirit of vengeance was still justifiable (and prisoners in orange jumpsuits were familiar from their own domestic prisons)—and the rest of the world, in which the unflinching support extended to the US in the wake of 9/11 began to be questioned.[7]

Soon after the arrival of the first prisoners, senior figures in the US administration and the US military reinforced this gulf, making a number of hyperbolic statements that were to come back to haunt them—in the media, if not politically. Brigadier-General Mike Lehnert of the Marines, who was in charge of the camp, told reporters, "These represent the worst elements of al-Qaeda and the Taliban. We asked for the worst guys first," and General Myers, the chairman of the Joint Chiefs of Staff, explained that the prisoners were restrained because, given the opportunity, they would "gnaw through hydraulic lines in the back of a C-17 [military plane] to bring it down." On January 22, Rumsfeld waded in. "These people are committed terrorists," he said. "We are keeping them off the street and out of the airlines and out of nuclear power plants and out of ports across this country and across other countries." On a visit to Guantánamo on January 27, he claimed that the prisoners were "among the most dangerous, best-trained, vicious killers on the face of the earth."[8]

Almost lost in the furore was the administration's more worrying decision to deprive the prisoners of the protections of the Geneva Conventions. Speaking on the day that Guantánamo opened, Rumsfeld stated, unequivocally, "They will be handled not as prisoners of war, because they're not, but as unlawful combatants. Technically, unlawful combatants do not have any rights under the Geneva Convention. We have indicated that we do plan to, for the most part, treat them in a manner that is reasonably consistent with the Geneva Conventions, to the extent they are appropriate."[9] Two weeks later, in a memorandum that did not surface until 2004, Alberto Gonzales, the President's Chief Counsel, spelled out the legal contortions that resulted in this unprecedented move. Noting that Bush had referred to the war on terrorism as a new kind of war, Gonzales wrote, "In my judgment, this new paradigm renders obsolete Geneva's strict limitations on questioning of enemy prisoners and renders quaint some of its provisions." Aware that the government was in dangerous new territory, he added that depriving al-Qaeda and the Taliban of their rights under the Geneva Conventions (GPW) "substantially reduces the threat of domestic criminal prosecution under the War Crimes Act," enacted by the US in 1996, which made it illegal to undertake grave breaches of the GPW, including "outrages upon personal dignity" and "inhuman treatment."[10] Lawyers in the State Department immediately sought to rein in Gonzales, arguing, prophetically, that a derogation from the Geneva Conventions would "undermine the protections of the law of war for our troops" and would have "a high cost in terms of negative international reaction, with immediate adverse consequences for our conduct of foreign policy," but it was to no avail.[11] President Bush put forward what appeared to be a compromise on February 7, declaring that the Geneva Conventions would apply to the Taliban prisoners, but not to those from al-Qaeda, and that, "to the extent appropriate and consistent with military necessity," all the prisoners would be treated "in a manner consistent with the principles" of the GPW, but it was hollow rhetoric. In fact, the administration continued to blur the distinctions between al-Qaeda and the Taliban, and continued to regard the GPW as "obsolete."[12]

Intelligence Failures

It took seven months until the first insiders questioned the assertions of guilt put forward by Rumsfeld, Cheney and his colleagues. In August 2002, a US intelligence official told the *Los Angeles Times* that the prisoners were "low-and middle-level" fighters and supporters, and not "the big-time guys" who might know enough about al-Qaeda to help counter-terrorism officials unravel its secrets; another official said that the authorities had netted "no big fish" in Guantánamo, and that some of the prisoners "literally don't know the world is round."[13] In the meantime, however, before the Pentagon's PR machine shut down all loose talk, reporters on the ground were presented with hints of the truth behind the rhetoric, as those in charge of Camp X-Ray admitted that they were struggling to comprehend who they had in their custody. In early February, toning down his earlier rhetoric, Mike Lehnert said, "A large number claim to be Taliban, a smaller number we have been able to confirm as al-Qaeda, and a rather large number in the middle we have not been able to determine their status. Many of the detainees are not forthcoming. Many have been interviewed as many as four times, each time providing a different name and different information."[14]

While these problems undoubtedly contributed to the administration's decision to deny GPW protections to the prisoners, so that they could be interrogated more thoroughly, the reasons why the administration knew so little about those in its control can largely be traced back to the inadequate screening processes conducted in Afghanistan. Although Chris Mackey explained that these failures were largely due to the punishing workload and the requirement that every Arab be sent to Guantánamo, others pointed out that the problem was more fundamental.

Lieutenant Colonel Anthony Christino III, a senior military intelligence officer, who retired in 2004 after 20 years' service, spent the last few years of his career coordinating intelligence support to the army in Afghanistan and Guantánamo, and working as a Senior Watch Officer for the intelligence unit known as "Joint Intelligence Task Force—Combating Terrorism," which was responsible for analyzing the intelligence produced from prisons including Guantánamo. He told David Rose that the screening process was "flawed from the get-go," and explained that, since Vietnam, the military had invested all its time and effort in the technological aspects of intelligence gathering, training its workers in "Combat Electronic Warfare Intelligence," which mainly involved analyzing communications intercepts, rather than learning the age-old skills of gathering intelligence from human sources (HUMINT). When the "War on Terror" began, of course, these skills were suddenly in demand, but Christino was adamant that, by

2001, all the senior personnel with the required skills had retired, and the younger generation, who had mostly learned "sloppy methods" in the Balkans, Haiti and Somalia, where they "did not have the benefit of senior leadership," were "far too poorly trained" to distinguish between real terrorists, Taliban foot soldiers, and those caught in the wrong place at the wrong time. Explicitly criticizing the caliber of interrogators employed in Afghanistan and Guantánamo, he pointed out that, although these young men and women were undoubtedly bright and enthusiastic, they lacked "meaningful" life experiences, and were expected to demonstrate advanced intelligence skills after just 16 weeks' training at Fort Huachuca. He compared the situation unfavorably to the recruitment of police detectives, who, typically, have a degree in criminal justice and spend up to five years doing routine police work before graduating to intelligence-based investigations.[15]

Christino also condemned the military for its reliance on interpreters, mainly sourced through corporate employment agencies, whose quality was "often abysmal," and this was confirmed in a highly critical report produced for the Pentagon in 2003 by a unit called the Center for Army Lessons Learned, whose director, Lieutenant Colonel Bob Chamberlin, concluded that the lack of competent interpreters "impeded operations" in Afghanistan and Iraq. "Laugh if you will," he wrote, "but many of the linguists with which I conversed were convenience store workers and cab drivers, mostly over the age of 40. None had any previous military experience." Most of the linguists, he insisted, only had "the ability to tell the difference between a burro and a burrito," adding that the majority were also made to work "to the point of burn-out."[16]

Camp X-Ray

These failings, when added to the familiar pressure to achieve intelligence results, created a claustrophobic atmosphere at Guantánamo. For interrogation, the prisoners were initially strapped to a gurney and wheeled to their destination, but when photos of these journeys caused another furore in the world's media, they were escorted on foot, even though the handcuffs and shackles bit deeply into their wrists and ankles. Although the interrogations were not particularly severe at this early stage, there was a crushing circularity to them. Interrogators from various agencies took turns with the prisoners, but as the Spaniard

Hamed Ahmed explained, "The questions were always the same: if I knew Osama bin Laden or someone of his inner circle, what I was doing in that region, who my contacts were, where I had fought, etc. This went on for two or three hours. They asked the same questions in different ways. They finally told me that if I wasn't more cooperative, I would never see my family again."[17]

Initially, the conditions of detention were the most severe obstacle facing the prisoners, prompting Asif Iqbal to declare that "the restrictions that were placed on us when we were in our cages were probably the worst things we had to endure." Importing tried and tested tactics from Afghanistan, the authorities prevented the prisoners from talking to one another and their cages were permanently floodlit. "I spent the first month in utter silence," Mohammed Saghir said after his release, and Hamed Ahmed added, "In the morning they woke us up at 8 o'clock with a song by Bruce Springsteen, 'Born in the USA,' which they played at full volume through the loudspeakers." The prisoners were allowed a handful of meager "comfort items"—two towels, a blanket, a sheet, a small toothbrush, shampoo, soap, flip-flops and an insulation mat to sleep on, as well as two buckets, one for water and one for use as a urinal—but if they wanted to defecate they had to be escorted to a portaloo by the guards, who unshackled one of their hands, but kept an eye on them the whole time. This was not only a source of humiliation for devout Muslims, but also, as Shafiq Rasul explained, "very often the guards would refuse to take us to the portaloo outside and therefore people started to use the buckets in the cells. Many of the people who were detained in Camp X-Ray were ill, often suffering from dysentery or other diseases and simply couldn't wait until the guards decided they would take them to the toilet ... The smell in the cell block was terrible." Asif Iqbal also described how, in the first few weeks, they were "not allowed any exercise at all," were only "allowed out for two minutes a week to have a shower and then returned to the cage," and were often only given a minute to eat their food before it was taken away.[18]

Although many prisoners said that the everyday violence that was common in Afghanistan was not replicated in Guantánamo, they explained that the psychological pressure was more intense, and that they were absolutely terrified during the first few weeks in Cuba. Shafiq Rasul explained, "During the whole time that we were in Guantánamo, we were at a high level of fear. When we first got there the level was sky-high. At the beginning we were terrified that we might be killed at any minute. The guards would say to us, 'we could kill you at any time.' They would say, 'the world doesn't know you're here, nobody knows you're here, all they know is that you're missing and we could kill you and no one would know.'" At this stage, no one—not even the British prisoners, who could readily understand the Americans—had any idea of where they were, and when Red Cross representatives made their first visit, on January 20, they pointed out that in many Arab countries orange jumpsuits were "a sign that someone is about to be put to death." While the ICRC visit led to a few improvements in the prisoners' treatment—they managed to get the no-talking ban lifted, for example, and secured a promise that the prisoners would be supplied with underwear—they were less successful in their attempts to get the authorities to address the prisoners' complaints about their lack of privacy at the portaloo, their requests for more food (2,100 calories a day was considered adequate, which it is not), and their requests to be allowed to exercise and to be placed near other prisoners who spoke the same language. The issue of the jumpsuits was addressed in an extraordinary memorandum written by a member of the Joint Task Force after the visit. "Should we continue not to tell them what is going on?" the author of the memo wrote. "ICRC says they are very scared. What are the benefits in keeping them in the dark vs. telling them what is happening? The detainees think they are being taken to be shot." As for telling the prisoners where they were, the author concluded, "This request will be considered after the first round of interrogations."

While the prisoners were subjected to less random violence than in Afghanistan, however, they soon discovered that regular punishment was built into the system at Guantánamo. Shafiq Rasul said that their "comfort items" would be removed for the most minor infringement of the rules—leaning against the mesh walls of the cell, for example. Many prisoners also pointed out that they were subjected to indiscriminate verbal abuse from large numbers of the military personnel. Briefed by their superiors that these were the most dangerous men on the face of the earth, many of the guards—two-thirds of whom were reservists or members of the National Guard—took the propaganda at face value. Asif Iqbal explained how, when the restrictions on talking to the guards were relaxed after the first few weeks, several told him they had been briefed that they were "wild animals," who "would kill them with our toothbrushes at the first opportunity, that we were all members of al-Qaeda and that we had killed women and children indiscriminately."[19]

The Extreme Reaction Force

The most extreme brutality came from a special unit called the Extreme Reaction Force, which was—and is—a five-man riot squad responsible for beating supposedly recalcitrant prisoners into submission, and its use was so prevalent that a new phrase—"to be ERFed"—was coined by the prisoners. Mohammed Saghir explained that, in the early days of Camp X-Ray, even prisoners who attempted to pray were ERFed. "They wouldn't let us call for prayers," he said. "I tried to pray and four or five commandoes came and they beat me up. If someone would try to make a call for prayer they would beat him up and gag him." Tarek Dergoul, who spoke at length about the ERF after his release, confirmed that their attacks were largely prompted by minor disciplinary infractions, which he described as "an act of deliberate provocation." Explaining what happened to him on one of the five occasions that he was ERFed—for refusing to agree to a third cell search in a day—he said:

> They pepper-sprayed me in the face and I started vomiting; in all I must have brought up five cupfuls. They pinned me down and attacked me, poking their fingers in my eyes, and forced my head into the toilet pan and flushed. They tied me up like a beast and then they were kneeling on me, kicking and punching. Finally they dragged me out of the cell in chains, into the rec yard, and shaved my beard, my hair, my eyebrows.[20]

Dergoul was the first released prisoner to point out that each ERF attack was filmed, by a sixth member of the team with a video camera, and this was confirmed by a spokesman for Guantánamo in 2004, who said that they were used to monitor whether or not excessive force had been used. He refused to discuss how many times the ERF had been used, but in July 2004 the Pentagon said that "only 32 hours" of the tapes showed the units using "excessive force."[21]

One of the most violent of all the ERF assaults took place in Camp X-Ray at the end of April 2002. The victim was Juma al-Dossari, and the attack was witnessed by Shafiq Rasul, Asif Iqbal, Feroz Abbasi and

David Hicks. The men from Tipton described al-Dossari as having mental health problems. "He used to shout all the time," they said. "The guards and the medical team knew he was ill. Whenever soldiers would walk past his cell he would shout out and say things to them. Not swearing but silly things. He would impersonate the soldiers. One day he was impersonating a female soldier. She called the officer in charge, [who] came to the block and was speaking to Juma." Rasul continued:

> There were usually five people on an ERF team. On this occasion there were eight of them ... The first man is meant to go in with a shield. On this occasion the man with the shield threw the shield away, took his helmet off, and when the door was unlocked ran in and did a knee drop onto Juma's back just between his shoulder blades with his full weight. He must have been about 240 pounds in weight ... [he] grabbed his head with one hand and with the other hand punched him repeatedly in the face. His nose was broken. He pushed his face and he smashed it into the concrete floor ... There was blood everywhere. When they took him out they hosed the cell down and the water ran red with blood. We all saw it.[22]

In late April, Camp X-Ray was closed down and the prisoners were moved to a new, purpose-built prison, Camp Delta. Made out of shipping containers, the camp consisted of blocks of 48 cells, arranged in two rows of mesh cages separated by a narrow corridor. Although the new cells were a small improvement—they were slightly larger than Camp X-Ray's cages, and each had a wall-mounted steel bed, a toilet and a tap—there was no improvement in the prisoners' general living conditions. The cells were cold at night, the piped water (from a desalination plant) was yellow, the lights still stayed on all night, and giant "banana" rats turned up to replace the snakes and scorpions that had plagued them in Camp X-Ray. The cells were similar to those in the US's notorious Supermax prisons, on which they were modeled, but there were still fundamental differences: not only had the inmates of America's harshest prisons been tried and convicted of crimes, they also, for the most part, were allowed regular visits by family members, and had unlimited access to books, TV, music, pens and paper. In contrast, the Guantánamo prisoners were still held in a legal limbo, with no access to lawyers, no access to their families, no books apart from the Koran, no other forms of recreation, and no notion of when, if ever, their detention would come to an end. What none of them knew at the time was that the worst was yet to come.

12
House Raids and Other Arrests in Pakistan

Random Arrests

In addition to the 180 prisoners captured crossing the Pakistani border in December 2001, 120 other prisoners were captured in various towns and cities in Pakistan between September 2001 and July 2002. From January 2002, the majority were seized in house raids based on intelligence gathered by the ISI, but in the previous months they were mostly random arrests, precipitated, no doubt, by the generous financial rewards offered to President Musharraf by the Americans.

The story of 39-year-old Mohammed al-Adahi is typical of these early arrests. Married with two children, al-Adahi had never left the Yemen until August 2001, when he took a vacation from the oil company where he had worked for 21 years to accompany his sister to meet her husband, who was working for a charity organization in Afghanistan. As he told his tribunal, "In Muslim society, a woman does not travel by herself." After flying to Karachi, they traveled to Kandahar, where his brother-in-law was living. Al-Adahi stayed in Afghanistan for a month, "to ease his sister's transition to life in Afghanistan," and then made his way back to Pakistan, where he was arrested by soldiers while traveling on a bus. "They were capturing everybody with Arabic features," he said. "I gave them my passport and that shows that I'm an Arab. They said, 'why don't you follow us, we need you at the Centre.' From that point on they brought us over here."[1]

While the circumstances of al-Adahi's arrest were reflected in other prisoners' stories, his reasons for being in Pakistan were unique. The majority of the other prisoners captured at this time had, like many of those who went to Afghanistan, traveled to teach or to learn the Koran, to provide humanitarian aid, or to establish a new life. A few also went for medical treatment, which was often considerably cheaper than it was in their home countries, and these included Isa al-Murbati, the 36-year-old Bahraini whose abuse in Kandahar was described in Chapter 8. Married with five children, al-Murbati was a grocer who had previously served in the army. Accused of traveling to Afghanistan in November 2001 with the intention of fighting, and of training to use an AK-47 in Kabul, he said that he had never been in Afghanistan and had traveled to Pakistan for medical treatment. He pointed out that he was issued with a medical visa—dated October 28, 2001 and valid for one month, it was included in his passport, which was held by the US authorities—and was arrested by the police on arrival in Pakistan.[2]

Those who were in Pakistan for religious reasons included Murat Kurnaz (released in August 2006), a 19-year-old apprentice shipbuilder who was born and raised in Bremen, Germany. The son of Turkish immigrants who had moved to Germany in the 1970s, he was accused of being "a member of al-Qaeda who had been trying to reach Afghanistan to fight against US forces." In fact, he went to Pakistan to study with Jamaat-al-Tablighi, and was captured on a bus in November 2001, in circumstances that were remarkably similar to those described by Mohammed al-Adahi. Transferred to Kandahar, he experienced many of the brutal methods of treatment described by other prisoners. He said that "interrogators repeatedly forced his head into a bucket of cold water for long periods" and "gave electric shocks to his feet," that he was "held for days shackled and handcuffed with his arms secured above his head," and that on one occasion an officer loaded his gun and pointed it at his head, "screaming at him to admit to being an al-Qaeda associate."[3]

Those who traveled to Pakistan to provide humanitarian aid included Mohammed al-Harbi, a 28-year-old Saudi, and Abdullah al-Ajmi, a 23-year-old Kuwaiti (released in November 2005). Al-Harbi, who had three businesses in Saudi Arabia selling fruit and vegetables, was accused of being a mujahideen fighter in Kandahar, although he insisted that he never went to Afghanistan. He said that he traveled to Pakistan in November 2001, taking $12,000 to provide humanitarian aid to the refugees fleeing Afghanistan, and added that he was only planning to stay for a few weeks, because his wife was pregnant. On arrival in Pakistan, he spent a week organizing how to help the refugees and, after hearing that there were problems on the border, decided to donate his money to the Red Crescent in Quetta, but was detained at a checkpoint, and questioned by Americans at a local police station. "I had a return ticket home and it was clear I wasn't planning to stay or ever cross into Afghanistan," he said. "The Pakistani police sold me for money to the Americans. This was part of a round-up of all foreigners and Arabs in that area." He also explained that, although the Saudi authorities intervened to help him while he was in custody, the ISI hid his passport to protect their reward money. Al-Ajmi told a similar story. A lance corporal in the Kuwaiti Army, he was accused of going AWOL "in order to travel to Afghanistan to participate in the jihad," and of fighting with the Taliban against the Northern Alliance, although he actually went to Pakistan as a member of Jamaat-al-Tablighi, and did not set foot in Afghanistan. As his family described it, he took a leave of absence in order to "rescue the needy and the poor" in Pakistan, and contacted them after a month to tell them that he was successfully carrying out aid work. Al-Ajmi also explained how the false allegations against him had come about, revealing the extent to which the Pakistani authorities needed convincing stories to sell to the Americans: "These statements were all said under pressure and threats. I couldn't take it. I couldn't bear the threats and the suffering so I started saying things. When every detainee is captured they tell him that he is either Taliban or al-Qaeda and that is it. I couldn't bear the suffering and the threatening and the pressure so I had to say I was from [the] Taliban."[4]

Mohammed al-Harbi was not the only prisoner seized in Quetta. Five other men were seized from the Saudi Red Crescent hospital in the city; two who were moved there at the request of the Saudi authorities, and three who were severely wounded. The first two men, Bessam al-Dubaikey, a 23-year-old Saudi (released in 2006) and Abdullah al-Utaybi, a 29-year-old Saudi, were, like al-Harbi, captured at a checkpoint. Al-Dubaikey, who traveled to Pakistan in November 2001 to look for rare books and old coins, refuted various allegations about attending al-Qaeda guest houses in Afghanistan, insisting that he had not set foot outside of Pakistan, and explaining to his tribunal why he was critical of religious fanatics. "I faced a lot of animosity in my own country," he said. "If I flirt with a girl or listen to [certain] songs

I face a lot of animosity from these people that grow long beards. They have a lot of authority in my country." Captured with al-Utaybi, who was accused of being the director of the al-Wafa office in Herat and of "possibly" having trained at Khaldan, al-Dubaikey expressed surprise. He said that he only met al-Utaybi a few days before, and the two men decided to stick together because they were both carrying money, and explained that he traveled to Quetta with al-Utaybi so that he could donate his money to the Saudi Red Crescent, which he thought was rather odd if he was working for a charity himself. Asked about the circumstances of his arrest, al-Dubaikey said, "They said that you are Arabs. Even when I talked to one of them in English, they said there is nothing against you, but he asked for $5,000. He said that the United States will buy you for $10,000; $5,000 per person." After his arrest, he and al-Utaybi were held by the ISI for five days, and were then taken to the hospital while the Saudi authorities tried to secure their release. A week later, they were taken to a Pakistani prison instead. Al-Dubaikey explained, "The Saudi Arabian embassy representative apologized. He said we couldn't do anything. The United States wants you. The United States is bigger than Saudi Arabia so you will be going with the Americans. They assured us that we would be free in a very short time."[5]

Of the wounded men, Amran Hawsawi, a 25-year-old Saudi, worked for a charity organization in Saudi Arabia, teaching the Koran, and went to Afghanistan to teach refugees in a camp near the border with Iran, where he suffered shrapnel injuries after a bombardment. He tried to cross the border, but was turned back by Iranian officials, and made his way to Pakistan instead, where he was arrested in the hospital, even though he was seriously ill. "The doctor refused but they took [me] by force," he explained. "He said you can release anybody but this one." The other two wounded men were humanitarian aid workers. Khalid Mohammed, a 28-year-old Saudi, traveled to help the refugees at Spin Boldak, on the Pakistani border, and was injured while buying food and supplies for the refugees in a market, when US forces began bombing the area, and Adel Fatouh El-Gazzar, a 36-year-old Egyptian accountant (cleared for release in 2007), was also injured in a bombing raid near a refugee camp. El-Gazzar explained that he had been in Pakistan for a year, and had visited the al-Aqsa training camp, which was run by the Pakistani militant group Lashkar-e-Tayyiba (LeT), but he denied that he was a member of the group, and gave his tribunal a brief history lesson about how the Pakistani Army had used LeT as one of its proxy armies in the Kashmir struggle, how LeT had a history of discord with the Taliban and al-Qaeda, and how unimpressive he found the group's arrangements in Pakistan. "I didn't train there," he said. "I was an Egyptian officer, I don't need that type of training. It is not actually a camp, it is a joke ... it is several tents on the top of a mountain." He also explained that LeT "take people from the streets and give them training on the AK-47 then send them to Kashmir to fight. About 95 percent of them are killed crossing the border by India." Speaking of his arrest, he said that in November 2001 he was working with the Saudi Red Crescent at a large refugee camp, when it was bombed by US forces: "I saw a light and heard a voice and then I lost consciousness. When I woke up I was in a Pakistani hospital. I lost my coat, my passport, my money, everything. And I lost my leg also. Then I found myself in Pakistani custody." Kept in the hospital for a month, he was visited by Pakistani army officers and even the governor of Quetta, who "told me not to speak to anybody about [LeT], don't tell anybody our secrets," and was then told that he would be taken to "a large modern hospital with good facilities and surgeons to take care of my leg," but was handed over to the Americans instead:

> Q: Do you have any theories about why the governor and the Pakistani intel folks would sell you out and turn you over to the Americans?
> A: Come on man, you know what happened. In Pakistan you can buy people for $10. So what about $5,000?
> Q: So they sold you?
> A: Yes.[6]

Those who went to Pakistan in search of a new life included Mohammed El-Gharani, who was only 15 years old at the time of his capture. Born in Saudi Arabia to parents from Chad, he was not regarded as a Saudi citizen and his opportunities for education and employment were therefore limited. In September 2001, he set off for Karachi, hoping to learn English and to undertake computer training, but was captured a month later during a police raid on a mosque. After his capture, he was treated brutally in Pakistani custody. For 16 hours a day over a three-week period, he was "hung by his wrists, naked apart from his shorts, with his feet barely touching the floor," and his interrogators beat him if he moved. He was also blindfolded the whole time, apart from a few minutes each day when he ate, and was "forced to drink lots of water before his interrogators tied his penis with string so that he could not urinate." Although he was a minor, and was captured in a random operation, this brutal treatment was only the start of his problems. Transferred to Kandahar, his treatment echoed that described by other prisoners, but with a few novel touches. He was "stripped naked and repeatedly beaten," was "doused in freezing water and left exposed to the elements for three or four nights," was "repeatedly called 'nigger' by US soldiers, a term of racist abuse he had never heard before," and said that a guard "held his penis with a pair of scissors and told him he would cut it off."[7]

Ahmed Sulayman, a 40-year-old Jordanian, was captured by bounty hunters. A member of Jamaat-al-Tablighi, he also worked for the International Islamic Relief Organization, the Saudi charity whose purported ties to terrorism were mentioned in Chapter 6, but whose activities indicate that it fulfills a role akin to that of Christian Aid and Oxfam. Sulayman described it as an organization which "helps poor people, immigrants and orphans and feeds people during Ramadan and Eid ul-Adha," and while the prisoners in Guantánamo were being subjected to the most spurious allegations about the charity, the IIRO was providing relief packages to the victims of the 2004 tsunami and to some of the most remote and inaccessible parts of Pakistan that were affected by the 2005 earthquake.[8] According to Clive Stafford Smith, who visited Sulayman's family in Jordan, he was working for the IIRO as a teacher, and had "moved his family to a tiny village near Peshawar, a four-hour walk from the nearest main road, to help teach the poorest of the poor there." He reported that he "was so much liked that when he fell ill with meningitis, the locals paid for his hospital bills and refused repayment from his family," and he also stated that during the US-led invasion he continued with his work, but "One morning, he left home for work, and simply did not come back. His wife worried that the meningitis had recurred and called around the hospitals. Six months later, the family received news that Ahmed was in Guantánamo."[9]

Three other prisoners, who had various non-militant reasons for being in Pakistan, were also captured by bounty hunters. Brahim Benchekroun, a 22-year-old Moroccan (transferred to Moroccan custody in August 2004), explained that he was "rounded up by the Pakistani security forces at the end of 2001" near Lahore, "at the time of the first round-ups of Arabs in the Koranic schools." He was taken into custody with Ahmed Errachidi (cleared for release in 2007), a 35-year-old Moroccan chef, who had been living in the UK for 18 years, and Karama Khamisan, a 32-year-old Yemeni soldier (transferred to Yemeni custody in August 2005), who went to Afghanistan as part of a drug-smuggling ring, and was held as a human guarantor until the deal was completed. Errachidi was captured in Islamabad, where he had been working in a jewelry store after visiting Afghanistan to provide humanitarian aid to those affected by the US-led invasion, and Khamisan explained that, after the US-led invasion began, the drug dealers fled, leaving him near the border with Pakistan, where he was captured by Pakistani villagers. Benchekroun described what happened to the three men once they were in Pakistani custody. "We were looking through the makeshift blindfolds that the Pakistanis had put on us," he said, adding that Errachidi spoke English and was following the negotiations, when "people showed up with black suitcases and started bargaining with the Pakistanis over the price for handing us over." When they agreed on a price of $5,000 a head, Benchekroun explained, they all applauded. He also said that Khamisan was singled out for unusual treatment: "The Pakistanis made him grow a beard and learn to pray. I taught him the basics about washing myself. We didn't understand that it was so that they could sell him to the Americans, too." In an interview with Amnesty International, Khamisan confirmed that Pakistani officials "refused him shaving goods and instead gave him oil for his beard and kohl which he was told to use for his eyes, in the style adopted by many Taliban fighters."[10]

Another Moroccan, 28-year-old Mohammed Mazouz (also transferred to Moroccan custody in August 2004), was captured at this time. An economic migrant, he studied at Leningrad University and then traveled to London, where he survived for a few years doing various odd jobs. After befriending a Pakistani, he arranged to marry his sister and traveled to Pakistan in August 2001 to meet his bride-to-be and to sort out the marriage. Four days after his marriage, on September 22, he was stopped in the streets of Karachi by members of the Pakistani security forces, who were "rounding up anything that looks even a little like an Arab." Held for five days in a police station, he was then moved to a hangar with numerous other prisoners, "beaten, denied meals, and questioned about Mullah Omar [and] Osama bin

Laden," and was then transferred to Kandahar, where he described daily interrogations, in which, "at the beginning, we were beaten, face on the ground, by insane soldiers," and the use of electric shocks.[11]

Khalid al-Asmar, a 38-year-old Jordanian (released in July 2005), was also captured by the Pakistani police. A former mujahideen fighter against the Soviet Union, he married an Afghan woman, Fatima, whose parents and sister had been killed in a Soviet bombing raid in 1984, and moved to Pakistan, where he supported Fatima and their seven children by selling herbs and honey. In 2000, they returned to Afghanistan, settling in Kabul, which, at the time, was relatively safe, but when the war came to the city in November 2001 and US bomber planes destroyed a warehouse behind their home, they bundled the children into their white Toyota Corolla and set off for Pakistan once more. Unfortunately, the US military associated white Toyotas with the Taliban, and, on the way to Pakistan, they were targeted twice by US bombers, narrowly avoiding death on both occasions when the Americans' rockets failed to hit their target. When they reached Islamabad, al-Asmar found work and also contacted a Libyan charity that arranged flights to Jordan, where his parents still lived, but the day before their proposed departure he called his wife to say that he had been detained by the Pakistani police, and told her to leave without him. "I wasn't worried," Fatima said, "because I knew Khalid had done nothing wrong," but seven months later she heard that he was in Guantánamo. Acknowledging that her husband may have aroused suspicion because he fought with the mujahideen, she said that he saw the Taliban's role as different to that of the mujahideen. "This was a war for power," she said. "Khalid wanted nothing to do with it. He said it was not for God."[12]

One of the most distressing arrests in this period—and a clear example of American bullying—was the capture of Sami al-Hajj, a 32-year-old Sudanese cameraman, married with a one-year-old child, who was working for al-Jazeera. Despite reservations, al-Hajj had been covering the US-led invasion of Afghanistan since October 2001. His brother said that he was "reluctant and nervous about going to the conflict zone, but decided that it would not be in his best career interests to turn down such a prestigious assignment." After the fall of Kabul, he left for Pakistan with the rest of the al-Jazeera crew, but when, having renewed their visas, they were returning to Afghanistan to cover the inauguration of the new government in December, al-Hajj was singled out and arrested by the Pakistani authorities, at the request of the US authorities. After a visit to al-Jazeera's headquarters in Qatar, Clive Stafford Smith explained that the US military seized al-Hajj "because they thought he had filmed the interviews with bin Laden—like so much of the intelligence in the 'war on terror,' this proved false." His brutal treatment at the hands of the Americans—in Bagram, Kandahar and Guantánamo—and the authorities' attempts to persuade him to work for them as an informer, are described in the following chapters.[13]

The First House Raids

The first house raids—based on intelligence that was often extremely suspect—took place in November 2001. One of the first prisoners was Mohammed Sulaymon Barre, a 37-year-old Somali, who had been living in Pakistan, as a UN-approved refugee, since fleeing his homeland during its ruinous civil war in the early 1990s. Arrested at his home in Karachi on November 1, 2001 by police and intelligence agents who had made two previous visits to check his papers, and who seem, therefore, to have seized him on this third occasion because they were looking for easy targets to hand over to the Americans, his troubles began when the Americans began investigating his occupation. Barre worked from his home as the Karachi agent for the Dahabshiil Company, a Somali organization with branches around the world, which provides essential money transfer operations for the Somali diaspora. According to the Americans, Dahabshiil was "closely related to al-Barakat, a Somali financial company designated as a terrorism finance facilitator," which was shut down under US pressure. Barre said that he knew nothing about this allegation, pointing out that his job only involved making small transactions on behalf of Somalis living in Pakistan. In fact, as was noted in a World Bank report in 2004, the enforced US-led closure of money transfer operations with suspected links to terrorism was "disastrous for Somalia, a country with no recognized government and without a functioning state apparatus. After the international community largely washed its hands of the country following the disastrous peacekeeping foray in 1994, remittances became the inhabitants lifeline. With no recognized private banking system, the remittance trade was dominated by a single

firm (al-Barakat)." Crucially, the report added that, although the US
authorities closed down al-Barakat in 2001, labeling it "the quarter-
masters of terror," only four criminal prosecutions had been filed by
2003, "and none involved charges of aiding terrorists." This has not
helped Barre, who was still in Guantánamo at the time of writing,
despite pointing out, "A lot of interrogators said to me that ... a lot of
mistakes were made and they must be corrected. They told me many
times that I am here by mistake."[14]

Two Afghan brothers, 41-year-old Abdul Rahim Muslim Dost
(married with nine children), and 31-year-old Bader Zaman Bader
(married with three children), were captured at Muslim Dost's house
in Peshawar on November 17, 2001. Both were talented and capable
men: journalists and gemstone dealers, Bader was also a university
professor and Muslim Dost operated eight non-Islamist schools in
Afghanistan and Pakistan. Held in solitary confinement in Pakistan
for three months, while the ISI cooked up charges against them and
offered them the opportunity to bribe their way to freedom—which
they refused on principle, as they had done nothing wrong—they were
then sold to the US authorities, who accused Muslim Dost of serving
as an al-Qaeda contact in Herat, which he had never even visited.
Released in 2004 and 2005, they were, without doubt, picked up by
the ISI and sold to the Americans because, although they had been
living in Pakistan since their family fled Afghanistan in 1982, they
had published several satirical magazines and had written newspaper
articles in which they not only criticized the Taliban but also pointed
out the role of the ISI in creating and supporting the regime. As Muslim
Dost said in his tribunal:

> I am not an enemy of the United States of America. I am against the
> Pakistanis. I think the Pakistanis sold me to you and all of these wrong
> allegations were made by the Pakistanis. The Pakistanis trained all the
> people who are going to Afghanistan to fight. You can believe me or not.
> Pakistanis are training al-Qaeda and the Taliban and then sending them to
> Afghanistan. My guilt was to defend Afghanistan.

On his release, Bader explained more about the reasons that he and
others were sold to the Americans, describing it as a common practice.
For the ISI, he said, "it was just a question of keeping the Americans
busy with false suspects. They never stopped playing the international
community." He also told the story of a taxi driver in Guantánamo,

who was sold for $5,000. "The Pakistanis had just made a raid to find Arabs close to al-Qaeda and hadn't found anybody, so they arrested him," he said. "The officer who sold him to the Americans told him, 'Look here, it's worth it to sell people like you to keep the Americans from coming to make war on Pakistan.'"[15]

Haji Wali Mohammed, a 35-year-old money exchanger, was also captured at his home in Peshawar, on January 24, 2002. Married with two wives and ten children, he was born in Afghanistan, but his family fled to Pakistan in 1978 and lived in refugee camps for the next ten years until he established himself as a successful moneychanger and moved to Peshawar in 1988. All was well until 1995, when he first lost a significant amount of money, and in 1998, after entering into a business deal with the Bank of Afghanistan that also failed, he ended up being blamed by the Taliban, who made him responsible for the whole debt—around $1 million—even though he only had a 25 percent stake in the deal. He explained to his tribunal that the ISI took his car in November 2001 and then returned in January, because they knew he was "a very famous money exchanger" and assumed that he would pay them a bribe of at least $100,000. When he said that he actually owed a lot of money to other people and was unable to pay, he was told, "If you don't have a car and you don't have the cash, sell your house and give us half of it to save you from the bad ending." Three days later, he was handed over to the Americans, purportedly as a drug smuggler, although his new captors soon decided that he bought surface-to-air missiles for Osama bin Laden and—despite his abysmal financial record since 1995—was entrusted with $1 million by Mullah Omar. Explaining that he did not know bin Laden and had no time for the Taliban, who had ruined his life, he said, "We were businessmen, their ways and our ways were different. That's why they didn't like us and we didn't like them. Because a businessman does not have a beard and listens to music in his car, and he watches television and they didn't like that."[16]

Two more prisoners—who were regarded as highly significant by the US authorities—were also captured at their homes in January 2002. Mullah Abdul Salam Zaeef, the Taliban's former ambassador to Pakistan (released in September 2005), was seized from his home in Islamabad in a night raid on January 3, 2002. Married with eight children, the 34-year-old, who was reportedly a childhood friend of Mullah Omar but had a reputation as one of the Taliban's more moderate leaders, issued daily press briefings after the US-led invasion began, condemning American aggression and defending Afghanistan's "dignity," until the Pakistani authorities closed down the embassy in November, officially severing all ties with the Taliban regime that they had done so much to support. Fearing for his family's safety, Zaeef then applied for asylum, but his application was rejected, and from then on it was only a matter of time before the Americans got hold of him. One of only a handful of prisoners interrogated on board the USS *Peleliu*, he was then moved to Kandahar, where he was held for seven months before being transported to Guantánamo.[17]

The other supposedly significant prisoner seized at this time was Moazzam Begg, a 31-year-old Briton with dual British-Pakistani nationality. The father of four children, whose youngest was born after his capture, Begg was released in January 2005, and has become an articulate commentator on the plight of the remaining prisoners, also writing a book about his experiences. Something of an idealist, he supported the rights of Muslims to defend themselves militarily—in Bosnia and Chechnya, for example—and toyed with volunteering to fight himself, until he realized that he was not a warrior. He did, however, visit Bosnia to provide humanitarian aid, and also managed to arouse the interest of MI5 on three separate occasions: once in connection with a bookshop in Birmingham that he helped establish; once when he was stopped at the airport en route to Turkey, during a particularly ill-advised attempt to visit Chechnya; and another time in connection with a Tunisian he had met in Britain, who phoned him from Dubai and asked him to send him money, because he had no one else to turn to, and had just escaped from the custody of the security forces, who wanted to torture him.

In 2001, at the urging of a Palestinian friend who had moved to Afghanistan to provide humanitarian aid, Begg began funding well-digging projects in Afghanistan, and soon decided to move his entire family to Kabul. Settling in a large house, he continued his well-digging projects, gaining a particular satisfaction from seeing the effects first-hand, and was soon joined by a good friend from Britain, 33-year-old Shaker Aamer, who also brought his family. Married to a British woman, and, like Begg, the father of four children, the youngest of whom was also born after his capture, the Saudi-born Aamer had been a UK resident since 1996, and had applied for British citizenship before setting off for Afghanistan. An enormously charismatic figure (his status in Guantánamo is discussed in Chapter 19), he had worked in the UK as a translator for a solicitor who dealt with immigration cases, but he relished the opportunity to find a new life in Afghanistan.

9/11, of course, shattered their dreams. As the country descended into chaos, the two men's families escaped safely, but Aamer, who made it as far as Jalalabad, where he was taken in by an Afghan family, was captured by bounty hunters, who sold him to the Northern Alliance, who, in turn, sold him to the Americans. Begg was initially more fortunate. After crossing the mountains into Pakistan, he was reunited with his family in Islamabad at the end of November 2001, but two months later he was abducted at gunpoint by US and Pakistani agents, who took him from his house at midnight on January 31, 2002. For the next few weeks, until he was transferred to Kandahar, he was held in the villa described in Chapter 7, where he was interrogated by the Americans, and, on one occasion, by members of MI5, and where, on a toilet break, he managed to speak briefly to a number of Arab prisoners, including three Libyan students, who had been imprisoned for several months in squalid cells beneath the house.[18]

The Capture of Riyadh the Facilitator

While the Americans were chasing shadows with the arrests of most of the men described above, they apparently secured two significant victories on February 7, 2002, when Khairullah Khairkhwa, the 34-year-old governor of Herat, was captured in the border town of Chaman, and Abdu Ali Sharqawi, a 27-year-old Yemeni (more commonly known as Riyadh the Facilitator), was captured in a house raid in Karachi. Whether Khairkhwa lived up to his promise is debatable. Although he had been the Taliban's interior minister and was described by the *Pakistan Daily Times* as one of the six most prominent hardliners loyal to Mullah Omar, he was adamant that he had nothing of value to offer the Americans. "My only purpose," he said, "was to make transportation and communication easy for the people and to make bribery go away."[19]

Sharqawi, however, was a significant catch. Regarded as "a serious logistician" for al-Qaeda, according to an intelligence source, he was

captured after the Pakistani authorities took out newspaper advertise-
ments offering "rewards for tips about strange foreigners." According to
US News, "Riyadh's neighbors had noticed the odd comings and goings
of people who entered his small home," and tipped off the authorities.
He was one of the first apparently significant al-Qaeda operatives to be
subjected to the process known as "extraordinary rendition." Discussed
in detail in Chapter 16, this involved the CIA rendering supposedly
"high-value" terrorist subjects to its own secret global network of
prisons, or to other countries, where they could be interrogated by
proxy torturers without the CIA operatives having to lift a finger to
incriminate themselves in their treatment. Rendered to Jordan within
days of his capture, Sharqawi remained there until January 2004, when
he was rendered back to a CIA facility in Afghanistan. Although he was
moved to Guantánamo in September 2004, so little was known about
his capture and subsequent imprisonment that in December 2005,
when Human Rights Watch issued its first major report on the "ghost"
prisoners in CIA custody, his location was listed as "unknown." It was
not until April 2006, when the Pentagon finally released the names,
nationalities and ISN numbers of the Guantánamo prisoners, that it
was possible to identify the allegations against him, which included
claims that he operated an al-Qaeda safe house in Karachi in 2001,
and "assisted on average five to 15 mujahid per week gain entry into
Afghanistan," that he "traveled extensively throughout Europe, the
Middle East and Eastern Africa, during the period 1995 through
2001, for the purpose of participating in jihad," that he "served as an
intermediary in obtaining false travel documents for jihad leaders in
the Philippines," that he "traveled with Osama bin Laden for a period
of two months after the bombing of the USS Cole in 2000," and that
he "was present with top al-Qaeda leadership at Tora Bora."[20]

Fifteen other prisoners were captured at the same time as Sharqawi,
although all of them seem to have been captured, not in Sharqawi's
house, but in another purported safe house, and, in one case, a school.
Chris Mackey, writing of their subsequent arrival in Kandahar, declared
that they were "found in a couple of safe houses in an ethnically Arab
district."[21] Unlike Sharqawi, they were all transferred to Guantánamo
after processing and interrogation in Afghanistan, but it was far from
clear that any of them had any involvement with terrorism. Most seem
to have ended up at the safe house because it was one of many used as

part of an impromptu system developed after the fall of the Taliban to help hundreds of Arabs including trained fighters, recent recruits and civilians to evade capture by Afghan or Pakistani forces.

Only two of those captured in the raids admitted to any kind of involvement with the Taliban, and their recruitment followed the depressingly familiar pattern described by Sharon Curcio in Chapter 6. Abdul Aziz al-Suadi, a 27-year-old Yemeni bus driver, was recruited by a sheikh, who encouraged him "to go to Afghanistan to participate in jihad against the Russians," and Hamoud al-Wady, a 36-year-old Yemeni, went to Afghanistan for jihad because he swore that he would do so if his wife bore him a child. In Afghanistan, however, he said that the "picture about the fight in my head"—which he conceived as a fight between Muslims and Communists, as it had been in the conflict between North and South Yemen—was incorrect, and his supposed enemies were all Muslims. After undertaking humanitarian work with an Arab who explained that "not everybody comes to Afghanistan for fighting," he fled to Pakistan after the US-led invasion began and stayed at the house of a Pakistani, whose phone number he had been given in Afghanistan, which was where he was arrested. "I did not plan to go to that particular house," he explained. "I had only the telephone number and I did not know if it belonged to a house or something else, a shop, for example."[22]

More serious allegations were leveled at Omar Abu Bakr, a 29-year-old Libyan. It was claimed that he traveled to Afghanistan in 1998, that he was a member of the Libyan Islamic Fighting Group (LIFG), who was "known to assist Osama bin Laden in purchasing weapons," that he was a military trainer for the LIFG, that he established a training camp in summer 2001, that he "was a military leader of Arabs," who fought against the Northern Alliance near Taloqan, that he "met with Taliban leaders to plan military operations," and that he and his group were directed to Tora Bora by Osama bin Laden. One of his lawyers, Edmund Burke, refuted all the allegations, however. He acknowledged that his client had been a member of the LIFG, and had worked for the Taliban as a mine clearer until 1998, when his right leg was severely damaged by a land mine, but said that he spent the ensuing years moving from hospital to hospital in Afghanistan to receive treatment for his leg, which was eventually amputated. He added that he moved to Pakistan in 2001, and was living in a school for boys when it was raided by Pakistani police. Pointing out that his client "can't bear his weight on his good leg and only hobbles about with the help of a walker or crutches," he explained, "It's very hard to imagine him as a combatant of any kind."[23]

The other men maintained that they had nothing whatsoever to do with military activities, and two of them also insisted that they had never been in Afghanistan. Jamal bin Amer, a 28-year-old Yemeni, was accused of training at the Libyan camp near Kabul, but said that he went to Pakistan "with some other people who were acting as missionaries to talk about religion in the villages." Married with a five-year-old daughter, he worked for a government ministry, and his brother, who noted that he had called home regularly from Pakistan, described him as being "far from a religious fanatic." Saad al-Azani, a 22-year-old Yemeni, went to Pakistan to train as an imam, after attending a school run by Jamaat-al-Tablighi in Yemen. Unable to come up with any evidence against him, the Americans resorted to declaring that a request for permission for him to preach Islam in Pakistan "was found in a collection of materials related to al-Qaeda," that the man who ran the Institute of Islamic Studies, where he studied, was "an al-Qaeda operational planner," and that the student population "consisted primarily of Afghani and Philippine Taliban members."[24]

The last three prisoners—and the only ones to have been released—gave other, non-militant explanations for being in an alleged safe house, which lend a certain credence to many of the other stories related above. Adel al-Zamel, a 38-year-old Kuwaiti (released in November 2005), became the manager of al-Wafa's Kabul office in 2001, and took his wife and their eight children to Afghanistan, unaware that the humanitarian charity was under suspicion for activities related to terrorism. He gave up his job in August after a disagreement with a more senior figure, who, he felt, was arrogant and was squandering money that had been given in good faith for charitable purposes; he moved his family to Pakistan in September, and then returned to help the family of Sulaiman Abu Ghaith move to Pakistan as well. He added that he had met Abu Ghaith on a few occasions in Kuwait, but insisted that he did not know, until after 9/11, "when he appeared on TV," that he was a spokesman for al-Qaeda. Speaking of his capture, he denied all knowledge that he was staying in a safe house, as alleged, and said that he had been there for 16 weeks awaiting the opportunity to return to Kuwait. Saad al-Azmi, a 22-year-old Kuwaiti friend of al-Zamel (also released in November 2005), spent three weeks with his friend in Kabul, and ended up with him in the Karachi house. "The people I was arrested with were civilians," he said. "They were not wearing uniforms. I did not know anybody there except al-Zamel."[25]

Richard Belmar, a 22-year-old Briton (released in January 2005), was born and brought up in Marylebone, in central London. After training as a mechanic, he worked for the Post Office, and converted to Islam in 1999. In July 2001, after spending some time in Pakistan, he traveled to Afghanistan to study at a religious school in Kandahar. Trapped in the city after the US-led invasion began, he made several unsuccessful attempts to leave the country—on one occasion wearing a burka, but still failing to escape because the driver of his car thought that it was too dangerous—before managing to cross the border in December by walking across the mountains. "I didn't want to be part of any war," he said. "I wanted to get out. I was seeing people who'd been bombed, pieces of them everywhere." In Karachi, he stayed in a hotel for a while, but was running out of money and had lost his passport, and was afraid of contacting the British consulate because he knew that "anyone who had been in Afghanistan was at risk of arrest." He then met an Arab who "promised to sort me out," and arranged for him to stay in "a large house," where he was captured. Taken to the ISI headquarters in Karachi, along with the other prisoners, he was interviewed by US intelligence operatives, whose superiors, finding his story credible, recommended his repatriation to the UK and asked MI5 to send some agents to see if they wanted to recruit him. Turned down by MI5, for reasons that were never explained, he was sent to Bagram instead.[26]

13

The Capture of Abu Zubaydah and its Aftermath

The Capture of Abu Zubaydah

Although the Americans made little fuss about the capture of Abdu Ali Sharqawi, they exulted in the capture of another senior al-Qaeda operative, Abu Zubaydah, after a shoot-out during a house raid in Faisalabad on March 28, 2002. Allegedly the facilitator of the Khaldan camp, responsible for screening recruits arriving in Pakistan and selecting those who were suitable for training, he was described in more breathless terms by *Time*, who called the 31-year-old Saudi-born Palestinian "al-Qaeda's chief of operations and top recruiter," and suggested that he would be able to "provide the names of terrorists around the world and which targets they planned to hit."

Zubaydah was traced to Shabaz Cottage, a recently rented house on the outskirts of the city, through the careless use of satellite phones, which "triggered electronic monitoring systems run by American intelligence." On the night of the raid, FBI agents, Pakistani commandoes and a hundred local police converged on the house, where the lead operatives broke down the gate of the house next door and made their way up an outside staircase, surprising Zubaydah and two companions as they leapt onto the neighbor's roof. In the shoot-out that followed, one of the men was shot dead, and the others were seriously wounded; Zubaydah reportedly received gunshot wounds in his stomach, one of his legs, and his groin.[1]

While Zubaydah was immediately rendered to a secret CIA prison (see Chapter 20), five other men who were captured in the house, plus

16 others who were captured during a separate raid on a guest house in another part of the city, were held in prisons in Lahore and Islamabad, where they were questioned by US and Pakistani agents for two months, and were then transferred to Guantánamo via Bagram and Kandahar. Three of the five men who were captured with Zubaydah—Ghassan al-Sharbi, a 27-year-old Saudi, Jabran al-Qahtani, a 24-year-old Saudi, and Sufyian Barhoumi, a 28-year-old Algerian—were put forward for trial by Military Commission in November 2005.

Al-Sharbi, who speaks fluent English and graduated in electrical engineering from Embry Riddle Aeronautical University in Arizona, is the only one to publicly declare membership of al-Qaeda. In his tribunal, he accepted all the allegations against him, which included claims that he received specialized training in the manufacture and use of remote-controlled explosive devices to detonate bombs against Afghan and US forces, that he "was observed chatting and laughing like pals with Osama bin Laden," and that he was known in Guantánamo as the "electronic builder" and "Abu Zubaydah's right-hand man." Al-Qahtani, a graduate in electrical engineering from King Saud University in Saudi Arabia, was accused of traveling to Afghanistan after 9/11, "with the intent to fight the Northern Alliance and the American forces, whom he expected would soon be fighting in Afghanistan," and of being part of a group at Zubaydah's house who were provided with money to buy the components to make remote-controlled explosive devices. Barhoumi, who was accused of being a trainer for the bomb-making group, denied the allegations. He admitted traveling to Afghanistan for military training in 1999, but pointed out that this was before 9/11, and insisted that, having been shown a video of atrocities in Chechnya at a mosque in the UK, where he lived for two years, his intention was to train to fight in Chechnya. He explained that, after leaving Afghanistan, he traveled "from house to house," ending up at the safe house in Faisalabad, but said that he was only there for ten days before the raid, and claimed that the allegations were the result of "hearsay" and of "people testifying against me." He said that his interrogators told him, "people are talking about you a lot," and added that, because he was arrested with Zubaydah, "they dumped everything on me and said I was al-Qaeda also."[2]

The fourth man, Noor Uthman Mohammed, a 36-year-old from the Sudan, was not accused of being part of the bomb-making group, but

was accused instead of helping run Khaldan, when those in charge—
"the Sheikh's son" and Zubaydah—were not around. Although he
accepted that he received extensive weapons training at Khaldan, and
also provided food and training to some of the recruits, he denied
an allegation that he was involved in running the camp, saying, "I
am not convinced of the fighting, all I just came over there for was
preparation," and insisting that the camp was "a place to get training"
that had nothing to do with either al-Qaeda or the Taliban. "People
come over to that camp, train for about a month to a month and a
half, then they go back to their hometown," he said, adding that what
the people did with the training they received was their own business:
"When the person gets the training and leaves the Khaldan camp,
he leaves the camp for [his] country, and he changes his mind about
the whole thing. God gives them responsibility to fight, we cannot
just prevent them from doing that." Describing the circumstances of
his arrest, he said, "I don't know anything about this house. What I
know is that I know Abu Zubaydah was the person in charge of that
safe house. He is the person that told me [to] go to that place until he
made the traveling arrangements." When asked if Zubaydah was his
boss or his friend, he added, "I don't know Abu Zubaydah until the
last times I was in that house."[3]

The fifth man arrested at the house, Ahmed Labed, a 43-year-old
Algerian, said that he was sent there accidentally. A former drug dealer
in Europe, he had been imprisoned many times in Germany and Italy,
and explained that he decided to go to Afghanistan in March 2001,
after someone he met at a mosque in Hamburg recruited him by
showing him videos of mujahideen in Afghanistan and Chechnya, but
he added that he actually hoped to buy heroin to sell in Europe so that
he could buy his own nightclub. After arriving in Afghanistan at the
start of September, he trained at al-Farouq for twelve days until the
camp closed, and then fought with the Taliban until December, when
he left for Pakistan with a group of twenty other people, staying for
three months in houses in Banuu and Lahore. He was then told to go
to Faisalabad and wait until some people came to give him his passport
and send him back to Germany, and explained that he was with two
other people, a Russian and a Yemeni, but that, after they arrived at
Shabaz Cottage, they were told that they had been brought there by
mistake and would be moved after the evening prayer. Labed insisted

that he didn't want to leave, because the previous houses had been crowded, whereas this house was "big and nice" and "everybody had their own room," and refused to leave in the vehicle that was brought in the evening. Several days later, he said, "The guy from al-Qaeda, Daoud [identified as Zubaydah] questioned me as to who I was, what I was doing here and who brought me. I said I'm from Germany waiting on my passport. When I get it, I will leave. He said, no problem, you can stay here for a week. I stayed there for about twelve days and the Pakistani police came. They took us to prison. Daoud was arrested with us, you can ask him about us."[4]

Those captured in the other raid, on the Crescent Mill guest house in Faisalabad (also referred to as the "Issa" guest house, after its owner, and "the Yemeni house," after most of its guests), seem, for the most part, to have been nothing more than students, youthful adventurers and others in search of cheap medical treatment, who were caught in the wrong place at the wrong time. Six of the 17 said that they were students at Salafia University, where they were studying the Koran, and that the guest house was actually a university dorm, and all were appalled that they ended up in Guantánamo. Twenty-year-old Mohammed Tahar explained what happened to him while he was in Pakistani custody: "The army translator and the interrogator from the Pakistani intelligence said, 'yes, all of what this man said … about his story in Pakistan is correct, and therefore that is why we are going to give him back his passport that we took' … I was really surprised that the American intelligence refused all of these proofs and they said no. 'We still need him,' they said, and then they took me."

Tahar's story was echoed by others in the house, including 22-year-old Emad Hassan, who was nearing the end of a seven-month trip to the university to study the Koran, and said that, while in Pakistani custody, "the person who was in charge came and told us we didn't have anything to worry about," and that "our sheet was clean." A similar appraisal was presented by a friend of his, 18-year-old Mohammed Hassen (cleared for release in 2007), who was not even living at the house. Caught up in the raid after visiting for dinner and staying the night, Hassen's only explanation for his arrest was that an interrogator told him "the house was suspected." Twenty-four-year-old Fayad Ahmed was also a student. After fending off an allegation that he was "recruited" by Jamaat-al-Tablighi, saying, "if you mean recruited as being someone who went to the mosque with them and prayed with them, everyone sat sometimes with Tablighi," he pointed out that he was persistently told he was arrested by mistake and would be released, both in Pakistan and in Guantánamo, where, he said, "The interrogator and the investigator about a month ago that met with me told [me] that there was nothing against me and that I am an innocent man and should [be] released." He was also critical of US policy after 9/11 and insisted that he and the others were sold to the Americans. "After the incident that happened to the United States," he said, "the Americans were very desperate like a hungry person. They wanted just to take anyone. The Pakistanis took advantage of you and just gave you anyone for an amount of money ... The Pakistanis said that we were worth $5,000."[5]

Others were simply bewildered. When a tribunal member asked 22-year-old Abdel Hakim, "If you were a student studying the Koran, how did you end up here?" he replied, "This is the question I always ask myself ... why was I captured there, and why did they bring me here?" Mohammed al-Zarnuki, who took a break from farming to preach with Jamaat-al-Tablighi, was equally confused, pointing out that he spent four months preaching and then spent a month and a half at the house, where he became ill, and 22-year-old Ala bin Ali Ahmed, who was staying at the house but had run out of money to enroll on a course, also had no clue about why he was captured. "All I know is all the people in the house were students," he said.[6]

This was not strictly correct, but most of the others who were not students were also unconnected with either militancy or terrorism. Twenty-four-year-old Fahmi Ahmed said that he went to Pakistan to buy fabrics, taking $3,500 that he had borrowed from his mother, but explained that he actually spent most of his time in Pakistan "like a wild man," drinking and smoking hashish. After staying for a year and a half, during which time his visa expired, he was eventually advised to go to Faisalabad, where there was a big Arabic community, and where he was told he would be able to locate people who could tell him how to bribe the government to renew his visa. He said he ended up staying for two months with a Pakistani family, but just as he was planning to call his family to arrange to return home, because the house he was staying in was too small, he met Ali Abdullah Ahmed al-Salami, another 24-year-old (whose death in Guantánamo is described in Chapter 19), who invited him to stay at a larger house, where he was also staying, and where "they were all university students," and added that al-Salami mentioned that he might know people who could help him with his visa.[7]

Two others said that they traveled to Pakistan for medical treatment. Abdul Aziz al-Noofayee, a 25-year-old Saudi, said that he went to receive treatment for a back problem, and 21-year-old Mohammed Salam said that he went for treatment on his nose. After explaining that a "generous person" paid for his trip, the following exchange took place, which demonstrated, yet again, how wide the cultural gap was between the Americans and Muslims from the Gulf:

> *Tribunal Member*: I don't know your culture very well, but ... in our culture people just don't step up and say, "I'll pay for the trip for you."
> *Detainee*: In our culture, in Islam, there is such a thing ... Indeed, it is an obligation for any Muslim who is rich to pay for someone who is poor.[8]

Out of all these individuals, the only one who had either been to Afghanistan or been anywhere near any kind of military activity was 18-year-old Ahmed Abdul Qader, who said that he went to Afghanistan "to help the needy and the poor," and tried unsuccessfully to establish a charity organization. He admitted that he visited the "back line," encouraged by friends in the Taliban, but insisted that he "never participated in any kind of military activities." After leaving Afghanistan before the US-led invasion began, he ended up in the house in Faisalabad, where he became friends with Fahmi Ahmed. "We shared the same vision and he has the same opinions," Ahmed said, adding, "He used to use hashish with me," whereas the other students in the house "were trying to inspire me to do the religious things, like look at my religion, because most of the students were studying the Koran and all things related to religious studies."[9]

The only connection between Abu Zubaydah and the Crescent Mill guest house was through the two other men—Ravil Mingazov, a 34-year-old Russian, and Jamil Nassir, a 31-year-old Yemeni—who were sent to Abu Zubaydah's house by mistake along with Ahmed Labed. Unlike the Algerian, the two men were moved to Crescent Mill, where several of the students recalled that a Russian had moved into the house. Little is known about these men. Mingazov was accused of training to use explosives and poisons in Afghanistan, and Nassir was accused of staying at a Taliban guest house in Kandahar, but Labed's story, and one statement in particular—that, because the three men "did not have a connection or relationship with Abu Zubaydah," they "should have been placed in the Yemeni house"—confirms that, although Abu Zubaydah had some sort of contact with the house, it was, at best, a place where a few low-level fighters could be hidden alongside a group of students.[10]

Other House Raids

Emboldened by the capture of Abu Zubaydah, US and Pakistani intelligence operatives embarked on numerous house raids over the next few months, targeting various Islamic charities suspected of diverting charitable donations to al-Qaeda. With few exceptions, these raids succeeded only in capturing administrators and workers who were completely innocent of any wrongdoing. The biggest target was the Revival of Islamic Heritage Society (RIHS), a Kuwait-based NGO, with branches around the world, whose stated aim was "to improve the condition of the Muslim community and develop an awareness and understanding of Islam amongst the non-Muslim communities, by concentrating on youth and education." In January 2002, the Pakistani and Afghan offices of the RIHS were blacklisted by the US Treasury, along with the Afghan Support Committee (ASC), which had apparently been established by Osama bin Laden in the 1980s. According to Paul O'Neill, the Secretary of the US Treasury, the ASC's finance chief was Abu Bakr al-Jaziri, "formerly bin Laden's fundraiser," and the director of the Pakistani branch of the RIHS was Abdul Muhsin al-Libi, who also managed the ASC's office in Peshawar. Both men were on the FBI's "Most Wanted Terrorists" list, where they remain to this day, having managed to slip away unnoticed while US intelligence operatives prepared to raid the houses of their employees. Announcing the blacklisting, O'Neill stated that personnel in both groups, including al-Jaziri and al-Libi, "defrauded well-meaning contributors by diverting money donated for widows and orphans to al-Qaeda terrorists," and that members of the RIHS office in Pakistan "padded the number of orphans it claimed to care for by providing names of orphans that did not exist or who had died. Funds then sent for the purpose of caring for the non-existent or dead orphans were instead diverted to al-Qaeda terrorists."[11]

This may be the case, but those who took the blame were the RIHS's innocent workers, who were responsible for the lion's share of the organization's charitable work, which, in addition to the proselytizing mentioned above, included running schools and orphanages, drilling wells and building mosques. Five of the charity's workers—one Jordanian and four Sudanese—were captured in house raids in May 2002. With one exception, they were all subsequently released from Guantánamo, but not all of them have spoken about their ordeal. The Jordanian, 40-year-old Hassan Hamid, one of two Jordanian prisoners released in November 2003, was approached in 2005 by Clive Stafford Smith, who was on a fact-finding mission in Jordan. He reported that neither man consented to meet him and noted, "they were afraid that speaking out would only make their lives more difficult." Of the Sudanese employees, 28-year-old Mohammed al-Ghazali Babikir, an accountant, and 36-year-old Rashid Ahmad, married with four sons, have also not spoken about their experiences since their release in May 2004, but Ahmad's wife described the circumstances of her husband's arrest. She said that Pakistani soldiers, accompanied by Americans, "attacked the house in a terrifying manner, scaring the two children … A female Pakistani soldier that was with them attacked her in an attempt to remove her hijab, in order to ascertain her identity. She refused to uncover her face in front of the men. All of this happened in front of her children's eyes. He [Ahmad] had never been in Kabul or Kandahar, yet he was not safe from suspicion or capture."[12]

While the reticence of these men is understandable, the two other Sudanese employees of the RIHS spoke at length in their tribunals. Thirty-two-year-old Hamad Gadallah (released in July 2005) told the most complete story of the organization's activities, and obviously managed to impress upon the Americans that not everyone who worked for the charity was siphoning off money for al-Qaeda. Arrested at his home on May 27, 2002, by two Americans and representatives of Pakistani intelligence and the police, he explained that he had been working for the Central Bank in Sudan, when his brother, who worked for a bank in Bangladesh, told him that the RIHS in Peshawar had a vacancy for an accountant. He took leave from his job to investigate the organization in January 2001, and, after seeing that they were "all good people, with high standards, [who] love their work, and … perform their work faithfully," and that there were "no problems with the accountancy program," he handed in his notice at the bank and began working for the RIHS in March. Refuting allegations about the organization's inclusion in a US guide to terrorist organizations, he said, "I say that not every organization or person that is within that guide can be accused of being a terrorist. That requires a lot of evidence and proof ... I'm sure that the year that I was working for the RIHS in 2001, it had nothing to do with any terrorist acts." He added that the organization had an income of around $2.5 million in 2001, which came from mosques in Kuwait, and described it as a "huge organization" with one branch in Pakistan. He also explained the significance of his role and, crucially, how there were no underhand financial transactions during his time there:

Q: If your organization were transferring money to another organization, you would be aware of it?
A: That never happened.
Q: But if it had, you would know that?
A: Yes I would. Because I record everything that comes in and everything that goes out.[13]

Forty-three-year-old Salim Amir (cleared for release in 2007) was as perplexed as the other RIHS employees about his capture. A Pakistani resident, he explained that he traveled to Pakistan in 1991, "performed official lawful work for schools" for three years, and was then taken on by the RIHS, first as a schools inspector—visiting Afghanistan in 1998 to check on schools in Kunar and Jalalabad—and then in "the Orphanage Office of Administration." Responding to an allegation that the organization was "suspected of supporting extremist activity, and some employees are suspected of supporting terrorism," he said, "I have only known the Islamic organization to be associated with humanitarian efforts, never terrorism." He was baffled that his house was "identified as a suspected al-Qaeda residence," pointing out that he rented it from a Pakistani woman, and that "everything I did regarding the house was legal," and explained that, when he was arrested, in front of his wife and children, "the officer that arrested us said he was giving us to the American forces to avoid problems and keep our country safe."[14]

In his tribunal, Hamad Gadallah mentioned that his downstairs neighbor, who did not work for the RIHS, was also arrested, and this was Fethi Boucetta, a 38-year-old Algerian, who was released from

Guantánamo in November 2006. He was one of three teachers, working in a school run by the Saudi Red Crescent, who were also captured on May 27, 2002, under circumstances that were at least as dubious as those described above. A doctor who fled Algeria in 1996 to avoid military service, Boucetta sought asylum in Pakistan, where he was taken on as a teacher by the Red Crescent. Speaking of the circumstances of his arrest, his lawyer said that the Pakistani police "went to his house and asked to speak with somebody else [Hamad Gadallah], and Fethi said he didn't know that person and that he wasn't there. [They] came back with Americans in plain clothes, and they said they wanted to question him. That's when he was arrested." Despite being arrested by mistake, it took until May 2005 for the Americans to accept that he was a completely innocent man, and in the meantime the allegations that mounted up against him were staggering. It was alleged that he "reportedly was an active member of the Islamic Salvation Front" (the Algerian political party whose suppression by the army in 1992 provoked the civil war that began the following year), that he traveled to Afghanistan from the Yemen, where he taught from 1993 to 1996, "at the request of the Taliban" (he actually traveled to Pakistan and carried on teaching), that he "reportedly organized combatants to fight for the Taliban," and that he "reportedly has organized extremist networks in Arab countries and has contacts throughout the Middle East." The crowning irony in the Americans' treatment of Boucetta concerned his release from Guantánamo. Unwilling to send him to Algeria, because of fears that he would be mistreated, the only country that the Americans could persuade to accept him was Albania, where he—and two other wrongly detained prisoners released at the same time—joined the five Uyghurs described in Chapter 7, who were sent to a UN refugee camp in Tirana in May 2006. One of the other prisoners released in Albania with Boucetta was Ala Salim, a 34-year-old Egyptian religious scholar, who became an influential figure to the Arabs in Guantánamo. Salim had lived in Egypt until the age of 22, where, like thousands of other young men, he was arrested several times but never charged, and after living in Saudi Arabia he moved to Pakistan, where he was distributing humanitarian aid to Afghanistan for the International Islamic Relief Organization (IIRO) at the time of his capture.[15]

The other teachers arrested with Fethi Boucetta were Mohammed Abdallah, a 57-year-old Somalian (and the father-in-law of Mohammed

Sulaymon Barre, the moneychanger described in the previous chapter), and Menhal al-Henali, a 38-year-old Syrian (released in November 2003). Boucetta described how they used to travel to work together in a bus that was provided for the teachers. Abdallah, who was still in Guantánamo at the time of writing, refuted an allegation that he was "arrested in a raid on suspected al-Qaeda residences and support facilities connected to the Afghan Support Committee." He pointed out that he had lived in Peshawar under UN refugee status since 1993, had never worked for the ASC, and had spent the two years prior to his capture teaching orphans in the Red Crescent school. He said that he rented a house where he lived with one of his daughters and her family, and denied having anything to do with any kind of terrorist organization. "If there is anybody here that should be called a terrorist," he said, "it should be the people that came to my house that took me at two o'clock in the morning in front of my children and grandchildren. The women were crying and the children were terrorized, crying and screaming." Called as a witness in his tribunal, Boucetta described him as "basically a family man [who] just goes from home to work and does not really associate with people, period. Very rarely do you see him with other people."[16]

As well as rounding up employees of the RIHS and the IIRO, the Americans also seized a Sudanese hospital administrator for another large Saudi charity, the World Assembly of Muslim Youth (WAMY), which they also regarded with deep suspicion, even though it has never appeared on a terrorism watchlist, and was one of the favored projects of the late Saudi King Fahd bin Abdul Aziz. Forty-three-year-old Adel Hamad (cleared for release in 2007) had been working for WAMY since 1999 and had been working for humanitarian organizations in Afghanistan and Pakistan for 17 years. He was arrested at his home on July 18, 2002 after returning from his annual vacation in Sudan with his family, and his description of his arrest reveals how indiscriminate the Americans were becoming after months of rounding up every Arab they found:

> I was arrested in my house at 1.30 at night when I woke up and found myself in front of policemen from the Pakistani Intelligence pointing their weapons in my face like I was in a dream or a disturbing nightmare. They were screaming at me, "don't move!" So I told them, "what is it, what do you want from me?" And with them was a tall man who did not look

Pakistani which I think he was American. So they handcuffed me and they told me, "where are your papers?" ... So the tall man checked my passport and he told me that I came back early from my trip. I told him yes. He spoke in poor Arabic. He saw a legal official Pakistani permit by the date that was in my passport which had a legal official authorization posted for two years ... So the guard hesitated at the end and asked the tall man, "do we take him?" And the man said, "yes, take him." So they took me and detained me in jail in Pakistan for six months and ten days. Later I was moved to Bagram and then to Cuba.

In his tribunal, Hamad poured scorn on the US authorities' allegation that WAMY "supports terrorist ideals and causes," pointing out that the organization provided food, medicine, clothes and education for Afghan refugees, and was responsible for digging wells and building schools, orphanages, clinics and hospitals. After condemning al-Qaeda, saying, "I hate them and I pray to God not to let people among the Muslims carry [out] their ideas," he told his tribunal, "If I was a member in al-Qaeda or if I had an association with them I would've not traveled in June 2002 to Sudan with my family on an annual vacation and after the vacation ended I voluntarily returned to Pakistan. If I was a criminal, with association to those criminals, why would I return to Pakistan knowing that Pakistani intelligence was arresting al-Qaeda members?"[17]

What makes Hamad's case all the more extraordinary is that, although he has finally been cleared for release, one of the members of his tribunal pressed for his release in 2004. The journalist Farah Stockman, who examined the documents relating to his tribunal, noted that an army major issued a dissenting opinion, in which, having taken into account the fact that WAMY does not appear on the State Department's list of terrorist organizations, he argued, "even assuming all the allegations ... are accurate, the detainee does not meet the definition of enemy combatant," adding, "These NGOs presumably have numerous employees and volunteer workers who have been working in legitimate humanitarian roles. The mere fact that some elements of these NGOs provide support to 'terrorist ideals and causes' is insufficient to declare one of the employees an enemy combatant." Stockman noted, however, that the major was overruled by his colleagues, one of whom—in a single line that effectively discredits the whole tribunal process—wrote that the case "passed the 'low evidentiary hurdle' set up by the rules of the hearings."[18]

Mammar Ameur, a 44-year-old Algerian (also cleared for release in 2007), who had been living in Pakistan since 1990, and had been a registered UN refugee since 1996, was captured at the same time as Adel Hamad; he and his wife and their four children lived in an apartment downstairs, and Hamad and his family lived upstairs. Specifically refuting an allegation that his house was "a suspected al-Qaeda house," he pointed out that it was a small, two-roomed apartment near an airport used by the military, in an area that was "full of police stations," and indicated that this was not an ideal location for al-Qaeda to operate in with any degree of safety. The allegations against Ameur were at least as weak as those against Hamad. Accused of being a member of the Armed Islamic Group (GIA), he said that he left Algeria before it was founded, serving as a mujahideen fighter against the Communist regime in Afghanistan in 1990–92, and stressed, "I don't believe in this ideology because it's against my religion. These people are criminals, like criminals everywhere." Unable to come up with any other allegations, the US authorities attempted to implicate him in the purported terrorist activities of the IIRO, because he knew someone who had been involved in the organization, and with WAMY, because of his neighbor. Cutting to the heart of this entire folly, Ameur described what he was told by one of the Pakistanis who arrested him: "I was told by Pakistan intelligence when they captured us that we were innocent ... but we have to do something for the Americans. We will have to give you as a gift to protect Pakistan." He added, however, "Americans themselves have detained me here for nothing; I thought it was a Pakistani mistake, but it was the Americans. They have fabricated allegations as reasons to keep me here."[19]

Another prisoner who has been held, in part, because of his associations with charitable organizations is Mustafa Hamlili, a 42-year-old Algerian who was captured at his home, in a village near Peshawar, on May 25, 2002. Hamlili's story is rather more complicated than that of the men described above, because one of his sons, Adil al-Jazeeri, who is also held in Guantánamo, is regarded as an al-Qaeda operative (see Chapter 16). Although there may be classified evidence which purportedly connects Hamlili to his son, no clues were forthcoming in his tribunal. Instead, the former university professor, who fought the Russians in Afghanistan, ran through his history in a dignified and eloquent manner, declaring his innocence, and explaining, "For the last 15 years, I have not [had] any problems with anyone in my village. Anyone in my village can verify that. I am 45 and I am not going to do anything foolish. If I were going to do these things, I would have done them when I was younger. I am a Muslim. Islam is against all terrorism, violence and problems between people." According to the timeline of events described by Hamlili, he traveled to Pakistan from Saudi Arabia in 1987 and took up a job with the IIRO, working in the Orphans' Department and looking after a school until it closed in 1990. He then supported himself and his family by working as a welder and a honey seller for the next ten years, traveling to the Yemen from 1995 through 1997, when he took the opportunity to study because he didn't need a visa. From June to September 2001, he said that he worked for al-Wafa in Kandahar, digging wells and remodeling mosques, until the office closed, adding that he "never suspected al-Wafa was a terrorist organization because they had blankets, medicine, hospitals, and equipment to repair roads." He also told his tribunal that he began working with al-Wafa because "I was told there was a Saudi organization that was looking for employees. The Arabs in Afghanistan didn't want to work for al-Wafa because they considered it working for [the] Saudi government. I was proud to be working for a humanitarian organization." While this may not be the whole story—at the time of his arrest, the police said that he had been in charge of Islamic schools in eastern Afghanistan during the Taliban years, and in 2005 his wife said that the family moved to Afghanistan in 1997, and that her husband taught in an Islamic school in Jalalabad—it was still unclear what he had done to be designated as an "enemy combatant," and in his tribunal his Personal Representative spoke up on his behalf, saying, "The Pakistani police and the Americans confiscated his audiotapes and books but found nothing to connect him with any terrorist activities." Hamlili himself summed up his predicament when asked why he thought he was arrested. "From what I understand," he said, "the Pakistani intelligence was under pressure from the Americans to deliver al-Qaeda operatives and other terrorists. The Pakistani intelligence arrested people (some were poor and innocent) so they could show Americans they were working with them. The Pakistani officer that arrested me said I had nothing to worry about. I would be released

shortly since they were looking specifically for al-Qaeda members."
At the conclusion of his hearing, when asked, "Have you ever worked
for al-Qaeda or supported them in any way?" he seemed to reinforce
the case for his innocence by delivering the following stinging rebuke:
"No, I would rather starve than work for that organization. They try
to control you and do things to your religion."[20]

Hussain Mustafa, a 48-year-old Jordanian, who was born in
Palestine, was another innocent victim of house raids based on dubious
intelligence. Released in August 2004, he was interviewed by Clive
Stafford Smith, and explained that he had taken a Masters degree in
Islamic Law in Saudi Arabia, and had taught at the University of Galilee
until 1984, when he moved to Pakistan, where he lived with his family
near the Afghan border, teaching refugees. He told Stafford Smith that
on the evening of May 25, 2002, after returning home with his son
Mohammed, the doorbell rang. "I asked Ibrahim, my youngest son
to answer the door," he said. "He came back scared, calling, 'Police,
Police!' He was crying. As soon as he came in the room, the Pakistani
police followed, armed and with their guns pointing at us ... I asked
the officer what he wanted and he said he needed Hussain. I said, 'I am
Hussain.'" He added that he had a refugee card from the UN, but that,
although the police looked at it, they took him and his son away.[21]

Three unfortunate Tajiks—21-year-old Muhibullo Umarov, 27-year-
old Abdughaffor Shirinov and 22-year-old Mazharuddin (all released
in April 2004)—were not even captured in a house raid, but were,
instead, seized from an improvised dormitory in the library of Karachi
University. In 2006, the journalist McKenzie Funk met Umarov by
chance while reporting from Tajikistan, when a farmer in the remote
Obihingou valley told him, "There's a man in the valley who has been
to America. Really. He was in a prison. They made a mistake." After
tracking Umarov down to his tiny, mud-walled home, Funk heard
how, during the civil war, when he was 14 years old, his father took
him and his two younger brothers to Pakistan and installed them in
madrassas for the duration of the war. Six years later, he returned
to his home village, diploma in hand, and began helping the family
with their harvest of apples, potatoes and walnuts, "but then America
bombed Afghanistan and the whole world went crazy." Sent back to
Pakistan to raise money to bring his brothers home, he found odd jobs
in the bazaar in Peshawar and on May 13, 2002, in search of a better

job, set off for Karachi, where his friend Abdughaffor Shirinov, who was working at the library, had a place for him to stay. Mazharuddin was also staying there, and at night the three men hung their T-shirts on the bookcases and slept on thin carpets on the floor. Six days after his arrival, in the wake of Pakistan's first suicide bombing, Pakistani intelligence agents raided the library, using the men's T-shirts to tie them up and blindfold their eyes, and took them away. Held for ten days by the Pakistanis, Umarov was moved to a secret prison—in what appeared to be a luggage factory—that was run by Americans, where he was questioned about al-Qaeda and was locked up for ten days in a concrete cubicle that was only a meter long and half a meter wide, and was "insufferably hot." "All my thoughts were about how my life was going to end," he told the journalist. He was then returned to his friends in the Pakistani jail, and the following day the three men were transported to Kandahar.[22]

Other Random Arrests

The other prisoners captured at this time were mostly seized in random arrests similar to those described in the previous chapter. Mohammed al-Amin, an 18-year-old Mauritanian (cleared for release in 2007), left his family and traveled to Saudi Arabia to study the Koran, with the intention of becoming a teacher. He then traveled to Pakistan to continue his studies, but was arrested in Peshawar in April 2002, and held for two months in a jail, where he was "subjected to beatings, held for prolonged periods in solitary confinement and denied adequate food," in an attempt to force him to confess that he was a Saudi Arabian national, and was then transferred to Bagram. Abbas al-Naely, a 33-year-old Iraqi (also scheduled for release in 2007), was captured in Balochistan (near the Afghan border) in April 2002. A refugee, he arrived in Afghanistan in 1994 and seems thereafter to have become something of a drifter. He was described by one of his compatriots in Guantánamo, Jawad Sadkhan, as a beggar with a hashish problem. Sadkhan said that when he came to his house begging for help, "I did not have anything to offer [him]. But when I looked at his overall look and his dirty clothing he had on, he looked so miserable. So I went to a friend of mine and asked him for money."[23]

Omar Deghayes, a 32-year-old British resident, was born in Libya but spent most of his life in the UK, where he was granted refugee status in 1987. His family escaped from Libya after his father, a prominent lawyer, was assassinated by Colonel Gaddafi, and twenty relatives and friends of the family were rounded up and imprisoned by the secret police. A devout Muslim, he studied law at Wolverhampton University, undertook prison visits and hoped to become a human rights lawyer, but in 2000 he became "curious about life under a strict Islamic regime" and set out to look for work abroad with a friend. After traveling to Malaysia and Pakistan, he ended up in Afghanistan, where he met and married an Afghan woman and had a son, even though he planned to return to Britain, because his application for citizenship was still pending. When the US bombing campaign began, he took his family to Pakistan, hoping to bring them back to Britain, but was arrested in Lahore in April 2002 by the Pakistani police, who subsequently sold him to the Americans for $5,000. Like al-Amin, he was treated brutally in Pakistani custody, where he was told that he was being held at the request of the US authorities: he "underwent systematic beatings," was "kept in a dimly lit room full of glass boxes with 'very large snakes' and threatened with being left in the room after the snakes had been released," and was "submerged under water until he believed he would drown."[24]

Of the thirty prisoners arrested in the months following the capture of Abu Zubaydah, only a handful had even the most tangential connection to the "War on Terror." The alleged terrorist activities of Aziz Abdul Naji, a 26-year-old Algerian ironsmith, concerned his involvement with Lashkar-e-Tayyiba (LeT). He admitted traveling to Pakistan with the intention of fighting in Kashmir, and attending a LeT training camp, but pointed out that he lost a leg when he stepped on a mine while trying to enter Kashmir with about forty other volunteers, and never actually got to fight; he also insisted that LeT was a large group, and that he was unaware that it was affiliated with al-Qaeda, as the Americans alleged. Given this information, it's probable that the Americans took an interest in him because of the intelligence that they thought he might be able to provide them with about LeT's operations in Kashmir.[25]

Twenty-two-year-old Jamal Kiyemba, who was born in Uganda, had been a British resident since the age of 14, when he was granted indefinite leave to remain in the UK following the death of his father, but he had never claimed British citizenship, and on his release (in February 2006), he was sent to Uganda and prohibited from setting foot in the UK again. He told Clive Stafford Smith, "I may not be British according to some bit of paper but in reality I am a Brit and always will be. My doctor, my local mosque, my teens, my education, employment, friends, taxes, home and above all else my family—it is all in Britain." He was arrested in March 2002 in Pakistan, where he went to study Arabic and the Koran because it was "very cheap," without ever having set foot in Afghanistan, although he admitted that he was taught how to use a Kalashnikov by a Pakistani he met, and that he "left England with the intention of finding a way to fight jihad" in Afghanistan, "to defend the Muslims who were being killed." After his arrest, he was held for two months, beaten by Pakistani intelligence officers, threatened with torture and then transferred to Bagram.[26]

14
Bagram

From Kandahar to Bagram

Bagram airbase, a gloomy Soviet relic 25 miles north of Kabul, was taken by Northern Alliance forces, with the help of US Special Forces, in late October 2001. By January 2002, when it began to be used as a prison for a handful of supposedly significant individuals, it was also home to around five hundred US soldiers, augmented by other coalition forces; by late March, when the prison operations at Kandahar airport were scaled back significantly, it became the main US prison in Afghanistan, which it remains to this day. Chris Mackey arrived at Bagram in May, marveling at the cooler temperature and the improved facilities, but he described the prison, which was housed in a disused aircraft machine shop, fitted out with five large wire pens and six plywood isolation cells, and with rusted metal sheets where the windows had once been, as "a dungeon."[1]

Before leaving Kandahar, Mackey watched the last scenes play out in the extraordinary saga of one of the prisoners held at Bagram in early 2002. Ayman Batarfi, the Yemeni doctor captured in Tora Bora, reprised much of what he revealed at Kandahar during his Guantánamo tribunal. A doctor during the mujahideen resistance to the Soviet occupation, he returned to Afghanistan in 2001, hoping to provide medical assistance to Chechen refugees, but instead found work with al-Wafa, renovating a hospital in Kabul, and traveling to Karachi to purchase medicine and equipment. Asked about al-Wafa's purported connection to al-Qaeda and the Taliban, he said that "the al-Wafa office worked well with the Taliban office, especially with the Ministry of Health and Ministry of Education because they built the hospital, the schools and the mosque there," but insisted, as had Mustafa Hamlili, that there was no relationship between al-Wafa and Osama bin Laden, and that bin Laden's people "believed al-Wafa was spying for Saudi Arabia, because some friends in Saudi Arabia support them financially." After the US-led invasion began, he made his way to Karachi, but returned almost immediately to Afghanistan, after al-Wafa's representative in Karachi was taken to Jordan "on a special flight," the organization's financier returned to the UAE, and he was told that his name was "on the wanted list" because he was purchasing medicine for al-Wafa. He then worked in a hospital in Jalalabad, but fled to the mountains when the city "collapsed within a half of an hour" and the Afghan doctors told him, "Arabs here have a very bad history; if they find you they will kill you. It would be best for you to go back to Pakistan." Hoping to rescue $11,000 in surgical equipment and medicine for the hospital—purchased when the Taliban agreed to open a new orthopedic department—he wrote to "the head of the mountains" for assistance, not knowing that it was bin Laden. After the tribunal got over its surprise, he explained that bin Laden was unable to help, and told him that "he didn't have any route to leave the mountains and he was stuck there himself," adding, "According to my knowledge he stays a maximum of three days in one location ... He was running from the bombing and he was trying to go to Pakistan."[2]

Whether or not this story was true, its effect on his tribunal, whose members were drawn in by his eloquence and the drama of his narrative, was echoed during his detention in Bagram, where he was recommended for release, and was given VIP status, including a private bedroom. When he was delivered to Kandahar, he was escorted by a 20-year-old, "wearing cool-kid skater clothes," who horsed around with him as though they were "a couple of junior high school chums." Unconvinced by this scenario, Mackey assigned his most subtle interrogator to Batarfi, who, over the following weeks, developed a rapport with the doctor, engaging him in educated conversation, bringing him gifts, playing chess with him, and slowly attempting to find out if there was more to his procurement of medicines than he had previously revealed. In response, Batarfi provided useful information on people he had met in Afghanistan, poured out more of his life story than before, and requested a second meeting with representatives of the CIA, who, he said, had approached him in Bagram and had offered him an opportunity to work as a spy. Unfortunately for Mackey and his interrogator, it was when a woman from the CIA turned up to talk to Batarfi that their weeks of careful work were undone. As Mackey described it, she launched into a sudden tirade, declaring that the agency knew that al-Wafa and al-Qaeda were "running an unconventional weapons program out of hospitals in Kandahar and Kabul," and alluding to suspicions that "there might be plans to put these substances to use." In response, Batarfi clammed up, the bond was broken, and he was soon sent to Guantánamo, where the truth of these allegations remains as opaque as it does in the cases of so many other prisoners.

As Kandahar wound down, Mackey was left with a dwindling prisoner population. One of the last things he saw was the return of "Crazy Bob"—the schizophrenic Abdul Razeq—who taxed the interrogators at Guantánamo to such an extent that they sent him back after just a few months. Mackey noted that he arrived "strapped down in the centre of the plane like Hannibal Lecter." The first prisoner to be released from Guantánamo, he was taken to a maximum security cell in a hospital, where the journalist Sami Yousafzai interviewed him. The ethnic Uzbek, a native of Mazar-e-Sharif, explained that he was captured a week after Mazar fell to the Northern Alliance. "The Americans stopped me near the city and asked me where I was from," he said. "I told them, 'I am an Afghan.' They didn't believe me. They said, 'No, you are a foreigner.' And they took me. They took me to America to treat my mental problems. I was taken to a very good hotel [Kandahar] and after a month they shifted me to a place where they kept Chechens and Pakistanis [Camp X-Ray]. I was the only Afghan. Afterwards, they flew me back to Afghanistan." Razeq had no complaints about his brief stay in Guantánamo, although he didn't know why he was persistently interrogated about the whereabouts of Mullah Omar and Osama bin Laden, but Yousafzai wondered why the US authorities took so long to diagnose his schizophrenia.[3]

Torture and Abuse

Some of the prisoners captured in Pakistan arrived in Bagram during Mackey's three-month tenure. He explained that the interrogators unearthed information about the passport-forging business in the cities, which did a roaring trade with Arabs who had either lost their passports or had been betrayed by their Afghan handlers, who took them for safe-keeping and then sold them on the black market. He also remained critical of the CIA, noting that they persisted in dropping off prisoners without providing any information, and snatching others when the interrogators were making a breakthrough, and the extent to which he and his team were kept in the dark by the CIA was revealed when 28 prisoners arrived from Pakistan in June 2002. Mackey believed that many of them were captured with Abu Zubaydah, whereas they were, for the most part, the charity workers rounded up in the months following Zubaydah's arrest. He also admitted that the pressure on interrogators increased during this time, and, while maintaining that he stuck to his principles—in particular that physical coercion was "illegal and ineffective," and that "you can't trust information gained by torture because prisoners will say anything to stop the pain"—he admitted that some of his colleagues began using painful stress positions, and that Special Forces introduced sleep deprivation, explaining to him that "hard-core prisoners were unlikely to start cracking until about 14 hours into an interrogation." Pressured to keep up with these methods, he introduced a new technique, which involved sessions that lasted as long as the interrogator could stay awake. Inspired by a member of his team, who said of the prisoners, "You've got to scare them, get right up in their face and *monster* them," they called it "monstering."[4]

While Bagram was a harsh place throughout Mackey's time there, the brutality that was directed towards the prisoners increased noticeably after he and his team were relieved of duty and 14 soldiers from the 525th Military Intelligence Brigade at Fort Bragg took over, led by Lieutenant Carolyn Wood, and were soon joined by six Arabic-speaking reservists from the Utah National Guard. Typically, the new recruits were unprepared for what awaited them. Some were counter-intelligence specialists with no background in interrogation, and only two had interrogated real prisoners before. They were also given few guidelines about how to behave. Speaking to the army's criminal investigation unit in 2004, one of the reservists said that President Bush's announcement, in February 2002, that the Geneva Conventions did not apply to al-Qaeda and that Taliban fighters did not have rights as prisoners of war, led the interrogators to believe that they "could deviate slightly from the rules." "There was the Geneva Conventions for enemy prisoners of war, but nothing for terrorists," he added, explaining that senior intelligence officers told them that the prisoners "were to be considered terrorists until proved otherwise."

Given carte blanche to treat the prisoners as they saw fit, and under persistent pressure to come up with intelligence, Wood's team adopted stress positions as a standard procedure, and pushed the policy of sleep deprivation further than Mackey had. Whereas "monstering" had never exceeded 24 hours, one former interrogator said that they "decided on 32 to 36 hours as the optimal time to keep prisoners awake and eliminated the practice of staying up themselves." It also became standard policy that new prisoners were hooded, shackled and kept in isolation for the first 24 hours of their imprisonment, and sometimes for the first three days. Writing about the army's report, the journalist Tim Golden noted that prisoners who were considered important or uncooperative were handcuffed and chained to the ceilings and doors of their cells, sometimes for several days. Although the Red Cross complained, the army report noted that senior officers toured the facility and saw it in operation, but never prohibited its use. In addition, Bagram became a place of even greater random brutality. Golden described how violence was sometimes used to extract information, or as punishment for rule-breaking, but that on other occasions "the torment seems to have been driven by little more than boredom or cruelty, or both." In statements to army investigators, soldiers mentioned a prisoner who was "forced to roll back and forth on the floor of a cell, kissing the boots of his two interrogators as he went," and another who was "made to pick plastic bottle caps out of a drum mixed with excrement and water as part of a strategy to soften him up for questioning."[5]

These and other violent and humiliating techniques—including forced nudity, sexual humiliation, sexual assaults, and the use of dogs and electric shocks—were described by numerous prisoners. Omar Deghayes, Richard Belmar, Jamal Kiyemba and Mohammed al-Amin were hung by their wrists for prolonged periods. Belmar explained that it happened to him when he was punished for breaking the prohibition on talking (which had migrated from Kandahar), al-Amin was tied by his hands to the ceiling "for days on end," and "whenever he lost consciousness a guard would forcefully pull him up to wake him," and Jamal Kiyemba recalled a 48-hour period, when he was "hung on the door for two hours and then allowed to sit for half an hour but never allowed to sleep," and was then taken for interrogation for two hours at a time, adding, "I had to kneel on the cold concrete throughout the interrogations with my cuffed hands above my head." He was also interviewed by MI5 officers, who showed him photos of supposed terrorists in the UK and told him they would only be able to help him if he helped them, but he didn't know any of them. He recognized Abu Hamza and Abu Qatada, but had only ever seen them on TV.[6]

Omar Deghayes compared Bagram to "Nazi camps that I saw in films." He said that beating and torture were "considered normal," and that he was subjected to forced nudity and food deprivation, and was "locked in a box with very little air for prolonged periods." He also said that the "guards forced petrol and benzene up the anuses of prisoners," which "would burn horribly." Somewhere between Bagram and Guantánamo, most of the allegations arose that have plagued him ever since—that he "went to Bosnia to join the mujahideen" (he actually went with a Canadian charity), that he trained at Khaldan in 1999, that he stayed at the guest house of a senior al-Qaeda leader, and that he "had a good relationship with Osama bin Laden"—although there was one more unpleasant surprise that was reserved especially for Guantánamo (as discussed in the following chapter). Mohammed al-Amin was sexually abused, and threatened with being sent to Egypt to face further torture. After two months, he said, "They wanted me to say I had come to join the jihad. Eventually I told them what they wanted to hear and the torture stopped." What they wanted to hear eventually surfaced in Guantánamo, where it was alleged that he traveled to Afghanistan to fight the Americans, having decided to "go on jihad after being angered over the US air attacks in Afghanistan," and that he trained with Lashkar-e-Tayyiba.[7]

Hussain Mustafa, the Jordanian teacher, told Clive Stafford Smith that he was repeatedly threatened that his wife would be brought to Bagram. "I felt a true anger," he said. "I was torn on the inside because of what they said. This was a terrible threat." He also said that prisoners were repeatedly threatened "with ghastly and immoral acts like rape," and explained that he thought that the worst moment in his life took place in Bagram, when, blindfolded and handcuffed, and with his ears plugged and his mouth covered, he was forced to bend down, while a soldier "forcibly rammed a stick up my rectum." Sami al-Hajj, the al-Jazeera cameraman, described the 16 days he spent in Bagram as "the worst in my life," and said that he was "severely physically tortured and had dogs set upon him." He was then transferred to Kandahar, where he was "subjected to sexual abuse by US soldiers, including being threatened with rape," and was "forced into stress positions, being forced to kneel for long periods on concrete floors." He added that he was beaten regularly by the guards, had all the hairs on his beard plucked out one by one, and was not allowed to wash for a hundred days and was covered with lice.[8]

Of the three prisoners captured by bounty hunters, Brahim Benchekroun, the Moroccan, described harassment that was familiar from Kandahar: "The soldiers came out of nowhere, sometimes several times in the same night, screaming bloody murder, throwing everything around on the pretext that there was a search, and rarely forgetting to throw the Koran on the ground, if they didn't tear it up." He also said that, when the Red Cross visited, "The ones who were the most bashed up were hidden in a storage room over the interrogation chamber." Karama Khamisan, the Yemeni drug mule, had an even tougher time. Kicked and beaten while hooded, stripped naked and beaten with batons, he was then transferred to Kandahar, where he was "threatened with electric shocks," and where, in a sign that Abu Ghraib-style abuse was already being practiced, "he and a group of other detainees were stripped and piled on top of each other naked, whilst the US officials, in full military uniform, laughed at them and took photographs of the pile of naked bodies."[9]

Of those captured in the raids that netted Riyadh the Facilitator, the Kuwaiti Adel al-Zamel said, "While walking to the place of interrogation, the guards would continuously hit me on my head with sticks, and every time I denied their accusations during interrogations [of being tied to al-Qaeda] the guards would hit me even more, hold me high up and then fling me to the floor." He added that he was hooded and "stripped naked in front of women officers while they clicked photos, laughing all the time," was intimidated by interrogators placing a gun on the table during interrogations, and was "suspend[ed] with one hand tied to the ceiling during interrogations, making it almost impossible to either sit or stand straight." Richard Belmar said that on the plane to Bagram he received a huge blow to the back of his head from a rifle butt, which gave him headaches "for a long, long time," and that in Bagram, where he spent more than six months and was interrogated repeatedly, he was sexually taunted by a woman interrogator, who fondled his genitals. "I told her she was ugly, cheap and I spat in her face," he said. "There were two guys in the room and I was shackled. They got me on the floor and started kicking me up, in the back, in the stomach, they gave me a real beating." In another interrogation, a pistol was forced into his mouth: "It tasted cold, bitter. I thought, 'Yeah, this is getting serious, there's a good chance they will pull the trigger.'" Eventually, he said, he gave the interrogators the confession they wanted, even though it was all lies. He told them he had listened to Osama bin Laden making a speech, but pointed out after his release, "How could I have done that? I didn't know a word of Arabic," and added that the interrogators "tried to make me confess to being at a training camp in 1998—when I never left Britain, and wasn't even a Muslim."[10]

Afghans Sent to Bagram

In some cases—especially with the many Afghans rounded up at this time—the established failings of the screening and interrogation processes were compounded by the activities of the Special Forces units. Hunting remnants of al-Qaeda and the Taliban in various southern and eastern provinces—particularly Paktia, Paktika and Uruzgan—they were swiftly engaged in a low-level insurgency conducted by the Taliban and hostile locals, and were also prey to the vagaries and self-interest of the dubious warlords and tribal leaders with whom they had cut deals to win their proxy war. Astutely grasping the extent of the confusion, Chris Mackey described how the interrogators were receiving the fallout from a largely invisible war: "Raids on compounds in the middle of the night. Transfers of prisoners from prisons in Pakistan you didn't even know existed. A steady stream of detainees from ... Afghan warlords pocketing a nice wad of cash for every prisoner they turned over." He singled out the Special Forces for particular criticism, noting how they, like their close colleagues in the CIA, delivered prisoners without any explanation of who they were, leaving the interrogators to conclude that they had no idea who they had captured. "They were bringing back a lot of fighters," he wrote, "but they were also bringing back a lot of farmers."

Between April and December 2002, at least fifty Afghans were sent to Guantánamo from Bagram. Mackey reported that the screening for Afghan prisoners was made more flexible in June, when the prison's commanders finally worked out how to release "worthless prisoners back to their farms and families." The process involved creating a new category of prisoner—"persons under US control"—who could be held for 14 days without being assigned a number that entered the system overseen by the overall commanders in Kuwait and the Pentagon, because, as noted in Chapter 9, once a prisoner was officially assigned a number, it was almost impossible for the interrogators to let them go.[11]

Despite this apparent improvement in the screening process, it actually remained as inept as ever, and at least three-quarters of the prisoners transferred to Guantánamo in this period were subsequently released. Some, like 70-year-old Haji Faiz Mohammed and 49-year-old Bismillah, were seized in raids by Special Forces in Uruzgan province. Mohammed, who thought that he was 105 years old, was seized by US forces in a clinic. Released in October 2002, he said, "I don't know why the Americans arrested me. I told them I was innocent. I'm just an old man." Bismillah (released in March 2003) was captured because he is hard of hearing. "At 2 am Americans came to our house and asked me to show them where the Taliban are," he said. "Since I am deaf, I couldn't understand what they said so they arrested me. It took them more than a year to realize I am innocent." Forty-five-year-old Khudaidad (released in February 2006) was captured in a night-time raid by Afghan soldiers in Uruzgan in April 2002. It was alleged that his compound was used by Mullah Berader, that he was a Taliban official and that he was supposed to "assume a prominent leadership role in Kandahar," but he was actually just a poor farmer.[12]

Others were betrayed by rivals. Thirty-one-year-old Haji Mohammed Akitar, a businessman who worked in the logging business after returning from Pakistan, where he lived with his family as a refugee during the Soviet occupation, was working for the Karzai government in Jalalabad, and had just returned to visit his family when he was arrested by US and Afghan forces after a rocket attack on a US base in Asadabad in September 2002. He said that he was betrayed by a long-standing enemy, who was with the Americans when he was arrested, as was his enemy's son-in-law, who was the commander of a local Afghan military division. In his tribunal, he explained that he was never told why he was arrested, and had only been interrogated "two or three times" in Guantánamo. The 25-year-old laborer Mohammed Nasim, who was accused of taking part in a rocket attack on Kandahar airport in August 2002, and who scoffed at an allegation that he was the governor of Zabul province under the Taliban, also said that he was betrayed, as part of the rivalry between two local commanders. Having agreed to work for one, he said that the other told him, "I will kill you and destroy your family," and arranged for his capture. Two brothers from Khost—39-year-old Niaz Wali, a cobbler, and 24-year-old Badshah Wali, a taxi driver—were "targeted for arrest by local people, who were their enemies from another Pashtun tribe." On their release in March 2003, they were "too scared to talk about their experiences."[13]

Two other taxi drivers, 19-year-old Said Abassin (released in March 2003) and 24-year-old Wazir Mohammed (released in March 2004), were captured by Afghan soldiers in April 2002. Abassin, an admirer of Western culture, who had been beaten up by the Taliban for playing music in his taxi, was traveling from Khost to Kabul when a loud explosion rocked the US garrison in Gardez. Stopped at a checkpoint and taken to the local police station with his passenger, 33-year-old car dealer Alif Khan (also released in March 2003), he and Khan were accused of being members of al-Qaeda, as was Mohammed, a friend of Abassin, who was captured after asking what had happened to his friend. According to Ashwin Raman, the governor called US Special Forces to take the men away without bothering to check the facts, and after their release they said that they were sold for bounty payments of several thousand dollars each. "My life is ruined," Abassin said. "Why? For which crime? I'd heard that in America or Europe when they arrest someone they have proof. I saw none of that. I was just driving. Arrested and taken to prison. My hands were tied behind my back. They put a sack over my head and took me away in a helicopter." Held in Bagram for 40 days, he described a regime of "sleep deprivation, 24-hour lighting and guards banging on cells and shouting to keep detainees awake." He said that he was not hit, but was forced to stand, sit and kneel for prolonged periods, and explained that "being forced to kneel for four hours a day felt worse than being beaten."[14]

Alif Khan, who was held in Bagram and Kandahar, described similar treatment, and said that the Americans made him kneel for an hour with his hands above his head. "One of them was standing in front of me, the other was pointing the Kalashnikov," he explained. "If we moved our face to the side they would make us stay for a further two hours. If we moved just slightly it would increase to three hours. We would become unconscious." What made his case more notable, however, was that he was mistakenly thought to be a cousin of the renegade warlord Pacha Khan Zadran, whose baleful influence extended to other prisoners. Qadir Khandan, a 32-year-old pharmacist (released in October 2006), was a victim of Zadran and his nephew, Jan Baz Khan, who lied about him to the Americans to get him arrested. Khandan insisted that he was "enemy number one of Jan Baz and Pacha Khan," and got into trouble with them because he realized, when they were working with the Americans, that they were using them for their own ends. Arrested at his home in September 2002 and accused of running a safe house for a bomb-making cell, Khandan pointed out that he was working for the Karzai government in the National Security Office in Khost, and that, as a pharmacist, bombs were "truly against my ideology." He also explained that he was badly abused by American soldiers in a prison in Khost. "They put tight round glasses around my eyes, had my ears shut with plugs and I was covered with a bag," he said, adding, "I was ordered to stand up 24 hours for 20 days in a row. I had blood coming out of my body and my nose for days because I was tortured so much." Describing what appear to be otherwise unreported murders in US custody, he also said, "I saw four people die right in front of me."[15]

Also captured at this time (and subsequently released) was a family of businessmen from Birmel, in Paktika province, who were caught up in what the Americans described as "a sweep of the Birmel town bazaar," which was as random as it sounds. Twenty-seven-year-old Abdul Salaam, his 50-year-old brother Haji Osman Khan and his 19-year-old cousin Noor Aslam ran a hawalla (a money exchange/forwarding business) with branches in Pakistan and the UAE. Salaam was arrested at his shop by US and Afghan soldiers, but he insisted that he was an honest businessman and had never received money on behalf of the Taliban or al-Qaeda; he explained that the money they received at the hawalla was from families outside the country who were supporting their families in Afghanistan. Twenty-eight-year-old

Qalander Shah (released in 2005 or 2006) was also captured in a house raid in Birmel, along with his uncle and a cousin. Accused of having a weapons cache and a false Pakistani ID card, he explained that the weapons were for protection and that he had the false ID because "the Taliban were running the government and we were in conflict with them." Two others who were picked up almost as randomly (and later released) were 25-year-old Naquibullah Shabeen and 23-year-old Mohammed Rasoul, brothers—and doctors—who returned from Pakistan to open a clinic, and were captured after a rocket attack on a US base in October 2002, because US forces mistakenly believed that someone entered their house after firing the rockets.[16]

One particularly bizarre story concerned two 40-year-olds, Haji Roohullah and Sabar Lal Melma. The commander of a long-standing anti-Taliban mujahideen group based in Kunar province, which was aligned with the Northern Alliance, Roohullah had fired the first salvo against the Taliban in Kunar after the US-led invasion, and was rewarded with an important position in the province's post-Taliban administration. Betrayed by a rival, who took advantage of the Americans' ignorance—and their unwillingness to investigate the backgrounds of those seized after tip-offs—he was captured by US forces in August 2002 (with Melma, his military aide, and eleven others) and taken to Bagram for questioning, where he was accused of being part of an Islamic extremist group and helping al-Qaeda fighters to escape from Tora Bora, even though he had numerous meetings with senior US officials and offered support for the Tora Bora campaign. Although the others were subsequently released, the Americans decided that Roohullah and Melma had sufficient intelligence value to be transferred to Guantánamo in August 2003, believing—despite overwhelming evidence to the contrary—that Roohullah "had strong links with Middle Eastern fighters in Afghanistan, particularly Saudi Arabians like Osama bin Laden." In his tribunal, Melma (who was cleared for release in 2007) pointed out the injustice of imprisoning him with members of the Taliban: "The only thing I want to tell you that is so ironic here is that I see a Talib and then I see myself here too, I am in the same spot as a Talib. I see those people on an everyday basis, they are cursing at me ... They say, 'See, you got what you deserved, you are here, too.'"[17]

Although the stories above demonstrate typical incompetence, the Americans claimed that two significant Taliban members—30-year-old Abdul Zahir and 34-year-old Rahmatullah Sangaryar—were captured in this period, although even these stories were not straight-forward. Zahir, who was captured in July 2002, was accused of being a translator and money courier for al-Qaeda, and of taking part in a grenade attack on a vehicle carrying foreign journalists in Zormat in March 2002. He was put forward for trial by Military Commission in January 2006, although he stated that he did not take part in the grenade attack. Sangaryar's story was more complicated. A former Taliban commander, who fought with them in an attempt to bring peace to his country, he said that he and his tribe turned against them before the US-led invasion, because they became too enamored of fighting for its own sake, and because they dug up the corpse of a prominent tribal leader and deposited it in the street as an affront to his tribe. When Gul Agha Sherzai took over Kandahar, Sangaryar and his men handed in their weapons, and he returned to his village. He was captured and turned over to the Americans by Jan Mohammed, the new governor of Uruzgan province, after Mohammed stopped the car of Ismatullah, a 25-year-old embroiderer, who admitted that he had just delivered a letter to Sangaryar from Abdul Razaq, the former Taliban minister of commerce. Ismatullah explained that he was going to Uruzgan to sell his car, and Razaq said that he would pay his petrol if he delivered the letter. Unable to read, he asked his 23-year-old cousin, Nasrullah, to read it, to check that there "wasn't any danger in it," and Nasrullah, who was also captured in the car, said that the letter asked Sangaryar to go to Quetta, but did not mention fighting, even though the Americans alleged that Razaq specifically asked Sangaryar to report to Quetta "to fight and avoid capture by the Americans." According to Sangaryar, the letter was a trap, designed to punish him for turning his back on the Taliban and to discredit him by making it appear that he was still involved with them; if this was the case then it was spectacularly successful, as all three men were still in Guantánamo at the time of writing.[18]

Other Foreigners Captured in Afghanistan

Of the twenty foreigners transferred to Bagram in this period, several were captured many months previously and were first held in Afghan custody. Mushtaq Ali Patel, a 39-year-old Frenchman, who was born in

India, explained after his release in March 2005 that, although his wife and child were living in France, he had been working in Iran, where he taught at an Islamic school and traded in clothes and jewelry. After setting out for Pakistan, via Afghanistan, in October 2001, he was abducted, in the countryside near Herat, by three Afghans, including a policeman, who stole his passport and his money; they beat him with their fists and with electric cables, and took him to a police station in Ghazni, where he was forced to say that he was a Saudi, born in Medina, and that his name was Haji Mohammed. After several months, he was taken to Kabul to "some kind of a house that was like a prison," where he was sold to the Americans for $5,000. He said that the Americans threatened him with death "and to cause problems to my family," and then transferred him to Bagram, where they had "very hard attitudes," and Kandahar, where he was "badly mistreated, interrogated in bad ways."[19]

Zakirjan Asam, a 27-year-old from Saratov Oblast, part of the Russian Federation bordering Kazakhstan, was one of the three prisoners released in Albania in November 2006 because the US authorities feared for their safety if they were returned to their home countries, although he was actually cleared for release in 2004. A refugee, he was deported from Kazakhstan to Afghanistan in spring 2001, and was betrayed, after the US-led invasion began, by Afghan villagers anxious to avail themselves of the reward money offered by the Americans for vulnerable individuals who could be passed off as members of al-Qaeda or the Taliban. He explained that the inhabitants of two villages in Kunduz province negotiated between themselves and asked him to pay them a $3,000 bribe or they would hand him over to the Americans. He said that "they knew they could sell me to the Americans for $5,000," and that they explained to him that "because I am a Muslim they lowered the price for me." Abdel Hamid al-Ghizzawi, a 39-year-old Libyan, who had been living in Afghanistan since the Russians left, had a similar experience. Married to an Afghan, and with a six-month-old daughter, he ran a shop in Jalalabad that sold bread and honey. When the US-led invasion began, he took his wife and daughter to his wife's parents' home in the country, to escape the bombing raids, but was picked out by some of the locals, who, seduced by American offers of free money for life, abducted him and sold him to the Northern Alliance, who, in turn, sold him to the Americans.[20]

Ibrahim Zeidan, a 25-year-old Jordanian, was the victim of even more ambitious kidnappers. After traveling to Afghanistan in 2000 to visit his brother, who was teaching in Khost, he stayed for about a year and a half until the US-led invasion, when he was captured by a group of Afghans, who imprisoned him, tortured him and demanded a ransom for his release from his family. According to Clive Stafford Smith, who visited his family in Jordan, he was working in Kabul for a Saudi charity at the time of his capture, and was kidnapped before the war even reached the city. The gang who abducted him "apparently hoped for a far larger return than that offered by the US," because he was working for "a well-heeled Saudi charity," and rang his family demanding a ransom of $150,000, telling them that "his organs would be removed one by one" if they didn't pay. Although the family ran an appeal in a Jordanian newspaper and raised several thousand dollars, there was no way that they could raise the money demanded by the gang. After eight months, however, Zeidan managed to escape from his prison, although he was then captured in Jalalabad by government officials who handed him over to the Americans.[21]

Two other prisoners were freed from a Taliban jail, only to be seized by the Americans. Timur Ishmuradov, a 26-year-old from Tyumen Oblast (part of the Russian Federation, in the Urals), was imprisoned by the Taliban in summer 2001. Released in March 2004, he was particularly incensed at the treatment he received at the hands of the Americans. "I have traces of their tortures on my body [and] scars on my back after being dragged on the ground," he said. "They would beat me during interrogations and also while taking me from one place to another." Arkan al-Karim, a 25-year-old Iraqi, underwent a particularly strange journey. After deserting the Iraqi Army in 1994, he traveled to Iran, where he found work in a shoe factory, but was arrested when the government began clamping down on illegal workers. Hiding his Iraqi identity, he was deported to Afghanistan, where he approached the Taliban for help in returning to Iran, but was told, "You need to be with us a few months, and then you will get salary, some money, and go outside Afghanistan." While serving with the Taliban, he met Abdul Rahim al-Ginco (see Chapter 10) in a guest house in Kabul, and explained that, when al-Ginco was imprisoned by the Taliban as a spy, and was tortured to admit who had helped him, "he said a lot of names, and one of them was me. He said that I was spying with him for the United States. This is how they caught [me] in Kabul." Imprisoned in Kandahar in January 2000, he explained that, when the Taliban left and representatives of the new government came to the prison, he was moved to Kabul, where he stayed for another three months until the Americans found him. Conceding that it may have been a mistake to tell them that he knew some Arabs in Afghanistan and that "I have some information and if you want to know it, you will take me from this prison," he was taken to Bagram and Kandahar before being transferred to Guantánamo.[22]

While the stories above demonstrate the continuing unreliability of the screening process in Afghanistan, not everyone who was captured at this time was quite so divorced from military activity. Abdullah al-Qahtani, a 22-year-old Saudi (released in 2006), cheerfully admitted that he went to Afghanistan in September 2000 to take part in the jihad, which he described as "skirmishes with the Russians and allies such as Ahmed Shah Massoud." When the US-led invasion began, he and a number of other Arab fighters set up a base near Kabul but then negotiated a surrender with the Northern Alliance, and were surprised when they were handed over to the Americans. Although it's clear that al-Qahtani was nothing more than a typical foot soldier from the Gulf, his release was something of a surprise, considering how many other Saudis in Guantánamo were never involved in any kind of fighting.[23]

One dubious example of a "fighter" captured at this time was Omar Khadr, who was shot three times by US soldiers during a firefight near Khost on July 27, 2002, and is nearly blind in one eye as a result of his injuries. According to the US military, he killed a US soldier during the fight, and as a result, even though he was seriously injured, his interrogation began as soon as he was taken into custody. His case was later mentioned by a US official, who claimed that prisoners were so scared of abuse by US soldiers that they would talk without prompting: they "sometimes think we are going to cut out their livers," he said, citing Khadr as an example of a prisoner "singing like a bird." According to Khadr, the abuse was all too real. During his detention in Afghanistan, he "asked for pain medication for his wounds but was refused," was threatened with dogs while hooded during inter-rogations, and was "not allowed to use the bathroom and was forced to urinate on himself." Like many other prisoners, he was also hung from his wrists, and he explained that "his hands were tied above a door frame and he was forced to stand in this position for hours." His case is complicated for two reasons: first, because he was only 15 years old at the time of his capture, and should, therefore, have been treated as a juvenile, and second, because he is a member of the notorious Khadr family.[24]

Based in Canada after emigrating from Egypt in 1977, the family's patriarch, Ahmed Khadr, had fought with Osama bin Laden in Afghanistan in the 1980s and was reportedly a financier for al-Qaeda. In 1996, after bin Laden returned to Afghanistan from Sudan, he moved the family to Jalalabad, where they lived in a compound with bin Laden's family, and where he insisted that his sons—Abdullah, Abdurahman, Omar and Abdul Karim—undertook military training, even though they were only children. Despite the family's alleged status, however, they did not survive unscathed in the post-9/11 world. As well as losing Omar to the US military, the father was killed in a shoot-out with Pakistani forces in October 2003, when his youngest son Abdul Karim was paralyzed from the waist down; his eldest son Abdullah has been imprisoned in Canada since December 2005 at the request of the US authorities, who want him extradited on terrorism charges relating to Afghanistan, and Abdurahman was captured by Afghans in Kabul in November 2001, when he was 20 years old, and was then handed over to the Americans. Describing himself as the "black sheep" of the family, who saw no value in the radical beliefs of the rest of his family, Abdurahman agreed to work as a spy for the CIA in Kabul, and then in Guantánamo, but was told that, to protect his cover, he would have to be treated like all the other prisoners. He said that his imprisonment at Bagram—where he was stripped, photographed naked and subjected to an anal probe—was the start of "the longest and most painful ordeal of his life," and that he "had no idea what he was getting into." After ten days at Bagram, he was flown to Guantánamo, where, he said, he arrived "a broken man," and was then kept in isolation for a month before being moved to a cell near other prisoners. The plan, as he described it, was that "they could put me next to anyone that was stubborn and that wouldn't talk and I would talk him into it. Well, it's not that easy—lots of people won't talk to anyone because everybody in Cuba is scared of the person next to him. I couldn't do a lot for them." Unable to cope with his situation, he spent the rest of his time in Guantánamo in a "luxurious" private cell, and was then sent to Bosnia, where his mission was to infiltrate radical mosques and gather information on al-Qaeda's activities. When the CIA wanted to send him to Iraq, however, he decided that he couldn't take the pressure any more, and after resigning from the agency he returned to Canada, where his most salient comments concerned the prisoners in Guantánamo. He said that he told the CIA that the vast majority of the prisoners were innocent, and that it was "a huge mistake for the US military to offer large cash rewards for the capture of al-Qaeda suspects when they first arrived in Afghanistan." "There's 10 percent of them that should be kept there and 10 percent of them who might go back to being al-Qaeda if they had the chance," he explained. "But only 10 percent of the people there are really dangerous. The rest are people that don't have anything to do with it, don't even understand what they're doing there."[25]

A particularly distressing story is that of Fawaz Mahdi, a 21-year-old Yemeni who should never have been sent to Guantánamo at all, because, as the authorities have noted, he is "severely, psychiatrically ill," and has been seen over seventy times by psychiatrists since his arrival in June 2002. In his tribunal, he confirmed the precarious state of his mental health, explaining that he went to Afghanistan "because I was told only the jihad places had magic things inside ... I went to fight jihad as a last resort to fight the spell that was making me mentally ill," and also saying, "I have witnesses in Saudi Arabia and Yemen. I was told I have [a] magic disease." Although he admitted training at al-Farouq and being on the front lines, he said that he never fired his weapon, and in response to the most serious allegation against him, that he "signed an oath of loyalty to Osama bin Laden," he said, "I accused myself in front of the interrogators of many things to hasten my assumed execution rather than going to prison."[26]

Murders in Bagram

As Carolyn Wood and her team settled in at Bagram, they were joined, in late August, by a new military police unit—mostly reservists—who had received very little training, and who brought with them a new technique, the common peroneal strike, described by Tim Golden as "a potentially disabling blow to the side of the leg, just above the knee," which soon became widely applied. In the army report cited earlier in this chapter, the MPs claimed they were never told that it was not an accepted army technique, and most said they never heard one of their trainers in the US—a former police officer—telling a soldier "he would never use such strikes because they would 'tear up' a prisoner's legs."

In early December, the unfettered violence finally spilled over into homicide. The first victim was Mullah Habibullah, who was apparently the brother of a Taliban commander from Uruzgan. Stout and well-presented, he was described as "very confident" by the major in charge of the MPs. After kneeing a soldier in the groin during his anal probe, three guards took him to an isolation cell and shackled his wrists to the wire ceiling, and on the following two days, when he was still "uncooperative," he was given several peroneal strikes by one of the soldiers, whose lawyer later noted that his client was "acting consistently with the standard operating procedure that was in place at the Bagram facility." By the fourth day, he was coughing and complaining of chest pains, and his interrogator allowed him to sit on the floor because he was unable to bend his knees to sit down. Despite this, the violence increased the next day, when two MPs gave him nine peroneal strikes while he was handcuffed to the ceiling in one of the isolation cells. When three soldiers came to his cell later in the day and pulled off his hood, he was already dead. A medic told the military investigators, "It looked like he had been dead for a while, and it looked like nobody cared."

The second victim was a taxi driver named Dilawar, who was brought in the day after the death of Mullah Habibullah. According to his elder brother, he was "a shy man, a very simple man," who lived a quiet life with his wife, his young daughter and the rest of his family. On the day of his capture, he picked up three passengers and was passing Camp Salerno, a US base, when he was stopped at a checkpoint by soldiers serving under Jan Baz Khan, the nephew of Pacha Khan Zadran, who were looking for the men who had launched a rocket attack on the base earlier that day. Finding a broken walkie-talkie on one of the passengers and an electric stabilizer for a generator in the boot of the car, they delivered the four men to the Americans at Bagram as suspects. They were among the last men to be implicated by Jan Baz Khan, and Dilawar's passengers—Parkhudin, a 25-year-old farmer, Abdul Rahim, a 27-year-old baker, and Zakkim Shah, a 19-year-old farmer—were certainly the last three to be sent to Guantánamo on Khan's advice, because the Americans finally realized that their supposed ally was actually using them for his own ends, and imprisoned him in Bagram in February 2004.

All this, however, came too late for Dilawar. After the first night, when the four men were handcuffed to a fence, to prevent them sleeping, their interrogations began. Although Dilawar was only a small, frail man, he was regarded as non-compliant, when he apparently spat in the face of a soldier, who gave him a couple of peroneal strikes, which made him cry out, "Allah!" The soldier explained, "Everybody heard him cry out and thought it was funny. It became a kind of running joke, and people kept showing up to give this detainee a common peroneal strike just to hear him scream out 'Allah.' It went on over a 24-hour period, and I would think that it was over 100 strikes." Over the next two days, Dilawar was subjected to brutal interrogations, in which few words were actually spoken. Unable to assume a stress position in the first session, because his legs were so damaged, he was repeatedly thrown against the wall, and, according to the interpreter, a violent female interrogator stamped on his bare foot with her boot, and kicked him in the groin. The following day, after being chained to the ceiling once more, he was unable to kneel and kept falling asleep. After asking for a drink and being sprayed with water until he gagged, he was returned to his cell and chained up once more, and by the following morning he was dead.[27]

How long it would have taken the US military to investigate the murders, if left to their own devices, is unknown. Instead, they issued a press release, announcing that a prisoner had died of a heart attack, and then refused to release any further information. Investigating further, the journalist Carlotta Gall traced Dilawar's family and was shown his death certificate, on which an army pathologist stated unequivocally that, although he had coronary artery disease, his heart failed because of "blunt force injuries to the lower extremities." The extent of his injuries was later summed up by two coroners: one said that his legs had "basically been pulpified," and the other said, "I've seen similar injuries in an individual run over by a bus." Gall's article provoked an investigation into the murders, which, in 2005 and 2006, led to various minor punishments and reprimands for the soldiers involved, although at no point, as with the torture and abuse at Abu Ghraib, was anyone encouraged to look higher up the chain of command to explain why it was that such murderous treatment had become "standard operating procedure."[28]

Others who were aware of the murders were other prisoners who had been in Bagram at the time. Dilawar's passengers, who were released from Guantánamo in March 2004, explained that his family asked them to describe what had happened, but "they could not bring themselves to recount the details," and Parkhudin said, "I told them he had a bed. I said the Americans were very nice because he had a heart problem." Moazzam Begg also reported that he witnessed a death at the end of 2002, but what is even more disturbing is that Begg, Richard Belmar and Jamal Kiyemba reported another death in July that has never been investigated. All three said that a young Afghan was killed after he tried to escape. Belmar said, "He was fine when they brought him in. They had immobilised him, and the next thing they were carrying him out on a stretcher," and Kiyemba, who was clearly not talking about either Habibullah or Dilawar, because he was transferred to Guantánamo in October 2002, explained that the murder was used as part of the pressure that was exerted on him to make a false confession: "The only way out, I was told, was to confess. I heard and saw other torture—banging, screaming, cries, barking dogs and a dead guy who had tried to escape. One of the MPs said, 'Who's next?' So I confessed to be left alone."[29]

The most complete story of this unacknowledged murder was told by Moazzam Begg, who spent ten months at Bagram, where, in addition to the usual abuse, he was threatened with being sent to Egypt for torture, enticed to become a CIA agent, and, at a particularly low point, convinced that a woman who was screaming in a cell next to him was his wife. He reported that a guard he knew from Kandahar told him about the murder, admitting that he "started hitting the detainee so hard that he felt he had fractured something," and that another guard used "Thai-style elbow- and knee-techniques." He added, "I didn't know whether they knew that had killed him," and pointed out that another guard confirmed the murder, but later tried to deny it, saying, "Oh no, he didn't really die, the reason they covered his face was just to scare people."[30]

Torture, Abuse and False Confessions in Guantánamo

The Abusive Reign of Geoffrey Miller

While it was clear that abuse was commonplace at Guantánamo during the first ten months of 2002 (particularly through the seemingly indiscriminate use of the Extreme Reaction Force), the Pentagon's decision to replace Brigadier General Rick Baccus as the commander of the Joint Task Force and appoint Major General Geoffrey Miller instead created, almost overnight, a far harsher regime. "I was mislabelled as someone who coddled detainees," Baccus said after his dismissal. "In fact, what we were doing was our mission professionally." Baccus had apparently infuriated military intelligence officers by granting privileges to the prisoners—including distributing copies of the Koran and adjusting meal times for Ramadan—and had also disciplined prison guards for screaming at inmates. The main source of dissatisfaction with his regime, however, was his refusal to introduce more coercive interrogation techniques. "In no way did I ever interfere in interrogations," he explained, "but also at that time the interrogations never forced anyone to be treated inhumanely, certainly not when I was there."[1]

Under Baccus, the intelligence from Guantánamo was negligible. There was, of course, one particularly compelling reason why this was the case: the majority of the prisoners—the Taliban foot soldiers and those who were completely innocent—had absolutely nothing to offer. Miller, however, set out to increase the yield of intelligence, even though he had spent 27 years in the army dealing with artillery and had no experience in intelligence gathering. Backed up by the Pentagon, who admired his "can-do" approach and his reputation as a strict disciplinarian, he decided that the intelligence was so poor because the activities of the two elements that made up Guantánamo's personnel—the Joint Detention Group (the guards) and the Joint Intelligence Group (the interrogators and intelligence analysts)—were not coordinated. His flash of morbid inspiration came when he decided that their functions should be merged, and that the guards should be responsible for "setting the conditions" for the interrogations; in other words, that every aspect of the prisoners' physical existence—their conditions of detention, their food, their medical support, and every single "comfort item," which now included their solitary Styrofoam cup—would be geared to the interrogators' requirements. Miller insisted that this system was primarily directed towards rewards for cooperative prisoners, but it concealed a darker truth: not only was Guantánamo now the most oppressive of prison environments, but those who refused to cooperate—or were unable to cooperate, because they had no information —were subjected to horrendous abuse.

Under Miller's watch, incidents of abuse during interrogations became widespread, as did acts of violence from the guards. Although much of this violence was tied in to the total control of the prisoners, other incidents were purely gratuitous. Asif Iqbal, for example, heard an MP boasting that he had "beaten someone in isolation with a large metal rod used to turn on the water to the blocks," because "there was no one to tell," and the Bahraini Isa al-Murbati said that on one occasion, after an interrogation, the guards dragged him back to his cell by his shackles, causing his ankles to bleed, and then forced his head into the toilet and flushed it, and described another occasion when the lights in his block were suddenly turned off at night, and a group of guards, accompanied by a dog, entered his cell and sprayed mace in his eyes. David Hicks reported that he was repeatedly beaten, once for eight hours, and frequently while he was restrained and blindfolded. "I have been beaten before, after and during investigations," he said, adding that he had also been "menaced and threatened, directly and indirectly, with firearms and other weapons before and during investigations."[2]

As a result of the increased violence, several prisoners were hospitalized. The Kuwaiti Saad al-Azmi said that, during an interrogation, the guards beat him so hard that they broke his leg, and Sami al-Hajj, the al-Jazeera cameraman, reported that another set of guards "shattered his knee cap by stamping on his leg." When Isa al-Murbati's lawyers first met him in October 2004, he was wearing a cast on his arm as the result of a series of incidents of escalating brutality that had been provoked when he asked one of his guards—a young, white sergeant with "a reputation for being difficult"—for a spoon. A few days later, when he was returned to his cell after an interrogation session and, as usual, put his shackled hands through the slot in the door so that the shackles could be removed, the sergeant grabbed the belt attached to the shackles and "pulled it violently, even putting his foot against the cell door to create greater leverage," which caused him "significant injury." In addition, at least one prisoner suffered irreparable physical damage. During one session, interrogators stomped on the back of the Egyptian Sami El-Leithi, dropped him on the floor and repeatedly forced his neck forward, which resulted in two broken vertebrae and his confinement to a wheelchair. He was then "denied the necessary treatment and operation that would have saved him from permanent paralysis."[3]

As well as these attacks, the regular savagery of the ERF teams continued unabated. Sami al-Hajj, for example, was ERFed six times in ten days, and Omar Deghayes was permanently blinded in his right eye during another ERF attack. James Yee, a US army captain, served as the Muslim chaplain at Guantánamo from November 2002 until September 2003, when, astonishingly, he was arrested on leave, accused of spying, and held for 76 days in solitary confinement before being cleared of all charges; he was particularly upset by the activities of the ERF teams. He noted that "the use of the teams should have been kept to the bare minimum and carried only when necessary, but there were weeks when it occurred every day," and complained about the "excitement" that followed each attack: "The guards were pumped … They high-fived each other and slammed their chests together, like professional basketball players. I found it an odd victory celebration … I wasn't accustomed to seeing such an open and violent display of strength versus weakness." In a vivid demonstration of quite how brutal the ERF's tactics were, in January 2003, Sean Baker, a military policeman, took part in an ERF exercise in which he pretended to be a prisoner. Beaten mercilessly until he managed to give the code word that revealed that he was actually a soldier, he later developed seizures, and was treated for a traumatic brain injury and discharged from the military in April 2004.[4]

"Setting the Conditions"

Although the abuse described above was directed at prisoners who were presumed to be significant suspects, it's clear that many other prisoners who have not spoken about their experiences also suffered brutal treatment. Not everyone was abused by their interrogators or picked on by the guards, but the new regime took as its starting point the presumption that the majority of the prisoners had something to hide, and came up with new forms of abuse, in an attempt to "break" them, which, according to a former interrogator, were applied to one-sixth of the prisoners in Guantánamo; in other words, to at least a hundred prisoners. He explained that "when new interrogators arrived they were told they had great flexibility in extracting information from detainees because the Geneva Conventions did not apply at the base."[5]

Describing this period, Shafiq Rasul, Asif Iqbal and Rhuhel Ahmed, who were rarely subjected to physical brutality, said that they became aware of the changes when the frequency and the length of their inter-rogations increased, and explained that they were each interrogated on about five occasions in 2002, but that from January 2003 until their release in March 2004 they were subjected to over two hundred interrogations. These kinds of figures have been confirmed by other prisoners, including, to cite just a few examples, the Moroccan Younis Chekhouri, who was interrogated over 150 times, the Frenchman Khaled bin Mustafa, who was interrogated over a hundred times, and—to demonstrate that the changes were not only directed at prisoners who were regarded with great suspicion—a 29-year-old Afghan, Abdel Rahman Noorani (released in July 2003), who said that he was "badly punished 107 times," and added that "during his 20 months at Guantánamo, his captors had chained his hands and feet and had beaten him with a metal rod on his legs and back."[6]

What made the prisoners' experiences even more disturbing, however, was the new framework in which the interrogations were couched. Before the interrogations, prisoners were frequently moved into isolation blocks, where they remained for days, weeks, or even months, and where the air conditioning was usually turned up full, so that the cell was freezing. Aryat Vakhitov recalled, "During the interrogations they left you in a cold room for a few weeks ... We weren't given anything to lie on—no carpet. All of us have problems with our kidneys because we slept on the iron [floor] with [the] air conditioning on. It was freezing cold. The ceilings began to be covered with condensation from the cold. We were held like that for months. I was in the isolation ward for five months." Mehdi Ghezali, the Swede, who was interrogated daily for the first six months, but gave up talking when his interrogators kept asking the same questions, was subjected to Miller's regime in the three months before his release in July 2004: "They put me in the interrogation room and used it as a refrigerator. They set the temperature to minus degrees so it was terribly cold and one had to freeze there for many hours. 12–14 hours one had to sit there, chained." Similar experiences were reported by many other prisoners, and, demonstrating yet again that these techniques were not only applied to those who were regarded as being of particular significance, Parkhudin, the Afghan farmer, who had already been traumatized when his friend Dilawar was murdered in Bagram, said on his release, "They made me stand in front of an air-conditioner. The wind was very cold," and added that he was interrogated for up to twenty hours at a time. On other occasions, the authorities used heat instead of cold, and several prisoners reported this technique, including Isa al-Murbati, who was not only repeatedly held in a cell in which the air conditioning had been turned off, but said that on several occasions the floor was "treated with a mixture of water and a powerful cleaning agent," which was then thrown on his face and body, "causing great irritation" and making it difficult to breathe.[7]

Prisoners were also subjected to loud music, sustained noise and strobe lighting, which were clearly designed to "break" them. Isa al-Murbati was played songs "that had Arabic language lyrics praising Jesus Christ," and on other occasions "very loud music and white noise was played through six speakers arranged close to [his] head" for twelve hours, and "multiple flashing strobe lights were used as well," which were so strong that he "had to keep his eyes closed." These reports have been corroborated by other prisoners, including Asif Iqbal, who was forced to listen to Eminem, Bruce Springsteen and techno music, accompanied by strobe lighting, and Mehdi Ghezali, who was "exposed to powerful flashes of light in a dark room, and to very loud music and noise." Military whistle-blowers who spoke out in 2004—either because they "objected to the methods" or because they "objected to what they regarded as a chaotic and badly-run system"—added that they also played tracks by Li'l Kim and Rage Against the Machine, and tapes consisting of "a mix of babies crying and the television commercial for 'Meow Mix' in which the jingle consists of repetition of the word 'meow.'"[8]

These techniques usually took place while the prisoners were subjected to another humiliation. Several described how, when they were supposedly being taken for interrogation, they were actually left alone for many hours, and were often forced to soil themselves as a result. Tarek Dergoul explained that the authorities came up with a new phrase for these occasions—"You have a reservation"—and added that it happened to him every day for a month in 2003, and that he was mostly left alone for eight hours. "Eventually," he said, "I'd need to urinate and in the end I would try to tilt my chair and go on the floor. They were watching through a one-way mirror. As soon as I wet myself, a woman MP would come in yelling, 'Look what you've done! You're disgusting.'" After being taken back to his cell for three hours, he said that the whole process began again. The prisoners were also short-shackled while this took place, tied with an especially short chain from their handcuffs to a ring on the floor. "After a while," Dergoul explained, "it was agony. You could hear the guards behind the mirror, making jokes, eating and drinking, knocking on the walls. It was not about trying to get information. It was just about trying to break you." Omar Khadr, who arrived in Guantánamo in October 2002, a few weeks after his 16th birthday, was almost immediately subjected to similar humiliation. Short-shackled and left in a room for six hours, he said that "occasionally a US officer would enter the room to laugh at him." Once, the guards left him until he urinated on himself, and then "poured a pine scented cleaning fluid over him and used him as a 'human mop' to clean up the mess." As if further humiliation was required, he added that he was "not provided with clean clothes for several days after this degradation."[9]

Another of the authorities' favored techniques was sleep deprivation, which was achieved either by waking the prisoners whenever they fell asleep or, more commonly, by moving them repeatedly from cell to cell over a period of weeks or months. Abdul Malik al-Rahabi was subjected to prolonged periods of sleep deprivation, David Hicks was subjected to sleep deprivation "as a matter of policy," and Mourad Benchellali explained, "We were treated differently depending on whether or not we responded to questions. Those who did not 'cooperate' were awakened every hour with the aim of preventing them from sleeping at all costs." The prisoners who were moved from cell to cell—the "frequent fliers," as the men from Tipton described them—included the Kuwaiti Fouad al-Rabia, who, they said, was picked on like all the prisoners who had spent time in the US, and was moved every two hours, leaving him "suffering from serious depression, losing weight in a substantial way, and very stressed because of the constant moves, deprived of sleep and seriously worried about the consequences for his children." Mehdi Ghezali was "deprived of sleep for about two weeks by the constant switching of cells and interrogation," and Isa al-Murbati was "moved from cell to cell in the Tango and Oscar [isolation] blocks, typically on an hourly basis." As a result, he said, he was "never able to sleep for more than short periods." Mohammed Khan Achakzai, a 24-year-old Afghan businessman (who was sold to the Americans by the Northern Alliance after the fall of Kunduz) said on his release in March 2004 that some prisoners had been deprived of sleep for up to 45 days at a time, and one particularly unfortunate Yemeni, Mohammed Ghanim (who was in the first group of prisoners captured crossing from Afghanistan to Pakistan in December 2001, but does not seem otherwise significant) was apparently moved between cells and blocks every two hours for a total of eight months, as a result of which he lost a lot of weight—and, presumably, found it increasingly difficult to keep a grip on his sanity.[10]

The authorities also made use of prisoners' phobias, either through the use of dogs, as in the case of Saad al-Azmi, who was bitten by dogs while being hooded, or, as was more common, through sexual humiliation. Shafiq Rasul, Asif Iqbal and Rhuhel Ahmed explained that it happened "to the people who'd been brought up most strictly as Muslims," and that they were frequently so ashamed that it took them some time to tell their neighbors about their experiences. Although the men from Tipton were referring primarily to the Gulf prisoners, very few of them have spoken about their experiences, although the Yemeni Yasin Ismail reported that when he refused to talk during an interrogation, a female soldier entered wearing a tight T-shirt. "Why aren't you married?" she asked him. "You are a young man and have needs. What do you like?" Ismail said that she "bent down with her breasts on the table" and her legs almost touching him, and asked, "Are you going to talk, or are we going to do this for six hours?" Murat Kurnaz was one of many other prisoners subjected to similar treatment. He said that in one interrogation, after a young woman "began to caress him from behind, he jerked his head back, hitting her head." An ERF team then beat him up, pepper-sprayed him, and took him to an isolation cell. As in Kandahar and Camp X-Ray, one of the prisoners who suffered the most abuse was Juma al-Dossari. As well as being held in isolation for five months and subjected to random brutality on a regular basis, he reported that he was forced to watch two interrogators have sex, and was also offered sex in return for cooperation. He was also subjected to a particularly notorious example of anti-Muslim humiliation, when, during one of his interrogations, he was wrapped in the flags of Israel and the US, and was told by his interrogator that "a holy war was occurring, between the Cross and the Star of David on the one hand, and the Crescent on the other."[11]

The final part of Miller's program of total control was the introduction of four levels of overall treatment, which were entirely dependent on the prisoners' cooperation with the interrogators. The most compliant, in Level 1, kept all their "comfort items" and also received a bottle of water a week, and the levels were graded down to Level 4, which involved prolonged isolation, in which the supposedly uncooperative prisoners were held completely naked, or were allowed just a pair of shorts, and all other "comfort items" were removed. Those who experienced Level 4 deprivation included Saad al-Azmi, who was held naked for two months, the Bahraini Sheikh Salman al-Khalifa, who was treated "very badly," and was "kept in the worst prison for being silent and considered uncooperative," and the Yemeni Karama Khamisan, who ended up in isolation after being sexually threatened. He explained that on one occasion he was "taken to the shower room where guards attempted to sexually abuse him. As he pushed them away, ten guards entered the room and beat him before transferring him to a solitary cell where he was held for 25 days, naked. He said that he was only taken to use the toilet and shower once in this entire period and that he ate no solid food in order to avoid having to defecate in his cell."[12]

Torture and the Pentagon

While Miller can clearly be condemned for implementing egregious human rights abuses in Guantánamo, it was also obvious that he was not operating in a vacuum. His arrival at Guantánamo followed intensive discussions, in the Pentagon and the Attorney General's office, about the treatment of prisoners, and, in particular, about the definition of torture, which centered on an extraordinarily detailed memorandum—issued on August 1, 2002 and commonly known as the "Torture Memo"—in which the finer points differentiating "cruel, inhuman and degrading" practices from those which are "extreme, deliberate and unusually cruel" (and which therefore constitute torture) were dissected in relation to judgments about torture in cases from around the world, including Bosnia and Northern Ireland. The memorandum was notable for the suggestion that, for interrogation to count as torture, the pain endured "must be of an intensity akin to that which accompanies serious physical injury such as death or organ failure," and for the opinion that, as Commander-in-Chief exercising his wartime powers, the President could authorize torture, if he so desired. Signed off by Assistant Attorney General Jay Bybee, the memo was actually drafted by a handful of hard-liners close to Dick Cheney; in particular, David Addington, his Chief of Staff, and an influential young lawyer named John Yoo. Addington's relationship with Cheney dated from the Reagan years, when both men had sought to derail a law that prevented Reagan from supplying covert aid to the Contras in Nicaragua, arguing that it was an "unconstitutional infringement of Presidential prerogative." Unfettered executive power was something that Cheney had sought from early in his career, when he worked briefly for Richard Nixon, and both he and Addington found a soul-mate in John Yoo. According to the journalist Jane Mayer, the Yale-educated lawyer believed that "liberal congressional overreaction to the Vietnam War and Watergate had weakened the Presidency, the CIA, and the military," that, as Commander-in-Chief, the President had "virtually unlimited authority" to act as he saw fit, and that the cruel, inhumane, and degrading treatment of prisoners at Guantánamo should be authorized with very few restrictions.[13]

Through an unhappy coincidence, Bybee's "Torture Memo" was circulating at the same time that senior officers at Guantánamo began expressing their dissatisfaction with the intelligence that was being produced. Immune, like Miller, from doubts that this might have been because they had rounded up the wrong people, they outlined their frustrations on October 11 in a memorandum by Lieutenant Colonel Jerald Phifer, which soon made its way up the chain of command to Donald Rumsfeld's desk. "Problem," Phifer wrote, "The current guidelines for interrogation procedures ... limit the ability of interrogators to counter advanced resistance." He proposed three sets of additional techniques. Those in Category I, which could be used at will, included yelling and mild forms of deception. Those in Category II, which required approval by an "interrogator group director," included isolation for up to 30 days, removal of clothing, sensory deprivation and hooding, 20-hour interrogations, the use of stress positions for up to four hours, removal of comfort and religious items, forced grooming, and playing on prisoners' phobias, such as a fear of dogs, to induce stress. Those in Category III, which, Phifer suggested, would be reserved for a "very small percentage of the most uncooperative detainees" and would require permission from the commanding general before being used, included convincing prisoners that death or severely painful consequences were imminent for themselves or their family members, exposing them to cold weather or water, using a wet towel and dripping water to "induce the misperception of suffocation" (the reviled torture technique known as "waterboarding"), and using mild, non-injurious physical contact like grabbing or poking. Rumsfeld issued his response on November 27, having discussed the proposals with his deputy, Paul Wolfowitz, Under-Secretary Douglas Feith, and General Richard Myers, the Chairman of the Joint Chiefs of Staff. The only Category III technique that he authorized was the use of mild, non-injurious physical contact, but he approved all the proposed Category II techniques, and even added a hand-written note about the use of stress techniques—"I stand for 8–10 hours. Why is standing limited to four hours?"—which, at best, suggests that he had no idea of the pain that results from enforced stress positions, as opposed to standing freely at a lectern for ten hours a day, which was his preferred method of working.[14]

The arrival of Rumsfeld's memorandum at Guantánamo adds to the picture of a brutal, lawless prison experiment that was presented at the start of this chapter, and establishes the grim truth that, although Miller had the idea of merging the functions of the guards and the interrogators to create an environment of total dependency for the prisoners, the regime that followed was especially cruel and humiliating because it coincided with explicit authorization, from the very top of the chain of command, to use techniques that were previously considered off-limits. The ways in which the enhanced techniques were applied to Mohammed al-Qahtani are described below, and they represent a particularly low point in the moral standing of the United States, but the extended cruelty of his treatment should not blind us to the fact that the sustained abuse of at least a hundred other prisoners, whose presumed guilt was rarely based on any kind of evidence, also represented a colossal and corrosive moral failure. It's also clear that, on the ground, the boundaries of the new system were more blurred than ever. The approval of the use of mild, non-injurious contact was risible—because, as is well documented, extreme physical violence was ever-present in all of the US's "War on Terror" prisons—but it's also noticeable that the 30-day limit on isolation was regularly exceeded, that—perhaps with Rumsfeld's tacit blessing—the four-hour limit on stress techniques was also broken, and that the supposedly prohibited Category III technique of exposing prisoners to cold weather was actually deployed on a regular basis. Looked at as a whole—and bearing in mind how much more severe these individual techniques were when they were combined, as they usually were—the only conclusion that can be drawn is that, from the end of 2002, Guantánamo changed from being an illegal offshore interrogation camp and became, instead, a prison devoted to torture.

It's also apparent that Miller's role should not be underplayed. His innovations in Guantánamo were so well received in the Pentagon that in August 2003 he was sent to the main US prison in Iraq—Abu Ghraib— "to review current Iraqi Theater ability to rapidly exploit internees for actionable intelligence," where he promptly "called for the military police and military intelligence soldiers to work together cooperatively, with the military police 'setting the conditions' for interrogation," as they had in Guantánamo. This quote, and the central phrase—"setting the conditions"—that was used above to describe what was required of the guards in Guantánamo, came not from Miller, but from former defense secretary James Schlesinger, in a report that was published in August 2004, a year after the migration of Miller's techniques was responsible for encouraging interrogators in Iraq to strip their prisoners, to hood them, to beat them mercilessly, to hang them from the walls of their cells for days, to set dogs on them, to lead them around the cell block on leashes, to pile them up in grotesque naked pyramids and, on one notorious occasion, to place a hooded, dark-robed figure on a box, with his arms outstretched, and with wires trailing from his fingers. Schlesinger's report was critical, but, as in other reports commissioned in the wake of the Abu Ghraib scandal, he pointedly refused to gaze up the chain of command to investigate where, ultimately, the responsibility lay for authorizing these techniques. Echoing Bush and Rumsfeld, who blamed the abuse on a "few bad apples," Schlesinger concluded that it was the result of "Animal House on the night shift," although he conceded that "techniques effective under carefully controlled conditions at Guantánamo became far more problematic when they migrated [to Iraq] and were not adequately safeguarded."[15]

Noticeably, however, the changes authorized by Rumsfeld did not meet with universal approval in Guantánamo. Shafiq Rasul, Asif Iqbal and Rhuhel Ahmed noted that many of their guards, who kept them briefed about developments in the camp, "felt ashamed of the Army that these things were going on." More crucially, several major players in the US administration were also dismayed. Colin Powell's State Department remained implacably opposed to all the developments that sprang from the jettisoning of the Geneva Conventions, and Colonel Lawrence Wilkerson, one of Powell's Chiefs of Staff, was particularly incensed by Rumsfeld's note about standing for eight to ten hours, telling Jane Mayer, "It said, 'Carte blanche, guys.' That's what started them down the slope. You'll have My Lais then. Once you pull this thread, the whole fabric unravels."

The most trenchant criticism, however, came from two of the biggest law enforcement agencies, the FBI and the Naval Criminal Intelligence Service. The NCIS's battle was led by Alberto J Mora, the Navy's general counsel, who was informed about the abusive environment at Guantánamo in December 2002 by his colleague David Brant, who was overseeing a team of NCIS agents working with the FBI. In contrast to the military interrogators and the CIA—who were seeking to "break" al-Qaeda, and whose road to torture was paved by the highest powers in the land—the NCIS's mission was to seek out evidence that could eventually be used in military tribunals and civilian courts. Brant told Mora that the military interrogators, most of whom were poorly trained, were "engaging in escalating levels of physical and psychological abuse," and he later told Jane Mayer that "repugnant" would be a good word to describe the tactics he had heard about. He ordered his men to "stand clear and report" any abusive behavior that they saw, and explained that he didn't want them to "observe, condone, or participate in any level of physical or in-depth psychological abuse. No slapping, deprivation of water, heat, dogs, psychological abuse. It was pretty basic, black and white to me. I didn't know or care what the rules were that had been set by the Department of Defense at that point. We were going to do what was morally, ethically, and legally permissible." He also explained to Mayer that he "doubted the reliability of forced confessions" and feared that the use of brutal methods would "taint the cases his agents needed to make against the detainees, undermining any attempts to prosecute them in a court of law." Moreover, he added, "it just ain't right."

Mora was equally appalled, especially by Brant's revelation that the abuse wasn't "rogue activity," but was "rumored to have been authorized at a high level in Washington." He concluded that the interrogation techniques were "clearly contrary to everything we were ever taught about American values," that the arguments used to justify the new regime were fatally flawed, and that the administration could one day face criminal charges for its activities. On December 20, he confronted his immediate superior, William J Haynes II, the Pentagon's general counsel (and a protegé of David Addington), telling him that, "whatever its intent, what Rumsfeld's memo permitted was torture." Haynes disagreed, but Mora then asked him to think about its ramifications: "What did 'deprivation of light and auditory stimuli' mean? Could a prisoner be locked in a completely dark cell? If so, could he be kept there for a month? Longer? Until he went blind? What, precisely, did the authority to exploit phobias permit? Could a detainee be held in a coffin? What about using dogs? Rats? How far could an interrogator push this? Until a man went insane?"[16]

Mora's appeal was ultimately unsuccessful, but it remains to be seen whether his fears about the administration's legal culpability for its actions will one day come true. Noticeably, however, his fears over the direction that his country was taking in the "War on Terror," and his revulsion at the tactics that were being employed, were echoed by the FBI. As early as November 2002, senior FBI officials complained that the coercive interrogation techniques were "not permitted by the US Constitution," and warned that "several of the proposed tactics could constitute torture, depending on how a judge viewed the intent of the interrogator." Convinced that overstepping the existing boundaries was illegal, immoral and counter-productive, the FBI, like the NCIS, instructed its agents not to take part in interrogations where the guidelines were broken. The FBI's position was later derided in a report by Air Force Lieutenant General Randall Schmidt, who noted, as though reading from a script prepared by Donald Rumsfeld, that "FBI agents seek information admissible as evidence in US courts, which generally excludes information gained coercively," whereas the military "seeks 'actionable intelligence' to thwart future terrorist attacks and to defeat terrorist cells."[17]

As I have sought to demonstrate throughout this book, however, both the NCIS and the FBI were clearly correct to regard the unprincipled pursuit of "actionable intelligence" as a non-starter. Schmidt's investigation took place after the FBI asked 493 agents if they had witnessed "aggressive mistreatment" at Guantánamo, and the 26 positive responses constitute one of the most significant documents in the whole of the "War on Terror." Confirming all the prisoners' stories outlined above—and adding new details, including the use of an isolated plywood shack near the abandoned Camp X-Ray for particularly aggressive interrogations—the agents reported that they had witnessed extreme physical violence, the use of heat and cold, the use of dogs and sexual humiliation, the use of extreme stress positions, and interrogations that ran to 24 hours, overstepping the new limits but presumably not causing any consternation to those in command.

One agent reported that, on several occasions, he saw prisoners in interrogation rooms "chained hand and foot in foetal position to floor w/no chair/food/water; most urinated or defecated on selves, and were left there 18, 24 hrs or more. Once, the air conditioning was so low that the barefoot detainee was shaking with cold. Another time, it was off so the unventilated room was over 100 degrees; detainee was almost unconscious on floor with a pile of hair next to him (he had apparently been pulling it out throughout the night)." Another agent reported that he "heard of technique (not allowed by FBI agents) where a difficult detainee who would not cooperate would be left in shackles for extended time (12 hrs or more) and the AC turned way low or off." It was noted that this was described as "environment down—doesn't seem excessive given DoD policy." Another agent reported that a civilian contractor asked him "to come see something. There was an unknown bearded long-haired detainee gagged w/duct tape that covered much of his head." The agent "asked if he had spit at interrogators, and the contractor laughingly replied that [he] had been chanting the Koran nonstop. No answer to how they planned to remove the duct tape." On another occasion, an agent saw a prisoner "in darkened cell in Naval Brig where they planned to interrogate him for 24 hours straight," and "was told the Secretary [Rumsfeld] approved this technique," and another "observed sleep deprivation interviews w/strobe lights and loud music. Interrogator said it would take 4 days to break someone doing an interrogation 16 hrs w/lights and music on and 4 hrs off." A handwritten note next to the typed synopsis of this interrogation stated, "ok under DoD policy." Another agent reported rumors that an interrogator "bragged about doing lap dance on detainee, another about making detainee listen to satanic black metal music for hours then dressing as a priest and baptizing detainee to save him," and another observed the open-ended use of a painful stress technique: "chains were adjusted to force detainee to stand in 'baseball catcher' position. Detainee was being questioned by 2 military officers. Detainee was previously held in brig and questioned for 2 months w/no results. Permission had been granted to use 'special interrogation techniques.'" In another submission, an agent saw Juma al-Dossari "sitting on floor w/Israeli flag draped around him, loud music and strobe lights," and suspected that this was a practice used by Department of Homeland Security operatives from the Department of Defense.[18]

The Torture of Mohammed al-Qahtani

Mohammed al-Qahtani, the alleged "20th hijacker" on 9/11, arrived in Guantánamo in February 2002, but refused to divulge anything—not even his name—to his interrogators. It was not until July, when his fingerprints were matched to those of the man deported from Orlando after trying to meet lead hijacker Mohammed Atta in August 2001, that he began to be interrogated intensively. A senior FBI interrogator was assigned to the case, who "slowly built a rapport" with al-Qahtani, "approaching him with respect and restraint," according to officials who spoke to the *New York Times*: "He prays with them, he has tea with them, and it works." Opening up to this skilled, and by now resolutely old-fashioned technique, al-Qahtani started to yield information, revealing that he had attended an important al-Qaeda meeting with two of the 9/11 hijackers in Malaysia in 2000, but officials in the Pentagon were frustrated that he failed to reveal anything else about al-Qaeda's plans. To the FBI, this was understandable: as one of the potential hijackers intended to provide the "muscle," subduing the passengers rather than piloting a plane, it was plausible that he had been kept deliberately in the dark, as had almost all of those recruited by Atta.[19]

Failing to take this into account, however, the Pentagon—convinced that he was "a particularly well-placed, well-connected terrorist," who was "capable of unlocking an enormous amount of specific and general insights into 9/11, al-Qaeda operations and ongoing planning for future attacks"—removed the FBI from the case in November 2002 and began its own interrogations, which were singled out for particular criticism by a senior FBI official in a letter to the Pentagon in June 2004 that first highlighted the other abuses discussed above. According to the FBI, al-Qahtani was "subjected to intense isolation for over three months" and began "evidencing behaviour consistent with extreme psychological trauma (talking to non existent people, reporting hearing voices, crouching in a cell covered with a sheet for hours on end)." As his interrogation progressed, it was documented, in meticulous detail, in a log that was leaked to *Time* magazine in 2005. Recording the interrogation over a 50-day period, from November 23, 2002 to January 11, 2003, it was described by a Pentagon official as the "kind of document that was never meant to leave Gitmo [Guantánamo]." The log began two weeks before the enhanced techniques approved by Donald Rumsfeld kicked in, when the interrogators were already questioning him in 20-hour sessions that regularly ran from 4 am to midnight. Although they managed to humiliate him by giving him water and then refusing to let him take a toilet break so that he urinated in his trousers, they were struggling to get him to talk. What was probably the most salient exchange was, of course, disregarded by the interrogator:

> *Interrogator*: Why did you go to Orlando?
> *Al-Qahtani*: I wasn't told the mission.

Once the enhanced techniques were approved, they were immediately implemented. From December 2 until the log ended six weeks later, al-Qahtani was interrogated for twenty hours every day, and was subjected to forced grooming and sexual humiliation: one game was known as "Invasion of Space by a Female," because the interrogators noticed that he became "especially agitated by the close physical presence of a woman," and on another occasion pictures of scantily-clad women were hung around his neck. The most outrageous incident was described by Erik Saar, a translator at Guantánamo, who later wrote a book about his time at the prison. Saar was translating when a female interrogator subjected him to a particularly humiliating experience, unbuttoning her shirt, touching her breasts, and asking, "Don't you like these big American breasts?" When al-Qahtani failed to respond, "She started to unbutton her pants and reached and put her hands in her pants and then started to circle around the detainee. And when she had her hands in her pants, apparently she used something to put what appeared to be menstrual blood on her hand, but in fact was ink." Saar added, "I know that the individual that we were talking to that night was a bad individual ... But I felt awful that night. I felt dirty and disgusting."[20]

On other days, al-Qahtani was threatened by a dog, strip-searched and made to stand naked, and compelled to bark like a dog and growl at pictures of terrorists. Whenever he fell asleep, he was woken by having water poured on his head—a game called "Drink Water or Wear It"—or by tapes of Christina Aguilera playing at full volume, and at one point he was "subjected to a 'fake rendition,' in which he was tranquilized, flown off the island, revived, flown back to Cuba, and told he was in a country that allows torture." The sessions were so intense that the interrogators worried that the cumulative lack of sleep and constant interrogation posed a risk to his health. Medical staff checked his health frequently—sometimes as often as three times a day—and on one occasion, in early December, the punishing routine was suspended for a day when, as a result of refusing to drink, he became seriously dehydrated and his heart rate dropped to 35 beats a minute. While a doctor came to see him in the booth, however, loud music was played to prevent him from sleeping.[21]

How long the interrogations continued in this vein after the log ended on January 11, 2003 is unknown. Five days later, Donald Rumsfeld revoked the harsh measures he had approved seven weeks earlier, when Alberto Mora drafted a memorandum to the Pentagon's chief counsel, in which he described the interrogations at Guantánamo as "at a minimum cruel and unusual treatment, and, at worst, torture," and threatened to issue the memorandum officially unless the harsh techniques were immediately suspended. Haynes rang him back the same day to say that Rumsfeld had agreed to suspend the techniques, but Mora's victory was short-lived. Almost immediately, Rumsfeld ordered Haynes to put together a working group to submit a report, which, with only a few minor adjustments, reiterated everything to which Mora had objected. Led by Air Force General Counsel Mary Walker, the group comprised senior civilian and military lawyers from each military branch and consultants from the Justice Department, the Joint Chiefs of Staff, the Defense Intelligence Agency and other intelligence agencies. John Yoo was assigned to compile the report, and one of the group's members described how they "sought to assign to the President virtually unlimited authority on matters of torture—to assert presidential power at its absolute apex." Cut out of the loop, Mara was later shown a draft, and was shocked to realize that there was "no language prohibiting the cruel, degrading and inhuman treatment of detainees." When the report was issued officially in April 2003, however, he was not even told, and it was only as the Abu Ghraib scandal unfolded a year later that he realized what had happened. "I felt saddened and dismayed," he said. "Everything we had warned against in Guantánamo had happened—but in a different setting. I was stunned."[22]

Although the "Torture Memo" did not become public until after Abu Ghraib, Milton Bearden, a former CIA bureau chief, was dismissive of the administration's subsequent attempts to downplay its significance, saying, "It doesn't matter what distribution that memo had or how tightly it was controlled. That kind of thinking will permeate the system by word of mouth. Anyone who suggests that this and other official memos on this subject didn't have an impact, doesn't know how these things work on the ground."[23] Although the April 2003 report purportedly restricted certain techniques—the use of nudity and the use of dogs, for example—it's clear from the accounts of the prisoners in Guantánamo, as well as those who were soon to be detained in a similar manner in Iraq, that Bearden's analysis was accurate, and that, once unleashed, it was almost impossible to rein in the use of abusive techniques. When Mehdi Ghezali, for example, was subjected to a battery of the same enhanced techniques from April to June 2004, there was no evidence that anything had changed since the year before.

Whether al-Qahtani's interrogation produced any "actionable intelligence" is disputed. The Pentagon claimed that he named people and financial contacts in several Arab countries, described terrorist training camps where bin Laden lived, provided details of meetings with bin Laden, and explained how he may have escaped from Tora Bora, but this, at best, is a small amount of administrative detail, none of which was strictly necessary, and it reinforces the notion that, although committed to the al-Qaeda cause, he was nothing more than a "muscle" hijacker who did not even succeed in the mission that was chosen for him. What's clear, however, is that the interrogators eventually focused his attention on his fellow prisoners at Guantánamo, and it was in this context at least that he attained a certain notoriety. Shown the photos of prisoners captured around the same time as him—from the so-called "family album" of prisoner mug-shots, which had been used from Kandahar onwards—he declared that thirty of them were Osama bin Laden's bodyguards.[24]

False Confessions

Al-Qahtani recanted his confession in 2005, during a visit by his newly-appointed lawyer, Gitanjali Gutierrez of the Center for Constitutional Rights. Gutierrez reported that he "repudiated all of his previous statements," claiming, with some justification, that they were "extracted under brutal torture," and said that he appeared to be "a broken man, fearful and at times disoriented—someone who has 'painfully described how he could not endure the months of isolation, torture and abuse, during which he was nearly killed, before making false statements to please his interrogators.'"[25] While this was not exactly a surprising development, it was too late for "Osama's bodyguards," and their cases demonstrate that, once an allegation is lodged in a prisoner's file, it's almost impossible to remove it. The Taliban foot soldiers, humanitarian workers and religious teachers accused by al-Qahtani duly came up against the allegations in their tribunals, and were, of course, appalled.

A typical example was Samir Moqbel, the Yemeni who claimed that he was tricked into going to Afghanistan by a friend:

> These accusations make you laugh. These accusations are like a movie. Me, a bodyguard for bin Laden, then do operations against Americans and Afghanis and make trips in Afghanistan? I don't believe any human being could do all these things ... This is me? I have watched a lot of American movies like *Rambo* and *Superman*, but I believe that I am better than them. I went to Pakistan and Afghanistan a month before the Americans got there ... How can a person do all these operations in only a month?[26]

Mahmoud al-Mujahid, another Yemeni, explained to his tribunal, "I never knew Osama bin Laden. When the interrogators kept bothering me with this question, I told them, 'I saw him five times, three on al-Jazeera, and twice on Yemeni news.' After this they kept after me really hard. I told them, 'OK, I know him, whatever you want. Just give me a break.'" While al-Mujahid's story has rightly been touted as one of the absurdities of the tribunal system, the most revealing story is that of Farouq Saif, who went to Afghanistan to teach the Koran. Saif was judged as an "enemy combatant" not only because of the allegation that he was one of bin Laden's bodyguards, but also because of another allegation that he was seen at bin Laden's private airport in Kandahar, where he was "wearing camouflage and carrying an AK-47." On this latter point, his Personal Representative, a lieutenant colonel in the army, was so disgusted with the verdict that he submitted a written protest, in which he stated that the government's sole evidence that he was at bin Laden's airport in Kandahar was the statement of another prisoner, who was a notorious liar, according to an FBI memo that he presented to the tribunal, in which it was stated that he "had lied, not only about Farouq, but about other Yemeni detainees as well. The other detainee claimed he had seen the Yemenis at times and in places where they simply could not have been." The lieutenant colonel wrote, "I do feel with some certainty that [he] has lied about other detainees to receive preferable treatment and to cause them problems while in custody. Had the tribunal taken this evidence out as unreliable, then the position we have taken is that a teacher of the Koran (to the Taliban's children) is an enemy combatant (partially because he slept under a Taliban roof)."[27]

The "known liar" actually made allegations against sixty prisoners in total, as was revealed after the tribunal of Mohammed al-Tumani, the young Syrian refugee who, with his father, was tortured in Pakistani custody. When al-Tumani's Personal Representative, curious that he had strenuously denied an allegation that he attended al-Farouq, looked at the classified evidence, he found that only one man—the same prisoner mentioned above—claimed to have seen him at al-Farouq, and that he identified him as being there three months before he arrived in Afghanistan. As Corine Hegland wrote in the *National Journal*, "The curious US officer pulled the classified file of the accuser, saw that he had accused 60 men, and, suddenly skeptical, pulled the files of every detainee the accuser had placed at the one training camp. None of the men had been in Afghanistan at the time the accuser said he saw them at the camp."[28]

Two particular prisoners—an Iraqi and a Yemeni, one of whom may be the man mentioned above—were also revealed in the tribunals as frequent liars. To give just a few examples, Abdullah Khan, an Afghan Uzbek who was captured in Pakistan at the house of an acquaintance who was reportedly connected to al-Qaeda, refuted a statement made by an Iraqi prisoner who said that he saw him at a guest house on the Taliban front lines in Kabul in 1999 or 2000, explaining, "About two years ago, I was prepared to be released from here. At that point I lived with some Iraqi people and because they disliked me they were lying, they were throwing some allegations on me and that's why my process has stopped and that's why I have not been released." Yahya al-Sulami, one of the thirty men accused of being bin Laden's bodyguards, thought that this and other allegations against him had been made by the Yemeni, who he described as "mentally unstable and on medication," and Abbas al-Naely, the Iraqi beggar with a hashish problem, who attended the tribunal of his fellow Iraqi Jawad Sadkhan, named both the Iraqi and the Yemeni as being responsible for a swathe of allegations against Sadkhan. A taxi driver who had been living in Afghanistan with his family for three years, Sadkhan said that he helped General Dostum during the US-led invasion by "pointing out Taliban locations," putting "my life, my wife's life and the life of my children in danger in order to help the Northern Alliance," but he was accused of being a Taliban commander, of being "heavily involved in the heroin trade for the Taliban," and of receiving funds from Osama bin Laden that were "funnelled through the al-Wafa organization."[29]

In other cases, prisoners were subjected to ludicrous allegations whose provenance was not disclosed, but which were clearly implausible. Abdul Halim Sidiqi, for example, a 33-year-old Pakistani, who was married with a baby daughter, ran a small store in Pakistan. Caught up in the fall of Kunduz, after traveling to Afghanistan to look for his brother, he spent a year in Sheberghan and another three years attempting to convince the Americans that he was not a military commander who ran a "network of madrassas," through which he was able to recruit 2,000 fighters for al-Qaeda, and that he had led this vast fighting force—which included "300 Arab al-Qaeda operatives"—in combat against the Northern Alliance until he was captured in Kunduz. In his review in November 2005, he said, "The person who made these allegations, either he was drunk or he doesn't even have a brain," and finally someone believed him. A Board Member told him, "I don't believe that you were a mastermind, or a great general, or this person who could command 2,000 recruits to come with you on a moment's notice. I believe you." He was released in October 2006.[30]

Ahmed Sulayman, the Jordanian who was captured in Pakistan while working for the IIRO and had never set foot in Afghanistan, also had to contend with a barrage of wild allegations, which included claims that he was at Khaldan from 1994 to 1999, and that he was "a senior commander and trainer for al-Qaeda," in contact with Osama bin Laden and Abu Zubaydah. In his review board, the source of these allegations was touched upon, but never explained. A Board Member told him, "Some other detainees ... identified you as belonging to al-Qaeda," but when Sulayman asked him for details he was unable to provide any other explanation. Other bizarre allegations involved the Kazakh Ilkham Batayev, who was reportedly caught smuggling $600,000, which, if true, suggests that he managed to keep the money safe while trying not to drown in the basement of the Qala-i-Janghi fort, and the Palestinian Mahrar al-Quwari, who responded to an allegation that he attended al-Farouq, where he was "in charge of delivering food to caves," by saying that he asked one of the prisoners who had been at al-Farouq to describe it, and was told that "the camp did not have any caves."[31]

While some of the allegations above were obtained through coercion, others undoubtedly arose through General Miller's much-touted rewards system, which, although kinder on the informers than coercion—allowing them to move to Camp 4, where they shared dormitories with nine others, ate communally and were allowed to play sports together—was just as damaging in terms of the value of the intelligence produced.[32] Numerous prisoners were, of course, aware that other prisoners were telling lies in the hope of being released, but Miller was oblivious to it, proudly telling David Rose that his graduated system of 29 extra "comfort items" for cooperative prisoners had contributed to the 600 percent increase in intelligence under his watch, all of which, he maintained, was "enormously valuable intelligence," which was "distributed around the world." This was clearly nonsense—Anthony Christino said that he saw no dramatic improvement in the quality of the intelligence, but noted an increase in quantity and an attempt to "improve the way it was packaged"—but although it was more palatable to sell bribery as the key tactic that had apparently transformed Guantánamo, the blunt truth was that coercion—combined with a credulous approach to "evidence" on the part of the authorities—had played a more prominent part.[33]

It's uncertain quite how many prisoners were presented with patently false information that they either refuted, leading to horrendous punishment, or accepted under duress, producing self-incriminating false confessions, but the examples of several of the British prisoners suggest that both the scenario and its responses were widespread. It was in Guantánamo, under Miller's command, that Omar Deghayes was unexpectedly confronted with a grainy video of Chechen militants, in which, it was alleged, he was a prominent player, even though it has been established that the man in the video was actually a militant who died in Chechnya in 2004,[34] and it was under Miller that Shafiq Rasul, Asif Iqbal and Rhuhel Ahmed suddenly found themselves under intense suspicion when another grainy video surfaced purporting to show them in the crowd at a meeting between Osama bin Laden and Mohammed Atta in Afghanistan. In the case of the three men from Tipton, British intelligence agents, having been useless up to that point, finally intervened to confirm that Rasul's alibi—that he was working in an electrical store in the West Midlands at the time—was the truth, and not, as alleged, a devious cover story concocted by a hardened terrorist. This, in turn, led to their release, but not until all three men cracked under the pressure and "confessed" that the allegation was true. In a similar scenario, Ahmed Errachidi, the Moroccan chef, was

accused of training at al-Farouq in July 2001, and it was not until his
lawyers provided proof that he was working at a hotel in London at
the time that the authorities began to doubt his status as a terrorist.
The final Briton to be considered—Moazzam Begg—made a false
confession shortly after arriving in Guantánamo in February 2003.
Begg wrote that he was appalled by the allegations that were presented
to him—that he was a recruiter and financier for al-Qaeda, that he had
received "extensive training" at al-Qaeda camps since 1993, and that
he had been in Tora Bora—but stated that he was desperate to find
a way out of his predicament and presumed that "there was no way
that any competent court in the world was going to look past the first
sentence of the confession." Instead, he was rewarded with 600 days of
solitary confinement in Camp Echo, with only his guards for company,
which lasted until shortly before his release in January 2005.[35]

16
"Extraordinary Rendition,"
"Ghost" Prisoners and
Secret Prisons

"Extraordinary Rendition"

The process of capturing fugitives abroad and rendering them to the United States for trial has a long history, dating back to the 1880s, although its current incarnation only dates from 1995, when it began "in desperation," according to Michael Scheuer, the former head of the CIA's bin Laden unit. Frustrated that the government refused to address the growing problem of Islamist militants and effectively told the CIA to come up with their own solution, Scheuer said, "We knew where these people were, but we couldn't capture them because we had nowhere to take them ... we had to come up with a third party." The "third party" was Egypt, a key US ally in the Middle East, with a brutal reputation for suppressing dissent, and the arrangement was mutually satisfactory, as many of al-Qaeda's top operatives were Egyptian. A number of successful covert operations followed, in which suspects were rendered to Egypt from various countries. Assurances that suspects would not be tortured—which were required under US law—were, however, dealt with vaguely, if at all, although Scheuer pointed out that "a legal process" underpinned the renditions, because every suspect had been convicted in absentia and the CIA's legal counsel approved every operation.[1]

After 9/11, however, the program expanded beyond recognition. In much the same way that the definition of "enemy combatants" mutated, in the last months of 2001, from a handful of senior al-Qaeda leaders to encompass the whole of the Taliban, the rendition program was also transformed. What had been a tightly-controlled project aimed at a small group of significant suspects with outstanding arrest warrants became an additional tool in the "War on Terror," enabling the CIA to kidnap, render and facilitate the torture of large numbers of suspected "enemy combatants" with complete impunity, using the same shockingly vague parameters that were applied to all the other "enemy combatants" in Afghanistan and Pakistan. The intention was spelled out by Dick Cheney, in an interview on September 16, 2001, when he explained, "We ... have to work [through] sort of the dark side, if you will. We're going to spend time in the shadows in the intelligence world." According to a former CIA official, opening up to "the dark side" led to nothing short of "an abomination."[2]

Several dozen prisoners in Guantánamo—and another 14 "high-value" captives, who were transferred to Cuba from secret prisons in September 2006 (see Chapter 20)—were subjected to "extraordinary rendition." Captured in countries far from the battlefields of Afghanistan, including Pakistan, Egypt, Thailand, Indonesia, Bosnia, the Gambia, Mauritania, Zambia and Iran, some were sent to prisons in Jordan, Egypt and Morocco, where, as an official involved in the process explained, the understanding was, "We don't kick the shit out of them. We send them to other countries so *they* can kick the shit out of them"; others were held in brutal secret prisons in Afghanistan that were run by the CIA.[3]

The al-Wafa Prisoners

The first Guantánamo prisoner to be rendered was Jamal Mar'i, a 31-year-old Yemeni, who was kidnapped from his house in Karachi by US operatives on September 23, 2001. Married with four children, Mar'i studied petroleum engineering in Azerbaijan in 1994–98, but found no work in his chosen field, and worked in his family's store in Yemen until 2001, when he was employed by al-Wafa's Emirates-based financier to buy medicine for the organization in Karachi. He explained that this involved him traveling to Kandahar in May 2001 "to find out how the work was done and how the medicine is distributed," and that he was then responsible for purchasing medicines from specialist stores in Pakistan. Although there is no reason to doubt Mar'i's story, he probably came under suspicion because he was working for Ayman Batarfi, the Yemeni doctor discussed in Chapter 14, who, in turn, was almost certainly referring to Mar'i when he said that al-Wafa's representative in Karachi "was taken to Jordan 'on a special flight.'" After his kidnapping, Mar'i was indeed sent to Jordan, where he was held by the notorious General Intelligence Directorate (GID) for four months before being sent to Guantánamo. Despite the shock of his rendition, he was fortunate that he was not tortured by the Jordanians, although he told his lawyer, Marc Falkoff, that he was "hidden from visiting Red Cross inspectors." His current status in Guantánamo is unknown. In June 2006, Falkoff said, "When I first met Jamal, he said all he needed was to have his case heard and everyone would see that he was innocent. Now he won't even meet with us. He said that we initially brought him hope but that we're now like a mirage in the desert and he can no longer live with hope."[4]

Two and a half months after Mar'i's kidnapping, al-Wafa's founder and director, Abdul Aziz al-Matrafi, was also abducted by the Americans. A charity worker who had directed a fund-raising committee in Bosnia, and had then worked as an imam in Mecca, the 38-year-old father of three stayed on in Kabul after the US-led invasion began, even though al-Wafa's stores were the targets of bombing raids, in which seven aid workers were killed. He finally left the capital when he was seriously injured in a bombing raid, and his family last heard from him on December 10, 2001, as he was about to board an Emirates flight from Lahore to Dubai. Although he apparently boarded a second flight from Dubai to Jeddah, he never arrived at his destination. Somewhere between Lahore and Jeddah, he was abducted by US agents, rendered to Afghanistan and then put on the first flight to Guantánamo. Little has been heard about him in Guantánamo, although it's clear that the authorities regard him as a major supporter of terrorism, alleging that he was close to bin Laden, that his plan to provide funds to bin Laden for training caused disagreement within al-Wafa, that he admitted that al-Wafa purchased weapons and vehicles for the Taliban, and that he "negotiated a deal that allowed the Taliban to direct al-Wafa's activities."[5]

In October 2001, prior to his capture, al-Matrafi appeared on al-Jazeera, after al-Wafa was blacklisted by the US, arguing his innocence

Although Habib's freedom came at a price—the Australian authorities took his passport away, and he continues to be regarded with suspicion—he was more fortunate than the other Guantánamo prisoner who was in Egypt with him. Twenty-four-year-old Mohammed Saad Iqbal Madni, a Pakistani citizen and the son of a Saudi diplomat, was arrested in Jakarta by the Indonesian authorities on January 9, 2002, rendered to Egypt, where he was held for three months, and flown back to Afghanistan—with Habib—on April 12, 2002. Eleven months later, he was transferred to Guantánamo. Although he has not spoken of his treatment, several prisoners confirmed that he was tortured by the Egyptians. Rustam Akhmyarov said that he told him of his time "in an underground cell in Egypt, where he never saw the sun and where he was tortured until he confessed to working with Osama bin Laden," and added that he "recalled how he was interrogated by both Egyptian and US agents in Egypt and that he was blindfolded, tortured with electric shocks, beaten and hung from the ceiling." He also said that he was in a particularly bad mental and physical state in Guantánamo, where he "was passing blood in his faeces," and recalled that he overheard US officials telling him, "we will let you go if you tell the world everything was fine here." Mamdouh Habib confirmed Akhmyarov's analysis, recalling how Madni had "pleaded for human interaction." He said that he overheard him saying, "Talk to me, please talk to me ... I feel depressed ... I want to talk to somebody ... Nobody trusts me." [10]

Quite what Madni is supposed to have done to justify this torture and abuse has never been explained. The US authorities urged the Indonesians to arrest him after they claimed to have discovered documents that linked him to Richard Reid, the inept and mentally troubled British "shoe bomber," who was arrested, and later received a life sentence, for attempting to blow up an American Airlines flight from Paris to Miami in December 2001, but Madni has persistently denied the connections. In his tribunal—in which he pointed out that he is from a wealthy and influential family, is fluent in nine languages and is a renowned Islamic scholar—he maintained that he was betrayed by one of four Yemeni al-Qaeda members whom he met by accident on a trip to Indonesia in November 2001 to sort out family business after his father's death. According to the *Washington Post*, he rented a house in Jakarta, and did nothing more sinister than visiting the local mosque, handing out business cards "identifying him as a Koran reader for an Islamic radio station," and spending "hours on end watching television at a friend's house." Succinctly summing up what happened to him, he told his tribunal, "After I went to Indonesia, I got introduced to some people who were not good. They were bad people. Maybe I can say they were terrorists. When someone gets introduced to someone, it is not written on their foreheads that they are bad or good."[11]

Mohamedou Ould Slahi

Prior to picking up Madni in Indonesia, Mohamedou Ould Slahi, a 31-year-old Mauritanian, was rendered by the US to Jordan after handing himself in to the Mauritanian authorities on November 28, 2001. "My country turned me over, shortcutting all kinds of due process of law, like a candy bar to the United States," he said in his tribunal. Held for eight months in Jordan, where what happened to him was "beyond description" and he was tortured "maybe twice a week, a couple times, sometimes more," he was then transferred to Bagram for two weeks, and arrived in Guantánamo on August 4, 2002. Described in the *9/11 Commission Report* as "a significant al-Qaeda operative" who "recruited 9/11 hijackers in Germany," it was stated that Ramzi bin al-Shibh and three of the 9/11 hijackers—Mohammed Atta, Marwan al-Shehhi and Ziad Jeddah—were traveling on a train in Germany when they met a man named Khalid El-Masri, and "struck up a conversation about jihad in Chechnya." El-Masri told them to contact a man named Abu Musab (Slahi's alias) in Duisburg, but when they met him, he told them it was difficult to get to Chechnya because travelers were generally detained in Georgia, and advised them to go to Afghanistan for training instead. Slahi himself has disputed this story, denying an allegation that he "recruited for jihad," but even if it were true, it proves only that he was a recruiter for a war in Chechnya that was regarded by many Muslims as a legitimate struggle, who sent would-be recruits for training in long-established training camps in Afghanistan, and does not connect him in any meaningful way to 9/11.

Despite this, the US authorities have persistently presented his activities in Germany as more significant than the *9/11 Commission Report* suggested, choosing to ignore the official story—that the hijackers attracted bin Laden's attention once they were in Afghanistan—and claiming that Slahi arranged for one of them "to meet Osama bin Laden, and that this individual then swore allegiance to Osama bin Laden and became an important and influential al-Qaeda member." The authorities also attempted to implicate Slahi in all manner of other plots, in particular Ahmed Ressam's plot to blow up Los Angeles airport in 1999. Slahi said that he falsely confessed to being part of the plot while being tortured in Jordan, and explained that, although he moved to Canada in 1998, hoping to find work as an electrical engineer, he had nothing to do with extremists, and returned to Mauritania in January 2000 because he was kept under constant surveillance by the intelligence services: "Wherever I went I had people right behind me at the market watching my butt. I said what the heck? This is not the life I want to live."

Quite why Slahi was seized by the Americans in November 2001 has never been explained. It was not as if he was an unknown quantity. As well as being questioned in Canada, he had been investigated in Germany, had been questioned in Senegal on his way to Mauritania in January 2000, and had also been questioned on two occasions by the Americans themselves: by three FBI agents and "another guy from the Department of Justice" in Mauritania in February 2000, and again in October 2001, when an American agent took part in an interrogation and, according to Slahi, threatened to bring in "black people" to torture him.[12]

The Six Bosnians

In October 2001, another extraordinary and unprecedented story began to unfold in Bosnia, when the US embassy in Sarajevo asked the government to arrest six Bosnian citizens of Algerian origin—40-year-old Bensayah Belkacem, 33-year-old Sabir Lahmar, 34-year-old Mohammed Nechle, 32-year-old Mustafa Ait Idr, 36-year-old Lakhdar Boumedienne and 37-year-old Boudella al-Hajj—because of a suspicion that they were involved in a plot to bomb the US embassy. The Americans' request took the form of a diplomatic note, which contained no evidence to support the allegation, and the Bosnians refused to comply until the Americans threatened to close their embassy and withdraw peace-keeping forces unless the men were arrested. Human rights activist Srdjan Dizdarevic noted that "the threats from the

Americans were enormous. There was a hysteria in their behaviour."
Unwilling to defy the Americans, the Bosnians then arrested the men,
but after a three-month investigation, in which they conducted extensive
searches of their apartments, their computers and their documents, they
found "literally no evidence" to justify the arrests. The Supreme Court
ordered their release, and, with rumors circulating that the Americans
were going to seize them anyway, the Bosnian Human Rights Chamber
ruled that they had the right to remain in the country and were not
to be deported. On the night of January 17, 2002, a huge crowd of
supporters gathered outside the prison in Sarajevo to protect them on
their release, but riot police dispersed the crowd with tear gas, and
at dawn, as the men emerged, they were seized by American agents,
hooded, handcuffed and rendered to Guantánamo.

Since arriving in Guantánamo, the embassy plot has never been
mentioned. Instead, the six men have been subjected to relentless
allegations that they were associated with al-Qaeda. Although they
all traveled to Bosnia to support Muslims during the 1992–95 civil
war and were then granted citizenship, they married Bosnian women
and spent the next six years working with orphans for various Muslim
charities, including the Red Crescent, and, in the case of Lahmar,
an Islamic scholar, the Saudi High Committee for Relief, and there
was no evidence that any of them maintained a sideline dealing with
international terrorists. According to their lawyers, the source of the
false allegations was Lahmar's embittered ex-brother-in-law, who ran
a "smear campaign" against him. Another allegation made by the
Americans—that Belkacem made seventy phone calls to Afghanistan
after 9/11 and was "the top al-Qaeda facilitator" in Bosnia—has never
been substantiated, and there seems no doubt that all six men are
innocent. Manfred Novak, the UN Special Rapporteur on Torture,
explained, "It's implausible to say that they are enemy combatants.
They were fighters during the Bosnian war, but that ended in 1995.
They may be radical Islamists, but they have definitely not committed
any crime."[13]

Despite this, they have been treated brutally in Guantánamo. Shafiq
Rasul, Asif Iqbal and Rhuhel Ahmed reported that during Geoffrey
Miller's tenure, "They were treated particularly badly. They were
moved every two hours. They were kept naked in their cells. They were
taken to interrogation for hours on end. They were short-shackled for

sometimes days on end. They were deprived of their sleep." Ait Idr seems to have been singled out for particularly harsh punishment. During one cell search, "guards stuffed his face into the toilet and repeatedly pressed the flush button," and on another occasion "a garden hose was pushed into his mouth and the water turned on until [it] came out of his mouth and nose and he couldn't breathe." During an ERF, he had two knuckles broken, and was thrown onto crushed stones while a man jumped on the side of his head with his full weight, which led to him suffering a stroke that left one side of his face paralyzed. Despite requesting a hospital visit after this assault, he did not receive medical treatment for ten days.[14]

At the time of writing, the men remain in Guantánamo, where new allegations have sprung up to plague them, of which the most ludicrous is a claim that Boudella al-Hajj was with Osama bin Laden in Tora Bora, when of course, he was in jail in Sarajevo. The real reason that they are still in Guantánamo, however, is probably because of their supposed intelligence value. This was revealed by Condoleezza Rice in March 2005, when she responded to a request for their release from the Bosnian prime minister by stating that it was not possible because "they still possess important intelligence data," and it was explicitly stated by Mustafa Ait Idr in his tribunal in 2004. "The interrogator told me I was there to give up information," he said, explaining that he told him, "The story on the outside was I was captured because of terrorism, and now here you are telling me you want me to give up information about rescue organizations and Arabs and how the Arabs are living."[15]

The "Dark Prison"

Several prisoners were rendered to Afghanistan from Iran, where, like many of those captured in Pakistan, they were the victims of random arrests by the security services. Once in Afghanistan, they were seized by the CIA, who decided that they were high-profile al-Qaeda refugees and imprisoned them in a notorious underground prison near Kabul that was known as the "Dark Prison." Incarcerated in total darkness and shackled to the walls so that they were unable to lie down, they were subjected to loud music or other violent sounds, sometimes for weeks on end, beaten during interrogations, deprived of water and often given only rotten food to eat.[16]

Wisam Ahmed, a 25-year-old Jordanian (released in April 2004), ran a clothes shop in Jordan and traveled to Pakistan every year with a religious group. After getting married in 2000, he decided to take his wife and their newborn child to Pakistan for his visit in August 2001. In December, they were on a bus, traveling home, when they were stopped at a checkpoint in Iran, and Ahmed—under suspicion "because they associated [my] headdress with al-Qaeda and must have overlooked the fact that it was also my national dress"—was taken into custody. Rendered to Afghanistan on March 1, 2002, he was held in the "Dark Prison," in "unimaginable conditions that cannot be tolerated in a civilized society," and spent 77 days in a room that "was so dark that we couldn't distinguish nights and days. There was no window, and we didn't see the sun once during the whole time." He was then moved to another secret prison—"Prison Number Three"—where the food was so bad that he lost a significant amount of weight, and was then moved to Bagram, where, in the forty days before his transfer to Guantánamo, he was threatened by dogs, made to watch torture videos, and intimidated in other ways: "they used to start up an electric saw and while they were sawing we would hear cries of agony. I thought they would cut me into pieces sooner or later." His ordeal continued in Guantánamo. "We were beaten whenever the soldiers saw fit," he said. "If a prisoner didn't answer a question they would beat him, sometimes until he was unconscious." Speaking after his release, he said, "Sad to say, this is a statement that I make to ensure that history and humanity understand how we were treated by the Americans in the name of democracy and human rights. This treatment is all the more sad given the values that the US pretends to propagate."[17]

Walid al-Qadasi, a 22-year-old Yemeni (transferred to Yemeni custody in April 2004) was also captured in Iran, and was rendered to Afghanistan in January 2002. Describing his time in the "Dark Prison," he said, "The Americans interrogated us on our first night which we coined as 'the black night.' They cut our clothes with scissors, left us naked and took photos of us before they gave us Afghan clothes to wear. They then handcuffed our hands behind our backs, blindfolded us and started interrogating us ... They threatened me with death, accusing me of belonging to al-Qaeda." After this initial interrogation, he said, "They put us in an underground cell measuring approximately two meters by three meters. There were 10 of us in the cell. We spent three months in the cell. There was no room for us to sleep so we had to alternate ... It was too hot in the cell, despite the fact that outside the temperature was freezing (there was snow), because the cell was overcrowded." He added that they were only fed once a day, that loud music was used as "torture," and that one of his fellow detainees "went insane," and pointed out that, when Red Cross representatives were allowed to visit, the most severely disturbed prisoners were secretly moved to another cell that was off-limits. Transferred to Bagram after the "Dark Prison," where he was interrogated for a month, he was then flown to Guantánamo, where he spent another month in solitary confinement.[18]

Hussein Almerfedi, a 24-year-old Yemeni, and Aminullah Tukhi, a 29-year-old Afghan, were also held in the "Dark Prison," although neither of them mentioned being abused, perhaps because they were not regarded as being of particular significance. Almerfedi was held for a total of 14 months in three prisons in Afghanistan—"two under Afghani control and one under US control [Bagram]," although he added that they all "seemed to be under US supervision." A former student, he went to Pakistan in the hope of using members of Jamaat-al-Tablighi to help him emigrate to Europe, and insisted that he was "kidnapped" in Iran. He explained that he was only interrogated on three occasions in Afghanistan, and pointed out that on each occasion he was told that the authorities knew he was innocent and he would soon be released. Tukhi, an economics graduate from Herat, fled to Iran to escape the Taliban, and was working as a taxi driver when the Iranians began rounding up illegal immigrants towards the end of 2001. "That day President Bush had announced that Iran is not a good country," he said, "and everything wasn't normal. Police were everywhere and they were looking for everything." In US custody, he attracted the Americans' interest when it transpired that he had occasionally worked as a driver for Abdul Aziz al-Matrafi and other al-Wafa members, although he denied allegations that he forged documents for al-Wafa and helped smuggle members of the organization across the border. He added that ten prisoners in total—six Arabs, two Afghans, an Uzbek and a Tajik—were delivered to the Americans, although what happened to the other six is unknown.[19]

Another prisoner held in the "Dark Prison" was Rafiq al-Hami, a 33-year-old Tunisian, who had been working in restaurants in Germany, and had traveled to Pakistan in 1999 to study with Jamaat-al-Tablighi. The circumstances of his capture are unknown, but he also ended up in the hands of the CIA: "I was in an Afghan prison but the interrogation was done by Americans. I was there for about a one-year period, transferring from one place to another." He added that he was tortured for three months in the "Dark Prison," where, he said, "I was threatened. I was left out all night in the cold ... I spent two months with no water, no shoes, in darkness and in the cold. There was darkness and loud music for two months. I was not allowed to pray. I was not allowed to fast during Ramadan. These things are documented. You have them."[20]

In addition to al-Hami and those "rendered" from Iran, at least 16 other Guantánamo prisoners were held in the "Dark Prison" between 2002 and 2004, when the facility probably closed down, and the remaining prisoners were transferred to Bagram. The stories of several of these men are related below, but what's particularly shocking about many of the other cases is how little "evidence" of militant activity was sought by the CIA before they snatched prisoners from other facilities and subjected them to this gruesome torture: others who were sent there included the Saudi-born British resident Shaker Aamer, who suffered "particularly vicious torture," and Mohammed Khusruf, the 60-year-old Yemeni captured after Tora Bora, who told his tribunal that, after his arrest, he was moved from a jail in Jalalabad to "an underground prison" in Kabul, where "they would interrogate and beat us." He added that those who were wounded "were also there"—presumably some of the other Taliban foot soldiers, humanitarian aid workers and religious teachers captured after Tora Bora, who also ended up in Guantánamo.[21]

Rendered from Zambia

Martin Mubanga, a 29-year-old Briton, was rendered to Guantánamo from Zambia. Born in Zambia but brought up in London from the age of three, he became interested in Islam in his late teens. In 1995, he worked with a Muslim charity helping victims of the Serbs' ethnic cleansing in Bosnia, and in November 2000 he traveled to Pakistan, and then Afghanistan, where he studied at madrassas in Kabul and Kandahar. Although he was booked on a flight to the UK from Karachi on September 26, 2001, he discovered that the routes to Pakistan were closed after 9/11, and his passport and his will had gone missing. After finding a guide to take him to Pakistan, he phoned his family to ask them to post his Zambian passport to him, and then decided to visit relatives in Zambia, where he met his elder sister, who had arrived from the UK, in February 2002. A few weeks later, his sister's boyfriend phoned from London to say that the *Sunday Times* had run a story saying that a man named Martin Mubanga had been captured in Afghanistan while fighting for the Taliban. Although this explained what had happened to his passport, the sequence of events that followed was incomprehensible.

First, he was arrested by the Zambian security services, and then an American agent and an MI5 agent flew to Zambia and questioned him in a series of motel rooms. The British agent produced his passport, his will and a list of 33 Jewish organizations in New York, which, he said, had been found with the passport in a cave in Afghanistan, and suggested that Mubanga was planning to visit New York on behalf of al-Qaeda, to seek out Jewish military targets. Despite the absurdity of the situation, he was interrogated for another three weeks, and then, after unsuccessful attempts to recruit him to work as a spy in South Africa or the north of England, the American told him, "I'm sorry to have to tell you this, as I think you're a decent guy, but in ten or 15 minutes we're going to the airport and they're taking you to Guantánamo Bay."

In Guantánamo, he spent a year with prisoners who only spoke Arabic. "I always thought one of the main things they were trying to do was break you mentally, make you go crazy," he said after his release. "So I thought, either I sink or I swim. I decided to swim and that meant learning Arabic." Left behind after four Britons were released in March 2004—apparently because, under duress, David Hicks made false allegations against him, which he later retracted—he then faced his hardest test. First, he was moved to cell blocks that only contained Pashtu-speaking Afghans, and then, deprived of all "comfort items," he was held in solitary confinement and underwent many of the humiliations described in the previous chapter, subjected to searing heat or freezing cold in the interrogation rooms, and on one occasion left alone by an interrogator until he wet himself: "He comes back with a mop and dips it in the pool of urine. Then he starts covering me with my own waste, like he's using a big paintbrush, working methodically, beginning with my feet and ankles and working his way up my legs. All the while he's racially abusing me, cussing me: 'Oh, the poor little negro, the poor little nigger.' He seemed to think it was funny."

As a result, he refused to speak to any interrogators for seven months. Despite the harshness of his treatment, however, the authorities began to doubt his status as a terrorist. James Crisfield Jr, a military lawyer, suggested that there was sufficient doubt about his reasons for traveling to various countries to question his definition as an "enemy combatant," and said attempts should be made to contact his family, and several months later, the man who kept up the spirits of those in the cages around him by making up Jamaican-style raps about their predicament was finally released.[22]

Tortured in Morocco

The case of 24-year-old Binyam Mohammed al-Habashi is one of the most distressing of all the Guantánamo stories. Born in Ethiopia, he came to Britain in 1995 when his father sought asylum, and stayed behind, having been given indefinite leave to remain, when his father returned to Ethiopia. After rediscovering his religion in his late teens, following problems with drugs, he became a volunteer at a mosque in west London, and is remembered as "a very nice, quiet person who never caused any trouble." In June 2001, he traveled to Afghanistan, intending to see "whether it was a good Islamic country or not," and after escaping to Pakistan in December 2001, when he lost his passport and all his travel documents, he was arrested at Karachi airport as he attempted to leave the country on April 10, 2002. Ten days later, he attracted the attention of US agents, and it was from this point that his torture began. For reasons that have not been explained, the Americans believed that he was an accomplice of Jose Padilla, a former gang member from Chicago, who was arrested in Chicago on May 8, 2002 after returning from Pakistan, and that, with Padilla, he had been planning to detonate a "dirty bomb" in a US city, and had also been planning to rent a number of ground-floor apartments in a housing block, sealing them, filling them with gas and blowing them up with timed detonators. What seems likely, however, is that these allegations came from Abu Zubaydah, in the weeks after his capture in March 2002, from some of the other men captured with Zubaydah, or from Padilla, who has been held in solitary confinement and subjected to sensory deprivation since his arrest.

While the source of these allegations remains uncertain, however, it's clear that, in a concerted effort to get him to confess, he was tortured in Pakistan, Morocco and Afghanistan for two and a half years, and was then moved to Guantánamo, where he was put forward for a trial by Military Commission in November 2005. In conversations with his lawyer, he explained that, when first questioned by the Americans, he insisted on having legal representation, but was told by the FBI, "The rules have changed. You don't get a lawyer." When he then refused to speak, the Pakistani authorities beat him, hung him from leather straps, and threatened him with guns. He was also interviewed by British agents, but said that they were unable to help him: "They checked out my story, and they said they knew I was a nobody. They said they would tell the Americans. I have struggled to understand how I came to mean such a lot to them." Frustrated by his refusal to confess, the Americans then told him that he was going to be sent to an Arab country because "the Pakistanis can't do exactly what we want them to," and, after a last visit from the British agents, who gave him a cup of tea and advised him to add sugar because "where you're going you need a lot of sugar," he was rendered to Morocco, where the meaning of the Americans' threat became all too apparent:[23]

> They cut off my clothes with some kind of doctor's scalpel ... They took the scalpel to my right chest. It was only a small cut. Maybe an inch. At first I just screamed ... Then they cut my left chest. This time I didn't want to scream because I knew it was coming. One of them took my penis in his hand and began to make cuts. He did it once, and they stood still for maybe a minute, watching my reaction. I was in agony. They must have done this 20 to 30 times, in maybe two hours. There was blood all over ... One of them said it would be better just to cut it off, as I would only breed terrorists.

This torture was repeated once a month, but when he asked a guard, "What's the point of this? I've told them everything I possibly could," he was told, "As far as I know, it's just to degrade you. So when you leave here, you'll have these scars and you'll never forget.

So you'll always fear doing anything but what the US wants." In between the episodes of torture, which included "even worse things," which were "too horrible to remember, let alone talk about," he was interrogated once a fortnight, when the Moroccans "would tell me what to say." Even towards the end of his time in Morocco, he said that the interrogators were still "training me what to say," and one of them told him, "We're going to change your brain." In autumn 2002, after a brutal session in which three men in black masks beat him repeatedly, he was moved to another prison, where, presumably under instructions from the Americans, he was shackled and made to listen to Meat Loaf and Aerosmith played at full volume through earphones for days on end. Throughout the whole of his 18 months' imprisonment in Morocco, he never saw anyone apart from his torturers, never saw daylight, and was never allowed to sleep through the night.[24]

In January 2004, a group of Americans took him to the "Dark Prison," where photos were taken of his injuries, which, he was told, were "to show Washington it's healing," but although the specialized Moroccan torture came to an end, his suffering continued. Like others who experienced the CIA's Afghan dungeon, he described it as "pitch black," with "no lights on in the rooms for most of the time." Hung up almost permanently for the first three days, his legs swelled up and his wrists and hands went numb, and he was then forced to listen to Eminem's "Slim Shady" and Dr Dre for twenty days, followed by "horrible ghost laughter and Halloween sounds." Later, he was "chained to the rails for a fortnight," and throughout this period, "the CIA worked on people, including me, day and night ... Plenty lost their minds. I could hear people knocking their heads against the walls and the doors, screaming their heads off."[25]

The "Salt Pit"

On September 9, 2002, two Saudi-born Pakistani residents, 33-year-old Abdul Rahim Ghulam Rabbani and his 32-year-old brother Mohammed, were arrested by Pakistani operatives during a raid on an apartment in Karachi. According to the *9/11 Commission Report*, the elder brother was an "al-Qaeda member who worked closely with Khalid Sheikh Mohammed [the architect of 9/11, discussed in Chapter 20] in Karachi, and assisted many of the 9/11 hijackers," specifically by providing them with a safe house in 2000, after their training in Afghanistan and before they flew out to the United States. These allegations were reiterated in the brothers' tribunals at Guantánamo: Mohammed was presented as a junior partner, accused of being "a senior al-Qaeda operative," who knew Khalid Sheikh Mohammed and met Osama bin Laden on six or seven occasions, and who also moved mujahideen between Afghanistan and Pakistan and ran "an al-Qaeda guest house" with his brother, whereas Abdul Rahim was presented as a full-blown member of al-Qaeda, who acted as a facilitator for Khalid Sheikh Mohammed for three years, and was "a well-known Karachi-based al-Qaeda facilitator who had transported many al-Qaeda members from safe houses to the Karachi apartment." It was also alleged that he "operated or resided at six al-Qaeda safe houses in Karachi with a senior al-Qaeda lieutenant," and that he was a member of an al-Qaeda cell planning car bomb attacks against US forces. While there seems little doubt that the two men ran a safe house in Karachi, a Pakistani intelligence official cast doubt on the extent of their involvement with terrorism in October 2006. Speaking about the Pakistani prisoners in Guantánamo, he mentioned the brothers, saying, "Although they have served for Khalid Sheikh as his employees, they were not linked with al-Qaeda."[26]

Despite this, they were dealt with brutally in Pakistani custody, and were then rendered to Afghanistan, where they were held in another secret prison near Kabul, which, like the "Dark Prison," appeared to be run by Afghans but was actually supervised and paid for by the CIA. The existence of the "Salt Pit," housed in an abandoned brick factory north of the capital, remained a closely guarded secret until 2005, when two stories emerged to blow its cover. The first of these was a previously unreported murder, which was exposed by Dana Priest in the *Washington Post* in March 2005. Priest reported that in November 2002, a recently promoted CIA officer, who had been put in charge of the facility in the absence of any senior personnel who were willing to take the job, "ordered guards to strip naked an uncooperative young Afghan detainee, chain him to the concrete floor and leave him there overnight without blankets." Following their orders, the guards then dragged him around the floor before putting him in his cell, where he died of hypothermia during the night. According to a senior US official, he then "disappeared from the face of the earth": he was hastily buried in an unmarked grave, his family was never notified of his death, and the CIA officer in charge of the prison was promoted. The US authorities, meanwhile, showed no willingness to investigate the case further. "He was probably associated with people who were associated with al-Qaeda," one official said, even though nothing was known about him at the time of his death, apart from the fact that he was captured in Pakistan with some other Afghans.[27]

Although the Rabbanis have not spoken about the "Salt Pit," it was confirmed in the other story about the prison that emerged in 2005, that of Khaled El-Masri. A German citizen, who happened to share the same name as the man who directed Ramzi bin al-Shibh and the 9/11 pilots to Mohamedou Ould Slahi, El-Masri, a 41-year-old unemployed car salesman, was detained by the Macedonian authorities at a border checkpoint as he tried to enter the country for a holiday on New Year's Eve 2003, apparently because the other El-Masri was on a watchlist and they believed he had a forged passport. After being questioned at gunpoint about his connections with al-Qaeda, he was held in a motel for 23 days, and was then "released," only to be immediately abducted by seven or eight masked US agents, who beat him, stripped him, dressed him in blue overalls and rendered him to the "Salt Pit," where, he said, there were several other prisoners, including a Pakistani who had been there for two years, a Tanzanian and the Rabbani brothers. Describing the prison, he said, "Everything was dirty—a dirty blanket, dirty water like from a fish aquarium," and explained that on his first night he was repeatedly punched in the head and neck by the guards and was made to run up and down stairs with his arms shackled behind his back. As the weeks went by, he was regularly interrogated about his purported connections with the 9/11 hijackers, and was told by an interrogator, "Where you are right now there is no law, no rights, no one knows you are here, and no one cares about you," but it was not until February that the interrogators began to suspect that they may have rendered an innocent man, and it was not until April that CIA director George Tenet was briefed about the case. He apparently exclaimed, "You've got an innocent guy in the Salt Pit?" and urged his release. On May 29, the CIA added insult to injury by flying him to Albania, blindfolding him and putting him on a bus for seven hours, and then telling him to make his own way home, hoping, presumably, that no one would ever believe his incredible story.[28]

The Capture of Ramzi bin al-Shibh

While there are good reasons for suspecting that none of the prisoners described above were as significant as the Americans thought they were, they secured what appeared to be a significant victory on September 11, 2002—the first anniversary of 9/11—when, using documents that were apparently found on Abdul Rahim Rabbani at the time of his arrest, the Pakistani authorities were directed to another apartment in Karachi. After a four-hour firefight, they captured Ramzi bin al-Shibh, the original "20th hijacker," who was only prevented from dying a martyr's death on 9/11 because he was unable to obtain a US visa, but had since become a close associate of Khalid Sheikh Mohammed.[29]

While bin al-Shibh was immediately rendered to a secret CIA prison in Thailand, a different fate befell seven of the other prisoners who were captured with him. Seventeen-year-old Hassan bin Attash, a Saudi of Yemeni descent, was sent to the "Dark Prison" for a week, and was then rendered to Jordan, where, he said, he was severely tortured while being interrogated about the activities of his brother Waleed, a suspect in the bombing of the USS *Cole* in 2000, who was captured in Karachi six months later (see Chapter 20). After 16 months in Jordan, he was rendered back to US custody in Afghanistan on January 7, 2004 (along with Abdu Ali Sharqawi), and was transferred to Guantánamo on September 20, 2004, in a plane that also contained Sharqawi, Binyam al-Habashi and several other prisoners discussed below. Little is known about his treatment in Guantánamo, although the allegations against him surfaced in his tribunal, in which it was alleged that he traveled to Afghanistan "for jihad" in 1997 (when he was only 12 years old), received weapons and explosives training, and served as a foot soldier in Jalalabad. It was also alleged that he "took an al-Qaeda operative from Afghanistan to Pakistan to establish a safe house and organize an operation to plan al-Qaeda attacks against US naval vessels and US oil tankers in the Straits of Hormuz," and that he "forwarded money that allowed al-Qaeda operatives to travel to the UAE in support of the operation." Whether or not there is any truth in these allegations is impossible to ascertain. In June 2006, Marc Falkoff told the journalist Ken Silverstein, "I couldn't tell you whether he was guilty or innocent. I have no clue because we haven't been able to talk to him about anything other than the abuse he suffered."[30]

The other six prisoners—all Yemenis—were also transferred to Afghanistan, but managed to avoid rendition to a third country, probably because they were nothing more than recent Taliban recruits who ended up in Karachi as part of an extended safe-house system that was sheltering all Arabs from arrest, and not just those who were committed to al-Qaeda. Only two of them have spoken about the "Dark Prison," but it seems likely that all six spent some time there before being transferred to Bagram and then Guantánamo. Twenty-four-year-old Ha'il al-Maythali, who went to Afghanistan in November 2000 to "fight in the jihad," admitted ferrying supplies on the back lines near Kabul, but said that he was only on the front lines for a week because he had no military experience. He denied allegations that he trained at al-Farouq, saying that, after he was captured, he was taken to the "Dark Prison," where "there was very bad torture conducted on people," including himself, which was "so bad that he knew by making up and agreeing to the training it would stop the torture." He added that "his testicles were disfigured to the point where they cannot be repaired."[31]

Twenty-one-year-old Musab al-Mudwani arrived in Afghanistan in August 2001 and trained briefly at al-Farouq, until it closed. After spending a few months in guest houses in Afghanistan, he made his way to Pakistan via Khost, traveling with other Arabs, Pakistanis and Afghans, and then spent ten months being moved around various houses in Lahore, Quetta and Karachi, waiting for an opportunity to return home that never came. Explaining the situation in Karachi at the time of his arrest, he said, "The group I was arrested with were staying in two apartments. One person from each apartment refused to surrender and fought the Pakistani forces sent to arrest us. I was in the group that chose to surrender," and added that the Pakistanis were "thankful for our cooperation and surrendering without fighting." He then explained that there were seven men in his apartment, including one who was killed, who had only been there for about five days, and that two other men—presumably bin al-Shibh and bin Attash—shared the other apartment with a family. His only mention of the "Dark Prison" came when a Board Member asked him, "Are you holding anything back from the interrogators?" and he replied, "That is impossible, because before I came to the prison in Guantánamo Bay I was in another prison in Afghanistan, under the ground [and] it was very dark, total dark, under torturing and without sleep. It was impossible that I could get out of there alive. I was really beaten and tortured."[32]

The Yemeni Colonel

Eight days after the Karachi raid, Abdulsalam al-Hela, a 34-year-old Yemeni businessman, arrived in Cairo. The manager of a pharmaceutical firm, he was also the Yemeni representative of Egypt's biggest construction company, and had been invited to settle some financial disagreements, but within a week he was abducted by the Egyptian security services on behalf of the Americans. According to certain reports, an Egyptian militant in Yemen suggested that he had ties to al-Qaeda operatives, and it's possible that, when this information was passed on to the Americans, the decision was made to capture him. What seems more likely, however, is that the al-Qaeda story was a ruse, and that the Americans—now sufficiently emboldened after abducting and rendering whoever they felt like for over a year—decided to abduct him for his intelligence value. As well as being a businessman, al-Hela was a colonel in Yemeni intelligence, responsible for seeking asylum in other countries for the "Arab Afghans," including hundreds of former mujahideen who returned from Afghanistan to fight the Marxist rebels in South Yemen during the 1994 civil war, and some of the 30,000 other Yemenis who also went to Afghanistan over the previous twenty years. For the Americans, al-Hela had precious intelligence: he knew who had settled down and moved away from politics, who continued to be active, and who had left the country, and, as well as being familiar with members of the militant groups, he had a close relationship with Yemeni President Ali Abdullah Salih, and with numerous Arab and Western intelligence services.

After his abduction, al-Hela was interrogated in two hotels for a week, where he was subjected to "degrading treatment," and was then driven to an airport and handed over to masked US agents who stripped him, dressed him in blue overalls, chained his hands and feet, blindfolded him, and took him to the "Dark Prison," where, as well as being kept in permanent darkness, with "sharp metallic rock music" playing 24 hours a day, he was "regularly stripped naked and interrogated," was "suspended from the ceiling for prolonged periods," and had one of his hands "cuffed to the wall at all times making it difficult for him to sleep or go to the toilet." He added that "the only time he saw light was when a bright strobe light was flashed in his eyes during interrogation, temporarily blinding him," and that he lost 30 kg in weight. He was then transferred to another underground prison near Kabul called Malidu, a more modern facility where he was held for two and a half months and interrogated for 15 consecutive days, and was then taken to another secret prison, where he was held for 14 months, and where "his jailers told him he was being held at the behest of the US." Although he was also tortured in this unknown prison, he pointed out that "the psychological burden of being confined incommunicado was far worse than the physical abuse." He was then transferred to Bagram, where, he said, the conditions were "very, very bad," but did not wish to elaborate. While there, he managed to smuggle out a letter that was printed in a Yemeni newspaper, in which he pleaded for help and pointed out, acutely, "My only crime is that the Americans wanted information from me, but couldn't find any, so I was left in Afghani prisons. My last interrogation was a year ago." He was transferred to Guantánamo on September 17, 2004, in the plane full of supposedly significant suspects mentioned above, and has been held in Camp 5, reserved for prisoners who are considered to be dangerous or to have intelligence value.[33]

Rendered from the Gambia

Two British residents—33-year-old Bisher al-Rawi and 50-year-old Jamil El-Banna—were captured in the Gambia on November 8, 2002, and rendered to Afghanistan and then Guantánamo, under circumstances that reflect shamefully on the British intelligence services. Al-Rawi had been living in the UK since 1984, when his family fled Iraq after his father was tortured by Saddam Hussein's secret police. While the rest of his family became British citizens, he retained his Iraqi citizenship in the forlorn hope that the family might one day be able to reclaim its property in Baghdad. In the 1990s, he got to know the radical Jordanian cleric Abu Qatada, regarded by British and US intelligence as al-Qaeda's spiritual leader in Europe, because they attended the same mosque, and occasionally did some work for him, which involved either translating or undertaking house repairs. The day after 9/11, when two MI5 agents turned up at his house, he agreed to become an unpaid informer for them, keeping tabs on Qatada's whereabouts and eventually—when the British authorities decided to arrest him rather than keeping him under surveillance—helping MI5 capture him. His reward, and that of El-Banna, who helped out on one occasion, driving Qatada's wife and children to see him in his safe house, was imprisonment in Guantánamo, even though their lawyers noted that "British officers had thanked both men" when Qatada was arrested.

Married with five children, El-Banna was born in Palestine, but holds Jordanian citizenship. He moved to the UK with his family in 1994 from Pakistan, where he had worked at an orphanage in Peshawar, and, coincidentally, had also met Qatada. On the day after 9/11, he, like al-Rawi, received a visit from intelligence agents, although he refused to become an informer, but neither man was under suspicion when they planned a business trip to the Gambia, in autumn 2002, to help al-Rawi's brother Wahab set up a mobile peanut-processing plant. Ten days before leaving, MI5 agents again visited El-Banna—offering him a new life in an Islamic country if he became an informer—but telling him that there was no problem with his trip, and wishing him good luck with it, when he turned them down for a second time. When the men set off on November 1, however, they were detained in Gatwick and questioned about a supposedly suspicious electronic device in al-Rawi's hand luggage, which turned out to be nothing more than a battery charger, and as they prepared to fly out again on November 8 the British authorities sent US intelligence several telegrams, which were mostly full of lies. One informed them that the two men had been detained under the Terrorism Act, that al-Rawi was an "Islamic extremist," and that—contrary to the evidence—a baggage search had revealed a device that could possibly be used as "part of a car-based improvised electronic device," and another pointed out that they both knew Abu Qatada, and claimed that El-Banna was Qatada's financier.

With the stage set by MI5, al-Rawi, El-Banna and a British colleague were arrested as soon as they arrived in the Gambia on November 8, along with Wahab al-Rawi, who had traveled there the week before, and another colleague from the Gambia. Their investment—£250,000— disappeared, the plywood that was part of the materials exported by Wahab was used to make an improvised jail for the men, and, although the others were released after a few weeks, al-Rawi and El-Banna were rendered to Afghanistan, where they spent two months in the

"Dark Prison" and another two months in Bagram. They were then transferred to Guantánamo, where their interrogations, over the years that followed, focused exclusively on the lies and misrepresentations provided by MI5, and persistent attempts were made to recruit them as informers, using techniques that ranged from bribery to threats against El-Banna's family. For over three years, the British government refused to press for their release, and it was not until March 2007, when al-Rawi's MI5 connection could no longer be concealed, that he returned to the UK as a free man, although, at the time of writing, El-Banna remained in Guantánamo.[34]

Renditions in 2003

The 27-year-old Algerian Adil al-Jazeeri, the son of Mustafa Hamlili (see Chapter 13), was captured outside a restaurant in Peshawar on June 17, 2003 with five other men who were later released. After a month in Pakistani custody, he was rendered to Afghanistan on July 13, 2003, and was one of ten supposedly significant prisoners who were flown to Guantánamo on September 20, 2004. Regarded as an al-Qaeda facilitator by the US and Pakistani authorities, others were not convinced: a local described him as a member of the Takfiri group Jamaat-ul-Muslimeen, a violent, intolerant group, founded in 1994, which is fiercely anti-Western and anti-American. The truth is difficult to discern. Al-Jazeeri has been a thoroughly cooperative prisoner throughout his imprisonment, and, although he was presented with a barrage of allegations in his tribunal—including claims that he was involved with Algerian and Tunisian terrorist groups, and that he moved al-Qaeda fighters from Afghanistan to Pakistan—he refuted them all, saying that most were false statements that had been obtained under duress in Guantánamo, Bagram, or Kabul, where, presumably, he was held in the "Dark Prison," although he also pointed out that a few allegations were made by al-Qaeda prisoners. "All al-Qaeda members they lie," he said, "and most of them they really apologized to me in Camp 5. [One] asked for my forgiveness because he had had to do so. He had to say something like this because he was under pressure." In the end, all al-Jazeeri admitted was that he had been living in Pakistan since 1986, that he was married with four children, that he was expelled to Afghanistan in 2000 after spending a year in prison for having no legal papers, and that he subsequently found a job with the Taliban working in their media and translation department.[35]

Saifullah Paracha, a 55-year-old businessman and philanthropist from Karachi, was arrested after flying into Bangkok for a business trip on July 5, 2003. Rendered to Afghanistan, he spent 14 months in Bagram and was then flown to Guantánamo on September 20, 2004. A graduate in computer science from the New York Institute of Technology, he acknowledged that he had met Osama bin Laden twice, at meetings of businessmen and religious leaders in 1999 and 2000, but denied the allegations against him, which included making investments for al-Qaeda members, translating statements for bin Laden, joining in a plot to smuggle explosives into the US and recommending that nuclear weapons be used against US soldiers. These were indeed wild accusations for anyone familiar with his story. Deeply impressed by all things American, he had lived in the US in the 1980s, running several small businesses, and after returning to Pakistan had made a fortune running a clothes-exporting business in partnership with a New York-based Jewish entrepreneur (an unthinkable association for someone who was actually involved with al-Qaeda). His case is inextricably tied to that of his 23-year-old son Uzair, the eldest of his four children, who was detained in New York, where he was marketing apartments to the Pakistani community, four months earlier. Arrested by FBI agents, Uzair was accused of working with Ammar al-Baluchi and Majid Khan (two supposedly "high-value" suspects discussed in Chapter 20) to provide false documents to help Khan enter the US to carry out attacks on gas stations, and was convicted in a US court in November 2005—even though he said that he was coerced into making a false confession, and both Khan and al-Baluchi made statements that neither Uzair nor his father had ever knowingly aided al-Qaeda. Uzair was sentenced to 30 years' imprisonment in July 2006. His father remains in Guantánamo, where, although he has heart problems, he has refused to undertake an operation because he does not trust the prison's surgeons.[36]

Captured by the Russian Mafia

Two other prisoners—Soufian al-Hawari, a 31-year-old Algerian, and Omar al-Rammah (aka Zakaria al-Baidany), a 26-year-old Yemeni—were also captured far from the battlefields of Afghanistan. Al-Hawari, who said that he used drugs and stole from tourists in various European countries until he became a devout Muslim at the age of 27, traveled to Georgia in 2001 to meet an old friend from Algeria called Abdul Haq, and was captured on a bridge 50 miles from his friend's house under the most extraordinary circumstances: "The Americans didn't capture me. The Mafia captured me. They sold me to the Americans ... When I was captured, a car came around and people inside were talking Russian and Georgian ... We were delivered to another group who spoke perfect Russian. They sold us to the dogs. The Americans came two days later with a briefcase full of money. They took us to a forest, then a private plane to Kabul."

When asked who was with him, he replied, "There were four of us. Myself, my friend Abdul Haq, a Yemeni guy named Zakaria, and a Chech[en] driver, who was killed." According to a Cageprisoners report, they were sold to the Americans for $100,000. Al-Hawari has not spoken about his detention in either Afghanistan or Guantánamo (and al-Rammah has not spoken at all), but, according to two reports, al-Rammah has been subjected to brutal treatment in Guantánamo. Cageprisoners reported that he "would be held with his hand tied behind his back and his feet chained to the floor while being subjected to extremely cold temperatures. He would not be allowed to use the toilet or eat," and Juma al-Dossari described how he went on a hunger strike because of the abuse that he was subjected to during interrogations, but was still interrogated every day for more than twelve hours. He added that the interrogator ordered the guards to keep him awake and he was then placed in solitary confinement, and explained, "You have no idea of what the solitary isolation cells in Camp Delta are like; they cause psychological illnesses. They beat him in solitary and I heard his screams when they were beating him."[37]

The most extraordinary aspect of al-Hawari's story surfaced in 2007, when it was revealed that, despite having bought him as part of a $100,000 package, the authorities have cleared him for release from Guantánamo. Other intriguing facets of his story—in particular the fate of his friend Abdul Haq—surfaced in another extraordinary, and previously unreported document, which also sheds light on some of the other "ghost" prisoners who did not end up in Guantánamo. The document gave the names of twelve prisoners who were held in Bagram in 2005, and was issued in November 2005 by Abu Yahya al-Libi, one of four high-profile prisoners who escaped from Bagram in July 2005 (one of the others was Omar al-Farouq, who was captured in Indonesia in June 2002, and was killed in Iraq in September 2006). Al-Libi, who described a number of secret prisons in Afghanistan—including "la prisone tyrannique" (possibly the "Dark Prison"), Rissat, Rissat 2 and Panjshir (which is probably the Dohab prison in the Panjshir valley)—also described two other prisoners, in addition to al-Hawari and al-Baddah, who were transferred to Guantánamo: Tawfiq al-Bihani, a 30-year-old Yemeni, who was captured in Iran at the start of 2002, and Wissam Ahmed, the Jordanian shopkeeper mentioned above. He said that he met three of the men in Rissat 2, and, although he didn't specify where he met al-Baddah, he noted that he had "passed through all the prisons." He also reported what had happened to al-Hawari's friend Abdul Haq, noting that "we heard that he had been sent to Algeria but we are not sure," and added that, in February 2004, he and Abdul Haq had actually escaped from the Panjshir prison for a day and a half, before being recaptured in the "driving snow and freezing cold" of the mountains.

The other seven prisoners mentioned by al-Libi provide a fascinating insight into the parallel world of secret prisons running in tandem with Guantánamo. They are: Reda the Tunisian, captured in Karachi in May 2002; Amin al-Bakri, a Yemeni captured in Thailand at the end of 2002; Abu Houdayfa, a Tunisian captured in Peshawar at the end of 2002; Abu Nassim, a Libyan captured in Peshawar at the start of 2003; Issa, a Tanzanian captured in Mogadishu; Salah Din, a Pakistani captured in Baghdad in 2004; and, most shockingly, a Yemeni called Fadi, who was captured in Zabul province in Afghanistan at the end of 2004 and rendered first to Abu Ghraib and then Bagram. According to al-Libi, most of these men had, like Omar al-Baddah, "passed through all the prisons," where they had been subjected to "hard torture," and although three of them—Reda the Tunisian, Abu Houdayfa and Abu Nasim—were listed in a Human Rights Watch report in February 2007, I believe that the others have never been mentioned outside of al-Libi's original report. They are, of course, just a few of the hundreds of unknown prisoners who have been rendered to foreign prisons or held in other prisons ostensibly run by the host countries, but actually paid for and run by the CIA, and it's a world so far removed from the controlled operations pioneered by Michael

Scheuer and his colleagues that it would not be surprising to discover, as the whole enterprise unravels, that many of them—whether "guilty" of anything or not—will be the US's own "disappeared," subjected to not even the most cursory of paper trails, and written off as callously as the victims of other brutal regimes who are routinely condemned by the Americans themselves.[38]

17
Losing the War in Afghanistan

More Murders in US Custody

The murders at Bagram and the "Salt Pit" in 2002 heralded an increasingly barbarous US regime in Afghanistan. Although Hamid Karzai was sworn in as President after a loya jirga (grand council) in Kabul in June 2002, which was attended by 2,000 delegates from across Afghanistan, the US military—and, in particular, the Special Forces soldiers operating out of several forward operating bases around the country—behaved like a rogue army. In March 2003, journalists Adrian Levy and Cathy Scott-Clark traveled to Gardez to meet Dr. Rafiullah Bidar, the regional director of the Afghan Independent Human Rights Commission, recently established—with funding from the US Congress—"to investigate abuses committed by local warlords and to ensure that women's and children's rights were protected." Ironically, Bidar told the reporters that what his job actually entailed was registering complaints against the US military. "Many thousands of people have been rounded up and detained by them," he said. "Those who have been freed say that they were held alongside foreign detainees who've been brought to this country to be processed. No one is charged. No one is identified. No international monitors are allowed into the US jails. People who have been arrested say they've been brutalized—the tactics used are beyond belief." Speaking anonymously, a government minister also complained, "Washington holds Afghanistan up to the world as a nascent democracy and yet the US military has deliberately kept us down, using our country to host a prison system that seems to be administered arbitrarily, indiscriminately and without accountability."[1]

Throughout 2003, at least three more prisoners were murdered by Americans in three different forward operating bases that were part of this arbitrary, indiscriminate and unaccountable prison system. In Gardez, in March 2003, Jamal Naseer, an 18-year-old Afghan army recruit, was captured with seven other Afghan soldiers. After being treated "like animals" for 17 days, according to some of the other men, who said that they were hung upside down and struck repeatedly with sticks, rubber hoses and cables, immersed in cold water, made to lie in the snow, and subjected to electric shocks, Naseer's body, covered in bruises, was turned over to the local police with no documentation of his death and no autopsy results. Three months later, in Asadabad, 28-year-old Abdul Wali, who handed himself in voluntarily in connection with a rocket attack in which he was not involved, was beaten to death by David Passaro, a civilian contractor working with the CIA, who assaulted him "using his hands and feet, and a large flashlight" over a two-day period, and in November, at a base in Gereshk, another Afghan, Abdul Wahid, died from "multiple blunt force injuries," 48 hours after he was handed over by Afghan forces. As with the murders in 2002, the authorities were unwilling to pursue investigations. An inquest into Naseer's death did not begin until September 2004, after the story surfaced in the media, and in January 2007 the only outcome was that two soldiers received an "administrative remand" for failing to report the murder. In Abdul Wahid's case, the authorities absolved themselves of blame by claiming that his injuries were sustained in Afghan custody, and in Abdul Wali's case, David Passaro was charged with assault in June 2004, and was sentenced to eight years in prison in February 2007. This was little comfort to Wali's family, however, and Said Akbar, the governor of Kunar province, noted that his murder became a tool for terrorist recruiting and "created a huge setback for Afghanistan's national reconciliation efforts."[2]

Capturing Karzai's Men

At Bagram, meanwhile, the processing of prisoners for Guantánamo reflected both the desperation and the ignorance of US military operatives in the field. Hundreds of Afghan prisoners were held between December 2002 and August 2003, when the last of the Guantánamo prisoners were processed, but, although many were released and others continued to be held in Afghanistan, the ninety who were sent to Cuba were, yet again, almost entirely innocent. Around 60 percent—including at least 17 men who were working for the Karzai government—were betrayed by opportunistic rivals, who were all too aware that the Americans were both gullible and lazy, and would not make any attempt to investigate the men's histories; another 30 percent were bystanders rounded up arbitrarily after attacks on US forces.

Those who were working for the government included 40-year-old Haji Ghalib, the chief of police for a district in Jalalabad, and one of his officers, 32-year-old Kako Kandahari, who were captured together, after US and Afghan forces searched their compound and identified weapons and explosives that they thought were going to be used against them. Both men pointed out, however, that they fought with the Americans in Tora Bora. "I captured a lot of al-Qaeda and Arabs that were turned over to the Americans," Ghalib said, "and I see those people here that I helped capture in Afghanistan." He explained that he thought he may have been betrayed by one of the commanders in Tora Bora, because he "let about 40 [al-Qaeda] escape so I got on the phone and cussed at him and that is why I am here." Forty-year-old Khi Ali Gul, who was captured in Khost and accused of taking part in a bomb plot and being part of a Taliban assassination team, also said that he fought with the Americans in Tora Bora, and described one occasion when "the Americans were sleeping and we were guarding them." "If I were their enemy," he said, "I would have killed them all." He was captured at a checkpoint, where "there were some people that I had a dispute with," and said that they "told the American soldiers a lie," and he was then arrested.[3]

Six men captured in Gardez in July 2003 were also working for the government, and were resolutely opposed to the Taliban and al-Qaeda. Thirty-two-year-old Abdullah Mujahid Haq (cleared for release in 2007) was the police chief in Gardez and the security chief for Paktia province after the fall of the Taliban, and had just been promoted to a job protecting the highways of Kabul at the Interior Ministry. At the start of the US-led invasion, he met US Special Forces in Logar and invited them to Gardez, where he negotiated the rent of the camp that they used as their base, and he also fought alongside them during Operation Anaconda. According to his lawyers, he is so well respected that residents of Gardez and Paktia have sent several petitions to the

US administration, pointing out that he was "instrumental in helping establish schools, including schools for girls" in the region. Explaining the circumstances of his arrest, he said that two Americans detained him and asked him about two military commanders that he knew, who were accused of stealing. When he denied the story, he said that one of the men "told me that I wasn't telling the truth about these people, so you belong in Cuba," and added, "It appears that the decision was made to send me to Cuba already."[4]

Curiously, the theft that was responsible for getting Abdullah Mujahid Haq sent to Guantánamo seems to have been reported by Dr. Hafizullah Shabaz Khail, a 56-year-old pharmacist from Zormat, south of Gardez, who in turn blamed Haq for his imprisonment. Approached by the town elders after Karzai came to power, Khail served as the mayor for six months until an official appointment was made, and then continued to help out with security. "While I was mayor in Zormat," he said, "there were no problems with the Americans. I met with American commanders several times ... We even took pictures together." Arrested after capturing some thieves who were working for Taj Mohammed, the head of security in Zormat, he suggested that Haq, who was Mohammed's boss, then arranged for the Americans to arrest him. If this is the case—and lawyers for the two men have suggested that they were bitter enemies—then they were both in Guantánamo because of allegations they had made against each other; the fact that the US authorities failed to notice this indicates, yet again, that they had no interest in cross-referencing cases or investigating the truth of assertions made against those in their custody. Unlike Haq, however, Khail has not been cleared for release, even though, as with his rival, several local tribes sent a petition to the US authorities confirming his many contributions to their community.[5]

Also arrested at this time (and released in October 2006) was 43-year-old Dr. Said Mohammed Ali Shah, a Shia from one of the most prominent families in Gardez. A former mujahideen commander against the Russians, he fled to Iran during the Taliban's rule, where he qualified as a doctor, and after returning to his hometown in May 2002 he was chosen as the People's Representative for Gardez, and attended the loya jirga in Kabul the following month. He then returned to Iran to arrange for the return of his family, visited Saudi Arabia for the hajj, and was greeted by crowds of well-wishers when he returned to Gardez in August 2003. Two days later, however, he, like Haq, was arrested and taken to Bagram, where he was beaten regularly, kept awake by recordings of sirens that were played night and day, dragged around on a rope and subjected to extremes of heat and cold. The third man was 50-year-old Haji Mohammed Akhtiar (released in December 2006), who had also been a mujahideen commander against the Russians. After living as a refugee in Pakistan during the Taliban's rule, he returned to Gardez in 2002 but was captured by long-standing enemies loyal to Jalaluddin Haqqani, who only released him when he promised that he would not serve the Karzai government for the next nine months. When he finally took up a government post at the end of this period, recruiting personnel for the Afghan Army, he too was captured by the Americans and taken to Bagram. Haq, Ali Shah and Akhtiar all blamed long-standing Communist rivals—who were jockeying for positions of power in post-Taliban Afghanistan—for telling lies about them to the Americans, although Akhtiar also blamed one of Haqqani's commanders, who had become close to the Americans, and it's also possible that Pacha Khan Zadran was once more exercising his malign influence. Ali Shah recalled meeting him at the loya jirga, when he specifically told him that his enemies came from two particular villages—Ali Shah's, and that of Abdullah Mujahid Haq. Summoning up what had happened to him, Ali Shah told his tribunal: "I've been a good servant to my people ... and that's why they chose me as their representative. So these jealous, harmful and money-loving people, these spies, they created a fear for you ... In your country is it normal to keep someone for years just because somebody gave a report against them, without having any evidence? Or is it just us, the Afghans, that everybody should come and beat us up?"[6]

Nazar Gul Chaman was equally blameless. The 22-year-old (cleared for release in 2007) moved back to Afghanistan in April 2003, after living as a refugee in Pakistan, and was working for the government as a security guard at a fuel depot, when he was captured while staying in Mohammed Akhtiar's house. Following the script dictated to the Americans by Akhtiar's enemies, both men were accused of being members of Gulbuddin Hekmatyar's Hizb-e-Islami (HIG) party, which they were not, and when Chaman refuted the allegation, the following exchange took place:

> *Tribunal President*: I think you went there because Haji Akhtiar was a HIG and he needed fighters and you came to be a fighter for HIG with Akhtiar. That's what I think.
> *Detainee*: Why should I go over there just to kill myself?
> *Presiding Officer*: I don't know why. Many people do. I don't know why you all do it.[7]

Thirty-two-year-old Izatullah Nazrat Yar (also cleared for release in 2007) was also working for the government. A local tribal leader, he supervised the collection of weapons from his people, as requested by the Americans and the government, and was responsible for guarding them in a compound, but someone told a false story about him to the Americans and he was arrested. When his father, 78-year-old Haji Nazrat Khan (released in August 2006), heard about his capture, he made his way to the compound to ask why and was promptly arrested himself. A former commander for Sibghatullah Mojaddedi, who was President of Afghanistan for two months in 1992, Khan had been largely housebound since 1993, when his health deteriorated, and was scornful of allegations that he fought with the Taliban. "I was having problems with my legs," he said. "I could not get out of my home. How could I fight for the Taliban the way that I am?" He was particularly eloquent about Afghan history, and gave his tribunal a heartfelt summary of his people's woes, in which he explained that, after the Soviet Union fell,

> … we were expecting, waiting for Americans to help us to create and build up a new government. Unfortunately, they did not do it. Then the Taliban took over and they committed atrocities, killing, and any brutality they could. Talib means educated student or to learn things, but they were not that kind of people. Then, during the Taliban time, the opportunity opened for people to come from all over the world. The terrorist and any other kind of person came to Afghanistan and destroyed our honor and our dignity. Bin Laden, we hate him more than you guys and you people do not realize who is an enemy and who is a friend. When you came to Afghanistan everybody was waiting for America to help us build up our country. We were looking for you guys and we were very happy that you would come to our country. The people that hated you were very few, but you just grabbed guys like me. Look at me. Our very happiness, you turned it to bitterness. I am still

not mad at you guys, but in the future try to know the difference between your enemy and your friend.[8]

Other Betrayals

Elsewhere, incidents of betrayal were equally abundant. In Kandahar province, three villagers—43-year-old Haji Shahzada, 46-year-old Abdullah Khan, and 55-year-old Allah Nasir—were captured during house raids by Afghan soldiers on January 29, 2003 after an enemy of Shahzada, a prominent landowner and the local representative for the Karzai government, told a false story to the Americans. Shahzada explained, "In Afghanistan they heard that American forces are providing $25,000 to capture each Arab and $15,000 to capture each Afghan. Is it [that] you want to buy people with money? The enemy who sold me for $15,000 to you, I will charge him $200,000 and I will make sure that I hand all of his family to you, so they will work like me in Cuba." Warning that capturing innocent people like him was a sure way of turning the population against the Americans, he also said, "this is just me you brought but I have six sons left behind in my country. I have ten uncles in my area that would be against you. I don't care about myself. I could die here, but I have 300 male members of my family there in my country. If you want to build Afghanistan you can't build it this way ... I will tell anybody who asks me that this is oppression." Ludicrously, most of the allegations against Shahzada centered on Khan, a poor shopkeeper who had just sold him a dog. Captured at Shahzada's house, and accused of being Khairullah Khairkhwa, the governor of Herat (who had been in US custody since February 2002), he was also accused of being an airfield commander for the Taliban. The third man, Nasir, was an old family friend of Shahzada. An ethnic Uzbek, he was also a poor shopkeeper, and was also subjected to ludicrous allegations: that he worked for al-Wafa in Herat, and that he was involved in an international bomb plot. All three men were released in 2005 and 2006.[9]

Others were betrayed to the US forces, or were simply victims of US incompetence. Twenty-nine-year-old Janat Gul (released in 2005 or 2006) was captured at his home in Helmand province in January 2003. He worked for Ariana Airlines to avoid being conscripted to fight, but denied being a member of the Taliban, and explained that he quit his job several days after 9/11: "I was released from the oppression of the Taliban government. I came out of the darkness into the light ... even before the Americans came, I was in my own house and in my own land." Forty-year-old Abdul Ghafour was a teacher who ran a small school in his village in Paktia province, and rarely left the area because his mother was ill. When US and Afghan forces came knocking on his door in the middle of the night on February 7, 2003, he thought that they were robbers, and went to the roof and fired a few warning shots. When the Americans opened fire in response and summoned fighter jets, he realized he had made a mistake, and he then let them in and was arrested, but at no point did anyone explain to him why they wanted to search his house in the first place. Twenty-one-year-old Mohibullah, from Uruzgan, had a similar experience two weeks later. Woken in the night by the sound of firing, he went into his compound and fired three warning shots to ward off what he thought were burglars. Soon after, a US plane dropped a bomb on his compound, injuring him, and he was captured by Special Forces the following morning. "I never worked with the Taliban, or talked with them or ate with them," he said. "I was a bus driver." Taj Mohammed, a 21-year-old goat herder from Kunar province (released in October 2006), was betrayed by a relative. He said that he beat up his cousin, who was working for the Americans, after he installed water pipes for all the houses in the village except his. As a result, his cousin told the Americans that he was working with Gulbuddin Hekmatyar and planning an attack on a US base, and he was captured and taken to Bagram. "These are all lies about me," he said. "I was a shepherd, and I never can even go out very much, and I was always with my goats on the mountain." Another goat herder, 31-year-old Sharbat Khan, a nomad from the Kuchi tribe, was captured after an IED attack on US forces, for no reason other than the fact that there was no one else around. He was released in February 2006.[10]

These were not the only stories of betrayal and incompetence. Said Mohammed, a 25-year-old shopkeeper from a village near the Pakistani border, whose only crime seems to have been that his youngest brother once gave a small piece of dry bread to a passing Arab, was captured with his father, brother and two other villagers. "I was arrested at my home," he said. "I was irrigating my land and the guards [US Special Forces] were in my home. As soon as I got into the house, I saw the guards and I went to them and I said hello. They pushed me to the ground, covered my head with a bag and took me to Bagram." Two teachers—37-year-old Abdul Matin, and 50-year-old Mohammed Zahir—were also betrayed. Matin, a science teacher, had been living in Pakistan during the Taliban years, but returned to Afghanistan in February 2002 when the Karzai government called for people to help rebuild the country. He said that he was betrayed by local enemies, who knew that his father was wealthy, when he refused to pay a $30,000 bribe, and Zahir, who said that he was sold for just $100, taught math and languages at a secular school in Ghazni set up by the Karzai government, but received threatening night letters from Taliban sympathizers, who arranged for his arrest by telling lies to the US forces. The most outrageous ineptitude on the part of the Americans concerned Faiz Ullah, a 46-year-old Shia from Bamiyan province. Betrayed by a local leader who was frustrated in his efforts to marry his sister, he was accused of supporting the Taliban and being a HIG member. These allegations would have been insensitive enough in the case of any Afghan Shia, but in Faiz Ullah's case, as he pointed out, the Taliban killed hundreds of Shias in Bamiyan, including his uncle and his brother-in-law, and HIG members killed his mother and took his land, forcing him to become a refugee.[11]

Teenagers and Farmers

Those rounded up after attacks on US forces also had some distressing tales to tell. Eight prisoners were captured after a Special Forces raid, on December 11, 2002, on a compound near Zormat that was owned and run by a warlord called Samoud, and were subsequently transferred to Guantánamo, even though the youngest was only twelve years old, and others were only 13, 15 and 16. Captured after allegedly firing on US forces, they denied the accusations. Twenty-year-old Habib Rahman, a cook, thought it probable that the attacks were not directed against the Americans but against Samoud's many enemies, and 16-year-old Mohabet Khan, who said that he was forced into service, insisted that it was not even a raid. He explained that "they opened the doors to let the Americans come in and it really wasn't forceful or an impressive action." When it came to the most outrageous allegation—that the prisoners were "instructed to fight to the death" when US forces raided the compound—Habib Rahman said that this statement was obtained under duress by US forces in Gardez: "When we were in Gardez, they had taken all our clothes off. I was naked with eight other people … when I made that statement at that time. Americans were beating us really hard, and they had dogs behind us and they said if we didn't say this, they would release the dogs. After that, an American grabbed me by the throat and said, 'Has this happened to you?' and then I said 'yes,' and that is why I made the statement, 'Samoud told me to fight.'"

Nor were the youngest prisoners spared this treatment. Asadullah Rahman, the 12-year-old, was originally from Logar province, but moved to Paktia with his family when he was eight, after a feud over land, and had been working for Samoud since he was ten, when his uncle found him paid work serving food and washing dishes. Repeatedly kicked and beaten in his first five days in custody at Gardez, he was missing for seven months before his father found out that he was still alive. Naqibullah, the 13-year-old, was not even part of Samoud's group. The local imam's son, he was arrested after stumbling on the raid while cycling home from a friend's house. Subjected to brutal interrogation in Bagram, he said that his first ten days in Guantánamo were the worst ten days of his life. He and Asadullah Rahman were later moved to Camp Iguana, a special "juvenile detention facility," where, he said, he received "adequate treatment" as well as an education, but, whatever the Americans may claim, these are not circumstances in which children should be held. The boys were both released in January 2004, and the others were released in 2005 or 2006, while Samoud, according to Habib Rahman, was captured by the Americans and held in Bagram.[12]

These boys were not the only juveniles captured in Afghanistan in 2003. Two 14-year-olds—Abdul Qudus and Mohammed Ismail Agha—were sold to the Americans by Afghan soldiers. Agha said they had been looking for work, and ended up spending the night at an Afghan militia post in Gereshk. The following morning, Qudus said that the soldiers wanted to give them weapons and make them fight, and when they refused they were put in a car, delivered to the Americans, and accused of being with the Taliban. Although Agha was released with the other two boys in January 2004, Qudus was not freed until 2005 or 2006, and there is no evidence that he was ever held in Camp Iguana.[13]

A number of men who were captured because they were wearing olive drab jackets were seized after an alleged attack on US forces in Lejay, in Helmand province, on February 10, 2003. According to the Americans, US forces were "viciously attacked" by a 40-man pro-Taliban guerrilla unit led by Abdul Wahid, a local warlord, although the eight men who were sent to Guantánamo (out of at least seventy who were originally rounded up) were nothing more than poor farmers. Thirty-year-old Abdul Bagi and his 39-year-old uncle, Kushky Yar, were captured in the street near their homes while heading to the bazaar to buy parts for a tractor. Bagi denied that he was involved with the Taliban, saying, "My father and mother are dead and they left me small children. I am serving them. I have not served the Taliban or anybody else ... I have been home every night taking care of my brother and sister." He was remarkably restrained when it came to the ludicrous allegation that he was "apprehended wearing an olive drab green jacket consistent with the eyewitness accounts of the individual attacks," saying, "The green jackets are in the shops, hundreds of them, everybody can buy them and wear them." Fifty-six-year-old Alif Mohammed, who was accused of orchestrating the attack using a satellite phone, said that he was just a poor tinsmith, and pointed out that he would never work for Abdul Wahid because he killed his nephew and his nephew's pregnant wife, and Abdul Bagi spoke in his defense, saying, "Alif Mohammed is a drug addict and he is a very poor guy ... The Taliban beat [him] too much because he is a drug addict and was close to killing him. How could he be their commander?" Fifty-year-old Baridad told his tribunal, "I live in a place that if you see it, even an animal would not live there ... If you come back home and see my life, I bet you will cry. You will come back and ask why [they] pick up this poor innocent guy." He explained that on the day of his arrest, "I was sick ... I couldn't even go to the mosque and it was about eight feet away ... I was so cold I was just sitting in the sunshine and that is when the Americans captured me." The other four men—34-year-old Abdul Wahab, 20-year-old Rahmatullah, 29-year-old Hafizullah Shah and 22-year-old Naserullah—were captured in a minivan at a checkpoint and accused of wearing the infamous green jackets and suffering from hearing loss associated with the attack. At the time of writing, it was unclear how many of these men still remained in Guantánamo, as only Baridad (released in December 2006) had been mentioned by name.[14]

A Sad Conclusion

Having failed to round up a single Taliban leader throughout 2003, only one of the ninety men captured in this period was flagged as a significant catch—and even he turned out to be nothing of the sort. Sixty-two-year-old Haji Naim Kuchi, a tribal elder of the nomadic Kuchi tribe, was the object of a manhunt from the earliest days of "Operation Enduring Freedom," when the Americans bombed numerous locations in an attempt to kill him. Human Rights Watch reported that defense department officials told them that he "was a former Taliban official and a 'scumbag' involved in smuggling arms over the Pakistani border," but when he was finally captured by US forces, on his way to meet President Karzai to discuss a tribal dispute on January 1, 2003, his reputation seemed to vanish like a mirage. Instead of validating the Americans' concerns, this frail, unthreatening man, who suffered from diabetes and wore a surgical belt after one of his kidneys was removed, was so insignificant that he was released from Guantánamo in September 2004.[15]

Despite the litany of errors outlined above, my choice of the saddest Afghan story is that of 31-year-old Kakai Khan, for reasons that are unconnected with his alleged activities, and are solely to do with the attitude of one of his investigators at Guantánamo. For what it's worth, Khan was accused of being responsible for a rocket attack on the Gardez firebase, although he said that he was betrayed by personal enemies. His case stands out, however, because of comments made in 2005 by Jeffrey Norwitz, an investigator with the Defense Department's Criminal Investigative Task Force, one of the many organizations responsible for interrogating prisoners at Guantánamo for possible prosecution. Norwitz did not make a pronouncement one way or another on Khan's supposed guilt, regarding himself as part of an ongoing process—with no fixed conclusion—that bears no resemblance to established legal norms. After his final session in Guantánamo, he wrote, "I knew Kakai would never see the inside of a courtroom. Guilt 'beyond a reasonable doubt' is still a daunting challenge, whether in a federal courthouse or before a military commission at Guantánamo. Kakai's case could never meet that threshold." Even more astonishingly, Norwitz expressed his belief that being deprived of his liberty for years in a legal black hole was compensated for because, by being cooperative, Khan was well-fed, was being taught to read and write, and had received dental treatment, and suggested, moreover, that, in his case at least, Guantánamo was actually a benign beacon of democratic values. "Kakai will ultimately return home a healthier, more educated Afghan citizen," Norwitz wrote. "He will be prepared to participate in political change, engage in rebuilding his country, or return to herding livestock. The choice will be his, but it will be a choice based on options he would not have had if not for his time in Guantánamo."[16]

18
Challenging the Law

The First Challenges

The first legal challenge to Guantánamo began as soon as the camp opened on January 11, 2002. Within a week, a "Coalition of Clergy, Lawyers and Professors," including former Attorney General Ramsey Clark, filed a habeas petition on behalf of the Guantánamo prisoners. It was dismissed a month later, largely because the petitioners had no relationship with the accused, but by then the court's complaint had already been addressed. Breaking through the strict secrecy surrounding Guantánamo, the identities of three of the prisoners became known, and, with the support of the Center for Constitutional Rights (CCR), the parents of Shafiq Rasul, Asif Iqbal and David Hicks filed suit on behalf of their sons. *Rasul* v. *Bush* began its long journey to the Supreme Court on February 19, 2002. Noting that, despite regular interrogation by US agents, the three men had not been charged with an offense, put before a tribunal, or given access to lawyers, the petition challenged the legality of the November 2001 Military Order authorizing indefinite detention without due process, describing it as "unconstitutional and a violation of international law." Joseph Margulies, one of seven lawyers involved in the case, explained the significance of the petition: "We distinguish ourselves from terrorists only by our commitment to the rule of law, and the law is perfectly clear that the President can't order a person locked up indefinitely, without legal process. Unless the US says the law is simply a matter of convenience, something we are free to ignore whenever and wherever we choose, we have to change what we're doing in Cuba."[1]

In August 2002, the US District Court dismissed the case, ruling that the prisoners could not file habeas petitions because they were non-US citizens detained outside US jurisdiction. CCR then appealed, arguing that if US courts did not have jurisdiction to review the executive detentions at Guantánamo, "the US could act in any way it chose without being subject to any laws anywhere in the world." In March 2003, the Court of Appeals rejected the appeal, setting the stage for a showdown in the Supreme Court. CCR noted that the Court "ignored the fact that the detainees had not been declared 'enemies' of the United States by any lawful international or domestic tribunal" and were therefore "languishing in US military captivity without any legal basis," and Michael Ratner declared:

> The right to test the lawfulness of one's detention is a foundation of liberty that has roots going back to the Magna Carta. The US is not only denying the detainees fundamental rights, but is jeopardizing any claim that it is a country ruled by law. I fear for the rights of all of us. The court's ruling, that the US Constitution does not run to those jailed in territory over which the US has "complete jurisdiction and control," is utterly erroneous. Every detained person has a right to his or her day in court.[2]

In the meantime, another manifestation of the administration's new and legally untested detention policy was challenged in June 2002, when lawyers filed a habeas writ on behalf of Yaser Hamdi. Hamdi's case came to light in April 2002, when the authorities at Guantánamo discovered that he was a US citizen rather than a Saudi and transferred him to a naval brig in Virginia in an attempt to prevent federal court interference in the running of Guantánamo. *Hamdi* v. *Rumsfeld* centered on conflicting claims—the government's assertion that he was "affiliated with a Taliban military unit and received military training," and could therefore be held as an "unlawful combatant," without access to a lawyer or the court system, and Hamdi's assertion that he was not fighting for the Taliban, and was mistakenly captured while undertaking humanitarian relief work. Although the administration attempted to dismiss Hamdi's petition, Judge Robert Doumar, declaring that he would not be a "rubber stamp" for the government, questioned the meaning of "affiliation" and the level of "affiliation" that was "necessary to warrant enemy combatant status," and ordered officials to produce documents enabling the court to perform a "meaningful judicial review," including statements by the Northern

Alliance regarding Hamdi's capture, the dates and circumstances of his capture and interrogations, and a list of all the officials involved in the determination of his status as an "enemy combatant." Overturned by Appeal Court judges, Doumar's principled demands were never met, but the challenges meant that the case, like *Hamdi* v. *Bush*, also made its way to the Supreme Court.[3]

The third challenge came in July 2003, when the administration announced the names of the first six prisoners to be tried by Military Commission: David Hicks, Salim Hamdan, Ali Hamza al-Bahlul, Ibrahim al-Qosi, and, initially, Moazzam Begg and Feroz Abbasi. Although apparently authorized by the Military Order, the proposed Commissions attracted fierce criticism from the moment they were announced, for a number of obvious reasons, including the fact that the juries and presiding officers would be hand-picked by the administration, that evidence obtained through hearsay or torture would be allowed, and that both the accused and his lawyers could be prevented from seeing certain evidence. Despite hoping that the Commissions would proceed smoothly, the administration failed to realize that some of the military lawyers who were assigned to defend the prisoners might, like Charles Swift of the Judge Advocate General's Group (JAG), balk at what was required of them. Swift, who recognized immediately that the proposed system was monstrously flawed, ended up defending Salim Hamdan. "He had never been involved in any shootings or real violence," he told the journalist Marie Brenner in January 2007. "OK, so he was a driver to one of the worst men on earth. All that really links him is that he worked for a motor pool. He wasn't necessarily a henchman. I thought, I can work with this." What particularly disturbed Swift and the other JAG lawyers, as they learned more about Guantánamo and the proposed Commissions, was that they were primarily intended to sidestep the prohibition on torture and to secure prosecutions against men whose guilt had already been decided by the Executive. He told Brenner, "It took me about a month to understand: why a military commission? Because if you torture someone, it is the only way you can get their statements in and not have to admit it in public." "The whole purpose of setting up Guantánamo Bay," he continued, "is for torture. Why do this? Because you want to escape the rule of law. There is only one thing that you want to escape the rule of law to do, and that is to question people coercively—what some people call torture. Guantánamo and the military commissions are implements for breaking the law." With legal scholar Neil Katyal, Swift and others—including Michael Mori, who defended David Hicks—proceeded to challenge the Commissions, embarking on a legal journey that also ended up in the Supreme Court.[4]

Testimonies of Released Prisoners

While the legal challenges proceeded at a glacial pace, the prisoners in Guantánamo remained completely isolated from the outside world, as the administration intended, and the only outlet for information about the true nature of the prison, in the first two and half years of its existence, was from statements made by some of the two hundred prisoners who were released, or transferred to the custody of their home governments. Refusing to divulge the names of these prisoners, the administration hoped that they would return home quietly without speaking about their treatment, and many did just that, either because their governments asked them not to jeopardize future releases, or, in some cases, because the Americans terrified them into silence. Yuksel Celik Gogus, one of three Turks captured crossing from Afghanistan to Pakistan in December 2001, said on his release in November 2003, "They will come and take me away if I tell what happened in Guantánamo."[5]

Those who were bold enough to speak out included Mohammed Saghir, the Pakistani preacher, and Said Abassin, the Afghan taxi driver, but throughout 2003 there was little else to report. Some of the other 22 Afghans released with Abassin in March 2003 dropped hints that all was not right—mentioning arbitrary arrests, abuse of the Koran, brutal treatment in Kandahar and Bagram, and being sold for money—but most had not been subjected to particularly cruel treatment once they left Afghanistan, and although enterprising journalists and human rights activists traced some of the released men and encouraged them to tell more detailed stories, none of them grabbed the headlines. It was only in March 2004, when the first five British prisoners were released—Jamal al-Harith, Tarek Dergoul and the three men from Tipton—that Guantánamo once more hit the front pages, and within a month the stories that they told, of their wrongful arrests and the brutal regimes in Afghanistan and Guantánamo, were echoed and confirmed in the horrific photos of torture and abuse that emerged from Abu

Ghraib. With these reports—and the visceral impact of the photos—a wider tide of opinion finally began to turn against Guantánamo.

It was also apparent, from the earliest releases, that prisoners were not necessarily freed because they were presumed to be innocent, but because of negotiations between the Americans and their home countries. This was particularly true of the Europeans, but it was also noticeable that the release of 93 Afghans and 57 Pakistanis appeared to have been authorized more to boost support for two crucial US allies—Presidents Karzai and Musharraf—than it was to atone for the wrongful arrest and imprisonment of large numbers of innocent men. There were other examples, too. After four Saudis were transferred in May 2003, it was reported that they had been exchanged as a prisoner swap for six Britons and a Belgian imprisoned in Saudi Arabia,[6] and other deals were alleged to have accompanied the release of seven Russians in March 2004. Aryat Vakhitov said that a US military intelligence officer told him that the original terms of his release called for a prison sentence in Russia of 15 years, together with round-the-clock access for CIA and FBI investigators, but on their return they were swiftly released. Terrorism analyst Andrew McGregor explained that their release may have been "a public display of magnanimity," as Moscow sought the release of two Russian agents held in Qatar for the assassination of the Chechen president. Once the assassins were returned, however, he noted that the prisoners were no longer needed as pawns in Russia's foreign relations, and faced "a dark and uncertain future." This was indeed the case. Ravil Gumarov and Timur Ishmuradov were arrested in connection with a gas-line explosion in January 2005, and, after a trial that was regarded by observers as severely flawed, imprisoned for 13 and 11 years respectively, and Rasul Kudayev was arrested in October 2005 after 300 gunmen launched attacks on government installations in his home town. Despite protesting his innocence, a fellow prisoner reported that he was "given electric shock treatment, beaten, and bound up with tape and kicked around 'like a football.'"[7]

Landmark Decisions in the Supreme Court

On June 28, 2004, the Supreme Court finally delivered its verdict on *Rasul* v. *Bush*, ruling 6–3 that the Guantánamo prisoners had the right to challenge the legal limbo in which they had been held for nearly two and half years, and demolishing the administration's long-cherished belief that Guantánamo did not count as US territory. "They are not nationals of countries at war with the United States," the judges declared, "and they deny that they have engaged in or plotted acts of aggression against this country; they have never been afforded access to any tribunal, much less charged with and convicted of wrongdoing; and for more than two years they have been imprisoned in territory over which the United States exercises exclusive jurisdiction and control." In his majority opinion, Justice John Paul Stevens emphasized the importance of habeas corpus, citing a 1945 case in which it was described as "a writ antecedent to statute … throwing its roots deep into the genius of our common law," and a 1953 case dealing specifically with the detention of aliens in US custody: "Executive imprisonment has been considered oppressive and lawless since John, at Runnymede, pledged that no free man should be imprisoned, dispossessed, outlawed or exiled save by the judgment of his peers or by the law of the land. The judges of England developed the writ of habeas corpus largely to preserve these immunities from executive restraint."[8]

On the same day, the Supreme Court also delivered its verdict on *Hamdi* v. *Rumsfeld*, dealing another blow to the administration by ruling that, although US citizens designated as "enemy combatants" could be detained without trial, they, like the Guantánamo prisoners, had the right to challenge their detention in US courts. Justice Sandra Day O'Connor declared, "It is during our most challenging and uncertain moments that our nation's commitment to due process is most severely tested; and it is in those times that we must preserve our commitment at home to the principles for which we fight abroad." O'Connor also made the memorable comment that a state of war was "not a blank check for the President when it comes to the rights of the nation's citizens," and touched on the thorny issue of detaining prisoners for the purpose of interrogation: "An interrogation by one's captor, however effective an intelligence-gathering tool, hardly constitutes a constitutionally adequate fact-finding before a neutral decision-maker." Unwilling to take Hamdi's case further, the administration conceded defeat, and negotiated his repatriation to Saudi Arabia in October 2004, after he agreed to renounce his US citizenship and promised that he would not travel to the US, Israel, Palestine, Syria, Iraq, Afghanistan or Pakistan.[9]

Despite the success of *Hamdi* v. *Rumsfeld*, it had no impact on the other US nationals captured in the "War on Terror." John Walker Lindh was already in prison, and at the time of writing was the only American "enemy combatant" to have faced a trial. Although he was nothing more than a Taliban foot soldier, he was indicted in February 2002 on ten charges, which included contributing services to al-Qaeda and conspiracy to murder US citizens, even though the case was potentially humiliating for the government. Photos existed of his torture at the hands of US soldiers, and it was probable that a key piece of evidence—his confession—would have been excluded because it was obtained under duress, but the Justice Department somehow convinced him to accept a punitive plea bargain: if he pleaded guilty to just two charges—serving the Taliban and carrying weapons—and dropped claims that he was tortured by US military personnel, he would receive a 20-year sentence. Initially held in a medium security prison, he was then moved to the federal government's Supermax prison in Florence, Colorado—supposedly reserved for the most dangerous prisoners in the US—where he is held in solitary confinement for 23 hours a day and is prohibited from speaking Arabic for the duration of his sentence.[10]

In the case of the other American "enemy combatant," Jose Padilla, the administration ignored the impact of *Hamdi* v. *Rumsfeld* for as long as possible, and then switched tactics. Accused, like Binyam Mohammed al-Habashi, of being a member of al-Qaeda and of plotting to detonate a "dirty bomb" in the US, he was held for three and a half years as an "enemy combatant" in a military brig in South Carolina, and despite various challenges to his detention, it was not until November 2005, when the administration feared a challenge in the Supreme Court, that the "enemy combatant" label was dropped—along with all the charges—and he was indicted for conspiracy "to murder, kidnap and maim people overseas." Now held in a federal prison, his trial has been delayed, following allegations that five years of solitary confinement and sensory deprivation—held in a blacked-out cell with no contact with anyone except his guards and interrogators—have caused him to lose his mind. A forensic psychiatrist who examined him said that he "does not appreciate the nature and consequences of the proceedings against him, is unable to render assistance to counsel, and has impairments in reasoning as the result of a mental illness, i.e.

post traumatic stress disorder, complicated by the neuropsychiatric effects of prolonged isolation."[11]

Combatant Status Review Tribunals

For the lawyers who had spent so long fighting for the habeas rights of the Guantánamo prisoners, the verdict in *Rasul* v. *Bush* appeared to vindicate their belief that due process would triumph in the end over the abuse of executive power. However, while lawyers began filing habeas petitions in the hope that they would lead to trials, the administration refused to be derailed from its lawless mission. Although the authorities at Guantánamo could not refuse prisoners the right to meet lawyers and file habeas petitions—Gitanjali Gutierrez was the first lawyer to visit the prison, in October 2004, when she met Moazzam Begg and Feroz Abbasi, and a third of the prisoners had lawyers by May 2005—they did everything in their power to disable the process, from intimidating prisoners to obstructing the lawyers themselves. One lawyer noted that several prisoners told him "they had been interrogated by people who claimed to be their lawyers but who turned out not to be," Juma al-Dossari reported that several interrogators told him his lawyers were liars, and Fouad al-Rabia was told that "if he complained to his lawyers about conditions at Guantánamo Bay he would be kept there for life." Numerous lawyers have also pointed out that their security clearances are often held up for months and they are regularly prevented from meeting clients, and in October 2004, responding to their complaints, a US District Judge ordered the Pentagon to stop eavesdropping on lawyer–client conversations, which she described as a "bedrock" American principle.[12]

The administration also introduced its own response to the demand for greater transparency and accountability, announcing in July 2004 that the prisoners' status would be reviewed in Combatant Status Review Tribunals (CSRTs). As mentioned in Chapter 8, these resembled the "competent tribunals" demanded by the Geneva Conventions, which had taken place on or near the battlefield during every other US military operation, but at Guantánamo they were nothing more than hollow simulacra: prisoners were not allowed legal representation, were not allowed to see or hear secret evidence against them, and, given the "low evidentiary hurdle" mentioned in Chapter 13, the tribunals judged that all but 38 of the 558 prisoners whose cases they reviewed were properly designated as "enemy combatants." Moreover, the authorities refused to acknowledge that those who were recommended for release were innocent. In another sign of the evasive and self-righteous nature of the administration, they were, instead, designated "No Longer Enemy Combatants." In the parallel reality of the "War on Terror," no one who ended up in American hands was ever innocent.

Where the CSRTs also differed markedly from their battlefield predecessors was in the prisoners' right to call witnesses "if reasonably available." Although this was plausible for prisoners close to the time and place of capture it was, of course, extraordinarily difficult when the prisoners were in Guantánamo and no one was allowed to visit them. Shockingly, however, all the evidence indicates that the authorities had no intention of seeking out witnesses, other than occasionally allowing other prisoners in Guantánamo to speak on behalf of their friends or relatives. This disdain for the truth was particularly apparent in the cases of numerous Afghan prisoners, who provided names and phone numbers that could easily have been followed up if there was any intention of discovering the truth rather than rubber-stamping any false allegation that made its way into a prisoner's file. "The current government of Afghanistan, chief of the district, it would be very easy to find them," Rahmatullah Sangaryar said in his tribunal. "They have telephones." The police officer Swar Khan went one step further, providing the tribunal with the phone numbers required to prove his innocence, and in the case of the 63-year-old truck driver Abdul Razzak, who said that he was framed by a personal enemy who had already killed his father, his two brothers, his sister and two of his sons, the authorities said they could not locate Ismael Khan, the governor of Herat, whom Razzak claimed to have freed from a Taliban jail in 1999.[13]

In June 2006, the journalist Declan Walsh decided to find out how difficult it was to track down witnesses. Focusing on the case of Abdullah Mujahid Haq, the security chief from Paktia province, Walsh, who was in Afghanistan, started making phone calls, and within three days found three witnesses that the Pentagon had apparently been unable to contact. One was working in Washington DC, teaching at the National Defense University, and the other two were in Afghanistan. A call to President Karzai's office located Shahzada Masoud, an advisor on tribal affairs, who confirmed that Haq had accepted a job protecting the highways in Kabul and "was given a lavish transfer-of-power ceremony attended by government dignitaries," and Walsh obtained the phone number of Gul Haider, a defense ministry representative and former Northern Alliance commander, from a government official in Gardez. Haider confirmed that Haq sent thirty of his men to assist the Americans during Operation Anaconda, and said he had not heard anything to support the Americans' claims that he had turned against them. Pointing out that political rivalries were to blame for Haq's arrest, and that someone had made false allegations, Haider said, "Afghanistan has many problems—between tribes, Communists, the Taliban. That's why people like Abdullah, who are completely innocent, end up in jail."[14]

The First Military Commissions

A few weeks after the CSRT process began, the first Military Commissions—for Salim Hamdan, David Hicks, Ali Hamza al-Bahlul and Ibrahim al-Qosi—were convened in Guantánamo, reaching the wider world only when al-Bahlul announced, "As God is my witness, and the United States did not put pressure on me, I am an al-Qaeda member." Deborah Pearlstein, an observer for Human Rights First, filed reports from the hearings, which highlighted a number of alarming deficiencies in the system. Noting a widespread belief that "the US military leaders overseeing these trials are making much up as they go," she complained that, although the Presiding Officer was a retired Army judge, the other members of the Commission—the jury—had no legal experience, and seemed unable to understand the most basic aspects of the law. She also noted serious problems with the quality of the interpreters, and described a "stark and critical imbalance in the resources of the prosecution and defense attorneys," explaining that the prosecutors had an entire floor and a staff of researchers, clerks and paralegals, whereas the six defense lawyers shared a small office, with no support staff and only four computers.

Pearlstein's doubts about the system were upheld at the next session, in November, when, in response to a legal challenge by Charles Swift and his team—*Hamdan v. Rumsfeld*—District Judge James Robertson called a halt to the Commissions, on the basis that the tribunal system used to assess Hamdan's eligibility for trial by Military Commission—the CSRT—did not reach the level of a "competent tribunal," as demanded by the Geneva Conventions. Robertson also ruled that, until a "competent tribunal" determined that Hamdan was not a PoW, he had the right to be tried under the same judicial system as US soldiers, and that, even if he was determined not to be a PoW, the Military Commissions as they stood were inadequate and would not be allowed to proceed until their rules were revised to accord with the federal laws governing the trial of soldiers. In a final blow to the administration, he specifically addressed Hamdan's detention in Guantánamo, ruling that he was not to be held indefinitely in solitary confinement and should be returned to the rest of the prisoner population. This was a significant victory for those who had refused to support an unjust process, but, as with the other legislation relating to Guantánamo, his verdict was overruled in the Appeals Court (in July 2005), paving the way for another showdown in the Supreme Court.[15]

The Detainee Treatment Act

In the meantime, as *Hamdan* v. *Rumsfeld* made its way to the Supreme Court, Congress passed a fundamentally flawed piece of legislation dealing with the rights of prisoners captured in the "War on Terror." Introduced as an amendment to the Defense Appropriation Bill by Republican Senator John McCain, a long-standing opponent of the use of torture, the Detainee Treatment Act (DTA) was intended to ban the use of "cruel, inhuman and degrading" treatment by US personnel anywhere in the world, prohibiting interrogators from using any interrogation techniques other than those listed in the US Army Field Manual. McCain's most vocal critic was Dick Cheney, who demanded that he withdraw the amendment and, when he refused, insisted on an exemption for the CIA. For his efforts, Cheney was dubbed "Vice President for Torture" in a *Washington Post* editorial, but although the amendment was passed in November 2005, the administration had already stripped it of its power, first by encouraging McCain to compromise, including the exemption clause for the CIA, and then by incorporating another amendment, by Senator Lindsey Graham, which, on the basis that it was "necessary to eliminate a blizzard of legal claims from prisoners that was tying up Department of Justice resources," nullified the Supreme Court decision in *Rasul* v. *Bush* by once more preventing the prisoners from pursuing habeas appeals in the US courts. Tom Malinowski of Human Rights Watch explained how McCain's amendment had been gutted: "With the McCain amendment, Congress has clearly said that anyone who authorizes or engages in cruel techniques like waterboarding is violating the law. But the ... amendment leaves Guantánamo detainees no legal recourse if they are, in fact, tortured or mistreated." Human Rights Watch noted that the DTA not only hurled the Guantánamo prisoners back into their legal limbo, but was also "the first time in American history that Congress has effectively permitted the use of evidence obtained through torture."[16]

19
Suicides and Hunger Strikes

The Three Suicides

On the morning of June 10, 2006, three prisoners were found dead in their cells, having apparently hanged themselves in a coordinated suicide pact. They were Yasser al-Zahrani, a Yemeni captured after the fall of Kunduz, who was caught up in the Qala-i-Janghi uprising, Ali Abdullah Ahmed al-Salami, one of the Yemenis captured in the "Issa" guest house in Pakistan, and Mani al-Utaybi, a Saudi who was 25 years old when he was captured in Afghanistan. The administration's response to the deaths was extraordinarily callous. Rear Admiral Harry Harris, the commander of Guantánamo, said, "This was not an act of desperation, but an act of asymmetric warfare committed against us," and Colleen Graffy, the deputy assistant secretary of state for public diplomacy, described the suicides as a "good PR move to draw attention."[1]

Stung by international criticism, the administration rapidly back-tracked, and Cully Stimson, the deputy assistant secretary of defense for detainee affairs, stepped forward to say, "I wouldn't characterize it as a good PR move. What I would say is that we are always concerned when someone takes his own life, because as Americans, we value life, even the lives of violent terrorists who are captured waging war against our country." In an attempt to stifle further dissent, and to bolster their view that the three men were hardened terrorists, the Pentagon released details of the allegations against them, which served only to highlight almost everything that was wrong with the system at Guantánamo. As mentioned in Chapter 2, al-Zahrani was accused of being a Taliban fighter who "facilitated weapons purchases," but it was apparent that he was only 17 years old at the time of his capture, and that this scenario was highly unlikely. In al-Utaybi's case, the only "evidence" that he was an "enemy combatant" was his involvement with Jamaat-al-Tablighi, the vast worldwide Islamic missionary organization whose alleged connection to terrorism was duly exaggerated by the Pentagon, which had the effrontery to describe it as "an al-Qaeda 2nd tier recruitment organization." Heartless to the last, the administration also admitted that he had actually been approved for "transfer to the custody of another country" in November 2005, although Navy Commander Robert Durand said he "did not know whether al-Utaybi had been informed about the transfer recommendation before he killed himself." In the case of al-Salami, the Pentagon alleged that he was "a mid- to high-level al-Qaeda operative who had key ties to principal facilitators and senior members of the group."[2]

Although none of the men had taken part in any tribunals, more detailed allegations against al-Salami surfaced in the "evidence" for his Combatant Status Review Tribunal (CSRT), although a close inspection of the allegations reveals that they were mostly made by unidentified "members" of al-Qaeda, either in Guantánamo or in other secret prisons: "a senior al-Qaeda facilitator" identified him, another senior al-Qaeda figure—a "lieutenant"—identified him as being "associated with Khalid Sheikh Mohammed," the "al-Qaeda weapons trainer from Tora Bora" identified him from his time in Kabul and at Khaldan, and he was also identified as "an al-Qaeda courier," and as someone who "worked directly for Osama bin Laden's family." Shorn of these allegations—which summon up images of various "significant" prisoners being shown the "family album" in painful circumstances—the only other allegation was that the "Issa" guest house received the equivalent of jihadi junk mail: apparently, the residents of the house "routinely received endorsement letters from a well-known al-Qaeda operative" to attend the Khaldan camp.[3]

Other Suicide Attempts

The deaths of the three men were the first successful suicides at Guantánamo, but they were by no means the first attempts. Those that have been recorded include attempts by Mishal al-Harbi, the Saudi who suffered serious brain damage and was released in 2005, the Pakistani baker Shah Mohammed, who attempted suicide four times before his release in May 2003, and an Afghan Taliban conscript called Rostum (released in March 2003), who explained that he tried to hang himself because he was in a block of Arabs and Uzbeks who drove him to despair: "There were some very strange people, they were hitting their heads on the wall, insulting the soldiers, and that is why I hated it." Others who have tried to kill themselves, and who were still in Guantánamo at the time of writing, include the Syrian Abdul Rahim al-Ginco, who tried to harm himself "because of my emotional issues," and spent three years in the psychiatric ward, the former "ghost" prisoner Mohammed Madni, who tried to kill himself on the 191st day of his imprisonment, and Juma al-Dossari, who, disturbingly, has tried to commit suicide on at least 13 occasions. From January 2002 to July 2003, there were, officially, 28 suicide attempts by 18 different prisoners, which alarmed the authorities to such an extent that they began differentiating between "genuine" suicide attempts and incidents of "self-harm"—of which 350 were reported in 2003—which included "hanging gestures" and "manipulative, self-injurious behaviour."[4]

From the moment that Camp X-Ray opened, suicide attempts—along with hunger strikes—were the only avenues available for prisoners who were either in total despair, or were particularly incensed about the conditions of their detention: specifically, their day-to-day treatment, the crushing uncertainty of their fate, as they remained imprisoned without charge and without trial, with the ever-present possibility that they would be held for the rest of their lives, and the treatment of the Koran. While this latter point has been touched upon briefly in previous chapters, it's important to recognize that abuse of the Koran— which is widely documented throughout the "War on Terror" prisons, and is described in a report by Cageprisoners as an activity that was "systematic and institutionalized" in Guantánamo—had an impact on Muslim prisoners which was incomprehensible to Christian Americans, but was clearly used as a way of causing maximum psychological distress to the prisoners without having to lay a finger on them.[5]

Hunger Strikes and the Abuse of the Koran

These elements came together during the first month in Camp X-Ray, when several short hunger strikes took place in response to a guard stamping on the Koran. The strikes came to an end when a senior official delivered an apology over the prison's loudspeaker system, and the commanders, under Brigadier General Rick Baccus, made a decision to prohibit military personnel from handling the Koran except in emergencies, but a large-scale hunger strike, involving 194 prisoners, began on February 27, 2002—and continued until May 10—after an MP removed a home-made turban from a prisoner while he was praying. As the strike progressed, it became a protest against the prisoners' indefinite detention and their harsh living conditions, and by mid-March, when three strikers were forcibly given intravenous fluids, military officials acknowledged that the prisoners were protesting "the fact that they don't know what is happening to them," and were particularly concerned about "their murky future." By early May, only two prisoners, who had been fasting for over two months, were holding out, and the strike came to an end when they were force-fed through tubes that were pushed up their noses and into their stomachs.[6]

A second mass hunger strike took place in October 2002, and Tarek Dergoul reported that another strike—again prompted by mistreatment of the Koran—began in December and continued for six weeks. "People were fainting left, right and centre," he said, adding, "I felt very weak and ill and could only do a hunger strike for three days at a time." By now, the prisoners were even more concerned about their treatment, and FBI documents released under Freedom of Information legislation revealed the extent of their distress. One agent noted: "The mental condition of the detainees is to the point where [they] are all participating in a hunger strike. The detainees are upset with the way they are being treated by the guards. They are upset because they are being held as prisoners without being charged with a crime or released. The detainees think America is intentionally keeping people in custody for no other reason than as an attack on Muslims."

The FBI documents also revealed that several prisoners reported discussions about a mass suicide attempt as a political protest, which eventually took place during an eight-day period in August 2003, at the height of Geoffrey Miller's abusive regime, when 23 prisoners attempted to hang themselves in their cells. It was at this point that the authorities' redefinition of suicide attempts as "manipulative, self-injurious behaviour" came into its own. Only two of the attempts were classified as suicide attempts, and the authorities attempted to dismiss the entire episode by describing it as "a coordinated effort to disrupt camp operations and challenge a new group of security guards."[7]

The largest hunger strike, which involved at least two hundred prisoners, began in late June 2005 and continued for a month, although publicly the authorities denied it until two released Afghans announced it to the world's press on July 20. Conceived yet again as a political response to the conditions in which they were held, the organizers even had a manifesto: they called for "no violence, by hand or even words, to anyone, including guards," and declared that their protest was "a peaceful, non-violent strike until demands are met," which called for "starvation until death." In addition, some prisoners refused to wear clothes in solidarity with those who were held naked in the isolation cells. Spelling out specific grievances to a group of lawyers, the prisoners demanded religious respect, fair trials, proper food and clean water, the right to see sunlight, "real, effective medical treatment," the right not to have correspondence withheld, an end to the "levels" of privileges introduced by Miller, and the appointment of a neutral body to oversee conditions at Guantánamo.[8] This was extremely unlikely, of course, as Guantánamo would have ended up as a prison that met most of the conditions called for by the Geneva Conventions, but, to his credit, Guantánamo's new warden, Colonel Mike Bumgarner, who had assumed his post in April, decided to negotiate with the prisoners. "I was looking for a way to have a peaceful camp," he told Tim Golden, and said that his initial message was, "Look, I'm willing to give you things, to make life better, if y'all will reciprocate ... Just do not attack my guards."

Bumgarner's first point of contact was the British resident Shaker Aamer. Known in Guantánamo as "the Professor," Aamer had a reputation as a leader, who was all too capable of organizing campaigns of disobedience to demand rights for the prisoners, and Bumgarner spent five hours in his cell, listening to his life story and getting an insight into the man behind the number. Despite anger and unease from the Task Force interrogators—who still followed the rules laid down by Miller and the Pentagon, and warned him that there were few privileges at Guantánamo, and that they should be the ones handing them out in return for cooperation—he addressed a few outstanding complaints. Following an enlightening discussion with Ahmed Errachidi, he ordered the guards to stop referring to the prisoners as "packages"—Errachidi pointed out, "We are not 'packages.' We are human beings"—and he also turned down the lights at night on compliant blocks, and ordered guards not to disrupt prayer time, either by making noise or, as had been their habit, by playing "The Star-Spangled Banner."

Determined to bring the hunger strike to a halt, Bumgarner spoke again to Aamer, who told him that, although the prisoners' ultimate aim was to be brought to trial or sent home, they also demanded better medical and living conditions. "If you can get me to go around the camps," he said, "I can turn this off." Bumgarner agreed, and the following day the two men made their way through each of the blocks, with Bumgarner watching as Aamer spoke to other influential prisoners in Camp 5, including Sabir Lahmar, the Islamic scholar from Bosnia, and the Saudi Ghassan al-Sharbi, who was caught with Abu Zubaydah. In Camps 2 and 3, where generally compliant prisoners were moved after Camp 5 opened, Bumgarner noted that Aamer "was treated like a rock star." "I have never seen grown men—with beards, hardened men—crying at the sight of another man," he added. "It was like I was with Bon Jovi."

By July 28, the majority of the hunger strikers agreed to suspend their protests, and a calm descended on the prison, perhaps for the first time in its history. Bumgarner described it as the "period of peace." Over the following week, with Aamer and another influential prisoner, Mullah Abdul Salam Zaeef, the Taliban's former ambassador to Pakistan, he sat down and worked through some other complaints. Aamer produced a new menu, raising the calorific level of the meals from 2,800 to 4,200 calories, which was adopted and has been maintained ever since, Bumgarner did away with the loathed orange jumpsuits, replacing them with tan outfits instead, and the disciplinary system established by Miller was completely overhauled. Instead of the complicated system of rewards and punishments, all the prisoners started off with all their "comfort items" restored, and only those who subsequently broke the rules would have them taken away. In what seemed to be a confirmation that the new system was working, Bumgarner then allowed six of the prisoners—Aamer, Lahmar, al-Sharbi, Zaeef, and two Egyptians, the scholar Ala Salim, and the former army officer Adel Fatouh El-Gazzar—to meet unchained and unsupervised to discuss the future, and held two other meetings of the "Prisoners' Council," one on August 6, which he attended himself, telling the men, "This place ain't going away, so we might as well make the best of it," and another on August 8, when, suddenly, the whole project was closed down. According to Zaeef, the prisoners began making notes, but when an officer told them this was prohibited, and moved to confiscate them, several of the prisoners put the notes in their mouths and began chewing them.

Quite what happened that day has never been made clear. Tim Golden noted that officials suggested that al-Sharbi and Aamer were at odds, and that, surprisingly, it was Aamer who wanted to use the meetings to put pressure on the authorities to tackle the larger issues of the prisoners' continued detention without trial, but whatever the truth, the aftermath was a disaster. Prisoners in Camps 2 and 3 rioted and tore up their cells, the hunger strike resumed with a vengeance—inspired, in particular, by a violent assault on Hisham Sliti by an interrogator, who threw a mini-fridge at him—and, although Zaeef and Salim were soon released, and Bumgarner maintained an unlikely relationship with al-Sharbi, Aamer was placed in solitary confinement, where he remains at the time of writing, and Bumgarner never spoke to him again.[9]

Although previous strikes had required medical intervention, the hunger strike that resumed in August 2005 was so severe that dozens of prisoners were force-fed over the following months, and the reports of their treatment, issued after they were declassified by the military, made for shocking reading. The lawyer Julia Tarver Mason, who represents ten Saudi prisoners, visited Guantánamo in October 2005 and noted that three of her clients—Majeed al-Joudi (released in February 2007), Abdul Rahman Shalabi and Yousef al-Shehri—said that the feeding tubes, which were "the thickness of a finger," were regarded as objects of torture. She reported that they were forcibly shoved up the prisoners' noses without anesthetic or sedatives being provided, and that this resulted in prisoners "vomiting up substantial amounts of blood," but added that when they did so, "the soldiers mocked and cursed at them, and taunted them with statements like 'look what your religion has brought you.'" She also noted the prisoners' claims that they "were verbally abused and insulted and were restrained from head to toe" while the feeding took place, with "shackles or other restraints on their arms, legs, waist, chest, knees, and head," that attempts to give them intravenous medication were "often quite painful ... as inexperienced medical professionals seemed incapable of locating appropriate veins," and, most shockingly, that, while doctors, including the head of the hospital, were watching, "the guards took tubes from one detainee, and with no sanitization whatsoever, reinserted it into the nose of a different detainee. When these tubes were reinserted, the detainees could see the blood and stomach bile from other detainees remaining on the tubes."[10]

Medical Malpractice

With these methods—and the use of five "restraint chairs," which were ordered in December—the authorities succeeded in convincing the majority of the 84 hunger strikers who were holding out in early January 2006 to give up their protest by the end of the month, and by March only a few young Gulf prisoners, including Ghassan al-Sharbi, were still on strike.[11] It was noticeable, however, that both the methods used and the complicity of the medical staff raised uncomfortable questions about the role of the doctors in Guantánamo which had, up to that point, largely been concealed, even though numerous prisoners had spoken about the various ways in which, instead of maintaining a professional distance, the doctors and medical staff were intimately involved in every aspect of the prison's operations.

This had been apparent in a general sense from the beginning, when the prisoners were required to take unknown drugs on a regular basis. Shafiq Rasul, Asif Iqbal and Rhuhel Ahmed described an incident in August 2002 when medical staff toured the cell blocks asking the prisoners if they wanted an injection, "although they wouldn't say what it was for." They said that most of the prisoners refused, but the medical staff then returned with an ERF team who forced them to have the injections anyway. Ahmed said that the drug made him feel "very drowsy," and added, "I have no idea why they were giving us these injections. It happened perhaps a dozen times altogether and I believe it still goes on at the camp. You are not allowed to refuse it and you don't know what it is for." Abdullah al-Noaimi told his lawyers that within his first few days at Guantánamo he "was injected with an unknown substance which made him depressed and despondent. He was unable to control his thoughts and his mind raced. He was also unable to control his body and fell to the floor." He was then placed in isolation for three days, where medical staff administered an unknown medicine "that made him feel drunk," until he refused to take it any more, and on another occasion was given pills which "caused him to hear voices." When he told his interrogators that he "felt like he was losing his mind," their only response was, "Yeah, we know." Although the authorities have persistently maintained that there is nothing sinister about the injections administered to the prisoners, Sami al-Hajj believes that they are actually conducting horrendous medical experiments on the whole of the prison population, and claims that "the inoculations that have been forced on the prisoners ... are shots that contain diseases."[12]

Whether or not there is any truth in these claims, it's clear that the medical staff have persistently been used as an additional tool in the quest to "break" the prisoners, and that this role became more pronounced after Geoffrey Miller arranged for all the Guantánamo personnel—including the doctors and nurses—to "set the conditions" for the interrogations. This was achieved in two particular ways. The first and most common method involved withholding medical treatment until the prisoners cooperated with their interrogators. This has been reported by numerous prisoners, and has no doubt contributed to countless false confessions as a result. To give just a few examples, Sami al-Hajj, who has refused to bow to pressure from the Pentagon to falsely confess that al-Jazeera has connections to al-Qaeda, has complained that the authorities have consistently and systematically denied him access to the drugs he is supposed to take for the rest of his life to prevent a recurrence of the throat cancer he suffered in 1998, and Abdel Hamid al-Ghizzawi, the Libyan who was living in Afghanistan with his Afghan wife, has been refused treatment for liver cancer, presumably because he has refused to confess that he was a terrorist and not a shopkeeper.[13]

Others include David Hicks, who was refused treatment for a hernia at a time when the men from Tipton recalled that he had "gone downhill" and appeared willing to make any number of false confessions to alleviate his plight, Fouad al-Rabia, who suffered from serious stomach pains but was told that he "couldn't receive medication unless he cooperated," and Mohammed Ghanim, the Yemeni who was moved from cell to cell for a period of eight months, who was refused treatment for hemorrhoids unless he too agreed to cooperate. After submitting to this blackmail, he had an operation, which, disturbingly, was not carried out correctly, and when he again refused to cooperate he was held naked in solitary confinement. In the case of Omar Khadr, the men from Tipton reported that he was persistently refused painkillers for the wounds he sustained in Afghanistan, and that on one occasion, when he was "very badly ill" in an isolation cell, the medics "said that they couldn't see him because the interrogators had refused to let them."[14]

Released prisoners who found themselves unable to access medical treatment include the Kuwaiti Adel al-Zamel, who was beaten on the head with handcuffs, but was refused medical treatment for several weeks until his wound became infected, the Tajik Abdulrahman Rajabov, who developed hepatitis C after being denied "consistent medical care," and Mamdouh Habib, who was told by medics that he would only be given treatment for the internal bleeding he suffered in Egypt if he cooperated with his interrogators.[15]

The medical staff's second method of helping to "set the conditions" involved direct intervention in punishment. This has not been widely reported, but it formed the centerpiece of complaints by Douglas Cox, a lawyer for eleven Yemeni prisoners. According to Cox, two of his clients—Abdul Aziz al-Suadi and Saeed Jarabh—told him that medical staff were on hand to advise the ERF (Extreme Reaction Force) teams. Al-Suadi said, "The nurse participated with the riot squad by helping put something in my nose to make me unable to breathe, and this is the same nurse that dispenses medicines and makes diagnoses," and Jarabh said that, when he was "ERFed" in 2003, "one of the Guantánamo medical staff was in the room advising guards on how to beat him." As he described it, "He was regulating the process of the beating. This nurse who is regulating the beating process, he is the same person that was distributing medicine previously."

This is a loathsome betrayal of the medical staff's supposed impartiality, and it prompted Cox to complain that "medical staff at Guantánamo are violating state, federal and international ethics rules by participating in interrogations and abuse of detainees and by sharing detainees' medical records with interrogators, allowing interrogators to use this knowledge to coerce or threaten detainees."[16] It was hardly surprising, however, given how far removed Guantánamo was from internationally recognized laws and ethical standards, and in fact Cox's complaint touched on another aspect of medical malpractice—the inappropriate use of psychological pressure—that has been condemned not only by human rights groups, but also by medical and psychological practitioners. The most common example of interference by psychiatrists concerned the identification of phobias, which were then exploited by the interrogators, but the most notorious instance of inappropriate behavior—on the part of both psychiatric and medical personnel—took place during the torture of Mohammed al-Qahtani. The psychiatrist Dr. Darryl Matthews, who was brought to Guantánamo as an advisor after the suicide attempts in 2003, was so appalled by what he saw that he has since become an outspoken critic of the prison. Explaining why psychiatrists should play no part in any kind of interrogation, he told Jane Mayer, "As psychiatrists, we know how to hurt people better than others. We can figure out what buttons to push. Like a surgeon with a scalpel, we have techniques and we know what the pressure points are." Leonard Rubenstein, of Physicians for Human Rights, was even more outspoken. Pointing out that al-Qahtani's interrogation involved "conduct that's been considered forbidden for 30 years," he said of his colleagues in Guantánamo, "Of course they can't participate in coercive interrogations! It's clear as day. You can't advise, you can't develop plans, you can't review interrogations, you can't sign off on them, and you can't even be present in the room."

The influence of doctors and psychiatrists has been so prevalent, however, that several commentators, who have traced the involvement of Behavioral Science Consultation Teams at Guantánamo—referred to in a report by Geoffrey Miller in 2003 as psychologists and psychiatrists who are "essential in developing integrated interrogation strategies and assessing interrogation intelligence production"—have claimed that the teams' role is to "reverse-engineer" counter-resistance techniques that have been taught to the US military since the 1950s. Known as SERE (Survival, Evasion, Resistance, and Escape), the program trains military personnel to resist torture by simulating a number of extreme techniques—including hooding, sleep deprivation, forced nudity, sexual humiliation, extremes of heat and cold, the use of loud noise and religious abuse—which have, of course, all surfaced in the "War on Terror" prisons, and it seems likely therefore that SERE techniques have indeed been used in Guantánamo. Jane Mayer noted that Colonel Louie Banks, a psychiatrist connected to SERE, "played a significant advisory role in interrogations at Guantánamo," and Esteban

Rodriguez, the director of the Joint Intelligence Group, told Mayer that he was "a valuable adviser, particularly on the subject of 'resistance' to interrogation." More importantly, according to Mayer, SERE experts were consulted about the enhanced interrogation techniques that were approved for use on Mohammed al-Qahtani.[17]

In the end, however, even if Guantánamo is neither a giant medical laboratory nor a SERE-influenced psychological experiment, the human rights abuses that the hunger strikers have campaigned against have exerted a crushing toll on the prison's inmates. When the men from Tipton left Guantánamo in March 2004, 20 percent of the prisoners were on anti-depressants, and they estimated that at least a hundred detainees were "observably mentally ill as opposed to just depressed." They added that the behavior of at least fifty of these prisoners was "so disturbed as to show that they are no longer capable of rational thought or behaviour," and that it was "something that only a small child or an animal might behave like," and it's certain that the predicament of those remaining in Guantánamo has not improved in the years since. When Yasser al-Zahrani, Ali Abdullah Ahmed al-Salami and Mani al-Utaybi committed suicide in June 2006, several commentators—mindful of Islam's injunction against committing suicide—suggested that they had been murdered. While this remains a possibility, the main reason for doubting it is that in July 2005, at the height of that summer's desperate hunger strike, several prisoners had a vision, in which it was revealed that three men had to die for the rest to be freed. Like the "Ghost Dance" envisioned by the native Americans in 1890, which prophesied an end to white American expansion on the eve of the native Americans' final defeat, it seems that the visionaries at Guantánamo became so desperate that they came up with their own liberation myth. The only difference was that it took several centuries for the Paiute and the Sioux to come up with theirs, whereas the helpless prisoners of Guantánamo took just three and a half years.[18]

20
Endgame?

Another Landmark Decision in the Supreme Court

On June 29, 2006, the Supreme Court delivered its verdict on *Hamdan* v. *Rumsfeld*, shocking the administration by ruling 5–3 that the Military Commissions were illegal under US law and the Geneva Conventions. Concluding that Common Article 3 of the Geneva Conventions was "applicable" to Hamdan and others facing Military Commissions, Justice John Paul Stevens stated that it was Hamdan's right to be tried by a "regularly constituted court affording all the judicial guarantees which are recognized as indispensable by civilized peoples." Moreover, by confirming the importance of Common Article 3—which forbids "cruel treatment and torture" and "outrages upon personal dignity, in particular humiliating and degrading treatment"—the Supreme Court appeared to strike at the heart of the administration's lawless "new paradigm," and Justice Anthony Kennedy spelled out this position even more clearly, warning the administration that "violations of Common Article 3 are considered 'war crimes,' punishable as federal offences, when committed by or against United States nationals and military personnel." Those opposed to the system were overjoyed, although the euphoria was short-lived, as the administration's lawyers pursued the advice of Justice Stephen Breyer—"Nothing prevents the President from returning to Congress to seek the authority he believes necessary"—and drafted a shocking new bill which they presented to Congress just three months later. In the meantime, however, President Bush surprised everyone on September 2 by transferring 14 "high-value" prisoners to Guantánamo from secret prisons run by the CIA.[1]

The 14 "High-value" Prisoners

Heading the list of the 14 men were Abu Zubaydah, Ramzi bin al-Shibh and Khalid Sheikh Mohammed, with the rest apparently comprising a partial "Who's Who" of al-Qaeda and its affiliates. One was the Saudi Mustafa al-Hawsawi, captured with Khalid Sheikh Mohammed in Rawalpindi on March 1, 2003, who allegedly sourced funding for the 9/11 attacks from Dubai, and another was Majid Khan, a Pakistani who was captured a few weeks later. Khan attended high school in the US in the late 1990s and returned to Pakistan in 2002, where, it was alleged, he was being groomed by Khalid Sheikh Mohammed for a future terrorist attack on American soil, which, according to the Americans, involved Uzair Paracha and his father Saifullah. Waleed bin Attash (better known as Khallad), whose younger brother was already in Guantánamo, was also captured in Pakistan, in a house raid in Karachi on April 29, 2003. Described as a "pivotal figure in the USS *Cole* attack," it was also alleged that he played a part in the African embassy bombings in 1998, and that he was present at a meeting in Malaysia in 2000 that was attended by bin al-Shibh and two of the 9/11 hijackers (one of whom, in a major failure of pre-9/11 intelligence, was under US surveillance). One of Khalid Sheikh Mohammed's nephews, Ammar al-Baluchi (aka Ali Abdul Aziz Ali), was captured with bin Attash, and the two men were allegedly close to finalizing a bomb plot in Pakistan at the time of their capture. Ahmed Khalfan Ghailani, a Tanzanian, was also captured in Pakistan, after a gun battle in Gujarat in July 2004. Allegedly a coordinator of the African embassy bombings, it was also claimed that he ran a document-forging operation for al-Qaeda in Afghanistan. The last of the 14 to be captured in Pakistan was the Libyan Abu Faraj al-Libi, who was seized in the North West Frontier Province in May 2005. Regarded by Pakistani intelligence as the successor to Khalid Sheikh Mohammed, he became Pakistan's most wanted man after apparently organizing two attempts to assassinate President Musharraf in December 2003.

The last five prisoners were captured in other countries. Abdul Rahim al-Nashiri, a Saudi, was captured in the UAE in November 2002. Regarded as the mastermind behind the bombing of the USS *Cole* in 2000, he was allegedly al-Qaeda's operations chief in the Arabian Peninsula. Three others were captured in Thailand in 2003:

the Indonesian Riduan Isamuddin (aka Hamlili), who was believed to be the main link between al-Qaeda and its Indonesian counterpart, Jemaah Islamiyah, and was alleged to have been one of the planners of the Bali bombings in 2002, which killed over two hundred people, and two of his deputies, the Malaysians Mohammed bin Lep (aka Lillie) and Mohd Farik bin Amin (aka Zubair). The final prisoner was Gouled Hassan Dourad, a Somali, who was allegedly the head of a network in Mogadishu that supported al-Qaeda members in Somalia.[2]

Some of these prisoners—Abu Zubaydah, Ramzi bin al-Shibh and Khalid Sheikh Mohammed, in particular—were well-known. Not only had their arrests been well-publicized, but so too was some of the intelligence that had been gleaned from their interrogations, which was cited in the *9/11 Commission Report*. President Bush was so impressed by the information produced by these interrogations—and how it was extracted—that he discussed it during a televised address after the prisoners arrived at Guantánamo. Explaining that Zubaydah was wounded during his capture and "survived only because of the medical care arranged by the CIA," he said that he initially revealed Khalid Sheikh Mohammed's alias ("Mukhtar"), and information about a forthcoming plot in the US, but then refused to speak. As a result, Bush said, "the CIA used an alternative set of procedures" to interrogate him, which were "designed to be safe, to comply with our laws, our Constitution, and our treaty obligations," and explained that Zubaydah then identified bin al-Shibh, providing information that helped to lead to his capture, and that both Zubaydah and bin al-Shibh provided information that led to the capture of Khalid Sheikh Mohammed, who, in turn, identified Majid Khan as an intermediary between al-Qaeda and Jemaah Islamiya, and provided information that led to the capture of Hambali and the two Malaysians.[3]

Whether there was any truth in this account is open to dispute. According to other reports, the CIA may have saved Zubaydah's life, but only after using his wounds as a tool to facilitate interrogation, withholding pain relief unless he cooperated. More importantly, all the other allegations about Zubaydah were also disputed. The *Washington Post* pointed out that the *9/11 Commission Report* mentioned that the CIA identified Khalid Sheikh Mohammed's nickname in August 2001, but "failed to connect the information with previous intelligence identifying Mukhtar as an al-Qaeda associate plotting terrorist attacks, and identified that failure as one of the crucial missed opportunities before Sept. 11," and the *New York Times* disputed Zubaydah's importance in identifying bin al-Shibh, noting that officials identified his role in the attacks three months before Zubaydah's capture, in the indictment of Zacarias Moussaoui, another so-called "20th hijacker."[4] According to a former intelligence official, Zubaydah also had nothing to do with the capture of Khalid Sheikh Mohammed, who was actually captured through one of the intelligence services' oldest techniques: enticing a "walk-in" informer with reward money. The official said that an al-Qaeda insider gave away his location, collected a $25 million reward, and was now living under a new identity in the US.

The most explosive revelation, however, concerned Zubaydah's alleged role as a terrorist mastermind. The author Ron Suskind reported that, after his capture, he "turned out to be mentally ill" and was nothing like the pivotal figure that the CIA and FBI had supposed him to be. Investigating his diary, analysts found entries in the voices of three people—a boy, a young man and a middle-aged alter ego—which recorded in numbing detail, over the course of ten years, "what people ate, or wore, or trifling things they said." Dan Coleman, the FBI's senior expert on al-Qaeda, explained to one of his superiors, "This guy is insane, certifiable, split personality." According to Suskind, the officials also confirmed that Zubaydah appeared to know nothing about terrorist operations, and was, instead, a minor logistician.[5] This was something that Khalid al-Hubayshi, the Saudi prisoner who got to know Zubaydah while training at Khaldan in 1997, explained in Guantánamo, but his opinion was probably ignored because it did not fit the picture that the administration wanted. Al-Hubayshi explained that Zubaydah was responsible for "receiving people and financing the camp," that he once bought him travel tickets, and that he was the man he went to when he needed a replacement passport. He also suggested that Zubaydah did not have a long-standing relationship with bin Laden. When asked, "When you were with Abu Zubaydah, did you ever see Osama bin Laden?" he replied, "In 1998, Abu Zubaydah and Osama bin Laden didn't like each other", adding, "In 2001, I think the relationship was okay," and explaining that bin Laden put pressure on Zubaydah to close Khaldan, essentially because he wanted to run more camps himself.[6]

According to Suskind, when George Tenet reported the unpalatable truth about Zubaydah to President Bush, he responded by saying, "I said he was important. You're not going to let me lose face on this, are you?" Bush was reportedly "fixated on how to get Zubaydah to tell us the truth," asking one senior operative, "Do some of these harsh methods really work?" Intelligence officials explained that the "alternative set of procedures" which were then implemented included a range of techniques familiar from Guantánamo, including death threats, sleep deprivation and the use of noise and harsh lighting, and three particular "enhanced interrogation techniques," which were used by only a handful of trained CIA interrogators: "Long Time Standing," the "Cold Cell" and, of course, waterboarding. In the first, prisoners are forced to stand, handcuffed and with their feet shackled to an eye bolt in the floor for more than forty hours; in the second, they stand naked in a freezing cold cell and are repeatedly doused with cold water; and in the third, after being strapped to an inclined board, with their feet raised slightly higher than their heads, cellophane is wrapped over their faces and water is poured over them. This technique, which induces a terrifying fear of drowning, has a long history of drawing confessions out of its victims almost immediately. Subjected to these forms of torture, Zubaydah "confessed" to all manner of supposed plots—against shopping malls, banks, supermarkets, water systems, nuclear plants, apartment buildings, the Brooklyn Bridge, and the Statue of Liberty—and with each new tale, Suskind wrote, "thousands of uniformed men and women raced in a panic to each target ... The United States would torture a mentally disturbed man and then leap, screaming, at every word he uttered."[7]

Zubaydah was not the only "high-value" prisoner subjected to the "enhanced techniques" described above. According to an intelligence source who spoke to ABC News in 2005, they were applied to "around a dozen" prisoners, including Khalid Sheikh Mohammed, and this was confirmed in a confidential report by Red Cross representatives (the only outsiders to have met the 14 "high-value" prisoners), who stated that all of them "described highly abusive interrogation methods, especially when techniques such as sleep deprivation and forced standing were used in combination." ABC's intelligence source spoke of the waterboarding of Khalid Sheikh Mohammed, noting that CIA officers who subjected themselves to the technique lasted an average of 14 seconds before caving in, whereas Mohammed "won the admiration of interrogators when he was able to last between two and two-and-a-half minutes before begging to confess." Not only did this make a mockery of the authorities' persistent claims that they were not involved in torture—which was reiterated by Bush in his televised address, when he said, "I want to be absolutely clear with our people, and the world: The United States does not torture. It's against our laws, and it's against our values"—it also raised extremely uncomfortable questions about the quality of the intelligence that was produced by these experiments in torture.[8]

Predictably, some of this dubious intelligence migrated to Guantánamo, where it entered the prisoners' files along with the many false allegations made by their fellow prisoners. The authorities were, generally, careful to disguise the sources of this information, but the number of allegations attributed to "a senior al-Qaeda lieutenant" or "a senior al-Qaeda operative" are shockingly frequent, and, like the allegations made by other prisoners, are often transparent lies. A particularly notorious example is the case of Abbas al-Naely, the Iraqi beggar with a hashish problem. Al-Naely admitted serving the Taliban for a month and begging for money from Mullah Omar, but refuted numerous other allegations—including claims that he trained at al-Farouq and met Osama bin Laden on three occasions when he was "tasked" to conduct missions on behalf of al-Qaeda—which, he was told, were made by "a high-ranking member of al-Qaeda." When he attempted to dispute these allegations, his Presiding Officer declared that "the source who gave us this information is very reliable." Al-Naely, however, was more fortunate than some of his fellow prisoners. By 2007, the authorities seem to have realized that their source—presumably one of the 14 "high-value" prisoners—was actually less reliable than they had thought, and he was cleared for release.[9]

One prisoner whose status changed as a result of the capture of one of the "high-value" prisoners was Mohamedou Ould Slahi, who said that his life "changed drastically" after Ramzi bin al-Shibh was captured. Bin al-Shibh's "confessions" presumably led to the allegations about Slahi's supposed role as an intermediary between the 9/11 hijackers and Osama bin Laden, and he was interrogated daily by the FBI until May 2003, when he was assigned interrogators from the Defense Department's Defense Intelligence Agency—advocates of the "enhanced interrogation techniques" that were still favored by the most senior figures in the administration—who held him for four months in total isolation in a freezing cold cell, almost certainly subjected him to a range of abusive techniques that were also practiced on Mohammed al-Qahtani, and, on one particularly disturbing occasion in August 2003, took him out on a boat, where a team of Arabs beat him severely and then gave him medication, which left him unconscious "for two or three weeks." After that, he said, he told the interrogators whatever they wanted to hear, and the abuse stopped, although he has since recanted statements that he made at the time.[10]

I have only come across one instance when the name of one of the "high-value" accusers was not removed, but it helps to explain why so many new allegations emerged between the Combatant Status Review Tribunal (CSRT) and Administrative Review Board (ARB) processes, and reveals, explicitly, that the "family album" of prisoner portraits was shown to the "high-value" prisoners while they were held in the CIA's secret prisons. The Yemeni Mohammed al-Hanashi, who survived the Qala-i-Janghi massacre, admitted to his tribunal in 2004 that he arrived in Afghanistan eight or nine months before 9/11, and that he fought with the Taliban. By the time of his review in 2005, however, new allegations had been added, including the claim that Ahmed Khalfan Ghailani "identified him as having been at the al-Farouq camp in 1998-99 prior to moving on to the front lines in Kabul." In other words, although al-Hanashi admitted traveling to Afghanistan to serve as a foot soldier for the Taliban, a man who was held in extremely dubious circumstances in another part of the world was shown his photo and came up with a story about seeing him two or three years before his arrival in Afghanistan, which would, henceforth, be regarded as evidence against him.[11]

Another revealing exchange took place in the tribunal of Ibrahim Zeidan, the Jordanian who was kidnapped and held for ransom by a gang in Kabul. Refuting an extensive list of allegations against him—which included training at al-Farouq, appearing in a video about the bombing of the USS *Cole*, and attending a seminar for falsifying passports—he said, "A witness from the camp named Abu Zubaydah made these allegations against me that are not true," and added:

> This person also told lies about a lot of other people. We heard from the interrogators themselves that they used unusual methods to get information

from him. It is known that anyone that gives information under force should not be taken into consideration. Experience has shown that anyone that is subject to torture for long periods of time will say anything to stop the torturing. He may have talked about me under pressure or torture. He may have mistaken my identity for someone else. Anyway, the entire report is false.[12]

Zeidan's story is remarkable not only because he specifically named Zubaydah as a well-known liar, but also because he so confidently placed him at Guantánamo. This has never been admitted by the US administration, but it accords with a report in December 2004, which revealed the existence of a secret CIA facility within Guantánamo, where, presumably, Zubaydah was held at some point. A military official said that the facility was "off-limits to almost everyone on the base," another said that Mohamedou Ould Slahi was held there, and another said that it was used to house prisoners from several countries including Pakistan, West Africa and the Yemen. By the time the article was written, however, it had almost certainly been closed down, as the Supreme Court decision of June 2004 placed Guantánamo uncomfortably within the reach of the law.[13]

The Military Commissions Act

Although the transfer of the 14 "high-value" prisoners to Guantánamo appeared to be a desperate measure on the part of the administration, it was soon revealed as part of a cynical attempt to rewrite the rulebook yet again, which involved persuading a disturbingly supine Congress to pass a hideously flawed piece of legislation—the Military Commissions Act (MCA)—just a few weeks later. Overturning all the legal victories of the previous two years, the Act reintroduced the shameful system of Military Commissions that had been jettisoned by the Supreme Court in June, apparently nodding to the Supreme Court's concerns by incorporating Common Article 3 of the Geneva Conventions, but in fact allowing the President to define and apply it as he saw fit, and redefining the War Crimes Act to grant immunity to the many torturers employed over the previous five years. As Amnesty International described it, the MCA "narrow[s] the scope of the War Crimes Act by not expressly criminalizing acts that constitute 'outrages upon personal dignity, particularly humiliating and degrading treatment' banned under Article 3."[14] Another way of putting it would be that Bush passed legislation that confirmed that if a US representative tortured someone but said that he was only trying to get information, it wasn't actually torture.

The MCA also sought to retroactively nullify the prisoners' existing habeas petitions, stating, "No court, justice or judge shall have jurisdiction to hear or consider an application for a writ of habeas corpus filed by or on behalf of an alien detained by the United States who has been determined by the United States to have been properly detained as an enemy combatant or is awaiting such determination," and explained that an "enemy combatant" was either someone who has engaged in or supported hostilities against the US, or someone who "has been determined to be an unlawful enemy combatant by a Combatant Status Review Tribunal or another competent tribunal established under the authority of the President or the secretary of defense."[15] Considered in conjunction with the provisions described above, this blatant attempt to erase the prisoners' history was designed to smooth the way for around eighty prisoners to be tried by Military Commissions without the interference of civilian lawyers and without any inconvenient allegations of torture. The fact that over three hundred other prisoners, who, according to the authorities, would not be tried before the Military Commissions, now had no way of challenging their detention was considered irrelevant by the administration, and was completely overlooked by Congress.

No End in Sight

Whether the MCA will survive legal challenges is open to question, but in the meantime the situation at Guantánamo could hardly be worse for the 388 prisoners who remain there. Not only have they been deprived of their habeas rights, but many have been moved into a new camp, Camp 6, where, according to James Cohen, a lawyer who visited in February 2007, conditions are worse than in any Supermax prison on the US mainland. After noting that the men in Camp 6 include around a hundred prisoners who have been cleared for release, and who were previously held in the communal dorms of Camp 4, Cohen described a system of almost complete isolation, in which the prisoners are alone for 22 hours a day, and pointed out that, "although the prison was built with common areas, such as those where US maximum-security prison inmates are permitted to spend their time during the day, the prisoners of Camp 6 are not permitted access to these areas." He contrasted this with the conditions in maximum security prisons on the mainland, where "it is common for inmates to have jobs, to eat communally, to receive visits from family and friends and to have social contact with other inmates."[16]

The prisoners' response to the increased severity of their conditions was to embark on another hunger strike. In a document released in March 2007, Sami al-Hajj provided details of at least 42 hunger strikers, including three men who had been on strike for over a year: Abdul Rahman Shalabi, one of the Saudis who complained of torture when he was force-fed in October 2005, Tarek Baada, a Yemeni captured crossing from Afghanistan to Pakistan in December 2001, and the Saudi Ahmed Zuhair (also known as Handala), a little-known "high-value" suspect, who was apparently convicted in absentia by a Bosnian court for a car bombing in 1997. Al-Hajj also reported that Shaker Aamer, still held in total isolation in Camp Echo, was on hunger strike, and that the Saudi Murtadha Makram, an alleged Taliban foot soldier, who "has tried to kill himself many times," was now trying to starve himself to death. The report also contained a list of requests—including a plea that those held in total isolation, including Aamer, be "allowed to rejoin humanity," a call for an inquiry into the suicides in 2006, and a request that the US military "respects the religious rights of the prisoners." According to al-Hajj, "There continue to be routine violations of the prisoners' right to practice their religion freely and without denigration," and overall his reflections on the current state of Guantánamo, where prisoners are still routinely ERFed, given no news of the outside world and very little reading material, abused by "bad guards"—"and unfortunately there are plenty of them"—and held in isolation with the air-conditioning turned up full, serve only to confirm that the conditions in the prison remain an affront to decent human values.[17]

Despite this, the administration has been vigorously pursuing its post-MCA mandate. In March 2007, the first CSRTs were convened for the 14 "high-value" prisoners, to rubber-stamp their eligibility for trial by Military Commission. The first of these—the "confession" of Khalid Sheikh Mohammed—was released to the public almost immediately. Mohammed's claims—that he "was responsible for the 9/11 operation from A to Z," that he personally decapitated the American journalist Daniel Pearl in Pakistan in February 2002, and that he played a major part in thirty other plots—put Guantánamo back on the front pages, but the overall effect was not what the administration intended. A weary cynicism greeted the majority of his claims, with commentators not only noting that he was a notorious show-off—the *9/11 Commission Report* described him as a man who treated terrorism as theater, a "spectacle of destruction" with himself as the star—but also highlighting heavily redacted sections of his tribunal in which he said that he was tortured and admitted making false statements about other prisoners in US custody. Astute observers also noted that, by declaring a "war on terrorism" instead of treating terrorists as criminals, the administration allowed Mohammed to portray himself as a freedom-fighting warrior—comparing himself to George Washington, who, he said, would have been considered an "enemy combatant" if he had been captured by the British—and failed to condemn him for what he really was: a brutal criminal who deserved the same fate as serial killers—ignominious trial and conviction.[18]

By April 2007, CSRTs had been convened for most of the 14 "high-value" prisoners, with mixed results. Waleed bin Attash was the only one who came up with a "confession" akin to that of Mohammed. He said that he was the link between Osama bin Laden and the Nairobi cell during the African embassy bombings, and admitted that he played a major part in the bombing of the USS *Cole*, explaining that he "put together the plan for the operation for a year and a half," and that he bought the explosives and the boat, and recruited the bombers. Most of the others were less forthcoming: Mustafa al-Hawsawi admitted providing support for jihadists, including transferring money for some of the 9/11 hijackers, although he denied that he was a member of al-Qaeda; Ahmed Khalfan Ghailani, who also denied being a member of al-Qaeda, described himself as a peripheral character in the African embassy bombings, who was duped by others around him, although he admitted forging documents for al-Qaeda in Afghanistan; Hamlili said that he resigned from Jemaah Islamiya in 2000, and was not involved with al-Qaeda or with any bombings or plots; and Mohammed bin Lep denied all the allegations about his involvement with Jemaah Islamiya, admitting only that he had once transferred some money to Hamlili.

Ammar al-Baluchi was even more adamant that he had no involvement with terrorism, and was dismissive of the allegations that he worked on a bomb plot with Waleed bin Attash. Although he admitted transferring money on behalf of some of the 9/11 hijackers, he insisted that he had no knowledge of either 9/11 or al-Qaeda, and was a legitimate businessman, who regularly transferred money for Arabs, without knowing what it would be used for. His story was backed up by his uncle, Khalid Sheikh Mohammed, who stated, "Any dealings he had with al-Qaeda were through me. I used him for business dealings. He had no knowledge of any al-Qaeda links. Ammar is being linked to al-Qaeda because of me." In addition, two prisoners—Ramzi bin al-Shibh and Abu Faraj al-Libi—refused to take part in the process, and al-Libi challenged the legality of his detention in a written statement, arguing, as his Personal Representative put it, "that his freedom is too important to be decided by an administrative process," and demanding the right to be represented by a lawyer, and to challenge the evidence against him.

Only two prisoners—Abu Zubaydah and Abdul Rahim al-Nashiri—broached the subject of torture, but their claims added to the unease caused by Mohammed's "confession." Zubaydah, reinforcing most of the information that was provided by Ron Suskind and Khalid al-Hubayshi, said that he was tortured by the CIA to admit that he worked with Osama bin Laden, but insisted, "I'm not his partner and I'm not a member of al-Qaeda." He also said that his interrogators promised to return his diary to him—the one that contained the evidence of his split personality—and explained that their refusal to do so affected him emotionally and triggered seizures. Speaking of his status as a "high-value" prisoner, he said that his only role was to operate a guest house used by those who were training at Khaldan, and confirmed al-Hubayshi's analysis of his relationship with bin Laden, saying, "Bin Laden wanted al-Qaeda to have control of Khaldan, but we refused since we had different ideas." He explained that he opposed attacks on civilian targets, which brought him into conflict with bin Laden, and although he admitted that he had been an enemy of the US since childhood, because of its support for Israel, pointed out that his enmity was towards the government and the military, and not the American people.

In his tribunal, al-Nashiri said that he made up stories that tied him to the bombing of the USS *Cole* in 2000 and confessed to involvement in several other terror plots—including the bombing of a French oil tanker in 2002, plans to bomb US ships in the Gulf, a plan to hijack a plane and crash it into a ship, and claims that bin Laden had a nuclear bomb—in order to get his captors to stop torturing him. "From the time I was arrested five years ago," he said, "they have been torturing me. It happened during interviews. One time they tortured me one way, and another time they tortured me in a different way. I just said those things to make the people happy. They were very happy when I told them those things."[19]

For the administration's dwindling band of supporters, the confessions of Khalid Sheikh Mohammed and Waleed bin Attash have no doubt reassured them that they are "winning" the "War on Terror," but for those who are sickened that this whole malign experiment has not yet been closed down, it's distressing to report that at the time of writing the architects of this endless injustice were feeling especially buoyant. On the night of March 26, 2007, in the first of the new-style Military Commissions, a weary David Hicks accepted a plea bargain and declared that he was guilty of the only charge that was eventually raised against him: providing "material support for terrorism." For his cooperation, he was sentenced on March 30 to nine months' imprisonment, rather than the seven years that the prosecution had been seeking, and was told that he would be returning home in May 2007 to serve his sentence in Australia. This was some comfort for Hicks, but observers noted that the process was still fundamentally flawed. Australian lawyer Lex Lasry said that the court looked "pretty dysfunctional." He was not impressed when the judge, Marine colonel Ralph Kohlmann, eliminated two of Hicks' three lawyers, excluding one, Joshua Dratel, after he refused to agree in advance to court procedures that have yet to be drawn up, and he complained that when Hicks' remaining lawyer, Major Michael Mori, objected that Kohlmann was not sufficiently impartial, he "sat in judgment of himself" and "solemnly found that there were no grounds to find he was not impartial."[20]

While Hicks' story commanded the attention of the world's media, few commentators noticed that on the same day the administration announced that a new prisoner—Mohammed Abdul Malik, a low-level Kenyan terror suspect—was brought to Guantánamo from Kenya, raising the disturbing possibility that others will follow. Jennifer Daskal of Human Rights Watch noted that a US citizen, Daniel Maldonado, was recently extradited from Kenya to Texas to face prosecution in a federal court, and expressed fears that the administration was implementing a two-tier judicial system: "The vastly different treatment of these two terrorism suspects shows the US sees Guantánamo as a parallel criminal justice system for foreigners. Americans suspected of terrorism rightly go before US courts, while foreigners get sent to Guantánamo for indefinite detention and unfair proceedings."[21]

It remains to be seen whether the administration's renewed arrogance can last. My suspicion—and my hope—is that the commitment of decent Americans to the rule of law will prevail over that of the brutal and brutalizing forces who are currently in charge of their country's counter-terror policies. The voices of these decent people are not always heard over the shrill rhetoric of the administration's cheerleaders for torture, but I believe that they express not only what is wrong with the system that has been created at Guantánamo and beyond, but also how the administration will, in the end, discover that it has dug itself into a hole from which there is no way out. Bush and Cheney and their advisors were jubilant about David Hicks' "confession," but Hicks chose not to raise the issue of his treatment in US custody because he was informed that a guilty plea would enable him to return home. As a result, torture was never mentioned, and his lawyers proposed defense—that "material support for terrorism" is not a war crime as defined by the Geneva Conventions—was never tested. But what will happen when the administration comes to try Khalid Sheikh Mohammed, and tries desperately to keep quiet about what it did to him in the three and a half years that he was in their secret prisons? Can they really keep quiet about the waterboarding? Michael Scheuer thinks not. "The policymakers hadn't thought what to do with them," he told Jane Mayer, adding that once a prisoner's rights were violated there was no way of reintegrating them into the court system. "All we've done is create a nightmare," he added. "Are we going to hold these people forever?" Remarkably, doubts have also surfaced within the administration itself. One of the first proposals made by Robert Gates, who replaced Donald Rumsfeld as defense secretary in November 2006, was to close Guantánamo and conduct trials on the US mainland. Gates declared that Guantánamo's reputation was so tainted that any verdicts would lack legitimacy in the eyes of the international community, but although his opinion was backed by Condoleezza Rice and the State Department, he was overruled by Dick Cheney and the Attorney General Alberto Gonzales.[22]

In the end, torture, in the many forms in which it has been used by the administration since 9/11—ranging from waterboarding "high-value" individuals in secret locations to imprisoning hundreds of men without rights in an experimental prison in which violence, medical abuse and extreme isolation are prevalent—is no way to win this "war." Dan Coleman of the FBI, who spent his career understanding the value of building up relationships, even with suspects he despised, explained to Jane Mayer why he avoided embracing what Dick Cheney described as "the dark side." "Brutalization doesn't work," he said. "We know that. Besides, you lose your soul."[23] In the process of losing their souls, those in charge of America's "War on Terror" have been responsible for the catastrophic failure of justice chronicled in this book, which on every front—from Guantánamo, Afghanistan and Iraq to the Military Commissions and the still-unknown "ghost" prisoners subjected to "extraordinary rendition"—will haunt successive administrations for years to come.

Notes

Important Abbreviations Used in the Notes

"CSRT" and "ARB" refer to the Combatant Status Review Tribunals, which were held at Guantánamo from July 2004 to March 2005, and the Administrative Review Boards, annual reviews held from December 2004 onwards. For transcripts of these hearings, released by the Pentagon in March and April 2006 under Freedom of Information legislation, see <http://www.dod.mil/pubs/foi/detainees/csrt/index.html>.

In addition to the transcripts of the CSRT and ARB hearings, this page also provides access to the Unclassified Summaries of Evidence for over a hundred ARB hearings, listed as "ARB Factors."

"CSRB" refers to the Combatant Status Review Boards. These documents, which comprise the Unclassified Summaries of Evidence for 517 of the 558 CSRT hearings, were released by the Pentagon in 2005 under Freedom of Information legislation. See <http://www.dod.mil/pubs/foi/detainees/OARDEC_docs.html>.

For these transcripts, I have chosen a numbering system similar to that used for the CSRT and ARB hearings, so that, for example, "March 2005 Release" becomes "CSRB Set 3."

"ISN" refers to "Internment Serial Numbers," the unique number assigned to each prisoner in Guantánamo. For a list of the 558 prisoners (identified by name, nationality and ISN) who went through the CSRT process, see <http://www.dod.mil/pubs/foi/detainees/detainee_list.pdf>.

For a list of 759 prisoners, including the 201 released or transferred before the CSRT process began (identified by name, nationality, date and place of birth and ISN), see <http://www.dod.mil/pubs/foi/detainees/detaineesFOIArelease-15May2006.pdf>.

For the remaining 15 prisoners, see Chapter 20.

Preface

1. The administration refers to them as "detainees," but I have chosen to describe them as prisoners, which is more accurate. The 759 prisoners who arrived between 2002 and 2004 were from 43 countries and included 218 Afghans, 138 Saudis, 108 Yemenis, 67 Pakistanis, 82 prisoners from various North African countries, 43 from other Gulf countries, 33 from countries to the north of Afghanistan, and 30 Europeans.
2. "Guantánamo Bay: The legal black hole," Twenty-Seventh F.A. Mann Lecture, November 25, 2003.

3. Rear Admiral John D Stufflebeem, quoted in "US Gains Custody of More Detainees," *American Forces Press Service*, January 28, 2002.

4. Mark Denbeaux and Joshua Denbeaux, "Report on Guantánamo Detainees," Seton Hall University School of Law, February 2006 <http://law.shu.edu/aaafinal.pdf>. After analyzing the CSRB documents (which were mostly issued with the prisoners' identifying numbers removed), the Seton Hall team ascertained that 86 percent were captured by the Northern Alliance or Pakistani forces, 55 percent were not determined to have committed any hostile acts against the US or its allies, and only 8 percent were alleged to have had any kind of affiliation with al-Qaeda.

Chapter 1

1. "Bush: Bin Laden 'prime suspect'", CNN, September 17, 2001.

2. Jason Burke, *Al-Qaeda: The True Story of Radical Islam* (London: Penguin, 2004), pp. 173, 183–7; David Rose, *Guantánamo: America's War on Human Rights* (London: Faber and Faber, 2004), p. 25.

3. The Tajiks comprise 27 percent of the population, Uzbeks and Hazaras 9 percent each, and Pashtuns, who, crucially, are also found throughout Pakistan (and especially in the largely autonomous tribal areas in the west of the country), comprise 42 percent. All are Sunni Muslims apart from the Hazara, who are Shia Muslims.

4. According to Zbginiew Brzczinksi, Jimmy Carter's National Security Advisor, the US started funding the mujahideen six months before the Soviet invasion as a covert action aimed to induce Soviet military intervention.

5. It was not until 1991, when the Americans set up permanent bases in Saudi Arabia during the first Gulf War, that bin Laden's opposition to both the US and the Saudi royal family was first established.

6. Musharraf said that he was told this, shortly after 9/11, by Deputy Secretary of State Richard Armitage.

7. Steve Coll, "Flawed Ally Was Hunt's Best Hope," *Washington Post*, February 23, 2004.

8. It's probable that al-Qaeda underestimated the US response to 9/11, not thinking that they would invade Afghanistan.

9. Coll, "Flawed Ally Was Hunt's Best Hope."

10. Karzai initially supported the Taliban, describing them as "good, honest people," but recalled how, as early as September 1994, "others began to appear at the meetings—silent ones I did not recognize, people who took over the Taliban movement. That was the hidden hand of Pakistani intelligence" (Robert D Kaplan, "The Lawless Frontier," *Atlantic Monthly*, September 2000).

11. Of the dozens of training camps established in Afghanistan from the 1980s onwards, most were funded by Pakistan and wealthy donors in the Gulf countries. Some were run by Afghan warlords, others by Pakistani groups and others by militant groups from other countries. Although bin Laden had a few camps of his own, it was inappropriate to describe all the training camps in Afghanistan as "al-Qaeda camps."

12. Seymour Hersh, "King's Ransom: Exposing a Right Royal Mess," *New Yorker*, October 22, 2001.

13. "Afghan Scramble Begins Over Control After War," *International Herald Tribune*, October 11, 2001.

14. Gary Berntsen and Ralph Pezzullo, *Jawbreaker: The Attack on bin Laden and Al-Qaeda: A Personal Account by the CIA's Key Field Commander* (New York: Three Rivers Press, 2005), pp. 140, 168.

15. Justin Huggler, "Leaders in Kunduz linked to massacre," *Independent*, November 22, 2001; Seymour Hersh, "The Getaway," *New Yorker*, January 28, 2002.

16. "Al-Qaeda massacre Taliban," *Daily Telegraph*, November 19, 2001.

Chapter 2

1. Luke Harding, Simon Tisdall, Nicholas Watt and Richard Norton-Taylor, "Fatal errors that led to massacre," *Guardian*, December 1, 2001; Alex Perry, "Inside the Battle at Qala-i-Jangi," *Time*, December 1, 2001; Matthew Campbell, "The fort of hell," *Sunday Times*, December 2, 2001.

2. Colin Solway, "He's Got To Decide if He Wants to Live or Die Here," *Newsweek*, December 6, 2001.

3. Perry, "Inside the Battle at Qala-i-Jangi"; Campbell, "The fort of hell." Several prisoners escaped from the fort, although most were either shot by Alliance soldiers or killed by locals. One Yemeni, Fahed Mohammed (ISN 13), was more fortunate. The 19-year-old was recruited for jihad in Mecca, but told his tribunal, "I changed my mind [because] I saw some things there that were against my religion … like worshipping a cemetery where people have died," and explained, "I escaped during the fighting and turned myself in one day after. I went to the market to turn myself in" (CSRT Set 50, pp. 83–7; ARB Set 2, pp. 40–4).

4. "How Our Afghan allies applied the Geneva Convention," *Independent*, November 29, 2001.

5. "Taliban who escaped the fort of death," *Observer*, December 2, 2001.

6. Campbell, "The fort of hell"; Hamdi (ISN 9); "Taliban who escaped the fort of death."

7. Al-Rashid (ISN 74): CSRT Set 4, pp. 22–9; also see Adnan al-Saigh (ISN 105): CSRT Set 10, pp. 38–44 (released in May 2006).

8. Al-Atabi (ISN 122): ARB Factors Set 1, pp. 51–2; al-Harazi (ISN 79): ARB Factors Set 1, pp. 45–6; al-Yamani (ISN 206): ARB Set 4, pp. 11–15; al-Zahrani (ISN 93): "Pentagon identifies 3 Guantánamo Suicides," Associated Press, June 12, 2006.

9. Al-Oshan (ISN 112): CSRT Set 31, pp. 53–63; al-Sehli (ISN 94): CSRT Set 23, pp. 14–22; al-Rashid (ISN 74): CSRT Set 4, pp. 22–9; al-Rabiesh (ISN 109): CSRT Set 52, pp. 125–49. Thirteen other recent Taliban recruits (five Saudis and eight Yemenis) failed to mention being wounded, and may have escaped unscathed in the basement. They included Mishal al-Habiri (ISN 207), a 21-year-old Saudi, who drove a food truck for the Taliban, and was released in 2005, two years after he tried to commit suicide and suffered serious brain damage (CSRT Set 46, p. 20). Another Yemeni, 27-year-old Mukhtar al-Warafi

(ISN 117), said he "had nothing to do whatsoever with the Taliban," and had been working as a medic in Kunduz (ARB Set 3, pp. 72–3).

10. Al-Mutairi (ISN 205): CSRT Set 7, pp. 81–94; Ali (ISN 81): ARB Set 3, pp. 42–54.
11. Al-Tayeea (ISN 111): CSRT Set 43, pp. 46–69.
12. Don Van Natta Jr, "US Recruits a Rough Ally to Be a Jailer," *New York Times*, May 1, 2005.
13. Tourson (ISN 201): CSRB Set 3, p. 262; CSRT Set 38, pp. 2–14. Also see Arkin Mahmud (ISN 103): ARB Set 5, pp. 123–33.
14. Kudayev (ISN 82), Ogidov (ISN 211), Khazhiyev (ISN 209) and Gumarov (ISN 203): "From Russia to Guantánamo, via Afghanistan," *St Petersburg Times*, December 24, 2002.
15. Batayev (ISN 84): CSRT Set 10, pp. 47–54. Also see Rukniddin Sharipov (ISN 76), a Tajik: ARB Set 5, pp. 107–15.
16. "How Our Afghan allies applied the Geneva Convention"; Harding et al., "Fatal errors that led to massacre"; Perry, "Inside the Battle at Qala-i-Jangi."

Chapter 3

1. Rasul (ISN 86), Iqbal (ISN 87) and Ahmed (ISN 110): Rose, *Guantánamo*, pp. 15–16; "How we survived jail hell," *Observer*, March 14, 2004.
2. Babak Dehghanpisheh, John Barry and Roy Gutman, "The Death Convoy of Afghanistan," *Newsweek*, August 26, 2002.
3. Abdul Rahman (ISN 357): CSRT Set 49, pp. 46–67.
4. Saghir (ISN 143): <http://www.mindfully.org/Reform/2003/Guantanamo-Sagheer-USA-Moret31dec03.htm>; "To Hell and Back," *Newsline*, February 2004.
5. Rose, *Guantánamo*, p. 13.
6. Shah (ISN 119): "Afghans reveal Guantánamo ordeal," BBC News, March 25, 2003.
7. Rose, *Guantánamo*, p. 17; Robert Young Pelton, "Afghan War Eyewitness on Warlords, Future, More," *National Geographic News*, February 15, 2002.
8. Dehghanpisheh et al., "The Death Convoy of Afghanistan."
9. Jamie Doran, "A drive to death in the desert," *Le Monde diplomatique*, September 2002.

Chapter 4

1. Philip Smucker, "How bin Laden got away," *Christian Science Monitor*, March 4, 2002; Burke, *Al-Qaeda*, pp. 78, 160–1; Mary Anne Weaver, "Lost at Tora Bora," *New York Times*, September 11, 2005.
2. Weaver, "Lost at Tora Bora"; Smucker, "How bin Laden got away."
3. Berntsen, *Jawbreaker*, p. 307.
4. Rod Nordland, Sami Yousafzai and Babak Dehghanpisheh, "How Al-Qaida Slipped Away," *Newsweek*, August 19, 2002; Philip Smucker, "Bin Laden in Pakistan, Source Claims," *Christian Science Monitor*, December 12, 2001.
5. Smucker, "How bin Laden got away."

6. The stories of the Afghans (and a few Pakistanis) captured at this time are unknown, as they were either released—or otherwise dealt with—by the Afghans who captured them, or sent to Guantánamo but released before the tribunal process began.
7. Philip Smucker, "The hunt for bin Laden widens," *Christian Science Monitor*, December 19, 2001.
8. Al-Assani (ISN 554): CSRT Set 44, pp. 30–2.
9. Al-Anazi (ISN 514): conversation with his lawyer, Anant Raut, January 19, 2007; Zaid (ISN 550): ARB Set 3, pp. 75–80.
10. Al-Harbi (ISN 516): CSRT Set 44, pp. 100–5; ARB Set 7, pp. 44–56.
11. Zemiri (ISN 533): ARB Set 7, pp. 78–89.
12. Al-Kandari (ISN 552): ARB Set 2, pp. 146–57; and Nassir (ISN 244): Jon Lee Anderson, *The Lion's Grave: Dispatches from Afghanistan* (London: Atlantic Books, 2002), pp. 142–3.
13. Burke, *Al-Qaeda*, p. 105. Durunta became a camp that specialized in explosives training, where rudimentary research into chemical weapons also took place.
14. Nasseri (ISN 510): ARB Factors Set 2, pp. 5–7; Ourgy (ISN 502): CSRT Set 24, pp. 34–42.
15. Anderson, *The Lion's Grave*, pp. 143–5.
16. Al-Sawah (ISN 535): CSRT Set 44, pp. 82–92.
17. Al-Anazi (ISN 507): CSRT Set 37, pp. 20–30; Khusruf (ISN 509): ARB Set 7, pp. 1–12; al-Zuba (ISN 503): ARB Factors Set 1, pp. 84–5.
18. Al-Nahdi (ISN 511): ARB Set 7, pp. 13–28.
19. Khowlan (ISN 513): ARB Set 7, pp. 29–43; Ismail (ISN 522): CSRT Set 53, pp. 84–9; Dergoul (ISN 534): Rose, *Guantánamo*, pp. 34–7. Also see Mohammed Laalami (ISN 237): CSRT Set 33, pp. 72–4, and Salman al-Rabie (ISN 508): CSRT Set 53, pp. 40–2.
20. Al-Rabia (ISN 551): CSRT Set 7, pp. 113–51.
21. Al-Quwari (ISN 519): CSRT Set 31, pp. 1–8.
22. Philip Smucker, "US beefs up troops, but skips locals," *Christian Science Monitor*, January 16, 2002; Habeas petition <http://wid.ap.org/documents/detainees/fouadalrabia.pdf>.

Chapter 5

1. "7 Al-Qaida men, 8 Pak troops die in clash," *The Tribune, India*, December 20, 2001; "Pakistan holds senior Taleban official," BBC News, December 20, 2001.
2. Al-Bahlul (ISN 39): <http://www.globalsecurity.org/security/library/news/2004/02/d20040224al_bahlul.pdf>; al-Qosi (ISN 54): <http://www.globalsecurity.org/security/library/news/2004/02/d20040224al_qosi.pdf>; Tabarak (ISN 56): "Al-Qaeda Detainee's Mysterious Release," *Washington Post*, January 30, 2006; al-Qahtani (ISN 63): Adam Zagorin and Michael Duffy, "Inside the Interrogation of Detainee 063," *Time*, June 12, 2005.
3. Ghazi (ISN 26): CSRT Set 41, pp. 62–7; ARB Set 5, pp. 11–20.
4. Al-Zayla (ISN 55): CSRT Set 40, pp. 9–18; al-Sharekh (ISN 67): CSRT Set 13, pp. 35–42. Six other Saudis and Yemenis, who refused to take part in their

tribunals, were also accused of attending training camps and fighting with the Taliban, but without al-Qahtani's allegations they too were, at best, humble foot soldiers in an Afghan war that began long before 9/11.

5. Ghanim (ISN 44): CSRB Set 3, pp. 100–1; Idris (ISN 36): CSRB Set 3, pp. 150–1; al-Uwaydha (ISN 59): CSRB Set 3, pp. 110–11; al-Yazidi (ISN 38): ARB Factors Set 2, pp. 51–3. For Khaldan, see Burke, *Al-Qaeda*, p. 78. From 1990 onwards, Khaldan was a "clearing camp" for foreign volunteers, whose instructors selected able recruits for advanced training in other camps.
6. Moqbel (ISN 43): CSRT Set 47, pp. 63–9.
7. Mohammed (ISN 27): CSRT Set 8, pp. 112–14; al-Rahabi (ISN 37): CSRT Set 4, pp. 114–29; Saif (ISN 32): ARB Set 5, pp. 36–52.
8. Al-Sulami (ISN 66): CSRT Set 16, pp. 77–84; al-Mujahid (ISN 31): CSRT Set 52, pp. 186–95.
9. Al-Bawardi (ISN 68): CSRT Set 22, pp. 15–33. Also see Abdullah al-Yafi (ISN 34): ARB Set 5, pp. 53–62; CSRB Set 3, p. 259.
10. Al-Sebaii (ISN 64): CSRT Set 3, pp. 45–55.
11. <http://www.psywarrior.com/Herbafghan02.html>; Pervez Musharraf, *In the Line of Fire: A Memoir* (London: Simon and Schuster, 2006), p. 237.
12. Haji (ISN 60): CSRT Set 9, pp. 55–76; ARB Set 3, pp. 30–41.
13. Amin (ISN 65): CSRT Set 9, pp. 4–27.

Chapter 6

1. "15 killed as Osama men try to escape," *Dawn*, December 19, 2001.
2. Al-Rubeish (ISN 192): ARB Set 3, pp. 127–35; al-Fayfi (ISN 188): CSRT Set 1, pp. 10–13; al-Jabri (ISN 182): CSRT Set 52, pp. 2–9; ARB Factors Set 1, pp. 53–5. Ten other Saudi prisoners captured at this time were foot soldiers in the Taliban's war against the Northern Alliance, and a few others were training to fight in Chechnya.
3. Al-Jahdali (ISN 286): ARB Factors Set 3, pp. 58–9; Sharon Curcio, "Generational Differences in Waging Jihad," *Military Review*, July–August 2005, pp. 84–8.
4. Al-Harbi (ISN 265): CSRT Set 45, pp. 7–20; al-Jutayli (ISN 177): CSRT Set 43, pp. 1–9; al-Qurayshi (ISN 176): CSRT Set 52, pp. 167–8; al-Awfi (ISN 154): CSRT Set 1, pp. 14–26; ARB Set 2, pp. 20–9; al-Shurfa (ISN 331): ARB Set 6, pp. 67–85.
5. Al-Bidna (ISN 337): "Saudi Released From Guantánamo: Fatwas Prompted Me to Join the Jihad," *Al-Riyadh*, October 10, 2006.
6. Al-Amri (ISN 199): CSRT Set 46, pp. 21–2; al-Sharif (ISN 215): ARB Set 17, pp. 35–45; al-Qahtani (ISN 200): CSRT Set 33, pp. 100–11.
7. Al-Malki (ISN 157): ARB Set 5, pp. 180–94; al-Morghi (ISN 339): ARB Set 3, pp. 1–19.
8. Al-Baddah (ISN 264): ARB Set 6, pp. 25–40; I. al-Nasir (ISN 271): CSRB Set 3, pp. 57–8; A. al-Nasir (ISN 273): ARB Set 2, pp. 22–9; al-Ghanimi (ISN 266): CSRB Set 3, pp. 219–20. Also see Majid al-Frih (ISN 336), an aid worker (released in 2006) who came under suspicion because he was related by marriage to the manager of one of al-Wafa's offices (CSRB Set 3, pp. 95–6).

9. Al-Rushaydan (ISN 343): ARB Set 2, pp. 83–8. For more on the IIRO, see Chapter 12.
10. "Al-Qaeda Skimming Charity Money," Associated Press, June 7, 2004.
11. Al-Omar (ISN 338): CSRT Set 49, pp. 18–35; al-Qa'id (ISN 344): CSRT Set 49, pp. 1–17; al-Nurr (ISN 226).
12. Al-Juaid (ISN 179): CSRT Set 53, pp. 74–83; al-Bahuth (ISN 272): ARB Set 1, pp. 110–26.
13. Al-Khathami (ISN 191): CSRT Set 47, pp. 1–4; al-Amri (ISN 196): ARB Factors Set 2, pp. 69–71; al-Taibi (ISN 318): CSRT Set 10, pp. 27–32. Also see Abdul Rahman al-Hataybi (ISN 268): ARB Factors Set 2, pp. 92–3, and Adil al-Nusayri (ISN 308), a police officer who was held by the Taliban as a spy: CSRT Set 33, pp. 112–24.
14. Moqbill (ISN 193): ARB Set 1, pp. 77–85; ARB Factors Set 2, pp. 22–4; Sulayman (ISN 223): CSRT Set 18, pp. 23–31. Ten other Yemeni prisoners captured at this time were foot soldiers or support staff (cooks or guards) in the Taliban's war against the Northern Alliance.
15. Al-Busayss (ISN 165): ARB Set 17, pp. 14–16; al-Tays (ISN 162): CSRT Set 4, pp. 47–54; Basardah (ISN 252): ARB Set 5, pp. 233–44. Also see Saeed Hatim (ISN 255): CSRT Set 31, pp. 38–46, and Ali al-Raimi (ISN 167): CSRT Set 4, pp. 55–64.
16. Al-Jayfi (ISN 183): CSRT Set 13, pp. 14–22; al-Ansari (ISN 253): CSRT Set 44, pp. 128–38. Also see Sharaf Masud (ISN 170): CSRT Set 39, pp. 14–15, Mohammed al-Hamiri (ISN 249): CSRT Set 33, pp. 21–3, and Hani al-Shulan (ISN 225): CSRT Set 31, pp. 20–7.
17. Al-Khalaqi (ISN 152): CSRT Set 14, pp. 11–23. Also see Riyad al-Radai (ISN 256): ARB Set 18, pp. 82–5, and Fadil Hintif (ISN 259): CSRB Set 3, p. 67.

Chapter 7

1. Chris Mackey with Greg Miller, *The Interrogator's War: Inside The Secret War Against Al-Qaeda* (London: John Murray, 2004), pp. 7–13, 165–73.
2. Benchellali (ISN 161): "I Met Osama bin Laden," *Le Figaro*, February 14, 2006; Sassi (ISN 325): "Pakistan: Human Rights Ignored in the War on Terror," Amnesty International, September 29, 2006; Khalid (ISN 173): CSRT Set 7, pp. 52–64; bin Mustafa (ISN 236): "An Interview with Khaled bin Mustafa," *Le Parisien*, April 17, 2005.
3. Mourad Benchellali, "Detainees In Despair," *New York Times*, June 14, 2006.
4. CSRT Set 7, pp. 52–64; Yadel (ISN 371): <http://www.cageprisoners.com/prisoners.php?id=68>.
5. Al-Qadir (ISN 284): CSRT Set 42, pp. 63–70; Feghoul (ISN 292): Factual return for Habeas petition (author's copy); Sen (ISN 296): ARB Factors Set 2, pp. 1–2.
6. Saib (ISN 288): ARB Set 2, pp. 3–8; ARB Factors Set 2, pp. 90–1; Ameziane (ISN 310): ARB Factors Set 2, pp. 11–13; bin Mohammed (ISN 311): ARB Set 3, pp. 84–94.
7. Sameur (ISN 659): CSRT Set 51, pp. 38–52; ARB Set 8, pp. 28–45; "Profile: 'Forgotten' Cuba detainees," BBC News, October 5, 2006.

8. Belbacha (ISN 290): "I thought Britain stood for justice, but the British government has abandoned us," *Guardian*, October 3, 2006; ARB Factors Set 3, pp. 5–6; David Rose, "Pentagon Clears UK Detainees at Guantánamo," *Observer*, March 18, 2007.

9. Mabrouk (ISN 148): CSRT Set 50, pp. 48–58; Lagha (ISN 660): ARB Factors Set 2, pp. 45–7.

10. Hakimi (ISN 168): conversation with Zachary Katznelson of Reprieve, January 4, 2007; H. Sliti (ISN 174): CSRB Set 3, pp. 62–3; A. Sliti: "Footballer jailed at terror trial," CNN, September 30, 2003.

11. Al-Hubayshi (ISN 155): CSRT Set 1, pp. 65–78. Two Libyans—33-year-old Mohammed al-Futuri (ISN 194) and 30-year-old Ashraf Sultan (ISN 263)— were also associated with Jalalabad. Both denied allegations that they were members of the Libyan Islamic Fighting Group, presenting themselves as economic migrants, and al-Futuri was released in December 2006 (CSRT Set 46, pp. 29–34; CSRT Set 44, pp. 139–43).

12. Abderrahmane (ISN 323): "Danish detainee to join rebels," BBC News, September 30, 2004; "Pakistan: Human Rights Ignored in the War on Terror."

13. Kanouni (ISN 164): "6 Former Gitmo Inmates on Trial in Paris," *Washington Post*, July 3, 2006; Ghezali (ISN 166): "Freed Swede Says He Was Tortured in Guantánamo," Reuters, July 14, 2004.

14. Ahmed (ISN 267): "From Ceuta to Iran, In Search of the Taliban—A Spaniard in Guantánamo," *El Mundo*, July 31, 2004. Jailed in October 2005, he was cleared in 2006 by the Spanish Supreme Court, who ruled that he had not been considered "innocent until proven guilty," and castigated the government for using evidence collected at Guantánamo that "should be declared totally void and, as such, non-existent." ("Ex-Guantánamo Spaniard Cleared By Supreme Court," Reuters, July 25, 2006.)

15. Ahjam (ISN 326): CSRB Set 3, p. 232; Shaaban (ISN 327): CSRT Set 52, pp. 77–86; al-Hamawe (ISN 329): CSRT Set 44, pp. 18–25; ARB Set 6, pp. 56–66; Mouhammed (ISN 330): CSRT Set 18, pp. 32–42.

16. M. al-Tumani (ISN 312): CSRT Set 51, pp. 74–99; A. al-Tumani (ISN 307): CSRT Set 51, pp. 162–70.

17. Ben Moujan (ISN 160): ARB Set 1, pp. 100–6; ARB Factors Set 2, pp. 33–4; Boujaadia (ISN 150): CSRB Set 3, pp. 108–9.

18. Y. Chekhouri (ISN 197): CSRT Set 36, pp. 70–85; R. Chekhouri (ISN 499). The house outside Kabul was also mentioned in the tribunal of Mosa Zi Zemmori (ISN 270), a 23-year-old Belgian (released in 2005), who apparently traveled to Afghanistan in October 2000, but was unable to attend a training camp because he contracted malaria (CSRT Set 45, pp. 21–31).

19. Roy Gutman, "Guantánamo Justice?" *Newsweek*, August 28, 2002.

20. Al-Shammeri (ISN 217): CSRT Set 4, pp. 83–102.

21. Al-Odah (ISN 232): Habeas petition <http://wid.ap.org/documents/detainees/fouzialawda.pdf>.

22. Al-Kandari (ISN 228): CSRT Set 9, pp. 30–7.

23. Al-Daihani (ISN 229): CSRT Set 4, pp. 71–82; al-Mutairi (ISN 213): <http://www.kuwaitifreedom.org/>.

24. Al-Balushi (ISN 227): "Fourth Guantánamo detainee turned over to Bahraini authorities," dpa German Press Agency, October 15, 2006; al-Khalifa (ISN 246): CSRT Set 9, pp. 1–3; al-Noaimi (ISN 159): "Leaving Guantánamo: Enduring a Harsh Stay," National Public Radio (NPR), May 22, 2006; Habeas petition <http://wid.ap.org/documents/detainees/abdullahalnoaimi.pdf>.

25. Al-Dossari (ISN 261): ARB Set 6, pp. 1–22. Al-Dossari spent time in Lackawanna, in New York State, where he was regarded by the authorities—based on no evidence whatsoever—as an al-Qaeda recruiter who helped to persuade six impressionable young locals to attend al-Farouq. Regarded, improbably, as an al-Qaeda "sleeper cell," the "Lackawanna Six" were bullied into admitting "material support for terrorism"—using threats that they would otherwise be held indefinitely as "enemy combatants"—and were given prison sentences of six to nine years after a trial in 2003. It was also alleged that al-Dossari trained in Afghanistan in 1989 (when he was 15 years old), that he was involved in jihad in Bosnia and Chechnya, that he was involved in an attack on US forces in Saudi Arabia in 1996, and that he was in Tora Bora. He has denied all the allegations.

26. El-Leithi (ISN 287): "Deep Wounds," *Al-Ahram Weekly*, October 13–19, 2005.

27. Abdurehim (ISN 289): CSRT Set 20, pp. 9–17; Basit (ISN 276): CSRT Set 16, pp. 1–6; Ghappar (ISN 281): CSRT Set 43, pp. 34–45; Abbas (ISN 275): CSRT Set 20, pp. 18–25; Abdulquadirakhun (ISN 285): CSRT Set 20, pp. 26–39; Qassim (ISN 283): CSRT Set 12, pp. 39–48; Abdulhehim (ISN 293): CSRT Set 15, pp. 36–45.

28. Razak (ISN 219): CSRT Set 27, pp. 20–35; Adil (ISN 260): CSRT Set 12, pp. 56–61.

29. Ayub (ISN 279): CSRT Set 12, pp. 49–55. The Uyghurs in Chapter 2 have also been cleared for release.

30. "Pakistan: Human Rights Ignored in the War on Terror"; "Ending Secret Detentions," Human Rights First, June 2004.

31. CSRT Set 51, pp. 74–99, 162–70.

32. "Days of adverse hardship in US detention camps—Testimony of Guantánamo detainee Jumah Al-Dossari," Amnesty International, December 16, 2005.

Chapter 8

1. "Pentagon sends in the Marines," *South China Morning Post*, November 27, 2001.

2. <http://www.lindhdefense.info/20020613_FactsSuppSuppress.pdf>.

3. "Amnesty for all declared: No revenge, vows new chief," *Dawn*, December 6, 2001; "Kandahar celebrates the Taliban's departure," *Guardian*, December 8, 2001.

4. Peter Maass, "Gul Agha Gets His Province Back," *New York Times Magazine*, January 6, 2002; "Americans covered up massacre of 280," *Independent*, December 15, 2001.

5. Mackey, *The Interrogator's War*, pp. 3–4.

6. Saghir and Razaq (ISN 99): James Meek, "People the law forgot," *Guardian*, December 3, 2003.

7. "Guantánamo Bay Detainee Statements," compiled by Mark Sullivan and Joshua Colangelo-Bryan, Dorsey & Whitney, May 2005; "Days of adverse hardship ... ."

8. Mackey, *The Interrogator's War*, p. 117; "Enduring Freedom: Abuses by US Forces in Afghanistan," Human Rights Watch, March 2004.

9. "Days of adverse hardship ... ."

10. "Enduring Freedom"; Mackey, *The Interrogator's War*, pp. 66–7; "I Met Osama bin Laden"; "Danish former prisoner claims abuse," Reuters, June 6, 2004.

11. "Days of adverse hardship ... ."; "US detentions in Afghanistan: an *aide-mémoire* for continued action," Amnesty International, June 7, 2005; Shafiq Rasul, Asif Iqbal and Rhuhel Ahmed, "Composite statement: Detention in Afghanistan and Guantánamo Bay," Center for Constitutional Rights, July 23, 2004; Ehsanullah (ISN 350): "Out of Legal Limbo, Some Tell of Mistreatment," *Washington Post*, March 26, 2003.

12. Al-Murbati (ISN 52): "Guantánamo Bay Detainee Statements"; "Enduring Freedom."

13. "Case Sheet 13," Amnesty International, October 1, 2005; "Guantánamo Bay Detainee Statements."

14. CSRT Set 51, pp. 74–99; "Case Sheet 18," Amnesty International, October 1, 2006; "US detentions in Afghanistan."

15. <http://action.aclu.org/torturefoia/released/011206/>.

16. <http://www.unhchr.ch/html/menu3/b/91.htm>.

17. Rose, *Guantánamo*, pp. 26–7; Army Regulation 190–98, October 1, 1997.

18. Mackey, *The Interrogator's War*, pp. 158–9.

19. "I Met Osama bin Laden"; "Days of adverse hardship ... ."

20. Mackey, *The Interrogator's War*, pp. 87–98; Rasul, Iqbal and Ahmed, "Composite statement."

21. Rasul, Iqbal and Ahmed, "Composite statement."

22. Mackey, *The Interrogator's War*, pp. 81, 85; <http://www.fas.org/irp/world/para/manualpart1_4.pdf>.

23. "An Interview with Khaled bin Mustafa"; "US: Systemic Abuse of Afghan Prisoners," Human Rights Watch, May 13, 2004; "Enduring Freedom."

24. A lawyer representing a Saudi prisoner who was released from Guantánamo in 2006 told me that the released Saudis have been asked by their government not to talk about their treatment by the Americans, because it may hinder the release of other prisoners.

25. "Case Sheet 7," Amnesty International, May 1, 2005; CSRT Set 31, pp. 53–63; CSRT Set 52, 125–49; Haidel (ISN 498): CSRT Set 31, pp. 9–11.

26. CSRT Set 51, pp. 38–52.

27. "Days of adverse hardship ... ."; "Guantánamo Bay Detainee Statements."

28. "US detentions in Afghanistan"; "Days of adverse hardship ... ."; <http://action.aclu.org/torturefoia/released/011206/>.

29. Vakhitov (ISN 492): "They Couldn't Take Away My Dignity," *Guardian*, November 20, 2005; Andrew McGregor, "A Sour Freedom: The Return of Russia's Guantánamo Bay Prisoners," *Chechnya Weekly*, Vol. 7, Issue 22, June 1, 2006.

30. Mackey, *The Interrogator's War*, pp. 148–9.

Chapter 9

1. Mackey, *The Interrogator's War*, pp. 85–6, 161–3.
2. One was 16-year-old Yousef al-Shehri (ISN 114), who was captured between Mazar-e-Sharif and Kunduz with 120 other suspected fighters ("Case Sheet 19," Amnesty International, November 17, 2006). His 17-year-old cousin, Abdul Salam al-Shehri (ISN 132), who hid in the basement during the Qala-i-Janghi uprising and was released in June 2006, thought he was dead (ARB Set 5, pp. 158–79).
3. Bawazir (ISN 440): ARB Set 6, pp. 170–84. Two Tajiks were also transferred at this time: Wahldof Abdul Mokit (ISN 90): CSRT Set 3, pp. 31–44 (released in March 2007), and Maroof Salehove (ISN 208): CSRT Set 4, pp. 39–46.
4. Mohammed (ISN 107): "Low-risk prisoners freed from high-security hell," *Guardian*, October 30, 2002.
5. R. Khan (ISN 120): CSRT Set 12, pp. 62–3; ARB Set 3, pp. 114–23; A. Khan (ISN 118): CSRT Set 10, pp. 34–7.
6. Rauf (ISN 108): ARB Set 3, pp. 107–13; CSRT Set 50, pp. 99–101; <http://www.fairgofordavid.org/pubdocs/Ashwin_Raman_Paper.pdf>.
7. Tim McGirk and Rahimullah Yusufzai, "After Gitmo, A Talib Takes Revenge," *Time*, June 7, 2004; Tim Golden and Don Van Natta Jr, "US Said to Overstate Value of Detainees," *New York Times*, June 21, 2004. Golden and Van Natta also named three other Afghan Taliban commanders released by mistake, and in October 2004 another Afghan Taliban commander, Maulvi Abdul Ghaffar (released in March 2004), was killed in Uruzgan by Afghan soldiers, who believed that he was leading the Taliban forces in the province. Also released in March 2004 was a Pakistani Taliban commander, Abdullah Mehsud, captured in Kunduz, who had a false Afghan ID card and claimed that he was an innocent Afghan tribesman. After his release, he became the commander of a group of militants who kidnapped two Chinese engineers in South Waziristan in October 2004, and was killed by the Pakistani Army in March 2006 ("7 ex-detainees return to fighting," Associated Press, October 18, 2004; "Released Detainees Rejoining The Fight," *Washington Post*, October 22, 2004).
8. Sarjudim (ISN 358): "Out of Legal Limbo, Some Tell of Mistreatment." The reason that so few released Afghans spoke about their experiences was spelled out in April 2005, when Chief Justice Fazel Shinwari told 17 released Afghans, "Don't tell these people the stories of your time in prison because the government is trying to secure the release of others, and it may harm the chances of winning the release of your friends" ("17 Afghans, Turk Freed From Guantánamo Bay," Associated Press, April 19, 2005).
9. Burke, *Al-Qaeda*, pp. 168, 189–90.
10. Sattar (ISN 10): CSRT Set 41, pp. 68–9.
11. Syed Farooq Hasnat, "Afghan Crisis: A Dilemma for Pakistan's Security and International Response," *Perceptions: Journal of International Affairs*, Vol. X, Spring 2005, pp. 35–52.
12. Luke Harding, "Afghan massacre haunts Pentagon," *Guardian*, September 14, 2002.
13. Rafiq (ISN 495): CSRT Set 44, pp. 115–20.

14. Saeed (ISN 98): "17 ex-Guantánamo prisoners released," *Pakistan Daily Times*, June 28, 2005.

15. Khan (ISN 17): CSRT Set 41, pp. 70–1; Raza (ISN 299): CSRT Set 46, pp. 15–19; Ilyas (ISN 144); Anwar (ISN 524). 16-year-old Khalilur Rehman (ISN 301), who was also captured near Kunduz, said that he made a mistake in traveling to Afghanistan to fight, and explained, "When I left home it was an emotional decision. I had no sense at the time" (CSRT Set 11, pp. 9–10). Also see Fazaldad (ISN 142): CSRT Set 41, p. 61. All were subsequently released, except Khan and Fazaldad, who were still in Guantánamo at the time of writing.

16. Ul Shah (ISN 15): ARB Set 5, pp. 1–10.

17. Khan (ISN 23): "Former Guantánamo Bay detainees find that life doesn't get any easier," Associated Press, January 5, 2006; Mohammed (ISN 19): "Inside 'The Wire,'" *Time*, December 8, 2003; "Pakistani relives Guantánamo ordeal," BBC News, May 22, 2003.

18. Hicks (ISN 2): Meek, "People the law forgot"; "On His Lonesome at Guantánamo Bay," *The Australian*, December 9, 2006; "Case Sheet 4 update," Amnesty International, May 1, 2005; "Detainee Says He Was Abused While in US Custody," *New York Times*, March 20, 2007.

Chapter 10

1. Hamiduva (ISN 22): CSRT Set 47, pp. 70–80; Jamaludinovich (ISN 452): CSRT Set 33, pp. 1–10. Thirty-six-year-old Abdulrahman Rajabov (ISN 641), released in April 2004, was captured by the Northern Alliance after traveling to Afghanistan to search for his brother in late 2001. He explained that US military interrogators in Kandahar used psychological pressure to force him to falsely confess to fighting with the Taliban ("Released Guantánamo Detainee Says He Was Abused," Radio Free Europe/Radio Liberty, January 13, 2005).

2. Mert (ISN 543): "15 more Guantánamo detainees freed," Muslim Civil Rights Center, April 2004 Review; Mohammed (ISN 555): CSRT Set 31, pp. 107–21.

3. Kerimbakicv (ISN 521): CSRT Set 1, pp. 1–9; ARB Factors Set 2, pp. 43–4; Abahanov (ISN 526): CSRB Set 3, p. 273; Magrupov (ISN 528): CSRT Set 26, pp. 7–11.

4. Abbasi (ISN 24): Sean O'Neill and Daniel McGrory, *The Suicide Factory: Abu Hamza and the Finsbury Park mosque* (London: Harper Collins, 2006), pp. 196–214.

5. "Inmates Left by the Taliban Are Free, but Cannot Leave," *New York Times*, December 16, 2001.

6. Al-Harith (ISN 490): "Traveller who called Kandahar prison 'home,'" *Times*, March 11, 2004; "I was in the wrong place at the wrong time," *Daily Mirror*, March 12, 2004.

7. Al-Ginco (ISN 489): ARB Set 18, pp. 92–107.

8. Bukhari (ISN 493): CSRT Set 3, pp. 56–65.

9. Vakhitov (ISN 492): "From Russia to Guantánamo, via Afghanistan."

10. Turkistani (ISN 491): "Detainee Cleared for Release Is in Limbo at Guantánamo," *Washington Post*, December 15, 2005.
11. "I was in the wrong place at the wrong time."
12. Sadiq (ISN 349): Ashwin Raman, "Guantánamo: A Right to a Fair Trial," *Z Magazine*, Volume 17, Number 3, March 2004; Zumarikourt (ISN 348): "Inside America's Concentration Camp," *Counter Punch*, April 1, 2004; Shah (ISN 632) and Tahir (ISN 643): "Afghans Bitter Over Guantánamo Detention," Associated Press, May 9, 2003.
13. Barekzai (ISN 546): ARB Set 1, pp. 8–19; Rahman (ISN 496): CSRT Set 44, pp. 106–14; ARB Set 6, pp. 225–34; Peerzai (ISN 562): CSRT Set 14, pp. 24–34; ARB Set 7, pp. 134–43.
14. "Can Your Friend's Enemy Be Your Friend?" *Time*, August 26, 2002; "Flaws in US Air War Left Hundreds of Civilians Dead," *New York Times*, July 20, 2002.
15. A renowned cleric and mujahideen commander, whose defection to the Taliban paved the way for much of their later success, Haqqani was close to Osama bin Laden and had a number of important benefactors: the ISI, rich supporters in the Gulf, and, ironically, the Americans, who funded him extensively in the 1980s. Invited to Islamabad by the ISI after 9/11 and offered the presidency of Afghanistan, provided he broke all ties with Mullah Omar and established a "moderate" Taliban faction, he refused the offer, and has spent the years since resisting the Americans.
16. Sarajuddin (ISN 458): ARB Set 6, pp. 193–206; G. Zaman (ISN 459): CSRT Set 26, pp. 30–53; K. Zaman (ISN 460): ARB Set 6, pp. 207–15; Gul (ISN 457): CSRT Set 19, pp. 1–12.
17. "Former minister says fugitive Taliban leaders living life of luxury in Pakistan," *Guardian*, December 24, 2001.
18. "Urgent Need to Decide How to Prosecute Captured Fighters," Human Rights Watch, November 26, 2001; "Three Afghan Commanders Should Be Prosecuted," Human Rights Watch, December 3, 2001.
19. Fazil (ISN 7): CSRT Set 13, pp. 1–6; Noori (ISN 6): ARB Set 1, pp. 26–34; CSRT Set 4, pp. 35–8. Also in the car was 28-year-old Abdullah Gulam Rasoul (ISN 8). A Taliban recruit, who was seriously wounded in 1997, he said that he rejoined the Taliban in 1999 "to gain better medical attention," and went to Kunduz to fight the Northern Alliance in September 2001 (CSRT Set 42, pp. 1–2; ARB Set 3, pp. 95–100).
20. Berntsen, *Jawbreaker*, pp. 278–9, 287; "Al-Qaeda planning next phase," *Christian Science Monitor*, December 28, 2001; "Taliban intelligence chief killed in US attacks," *Guardian*, January 2, 2002.
21. Wasiq (ISN 4): CSRT Set 16, pp. 13–24; Ruhani (ISN 3): CSRT Set 42, pp. 7–12; ARB Set 1, pp. 152–63.
22. "Biker mullah's great escape," *Observer*, January 6, 2002; "Afghans let Taliban ministers wanted by US walk free," *Guardian*, January 10, 2002.

Chapter 11

1. "Kuwaiti Gitmo Detainees Speak Out About Abuse," *Kuwait Times*, December 1, 2006; Rose, *Guantánamo*, p. 5.

2. "Captured Taliban may face trial in Guam," *Guardian*, November 28, 2001. At the time the Pentagon claimed it was seeking a place where al-Qaeda suspects "could face trial beyond the US mainland" because it was "concerned about security."

3. <http://www.whitehouse.gov/news/releases/2001/11/20011113–27.html>.

4. Michael Ratner with Ellen Ray, *Guantanamo: What the World Should Know* (Gloucestershire: Arris Books, 2004), p. 24. Ratner also noted that the legal basis for detaining the majority of the prisoners in Guantánamo was the "Authorization for the Use of Military Force," a joint resolution passed by Congress and the House of Representatives on September 18, 2001, which gave the President the authority to use all "necessary and appropriate force" against those whom he determined "planned, authorized, committed, or aided" the 9/11 attacks, or those who "harbored such organizations or persons."

5. <http://www.whitehouse.gov/news/releases/2001/11/20011114–6.html>.

6. <http://www.defenselink.mil/Transcripts/Transcript.aspx?TranscriptID= 2696>.

7. <http://www.defenselink.mil/transcripts/transcript.aspx?transcriptid=2254>.

8. "Briton held in US camp as Al-Qaeda prisoner," *Observer*, January 13, 2002; "Rumsfeld Visits, Thanks US Troops at Camp X-Ray in Cuba," American Forces Press Service, January 27, 2002.

9. "US says detainees not protected by Geneva Convention," Reuters, January 12, 2002.

10. Memorandum from Alberto Gonzales to the President, January 25, 2002.

11. Memorandum from Colin Powell to Alberto Gonzales and Condoleezza Rice, January 26, 2002. Powell also argued that removing GPW rights "deprives us of a winning argument to oppose habeas corpus actions in US courts."

12. "Fact Sheet: Status of Detainees at Guantánamo," White House press release, February 7, 2002.

13. "No leaders of Al-Qaeda found at Guantánamo," *Los Angeles Times*, August 18, 2002.

14. "War captives baffle US interrogators," BBC News, February 10, 2002.

15. Rose, *Guantánamo*, pp. 43–8.

16. "Operation Outreach: Tactics, Techniques and Procedures," *CALL Newsletter* No. 03–27, October 2003.

17. "From Ceuta to Iran, In Search of the Taliban."

18. Rasul, Iqbal and Ahmed, "Composite statement"; Meek, "People the law forgot."

19. Rasul, Iqbal and Ahmed, "Composite statement"; Rose, *Guantánamo*, pp. 51–3, 58.

20. Meek, "People the law forgot"; David Rose, "They tied me up like a beast and began kicking me," *Observer*, May 16, 2004.

21. Rose, *Guantánamo*, pp. 73–4.

22. Rasul, Iqbal and Ahmed, "Composite statement."

Chapter 12

1. Al-Adahi (ISN 33): CSRT Set 28, pp. 22–30; "Suicide Bid by Yemeni Guantánamo Detainee after Torture Allegations," *Yemen Observer*, January 16, 2006.

2. Al-Murbati: Habeas petition <http://wid.ap.org/documents/detainees/issaalmurbati.pdf>. Also see Adnan Farhan Abdul Latif (ISN 156): CSRT Set 8, pp. 85–93; ARB Set 2, pp. 46–58.
3. Kurnaz (ISN 61): CSRT Set 9, pp. 38–47; "US Frees Longtime Detainee," *Washington Post*, August 25, 2006; "Case Sheet 6: Update," Amnesty International, May 1, 2005. Also see Said al-Farha (ISN 341): CSRB Set 3, pp. 92–3 (released in December 2006), and Mohammed al-Ansi (ISN 29): ARB Set 5, pp. 22–35.
4. Al-Harbi (ISN 333): CSRT Set 16, pp. 60–72; al-Ajmi (ISN 220): ARB Set 17, pp. 46–70; <http://www.kuwaitifreedom.org/>.
5. Al-Dubaikey (ISN 340): CSRT Set 29, pp. 22–30; ARB Set 6, pp. 86–105; al-Utaybi (ISN 243): CSRB Set 3, pp. 237–8.
6. Hawsawi (ISN 368): ARB Set 1, pp. 88–97; Mohammed (ISN 335): ARB Factors Set 3, pp. 49–50; El-Gazzar (ISN 369): CSRT Set 3, pp. 22–30.
7. El-Gharani (ISN 269): "Case Sheet 10," Amnesty International, July 1, 2005.
8. Despite its relief work, IIRO's branches in the Philippines and Indonesia were blacklisted by the US Treasury in August 2006.
9. Sulayman (ISN 662): ARB Set 2, pp. 175–86; Clive Stafford Smith, "Abandoned to their fate in Guantánamo," *Index on Censorship*, June 2006.
10. Benchekroun (ISN 587): "Two Moroccans in the Hell of Guantánamo," *Le Journal Hebdomadaire*, July 8–15, 2005; Errachidi (ISN 590): "Pakistan: Human Rights Ignored in the War on Terror"; Khamisan (ISN 586): "Guantánamo: Lives Torn Apart—The Impact of indefinite detention on detainees and their families," Amnesty International, February 13, 2006.
11. Mazouz (ISN 294): "Two Moroccans in the Hell of Guantánamo"; "Mohammed Mazouz—Survivor of Guantánamo," *La Gazette du Maroc*, April 11, 2005. Released on bail in March 2005, both Mazouz and Benchekroun were rearrested in November 2005 and accused of planning to join a new terrorist cell. Their current whereabouts are unknown.
12. Al-Asmar (ISN 589): CSRT Set 26, pp. 19–29; Stafford Smith, "Abandoned to their fate in Guantánamo"; Emily Bazelon, "Searching for Khalid," *Mother Jones*, March/April 2005.
13. Al-Hajj (ISN 345): "Case Sheet 16," Amnesty International, January 11, 2006; <http://www.reprieve.org.uk/resources-_28.03.06_Blog.htm>.
14. Barre (ISN 567): ARB Set 7, pp. 144–56; "Remittances: The New Development Mantra?" World Bank G-24 Discussion Paper Series No. 29, April 2004.
15. Muslim Dost (ISN 561): CSRT Set 17, pp. 1–16; Bader (ISN 559): "An Innocent Man in the Hell of Guantánamo," *Le Nouvel Observateur*, November 24, 2005. Disturbingly, after publishing a book about Guantánamo which was critical of the ISI's role, Muslim Dost was rearrested by the Pakistanis in September 2006. His current whereabouts are unknown.
16. Mohammed (ISN 560): ARB Set 7, pp. 111–27. Also see Saeed Abdur Rahman (ISN 581), a poor chicken farmer who was mistaken for a Taliban minister: CSRT Set 3, pp. 68–90.
17. Zaeef (ISN 306): <http://www.cageprisoners.com/prisoners.php?id=53>.
18. Begg (ISN 558): Moazzam Begg with Victoria Brittain, *Enemy Combatant: A British Muslim's Journey to Guantanamo and Back* (London: Free

Press, 2006), pp. 58–107, 1–19; Aamer (ISN 239): "British Residents in Guantánamo Bay," December 5, 2005: <http://www.cageprisoners.com/articles.php?id=10974>.

19. Khairkhwa (ISN 579): "Hunt on for Taliban spy chief," *Pakistan Daily Times*, June 2, 2003; CSRT Set 44, pp. 67–73.
20. Sharqawi (ISN 1457): David E. Kaplan, "Playing Offense: The inside story of how US terrorist hunters are going after Al-Qaeda," *US News*, June 2, 2003; Stephen Grey, *Ghost Plane: The Inside Story of the CIA's Secret Rendition Programme* (London: Hurst, 2006), pp. 250–7; "List of 'Ghost Prisoners' Possibly in CIA Custody," Human Rights Watch, December 1, 2005; CSRB Set 3, p. 153.
21. Mackey, *The Interrogator's War*, p. 191.
22. Al-Suadi (ISN 578): ARB Set 7, pp. 207–26; al-Wady (ISN 574): CSRT Set 39, pp. 1–13; ARB Set 7, pp. 199–206. Also see Abdul Hakim al-Mousa (ISN 565): ARB Factors Set 2, pp. 17–18.
23. Abu Bakr (ISN 695): CSRB Set 3, pp. 266–7; "Why is a Honolulu lawyer representing an admitted member of the Taliban?" *Honolulu Weekly*, April 24, 2006.
24. Bin Amer (ISN 564): Habeas petition <http://wid.ap.org/documents/detainees/jalalsalamawad.pdf>; al-Azani (ISN 575): ARB Factors Set 2, pp. 3–4. Also see Salah al-Zabe (ISN 572): CSRT Set 44, pp. 74–81, and Sabri al-Qurashi (ISN 570): ARB Set 7, pp. 187–98.
25. Al-Zamel (ISN 568): CSRT Set 7, pp. 101–5; al-Azmi (ISN 571): CSRT Set 7, pp. 95–100.
26. Belmar (ISN 817): David Rose, "Beatings, sex abuse and torture: how MI5 left me to rot in US jail," *Observer*, February 27, 2005.

Chapter 13

1. Tim McGirk, "Anatomy of a Raid," *Time*, April 8, 2002; John F. Burns, "The Fugitives," *New York Times*, April 14, 2002.
2. Al-Sharbi (ISN 682): CSRT Set 30, pp. 26–30; al-Qahtani (ISN 696): <http://www.defenselink.mil/news/Nov2005/-d20051104qahtani.pdf>; Barhoumi (ISN 694): CSRT Set 12, pp. 24–38.
3. Mohammed (ISN 707): CSRT Set 38, pp. 15–21.
4. Labed (ISN 703): ARB Set 8, pp. 107–26; CSRT Set 36, pp. 1–12.
5. Tahar (ISN 679): CSRT Set 3, pp. 100–15; Hassan (ISN 680): CSRT Set 7, pp. 106–12; Hassen (ISN 681): CSRT Set 7, pp. 65–80; Ahmed (ISN 683): CSRT Set 30, pp. 83–97.
6. Hakim (ISN 686): CSRT Set 19, pp. 15–21; al-Zarnuki (ISN 691): CSRT Set 16, pp. 41–59; Ahmed (ISN 692).
7. Ahmed (ISN 688): CSRT Set 4, pp. 103–13; ARB Set 3, pp. 168–77; al-Salami (ISN 693).
8. Al-Noofayee (ISN 687): CSRT Set 28, pp. 8–21; Salam (ISN 689): CSRT Set 27, pp. 13–19.
9. Qader (ISN 690): CSRT Set 51, pp. 5–12.
10. Mingazov (ISN 702): CSRB Set 3, p. 178; Nassir (ISN 728): CSRB Set 3, p. 122.

11. "Fact Sheet: The Continuing War on Terrorist Assets," US Department of the Treasury, January 9, 2002.
12. Hamid (ISN 711) and Ayman al-Amrani (ISN 169), the other released Jordanian: Stafford Smith, "Abandoned to their fate in Guantánamo"; Babikir (ISN 700): <http://www.cageprisoners.com/prisoners.php?id=369>; Ahmad (ISN 714): <http://www.cageprisoners.com/prisoners.php?id=267>.
13. Gadallah (ISN 712): CSRT Set 30, pp. 39–49.
14. Amir (ISN 710): CSRT Set 16, pp. 73–6.
15. Boucetta (ISN 718): CSRT Set 30, pp. 50–4, and Salim (ISN 716): "4 Men Cleared of Terrorism Links but Still Detained," *Washington Post*, May 20, 2006. Ibrahim Fauzee (ISN 730), a 23-year-old from the Maldives (released in March 2005), was arrested in similar circumstances to those described by Boucetta. A student of Islam, he was living in a house in which one of the other occupants was reportedly the father of an al-Qaeda suspect. A witness reported that on May 19, 2002, US agents came to the house in Karachi, and arrested Fauzee and the other man, whose whereabouts are unknown <http://www.cageprisoners.com/prisoners.php?id=276>.
16. Abdallah (ISN 704): CSRT Set 15, pp. 1–13; al-Henali (ISN 726).
17. Hamad (ISN 940): CSRT Set 52, pp. 37–46.
18. "Detentions over charity ties questioned," *Boston Globe*, August 31, 2006.
19. Ameur (ISN 939): CSRT Set 18, pp. 61–79; ARB Set 9, pp. 228–43.
20. Hamlili (ISN 705): CSRT Set 12, pp. 16–20; "Guantánamo Bay prisoners' wives live like widows in Pakistan," *Pakistan Daily Times*, January 10, 2005.
21. Mustafa (ISN 715): Stafford Smith, "Abandoned to their fate in Guantánamo."
22. Umarov (ISN 729), Shirinov (ISN 732) and Mazharuddin (ISN 731): "The Man Who Has Been to America: One Guantánamo Detainee's Story," *Mother Jones*, September/October 2006.
23. Al-Amin (ISN 706): "Case Sheet 17," Amnesty International, July 14, 2006; al-Naely (ISN 758): ARB Set 8, pp. 166–83.
24. Deghayes (ISN 727): <http://www.reprieve.org.uk/casework_omardeghayes. htm>; "Case Sheet 9," Amnesty International, June 1, 2005.
25. Aziz (ISN 744): ARB Set 3, pp. 162–7.
26. Kiyemba (ISN 701): CSRT Set 12, pp. 21–3; "I confessed to escape Guantánamo torture," *Mail on Sunday*, February 19, 2006.

Chapter 14

1. Mackey, *The Interrogator's War*, p. 247.
2. Batarfi (ISN 627): ARB Set 7, pp. 227–53.
3. Mackey, *The Interrogator's War*, pp. 208–37; Razeq (ISN 356): "The One That Got Away," *Newsweek*, May 20, 2002.
4. Mackey, *The Interrogator's War*, pp. 192–5, 345–50, 282–9.
5. Tim Golden, "In US Report, Brutal Details of 2 Afghan Inmates' Deaths," *New York Times*, May 20, 2005.
6. Rose, "Beatings, sex abuse and torture"; "Case Sheet 17"; "I confessed to escape Guantánamo torture."

7. "Case Sheet 9"; ARB Set 8, pp. 132–45; "Case Sheet 17"; CSRT Set 42, pp. 53–62.

8. Stafford Smith, "Abandoned to their fate in Guantánamo"; "Case Sheet 16."

9. "Two Moroccans in the Hell of Guantánamo"; "Guantánamo: Lives Torn Apart."

10. "Kuwaiti Gitmo Detainees Speak Out About Abuse"; Rose, "Beatings, sex abuse and torture."

11. Mackey, *The Interrogator's War*, pp. 113–15, 250–2, 153–4.

12. Mohammed (ISN 657): "Afghans Describe Life Inside Gitmo," Associated Press, October 29, 2002; Bismillah (ISN 658): "Guantánamo Bay Prisoners Complain of A Year Long Torture by US Military," *Khilafah*, March 26, 2003. Also see Qari Esmhatulla (ISN 591), the only prisoner captured after Operation Anaconda, a mission to oust al-Qaeda remnants from the Shah-i-Kot valley in Paktia province in March 2002, which involved 2,700 US and Afghan troops and was hailed as a major victory by the US, even though there was never any evidence of the bodies of the 500 al-Qaeda soldiers that the US military claimed to have killed (ARB Set 1, pp. 1–7).

13. Akitar (ISN 845): CSRT Set 14, pp. 1–10; Nasim (ISN 849): CSRT Set 43, pp. 10–18; N. Wali (ISN 640) and B. Wali (ISN 638): "A Tough Homecoming," *Afghan Recovery Report 55*, Institute for War and Peace Reporting, April 8, 2003.

14. Abassin (ISN 671) and Khan (ISN 673): "Inside Guantánamo," BBC Panorama, October 5, 2003; "The threat of a bad example"; Abassin and Mohammed (ISN 677): Ashwin Raman, "Guantánamo: A Right to a Fair Trial."

15. "Inside Guantánamo"; "A Tough Homecoming"; Khandan (ISN 831): CSRT Set 24, pp. 9–31. Also see Padshah Wazir (ISN 631): CSRT Set 36, pp. 28–36 (released in 2005 or 2006).

16. Salaam (ISN 826): ARB Set 8, pp. 259–65; Khan (ISN 818); Aslam (ISN 822); Shah (ISN 812): CSRT Set 30, pp. 31–8; Shabeen (ISN 834): CSRT Set 52, pp. 21–8; Rasoul (ISN 835): CSRT Set 36, pp. 13–27. Also see Abdul Nasir (ISN 874): CSRT Set 47, pp. 5–10 (cleared for release in 2007).

17. Roohullah (ISN 798): CSRT Set 30, pp. 16–25; Melma (ISN 801): CSRT Set 47, pp. 49–62; "Afghan religious leader moved to Guantánamo Bay for questioning," Associated Press, August 25, 2003.

18. Zahir (ISN 753): CSRT Set 12, pp. 1–8; Sangaryar (ISN 890): ARB Set 9, pp. 102–17; Ismatullah (ISN 888): ARB Set 9, pp. 89–101; Rahmatullah (ISN 886): ARB Set 9, pp. 78–88. Ironically, Razaq (ISN 1043), who was captured in April 2003, was cleared for release in 2007 (CSRT Set 19, pp. 39–45).

19. Patel (ISN 649): CSRT Set 18, pp. 8–14; "I was in some kind of cage," *Libération*, March 18, 2005. Also see the stories of two released Iranians— Mohammed Anwarkurd (ISN 676): ARB Factors Set 1, pp. 75–6, and Bakhtiar Bameri (ISN 623): <http://www.cageprisoners.com/prisoners.php?id=561>.

20. Asam (ISN 672): CSRT Set 29, pp. 1–14; al-Ghizzawi (ISN 654): H. Candace Gorman, "Why I am Representing a 'detainee' at Guantánamo," *Huffington Post*, September 19, 2006.

21. Zeidan (ISN 761): CSRT Set 11, pp. 29–36; Stafford Smith, "Abandoned to their fate in Guantánamo."

22. Ishmuradov (ISN 674): "Russians sue US government for torturing them at Guantánamo camp," Associated Press, February 4, 2005; al-Karim (ISN 653): ARB Set 8, pp. 1–22.
23. Al-Qahtani (ISN 652): "Life After Guantánamo," *Asharq Alawsat*, October 18, 2006.
24. Omar Khadr (ISN 766): "Case Sheet 14," Amnesty International, November 10, 2005.
25. Abdurahman Khadr (ISN 990): "The Khadr Family," CBC News Online, October 30, 2006.
26. Mahdi (ISN 678): CSRT Set 34, pp. 23–5; ARB Factors Set 3, pp. 68–9; "Urgent Action," Amnesty International, November 25, 2005.
27. Golden, "In US Report ... "; Parkhudin (ISN 896); Abdul Rahim (ISN 897); Shah (ISN 898).
28. Carlotta Gall, "US Military Investigating Death of Afghan in Custody," *New York Times*, March 4, 2003; Golden, "In US Report ... ."
29. Rose, "Beatings, sex abuse and torture"; "I confessed to escape Guantánamo torture."
30. Begg, *Enemy Combatant*, pp. 150–72.

Chapter 15

1. "Former Guantánamo chief clashed with army interrogators," *Guardian*, May 19, 2004.
2. Rasul, Iqbal and Ahmed, "Composite statement"; "Guantánamo Bay Detainee Statements"; "Case Sheet 4 Update." Juma al-Dossari reported that he and several other prisoners also had their heads flushed in the toilet, and other prisoners reported that they were threatened with guns.
3. "Kuwaiti Gitmo Detainees Speak Out About Abuse"; "Case Sheet 16"; "Guantánamo Bay Detainee Statements"; "Deep Wounds."
4. "Case Sheet 16"; <http://www.reprieve.org.uk/casework_omardeghayes.htm>; James Yee, *For God and Country: Faith and Patriotism Under Fire* (New York: Perseus, 2005), pp. 109, 70–1; Rose, *Guantánamo*, pp. 72–3.
5. "Fresh Details Emerge on Harsh Methods at Guantánamo," *New York Times*, January 1, 2005.
6. Rasul, Iqbal and Ahmed, "Composite statement"; CSRT Set 36, pp. 70–85; "An Interview with Khaled bin Mustafa"; Noorani (ISN 582): "Ex-Afghan Prisoners Describe Guantánamo," Associated Press, July 20, 2003.
7. "They Couldn't Take Away My Dignity"; "Freed Swede Says He Was Tortured in Guantánamo"; Golden and Van Natta Jr, "US Said to Overstate Value of Guantánamo Detainees"; "Guantánamo Bay Detainee Statements."
8. "Guantánamo Bay Detainee Statements"; Rose, *Guantánamo*, p. 102; "Freed Swede Says He Was Tortured in Guantánamo"; "Fresh Details Emerge on Harsh Methods at Guantánamo."
9. David Rose, "They tied me up like a beast and began kicking me," *Observer*, May 16, 2004; "Case Sheet 14."
10. "Case Sheet 7"; "Case Sheet 4 Update"; "I Met Osama bin Laden"; Rasul, Iqbal and Ahmed, "Composite statement"; "Freed Swede Says He Was Tortured in

Guantánamo"; "Guantánamo Bay Detainee Statements"; Achakzai (ISN 104); Ghanim (ISN 44): <http://www.cageprisoners.com/prisoners.php?id=219>.

11. Rasul, Iqbal and Ahmed, "Composite statement"; "Detainees Accuse Female Interrogators," *Washington Post*, February 10, 2005; "Case Sheet 6: Update"; "Days of adverse hardship ... ." Other regularly employed techniques involved shaving hair and beards, threats of rape, death threats (to both the prisoners and their families), and threats to send prisoners to other countries where they would be tortured.

12. "Kuwaiti Gitmo Detainees Speak Out About Abuse"; "Bahrain royal family member tortured at Guantánamo prison camp," Associated Press, August 10, 2004; "Guantánamo: Lives Torn Apart."

13. Memorandum from the Justice Department's Office of Legal Counsel for Alberto Gonzales, August 1, 2002; Jane Mayer, "The Memo," *New Yorker*, February 27, 2006.

14. Memorandum from Lieutenant Colonel Jerald Phifer to Major General Michael Dunlavey, October 11, 2002; Memorandum from William J. Haynes II for Secretary of Defense, November 27, 2002.

15. "Final Report of the Independent Panel to Review DoD Detention Operations (The Schlesinger Report)," August 2004.

16. Rasul, Iqbal and Ahmed, "Composite statement"; Mayer, "The Memo"; Wilkerson's mention of "My Lai" refers to a notorious massacre of villagers in My Lai by US troops in 1968, during the Vietnam War.

17. "Can the '20th hijacker' of Sept. 11 ever stand trial?" MSNBC, October 26, 2006; <http://usinfo.state.gov/dhr/-Archive/2005/Jul/15–641403.html>.

18. <http://foia.fbi.gov/guantanamo/122106.htm>.

19. Golden and Van Natta Jr, "US Said to Overstate Value of Guantánamo Detainees."

20. Zagorin and Duffy, "Inside the Interrogation of Detainee 063"; "The Interrogation of Prisoner 063," *Time*, March 3, 2006, <http://www.time.com/time/2006/log/log.pdf>; "Torture, Cover-Up at Gitmo," *60 Minutes*, May 1, 2005.

21. Zagorin and Duffy, "Inside the Interrogation of Detainee 063"; "Can the '20th hijacker' of Sept. 11 ever stand trial?."

22. Mayer, "The Memo"; "Pentagon Report Set Framework For Use of Torture," *Wall Street Journal*, June 7, 2004.

23. Rose, *Guantánamo*, p. 94.

24. Zagorin and Duffy, "Inside the Interrogation of Detainee 063."

25. Adam Zagorin, "20th Hijacker Claims That Torture Made Him Lie," *Time*, March 3, 2006.

26. CSRT Set 47, pp. 63–9.

27. CSRT Set 52, pp. 186–95; Corine Hegland, "Guantánamo's Grip," *National Journal*, February 3, 2006; ARB Set 5, pp. 36–52.

28. Corine Hegland, "Empty Evidence," *National Journal*, February 3, 2006.

29. Khan (ISN 556): ARB Set 7, pp. 98–110; al-Sulami (ISN 66): CSRT Set 16, pp. 77–84; Sadkhan (ISN 433): CSRT Set 43, pp. 91–8; ARB Set 6, pp. 136–69. Although I know the identities of the Iraqi and the Yemeni, I have chosen not to reveal them, but they are both Shias (as are the other Iraqis), whereas almost all the other prisoners are Sunni, and the conflict between the two groups is palpable. Both the "spies" and another Iraqi who admitted to "cooperating"

with the interrogators have been subjected to death threats, and Arkan al-Karim (ISN 653), an Iraqi who was imprisoned by the Taliban after Abdul Rahim al-Ginco identified him as a spy while being tortured, pointed out that the 23 allegations against him—which included claims that he was an al-Qaeda member, that he was close to bin Laden, that he had "taken up jihad in the Philippines, Chechnya and Bosnia," that he "went to London for al-Qaeda," and that he "had specific knowledge of the al-Qaeda organization and the attacks on the World Trade Center"—came about specifically because he was a Shia. "I have no friends in this camp at all," he explained. "Most of them, if they don't give me a hard time or they don't give me a problem, they will not talk to me. But also, they've threatened me more than five or six times. They will say things about me." He also shrewdly recognized that the Americans had used him for intelligence: "The reason they brought me to Cuba is not because I did something. They brought me from Taliban prison to get information from me about the Iraqi army before the United States went to Iraq" (ARB Set 8, pp. 1–22).

30. Sidiqi (ISN 1007): ARB Set 10, pp. 217–36.
31. ARB Set 2, pp. 175–86; ARB Set 5, pp. 116–22; CSRT Set 31, pp. 1–8. Other ludicrous allegations, which were leveled at large numbers of the prisoners, included claims that their Casio watches could be used as timers for improvised explosive devices, and that their names and aliases were discovered on various websites and documents recovered during raids on suspected al-Qaeda houses. Many pointed out that their names may have been leaked to websites—along with photos taken by the Pakistani authorities—to publicize their plight or as al-Qaeda propaganda, and others said that the intelligence about their supposed aliases was spectacularly unreliable.
32. Camp 4, in which the prisoners wore white clothing to confirm their cooperation, opened in February 2003, and eventually contained around a third of the prisoners, including most of the Afghans. Those who were slightly less cooperative were held in Camp 1, where they wore tan clothing, and those who were helping with intelligence or were regarded as the most dangerous prisoners (roughly 20 percent of the prisoners) were held in Camps 2 and 3, where they wore orange. Most of these were moved to Camp 5, a specially designed maximum security block, when it opened in May 2004.
33. Rose, Guantánamo, pp. 81, 84, 116.
34. <http://www.reprieve.org.uk/casework_omardeghayes.htm>. He was also visited by Libyan intelligence agents, who threatened to kill him (and several Uyghur prisoners were also threatened by Chinese intelligence agents).
35. Rasul, Iqbal and Ahmed, "Composite statement"; <http://www.reprieve.org.uk/resources_14.03.06_Blog.htm>; Begg, Enemy Combatant, p. 200. Camp Echo was—and is—a block used specifically for solitary confinement, where most of those facing Military Commissions were, like Begg, held for long periods.

Chapter 16

1. Grey, Ghost Plane, p. 120; Jane Mayer, "Outsourcing Torture," New Yorker, February 14, 2005.

2. "Meet the Press," NBC, September 16, 2001; Mayer, "Outsourcing Torture."

3. Dana Priest and Barton Gellman, "US Decries Abuse but Defends Interrogations," *Washington Post*, December 26, 2002.

4. Mar'i (ISN 577): CSRT Set 4, pp. 130–44; Habeas petition <http://wid.ap.org/documents/detainees/jamalmari.pdf>; Ken Silverstein, "US, Jordan forge closer ties in covert war on terrorism," *Los Angeles Times*, November 11, 2005; "Lawyer for detainees details violence and despair," *Harper's Magazine*, June 29, 2006.

5. Al-Matrafi (ISN 5): <http://www.cageprisoners.com/prisoners.php?id=37>; CSRB Set 3, pp. 190–1.

6. "Bin Laden tape challenges 9/11 conviction," *Guardian*, May 24, 2006. The tape was also noteworthy for the claim that "Our brothers in Guantánamo ... have no connection whatsoever to the events of Sept. 11" and that "some of them oppose Al-Qaeda's methods of calling to fight America," and for an additional comment that, of all the prisoners captured in the "War on Terror," only "two of the brothers" had any connection to 9/11.

7. "Saudi Charity Denies Kabul Office Was 'Terror Lab,'" Reuters, August 26, 2002.

8. Habib (ISN 661): "The torment of a terror suspect," *Los Angeles Times*, January 15, 2005; Habeas petition <http://wid.ap.org/documents/detainees/mamdouhhabib.pdf>.

9. Rasul, Iqbal and Ahmed, "Composite statement"; "Fresh Guantánamo torture claims," BBC News, February 13, 2005; "Under Suspicion," *60 Minutes*, February 13, 2005.

10. Madni (ISN 743): CSRT Set 1, pp. 46–58; "Guantánamo: Lives torn apart."

11. "US Behind Secret Transfer of Terror Suspects," *Washington Post*, March 11, 2002; CSRT Set 1, pp. 46–58.

12. Slahi (ISN 760): CSRT Set 41, pp. 28–38; ARB Set 8, pp. 184–218; *9/11 Commission Report* (New York: Norton, 2004), pp. 165–7, 437; "The case of Guantánamo detainee Mohamedou Ould Slahi," Amnesty International, September 20, 2006.

13. "Faces of Guantánamo," Center for Constitutional Rights, 2006; "At Guantánamo, Caught in a Legal Trap," *Washington Post*, August 21, 2006. The men's ISN numbers are 10001–10006.

14. Rasul, Iqbal and Ahmed, "Composite Statement"; "Case Sheet 8," Amnesty International, May 1, 2005.

15. Ait Idr (ISN 10004): CSRT Set 53, pp. 43–66.

16. "US Operated Secret 'Dark Prison' in Kabul," Human Rights Watch, December 19, 2005.

17. Ahmed (ISN 1018): Stafford Smith, "Abandoned to their fate in Guantánamo."

18. Al-Qadasi (ISN 1014): "Secret detention Case Sheet 3," Amnesty International, August 2005.

19. Almerfedi (ISN 1015): CSRT Set 28, pp. 31–40; Tukhi (ISN 1012): CSRT Set 42, pp. 71–7.

20. Al-Hami (ISN 892): CSRT Set 34, pp. 20–2; ARB Set 3, pp. 147–61.

21. <http://www.reprieve.org.uk/casework_shakeraamer.htm>; CSRT Set 48, pp. 11–22.

22. Mubanga (ISN 10007): David Rose, "How I entered the hellish world of Guantánamo Bay," *Observer*, February 6, 2005.

23. Al-Habashi (ISN 1458): Stephen Grey and Ian Cobain, "Suspect's tale of travel and torture," *Guardian*, August 2, 2005; "British Residents in Guantánamo Bay."

24. Benyam Mohammed, "One of them made cuts in my penis. I was in agony," *Guardian*, August 2, 2005.

25. "US Operated Secret 'Dark Prison' in Kabul."

26. A. Rabbani (ISN 1460): *9/11 Commission Report*, pp. 236, 437; CSRB Set 3, p. 164; M. Rabbani (ISN 1461): CSRB Set 3, p. 131.

27. Dana Priest, "CIA Avoids Scrutiny of Detainee Treatment," *Washington Post*, March 3, 2005.

28. Don Van Natta Jr and Souad Mekhennet, "German's Claims of Kidnapping Brings Investigation of US Link," *New York Times*, January 9, 2005; "CIA accused of detaining innocent man," NBC News, April 21, 2005. El-Masri was not the only innocent man held in the "Salt Pit." Laid Saidi, a 40-year-old Algerian, who ran the Tanzanian office of the Saudi charity al-Haramain, was arrested in Tanzania and handed over, in Malawi, to US agents who rendered him to Afghanistan, where he was held in the "Salt Pit," the "Dark Prison" and another secret prison, from May 2003 to June 2004. After his release, he explained that he, El-Masri and the Rabbani brothers spent several nights memorizing each other's phone numbers so that, if one of them were released, he would be able to contact the others' families (Craig S. Smith and Souad Mekhennet, "Algerian Tells of Dark Odyssey in US Hands," *New York Times*, July 7, 2006).

29. *9/11 Commission Report*, p. 168.

30. Bin Attash (ISN 1456): CSRB Set 3, pp. 274–5; "Lawyer for detainees details violence and despair."

31. Al-Maythali (ISN 840): CSRT Set 31, pp. 12–14.

32. Al-Mudwani (ISN 839): ARB Set 9, pp. 30–45.

33. Al-Hela (ISN 1463): "Cairo to Kabul to Guantánamo," Human Rights Watch, March 30, 2005; "Case Sheet 15," Amnesty International, January 11, 2006.

34. Al-Rawi (ISN 906): CSRT Set 8, pp. 2–84; El-Banna (ISN 905): CSRT Set 8, pp. 94–107; <http://www.reprieve.org.uk/press_APPG_public_hearing_30.03.06.htm>.

35. Al-Jazeeri (ISN 1452): ARB Set 11, pp. 315–34; "Al-Qaeda suspect arrested," *Dawn*, June 19, 2003.

36. Paracha (ISN 1094): CSRT Set 10, pp. 1–19; "Pakistani detainee enjoyed deep US roots," *New York Times*, August 18, 2003. One other inexplicable rendition was that of Feda Ahmed (ISN 1013), a 25-year-old Afghan, who paid a smuggler to help him get to the United States but was captured in a boat off the US coast, having traveled via Guatemala and Mexico. He was released in 2005 or 2006 (CSRT Set 19, pp. 13–14).

37. Al-Hawari (ISN 1016): CSRT Set 21, pp. 15–23; ARB Set 10, pp. 294–311; al-Rammah (ISN 1017): <http://www.cageprisoners.com/prisoners.php?id=518>; "Days of adverse hardship ... ."

38. Abu Yahya al-Libi, "Quelques Noms et Informations sur des frères Prisonniers à Bagram," November 1, 2005; al-Bihani (ISN 893); "Ghost Prisoner: Two Years in Secret CIA Detention," Human Rights Watch, February 2007. The Human Rights Watch report (on Marwan Jabour, another innocent man, who spent two and a half years in secret prisons, mostly in Afghanistan) also contained a list of 38 prisoners who may once have been held in secret CIA prisons, and although the stories of these prisoners are, in general, beyond the scope of this book, it's essential to relate one of them. Ibn al-Sheikh al-Libi, who ran the Khaldan camp, was captured in November 2001, and was fought over by the FBI, who wanted to play by the rules, and the CIA, who didn't. In the end, as happened in Guantánamo, the CIA took over, and he was rendered to Egypt, where he falsely confessed that Saddam Hussein had "offered to train two Al-Qaeda operatives in the use of 'chemical and biological weapons.'" He later recanted his confession, but in the meantime it was used as part of the "evidence" against the Iraqi leader in Colin Powell's notorious speech to the UN Security Council in February 2003. Dan Cloonan, a veteran FBI agent, was appalled. He told Jane Mayer, "It was ridiculous for interrogators to think Libi would have known anything about Iraq ... The reason they got bad information is that they beat it out of him. You never get good information from someone that way" (Mayer, "Outsourcing Torture").

Chapter 17

1. "One huge US jail," *Guardian*, March 19, 2005.
2. "US detentions in Afghanistan: an *aide-mémoire* for continued action"; "New Probe of Detainee Death," CBS News, September 21, 2004; "2 soldiers reprimanded for assaults," *Los Angeles Times*, January 27, 2007; "Ex-CIA contractor guilty of assault," Associated Press, August 16, 2006.
3. Ghalib (ISN 987): CSRT Set 35, pp. 1–10; Kandahari (ISN 986): CSRT Set 51, pp. 62–73; Gul (ISN 928): CSRT Set 52, pp. 47–58; ARB Set 9, pp. 196–205. Also see the stories of two pro-Karzai police officers—Swar Khan (ISN 933): CSRT Set 33, pp. 57–68, and Naibullah Darwaish (ISN 1019): CSRT Set 43, pp. 27–33 (released in April 2005), and the stories of two pro-Karzai military officers—Sharifullah (ISN 944): CSRT Set 1, pp. 79–97, and Said Amir Jan (ISN 945): CSRT Set 23, pp. 34–48.
4. Haq (ISN 1100): CSRT Set 41, pp. 1–21.
5. Khail (ISN 1001): CSRT Set 47, pp. 11–21.
6. Shah (ISN 1154): CSRT Set 51, pp. 110–35; Mahvish Khan, "Guantánamo Diary," *Washington Post*, April 30, 2006; Akhtiar (ISN 1036): CSRT Set 13, pp. 43–52; ARB Set 11, pp. 38–50.
7. Chaman (ISN 1037): ARB Set 11, pp. 51–63. The other two men were Mohammed Aman (ISN 1074): CSRT Set 47, pp. 31–48, and Mohammed Mussa (ISN 1165): CSRT Set 48, pp. 3–10, who was the last Afghan transferred to Guantánamo. For government workers betrayed in other provinces, see Haji Bismullah (ISN 968): ARB Set 10, pp. 83–94, and Sada Jan (ISN 1035): CSRT Set 32, pp. 1–13.
8. Yar (ISN 977): CSRT Set 52, pp. 101–6; Khan (ISN 1009): ARB Set 10, pp. 257–65.

9. Shahzada (ISN 952): CSRT Set 50, pp. 88–96; Khan (ISN 950): CSRT Set 52, pp. 14–20; Nasir (ISN 951): CSRT Set 51, pp. 28–37.

10. Gul (ISN 953): CSRT Set 29, pp. 31–48; Ghafour (ISN 954): ARB Set 10, pp. 9–22; Mohibullah (ISN 974): CSRT Set 1, pp. 27–44; Mohammed (ISN 902): CSRT Set 36, pp. 49–58; Khan (ISN 1051): CSRT Set 2, pp. 36–40.

11. Mohammed (ISN 1056): CSRT Set 2, pp. 82–5; Matin (ISN 1002): CSRT Set 48, pp. 23–50; Zahir (ISN 1103): CSRT Set 42, pp. 78–83; Ullah (ISN 919): CSRT Set 31, pp. 28–37.

12. H. Rahman (ISN 907): CSRT Set 31, pp. 84–9; Khan (ISN 909): CSRT Set 32, pp. 14–24; A. Rahman (ISN 912): "Cuba? It Was Great, Say Boys Freed From US Prison Camp," Guardian, March 6, 2004; Naqibullah (ISN 913): <http://www.cageprisoners.com/prisoners.php?id=245>. Also see Shardar Khan (ISN 914): CSRT Set 25, pp. 1–9.

13. Qudus (ISN 929): CSRT Set 41, pp. 22–7; Agha (ISN 930): "Three Young Afghans Return Home from Guantánamo," New York Times, March 12, 2004.

14. Bagi (ISN 963): CSRT Set 27, pp. 1–12; Yar (ISN 971): CSRT Set 18, pp. 89–98; Mohammed (ISN 972): CSRT Set 30, pp. 55–70; Baridad (ISN 966): CSRT Set 1, pp. 59–64; Wahab (ISN 961): CSRT Set 27, pp. 42–8; Rahmatullah (ISN 964): CSRT Set 16, pp. 33–40; Shah (ISN 965): CSRT Set 22, pp. 1–9; Naserullah (ISN 967): CSRT Set 43, pp. 70–9.

15. Kuchi (ISN 931): "Enduring Freedom."

16. Khan (ISN 1075): ARB Set 11, pp. 132–7; Jeffrey H. Norwitz, "Defining Success at Guantánamo: By What Measure?" Military Review, July–August 2005, pp. 79–83. Despite Norwitz's insensitivity, the Criminal Investigative Task Force, like the FBI and the NCIS, was one of the organizations that resisted the use of harsh interrogation techniques, warning that they "would not produce reliable information, could constitute war crimes, and would embarrass the nation when they became public knowledge" ("Battle over tactics raged at Gitmo," MSNBC, October 23, 2006).

Chapter 18

1. <http://www.ccr–ny.org/v2/legal/september_11th/sept11Article.asp?ObjID=ytOOAV96a7&Content=91>.

2. <http://www.ccr–ny.org/v2/rasul_v_bush/home.asp#rasul_v_bush>.

3. <http://www.humanrightsfirst.org/us_law/after_911/PDF/backgr_hamdi.pdf>.

4. Marie Brenner, "Taking on Guantánamo," Vanity Fair, March 2007.

5. "Guantánamo: Detainee Accounts," Human Rights Watch, October 2004.

6. Gogus (ISN 291): "Officials Detail a Detainee Deal by 3 Countries," New York Times, July 4, 2004.

7. McGregor, "A Sour Freedom"; "Russian Homeland No Haven For Ex-Detainees, Activists Say," Washington Post, September 3, 2006. It was also noticeable that, although 24 prisoners were released from other countries—Egypt, Iraq, Iran, Jordan, Morocco, Sudan, Syria, Tajikistan, Turkmenistan, Turkey and Uzbekistan—very few prisoners from the Gulf countries or other North African countries (who made up nearly half of Guantánamo's

population) were released. At the time of writing, this was still true of the Yemenis and the majority of the Algerians, Libyans, Sudanese, Syrians and Tunisians: 152 Afghans, 61 Saudis and 60 Pakistanis had been released, but only 18 North Africans and only eight Yemenis. One reason for the Yemenis' continued detention was spelled out in the ARB for Saeed Jarabh (ISN 235). Accused of training in Afghanistan, Jarabh said that he went to Pakistan to buy and sell honey and never set foot in Afghanistan, but the authorities were holding him partly because "Yemen is not a nation supporting the War on Terrorism" (CSRT Set 52, pp. 175–85; ARB Factors Set 1, pp. 60–2). Also see Ali al-Raimi (ARB Factors Set 1, pp. 88–9).

8. <http://www.supremecourtus.gov/opinions/03pdf/03–334.pdf>.
9. <http://www.supremecourtus.gov/opinions/03pdf/03–6696.pdf>.
10. Dave Lindorff, "Chertoff and Torture," *The Nation*, February 14, 2005; Tom Junod, "Innocent: The State of the American Man," *Esquire*, July 2006.
11. George Monbiot, "Routine and systematic torture is at the heart of America's war on terror," *Guardian*, December 12, 2006. The other "enemy combatant" held on US soil is a Qatari, Ali al-Marri, who came to the US to study in September 2001, bringing his family with him. Arrested in December 2001, he was charged with fraud and making false statements to the FBI, and was designated an "enemy combatant" in June 2003. He was then held incommunicado for another 14 months until the Red Cross was allowed to visit him in August 2004. He is accused of having connections to the al-Qaeda financier Mustafa al-Hawsawi (see Chapter 20) and of working as an "al-Qaeda sleeper agent" in the US, although the allegations have been denied by his lawyer, Mark Berman, who took his case in October 2004 but has been unable to end his legal limbo. His brother Jaralla (ISN 334) is held at Guantánamo. Accused of training at al-Farouq, he spent 16 months in isolation, and was hospitalized during a hunger strike in 2005 ("Ali Saleh Kahlah Al-Marri," Amnesty International, August 2, 2006; CSRT Set 10, pp. 20–3).
12. Thomas Wilner, "Guantánamo: American Gulag," *Los Angeles Times*, February 26, 2006; "Guantánamo Bay Detainee Statements"; "A timeline of legal developments at Guantánamo Bay," Knight Ridder, June 10, 2006.
13. CSRT Set 36, pp. 42–8; CSRT Set 33, pp. 57–68; Razzak (ISN 942): CSRT Set 18, pp. 55–9.
14. "Detainees not given access to witnesses," *Boston Globe*, June 18, 2006.
15. <http://www.humanrightsfirst.org/us_law/detainees/military_commission_diary.htm>.
16. "Senate Approves Limiting Rights of US Detainees," *New York Times*, November 11, 2005; "Landmark Torture Ban Undercut," Human Rights Watch, December 16, 2005.

Chapter 19

1. "Three Detainees Commit Suicide at Guantánamo," *Washington Post*, June 11, 2006; "Guantánamo suicides a 'PR move,'" BBC News, June 11, 2006; al-Utaybi (ISN 588).
2. "Pentagon identifies 3 Guantánamo Suicides."

3. CSRB Set 3, pp. 106–7.
4. "Inmates Released from Guantánamo Tell Tales of Despair," *New York Times*, March 25, 2003; ARB Set 18, pp. 92–107.
5. "Report into the Systematic and Institutionalised US Desecration of the Qu'ran and other Islamic Rituals," Cageprisoners, May 16, 2005 <http://www.cageprisoners.com/articles.php?id=7282>.
6. "The Guantánamo Prisoner Hunger Strikes & Protests: February 2002—August 2005," A Special Report by the Center for Constitutional Rights, September 8, 2005.
7. "The Guantánamo Prisoner Hunger Strikes & Protests"; "FBI Records," ACLU, May 25, 2005, <http://www.aclu.org/torturefoia/released/052505/>.
8. "The Guantánamo Prisoner Hunger Strikes & Protests."
9. Tim Golden, "The Battle for Guantánamo," *New York Times Magazine*, September 17, 2006.
10. Al-Joudi (ISN 25) and Shalabi (ISN 42): "Recently Declassified Notes Reveal Brutal Treatment of Hunger-Striking Detainees at Guantánamo," Common Dreams News Center, October 19, 2005. Al-Joudi and Shalabi were in the first group of men captured crossing from Afghanistan to Pakistan in December 2001.
11. Golden, "The Battle for Guantánamo."
12. Rasul, Iqbal and Ahmed, "Composite statement"; "Guantánamo Bay Detainee Statements"; "Case Sheet 16."
13. "Case Sheet 16"; Gorman, "Why I am Representing a 'detainee' at Guantánamo."
14. Rasul, Iqbal and Ahmed, "Composite statement."
15. "Kuwaiti Gitmo Detainees Speak Out About Abuse"; "Released Guantánamo Detainee Says He Was Abused"; Rasul, Iqbal and Ahmed, "Composite statement."
16. "Gitmo Captives Say Medical Personnel Approved, Participated in Abuses," *New Standard*, August 3, 2005.
17. Jane Mayer, "The Experiment," *New Yorker*, July 11 and 18, 2005.
18. Rasul, Iqbal and Ahmed, "Composite statement"; Golden, "The Battle for Guantánamo."

Chapter 20

1. Sidney Blumenthal, "The imperial presidency crushed," *Salon*, July 6, 2006.
2. "A Look at the 14 terror suspects sent to Guantánamo," Associated Press, September 7, 2006.
3. "President Discusses Creation of Military Commissions to Try Suspected Terrorists," White House press release, September 6, 2006.
4. "Secret World of Detainees Grows More Public," *Washington Post*, September 7, 2006; "Questions Raised About Bush's Primary Claims in Defense of Secret Detention System," *New York Times*, September 8, 2006.
5. "The Shadow War, In a Surprising New Light," *Washington Post*, June 20, 2006.
6. CSRT Set 1, pp. 65–78.

7. "The Shadow War, In a Surprising New Light"; "CIA's Harsh Interrogation Techniques Described," ABC News, November 18, 2005.

8. "CIA's Harsh Interrogation Techniques Described"; "Suspect at Guantánamo Claims Torture," Associated Press, March 31, 2007.

9. ARB Set 8, pp. 166–83.

10. "The case of Guantánamo detainee Mohamedou Ould Slahi."

11. ARB Factors Set 2, pp. 81–3. The source of another patently false allegation—that Osama bin Laden spoke to his group in Tora Bora—is unknown. Al-Hanashi was captured after the fall of Kunduz, and cannot possibly have been in Tora Bora with bin Laden.

12. CSRT Set 11, pp. 29–36.

13. Dana Priest and Scott Higham, "At Guantánamo, a Prison Within a Prison," *Washington Post*, December 17, 2004.

14. "Rubber stamping violations in the 'war on terror': Congress fails human rights," Amnesty International, September 29, 2006.

15. <http://thomas.loc.gov/cgi–bin/query/z?c109:S.+3930>.

16. "Cleared men, harsh facility," *National Law Journal*, February 23, 2007.

17. <http://www.cageprisoners.com/articles.php?id=19323>. It was alleged that Baada (ISN 178) traveled to Afghanistan in June 2001, trained at al-Farouq, fought near Kabul, and was a guard in Tora Bora (CSRB Set 3, p. 222). Zuhair (ISN 669) was also accused of being involved in the bombing of the USS *Cole* and the murder of a US official who was working for the UN in Bosnia, and has had a leg amputated in Guantánamo (CSRB Set 3, p. 99). Also see Makram (ISN 187): ARB Factors Set 1, pp. 56–7.

18. Mohammed (ISN 10024): "Release 9-11 Suspect's Description of Alleged Torture," Human Rights Watch, March 15, 2007; Rosa Brooks, "What impeccable timing, KSM!" *Los Angeles Times*, March 16, 2007. For the transcripts of the tribunals of the "high-value" prisoners, see <http://www.defenselink.mil/news/Combatant_Tribunals.html>.

19. Bin Attash (ISN 10014); al-Hawsawi (ISN 10011); Ghailani (ISN 10012); Hamlili (ISN 10019); bin Lep (ISN 10022); al-Baluchi (ISN 10018); bin al-Shibh (ISN 10013); al-Libi (ISN 10017); Zubaydah (ISN 10016); al-Nashiri (ISN 10015). In addition, Zubair (ISN 10021) attended his tribunal but did not respond to allegations about his involvement in Jemaah Islamiya. One other story that has only just begun to surface concerns other "ghost" prisoners who were captured with the 14 "high-value" prisoners. Two prisoners who were captured with Abu Zubaydah—Omar Ghramesh and an unnamed teenager—were rendered to Syria, where they were held and tortured in the notorious "Palestine Branch" prison, according to Abdullah Almalki, a Syrian-born Canadian who was also held and tortured in the prison. Almalki was one of three innocent Syrian-born Canadians—the others were Ahmed al-Maati, who, like Almalki, was captured by the Syrians on the Canadians' behalf, and Mahar Arar, who was rendered to Syria by the US, after being kidnapped at New York's JFK airport—who were abducted or rendered based on completely unjustified suspicions that they were connected with terrorist activities. All three were eventually released. Others captured with the "high-value" prisoners, whose whereabouts have not been explained, include at least two additional prisoners captured with Ramzi bin al-Shibh, a Yemeni

captured with Waleed bin Attash and Ammar al-Baluchi, "five other African or Pakistani Al-Qaeda suspects" captured with Ahmed Khalfan Ghailani, and "at least five other foreign Al-Qaeda suspects" captured with Abu Faraj al-Libi (Grey, *Ghost Plane*, pp. 4, 65–8; Jason Burke, "Brutal gun-battle that crushed 9/11 terrorists," *Observer*, September 15, 2002; "Bomb jitters in Pakistan too," *Asia Times*, May 21, 2003; "Pakistan Holds Top Al-Qaeda Suspect," *Washington Post*, July 30, 2004; "Pakistan catches Al-Qaeda chief," BBC News, May 4, 2005).

20. "Hicks May Go But Questions on His Treatment Remain," *Sydney Morning Herald*, March 31, 2007.
21. "Stop the Guantánamo Circus," Human Rights Watch, March 27, 2007.
22. Mayer, "Outsourcing torture"; "New to Pentagon, Gates Argued for Closing Guantánamo Prison," *New York Times*, March 23, 2007.
23. Mayer, "Outsourcing torture."

For updates and additional information, see the author's website <http://www.andyworthington.co.uk>.

Index